CRIME FICTION CRITICISM

GARLAND REFERENCE LIBRARY
OF THE HUMANITIES
(Vol. 233)

CRIME FICTION CRITICISM
An Annotated Bibliography

Editors:

Timothy W. Johnson
Julia Johnson

Associate Editors:

Robert Mitchell
Glenna J. Dunning
Susan J. Mackall

GARLAND PUBLISHING, INC. • NEW YORK & LONDON
1981

Library of Congress Cataloging in Publication Data

Johnson, Timothy W   1940–
  Crime fiction criticism.

  (Garland reference library of the humanities ;
v. 233)
  Includes index.
  1. Detective and mystery stories, English—History
and criticism—Bibliography.   I. Johnson, Julia,
joint author.   II. Title.
Z2014.F4J63   [PR830.D4]   016.823′0872′09   80-8497
ISBN 0-8240-9490-5

Printed on acid-free, 250-year-life paper
Manufactured in the United States of America

CONTENTS

INTRODUCTION

Most critics agree that mystery and detection fiction began in the middle of the nineteenth century, although a few argue that the genre dates back to biblical times. And despite predictions— some dating from the late nineteenth century—of the imminent demise of the genre, the popularity of mystery and detection fiction, in all its myriad forms, remains undiminished.

Early critics were unsure what to make of this new phenomenon. Much of the early criticism of mystery and detection fiction had a tendency towards apologia as literary men and women struggled to justify their attraction to this "disreputable" genre. Gradually, however, many skeptics were won over, and by the late 1960s and early 1970s mystery and detection fiction was being analyzed in "respectable" literary circles.

Crime Fiction Criticism is the first comprehensive, book-length bibliography of criticism of the genre, although there have been a number of primary bibliographies of mystery and detection fiction; Allen J. Hubin's *The Bibliography of Crime Fiction, 1749– 1975* (1979) is the latest and by far the most comprehensive.

Both Ordean A. Hagen's *Who Done It?: A Guide to Detective, Mystery and Suspense Fiction* (1969) and Jacques Barzun and Wendell Hertig Taylor's *A Catalogue of Crime* (1971) contain valuable compilations of criticism, but the primary mission of both books was to compile a bibliography of the fiction rather than the commentary on it. *Who Done It?* contains a fifteen-page list, largely unannotated, of crime fiction criticism, and *A Catalogue of Crime* contains a bibliography, with evaluative annotations, of about 240 works of mystery and detection criticism.

Crime Fiction Criticism, however, contains more than 2000 entries for over 1800 separate items, each with a descriptive annotation. A multitude of topics related to the genre as well as over 250 individual authors are covered. This bibliography is an endeavor to fulfill the need—long felt by the devotee and the scholar alike—for a genuinely comprehensive bibliography of mystery and detection criticism. This need is especially great because most crime fiction authors are not included in standard bibliographies such as *English Novel Explication* and *The Contemporary Novel*.

This work covers the criticism of all types of mystery and detection fiction, including thrillers and espionage stories. We have excluded critical works pertaining to true crime stories and to gothic or supernatural tales, since these genres are more properly the subjects of entirely separate bibliographies. For the same reason we have omitted items about crime fiction in cinema, television, and radio.

In addition to writers who have devoted all or most of their literary careers to mystery and detection fiction, we have also included relevant studies of the work of "mainstream" authors, such as Charles Dickens, Mark Twain, and William Faulkner, who have written some crime fiction. Only criticism that deals with the mystery or detection aspects of their works, however, is included. Thus, a hypothetical article entitled "*Hamlet* as Detective Story" would be included in this bibliography, although the vast majority of the criticism on Shakespeare's play would not. In addition to independent critical commentary, we have also included an author's commentary on his or her own work (either in an article or an interview) if that commentary contains useful critical insights.

We examined several thousand items (books, articles in periodicals and newspapers, and abstracts of dissertations) for possible inclusion in *Crime Fiction Criticism* and have included everything written about the genre or about individual authors that can be considered literary criticism. In adhering to this standard we have excluded the following categories: entries on the writing, editing, or publishing of crime fiction unless significant critical insights are provided, entries on the collection of crime fiction, entries devoted exclusively to manuscript or textual problems, parodies or other whimsical pieces, and news stories, obituaries, and other biographical items that contain no critical material.

Crime Fiction Criticism also excludes primary bibliographies unless they are book-length or unless they appear in *The*

Armchair Detective, the best-known, most respected, and most widely available of the periodicals devoted exclusively to mystery and detection criticism.

Finally, this work contains very few book reviews. For all but a few of the authors included these reviews tend to be brief and superficial. In addition, they are easily accessible through *Book Review Digest* and *Book Review Index*. Those book reviews that are essentially essay-reviews or that have been reprinted are included.

In compiling this bibliography we have collected citations to books, collections of criticism, articles in periodicals and newspapers, and dissertations. Many of the books were published in both American and European editions; others have been reprinted. We did not attempt to locate the original edition of each book, although a reprint issued significantly after the original publication date usually is noted in the annotation. In each case, the specific edition we examined is given in the citation. Where an article from a periodical or newspaper has been reprinted, we have cited the original source whenever possible, as well as the reprints. For frequently reprinted articles, however, we have been somewhat selective in the number of sources listed. Our intention in this matter is to be helpful, not exhaustive.

We have discovered, in the course of compiling this bibliography, that some of the more prolific critics have created special complications for the bibliographer. These critics (or their editors) have occasionally given identical titles to different articles. Other critics have, in essence, written the same article more than once, giving it a different title each time. Readers are advised to be guided by our annotations in determining whether the articles cited are originals, reprints (which will be noted in the citation), or variations on the same theme.

Crime Fiction Criticism is divided into two sections. In the first section are citations for works dealing with the genre of mystery and detection literature in general or specific topics within it. This general section is divided into four sub-sections: reference works, books, dissertations, and articles and portions of books. The second section contains items on individual authors of crime fiction. This second section is arranged alphabetically by the last name of the writer. Any significant examination of an individual writer in a general work is cited and annotated in the second section, with an item number to refer back to the main entry.

Each entry includes a short annotation summarizing its contents. It is important to note that our annotations are purely descriptive; they do not presume to evaluate the merits of the arguments they summarize. Each entry has been assigned only one item number; a work that contains criticism on more than one author is cited in full and numbered the first time it appears in the bibliography, and subsequent references to that same work give the item number in place of the publishing information. For example,

1897. Public, John Q. "A Question of Murder." *Murder Murder Murder* (item 1234), pp. 27–48.

Many authors of crime fiction write under one or more pseudonyms in addition to or instead of their own names. Also, the works of some authors have been published under one name and reprinted under another. Therefore, any writer who has written under more than one name is listed under his or her best-known name, whether it is a pseudonym or not, and the author's other important names are listed at the beginning of the main entry and cross-referenced throughout the author section. We have omitted unimportant or non-mystery pseudonyms. We have also occasionally noted the name of a writer's series character, but only when it will be an aid to understanding the annotations.

In order to find all relevant items we have searched four major college and university research libraries (at the University of Southern California, the University of Arizona, the University of California at Los Angeles, and the Claremont Colleges), the Los Angeles Public Library (which has a great many books and periodicals relating to crime fiction that are not available in the academic libraries), and some smaller public and academic libraries. Any item that was found in *any one* of these libraries is included. Items that are not in any of these libraries would, we believe, not be available to most users of this work. For the same reason we have confined our newspaper research to the London *Times*, the *New York Times*, and the *Los Angeles Times*. We have not included items in "fanzines" or other limited-distribution newsletters and society publications. Omitting these items is in no way a reflection on the worth or legitimacy of articles in such publications; it simply reflects the fact that virtually all of them are now difficult or impossible for a user of this work to find. Indeed, we look forward to the day when some of these periodicals are available in libraries and when their best articles are reprinted in book form.

We must emphasize that the number of citations for an author should not be interpreted as an indication of that author's popularity or importance in the genre. We have simply reported what has been published; we have not attempted to judge the importance of a writer and then exclude or include items on that basis. In the case of two writers whose representation in this work may appear especially disproportionate, we believe a further explanation is in order: Charles Dickens, who has, perhaps, more entries than one might expect, and Sir Arthur Conan Doyle, who has, perhaps, fewer.

Crime Fiction Criticism contains more citations on Charles Dickens than on any other author even though Dickens is not normally thought of as a mystery or detection writer. Two of Dickens's novels—*Bleak House* and *The Mystery of Edwin Drood*—contain elements of mystery and detection. In *Bleak House*, this element is perhaps secondary; in *Edwin Drood*, however, it is at the heart of the novel. Dickens is, of course, a titanic figure in nineteenth-century English literature, and his work, even in its secondary aspects, has naturally drawn a great deal of critical attention.

The situation is further complicated because Dickens died before he finished *Edwin Drood*, leaving that mystery forever unsolved. Scores of dedicated Dickensians have combed the extant portion of the novel for clues as to how Dickens would have resolved the story. Their commentary and speculation comprise a substantial portion of the citations in the section devoted to Dickens.

Sherlock Holmes, on the other hand, is undoubtedly the most famous figure in the literature of mystery and detection. Sir Arthur Conan Doyle's fiction has inspired well over 3000 books and articles on the exploits of the legendary sleuth. Some of this output is genuine literary criticism; most of it is not.

Baker Street whimsey has become a thriving industry among

Holmes fans. It began when Ronald Knox satirically applied the techniques of the higher criticism to Conan Doyle's works. This treatment caught on, and many "critics" began to write about Holmes and Watson as though they were real people; if Conan Doyle was mentioned at all, he was referred to as Watson's "literary agent." To give the user some idea of this side of Conan Doyle commentary we have included a few of the best-known examples of the whimsical or higher criticism (so indicated in the annotations), but nearly all of the section on Conan Doyle consists of items that are genuine literary criticism.

These two examples lead us to the following concluding observation: Our goal in compiling this bibliography was more than simply to publish a comprehensive list of the extant mystery and detection criticism. We also hope that scholars in this still fertile field will use *Crime Fiction Criticism* as a signpost to those authors and subjects in the mystery and detection genre that seem to invite further investigation. Despite the magnitude of scholarship represented by the citations in this bibliography, much work remains to be done.

Acknowledgment:

We wish to thank the Professional Development Committee of the University of Southern California Librarians for a grant to partially fund the typing of the manuscript.

Los Angeles and Tucson
April 1980

Section One
General Works

REFERENCE WORKS

1. Barnes, Melvyn. *Best Detective Fiction: A Guide from Godwin to the Present.* Hamden, Conn.: Linnet Books, 1975. 121pp.

   A primary bibliography arranged in narrative form "to give a superficial picture of the development of the genre" but "not intended as a complete history of detective fiction."

2. Barzun, Jacques, and Wendell Hertig Taylor. *A Catalogue of Crime.* New York: Harper and Row, 1971. 831pp.

   The largest portion is devoted to the authors' "inventory" of nearly three thousand works of mystery and detective fiction, each annotated with their personal comments. Also includes shorter sections on studies and histories of the genre, true crime stories, the literature of Sherlock Holmes, and ghost stories and the supernatural.

3. Breen, Jon L. *The Girl in the Pictorial Wrapper: An Index to Reviews of Paperback Original Novels in the New York Times' "Criminals at Large" Column, 1953-1970, and The Saint Mystery Magazine's "Saint's Ratings" Column, 1957-1959.* Dominguez Hills: California State College, Dominguez Hills, 1973. 50pp.

   Aptly described by the subtitle. An earlier edition (1972) included the *New York Times* only.

4. Gribbin, Lenore S. *Who's Whodunit.* Chapel Hill: University of North Carolina Library, 1968. 174pp.

   A listing of over a thousand pseudonyms used by mystery writers.

5. Hagen, Ordean A. *Who Done It? A Guide to Detective, Mystery, and Suspense Fiction.* New York: Bowker, 1969. 834pp.

   A listing of authors, titles, and themes. Contains a short secondary bibliography. Virtually all reviewers state that it contains a large number of errors.

6. Herman, Linda, and Beth Stiel. *Corpus Delicti of Mystery Fiction: A Guide to the Body of the Case.* Metuchen, N.J.: Scarecrow Press, 1974. 180pp.

    Intended as a guide to help "in compiling a balanced mystery fiction collection" and for those who want to know more about the genre, it is basically a list of fifty representative authors and their works with chapters on the "value of mystery fiction," "definition and terms," and the "history and development of mystery fiction."

7. Hubin, Allen J. *The Bibliography of Crime Fiction, 1749-1975.* San Diego: University Extension, University of California, in cooperation with Publisher's, Inc., 1979. 697pp.

    A primary bibliography "listing all mystery, detective, suspense, police, and gothic fiction in book form published in the English language." Does not include juvenile, magazine, or dime novel crime fiction. The dates of each author are given as well as the pseudonyms and names of series characters where appropriate.

8. McCormick, Donald. *Who's Who in Spy Fiction.* London: Hamish Hamilton, 1977. 216pp.

    Contains a brief overview of the field and a list of "abbreviations, titles and jargon used in espionage in fact and in fiction," but the body of the book is made up of short entries (one to five paragraphs long) on writers of spy fiction.

9. *Mysteries: A Bibliography of Detective, Mystery and Suspense Fiction and Criticism.* Sacramento: The Library, California State University, Sacramento, 1975. 52pp.

    An unannotated listing of the holdings of California State University, Sacramento, in the mystery and detection field. Includes works of criticism as well as anthologies and works by individual authors.

10. Penzler, Otto *et al. Detectionary.* Woodstock, N.Y.: Overlook Press, 1977. 299pp.

    "A biographical dictionary of leading characters in detective and mystery fiction ... and some of their most memorable adventures, as recounted in novels, short stories, and films."

11. Queen, Ellery. *The Detective Short Story: A Bibliography*.
    Boston: Little, Brown, 1942. 146pp.

    A primary bibliography of books containing detective
    short stories. Includes many annotations and evaluations.

12. Queen, Ellery. *Queen's Quorum: A History of the Detective-
    Crime Short Story as Revealed by the 106 Most Important
    Books Published in This Field Since 1845*. New York:
    Biblo and Tannen, 1969. 146pp.

    With the 1967 supplement included, this book lists 125
    important books in the field of mystery/detection short
    stories, with brief commentary on each. The criteria for
    selection are historical importance, literary quality, and
    desirability as a collector's item.

13. Smith, Myron J., Jr. *Cloak-and-Dagger Bibliography: An
    Annotated Guide to Spy Fiction, 1937-1975*. Metuchen,
    N.J.: Scarecrow Press, 1976. 225pp.

    A selected list of over 1,600 titles very briefly de-
    scribed, with symbols to indicate "humor a major feature,"
    "sex level lower than most," and "more suitable than most
    for under-10th-graders."

14. Steinbrunner, Chris, and Otto Penzler, eds. *Encyclopedia
    of Mystery and Detection*. New York: McGraw-Hill, 1976.
    436pp.

    The bulk of the six hundred entries (most of which are
    one to three paragraphs long) are for authors, but many
    entries for characters and topics are included. The illus-
    trations are chiefly from films.

15. Stilwell, Steven A. *The Armchair Detective Index*. New York:
    Mysterious Press, 1979.

    Indexes volumes 1-10 (1967-1977) of the quarterly journal
    Armchair Detective.

                              BOOKS

16. Adams, Donald K., ed. *The Mystery and Detection Annual
    1972*. Beverly Hills, Calif.: Donald Adams, 1972. 264pp.

    Consists of original articles and reviews. The articles
    are annotated individually.

17. Adams, Donald K., ed. *The Mystery and Detection Annual*
     1973. Beverly Hills, Calif.: Donald Adams, 1974. 337pp.

     Consists of original articles and reviews. The articles
     are annotated individually. (The third volume is scheduled
     for publication in late 1980.)

18. Aisenberg, Nadya. *A Common Spring: Crime Novel and Classic.*
     Bowling Green, Ohio: Bowling Green University Popular
     Press, 1980. 271pp.

     Contends that "there exist basic but unsuspected connec-
     tions between myth, fairytale, and the crime novel" and
     that "the detective story and the thriller have made an
     unacknowledged contribution to 'serious' modern literature."
     Supports this contention by using Dickens, Conrad, and
     Greene as examples of major writers who have "borrowed many
     important ingredients" from the crime novel.

19. Allen, Dick, and David Chacko, eds. *Detective Fiction:*
     Crime and Compromise. New York: Harcourt Brace Jovanovich,
     1974. 481pp.

     An anthology of works of mystery and detective fiction
     with one section devoted to reprints of some famous criti-
     cal essays.

20. Arnold, Armin, and Josef Schmidt. *Kriminal Roman Fuhrer.*
     Stuttgart, Germany: Philipp Reclam, 1979. 445pp.

     Consists chiefly of a listing of authors with both bio-
     graphical and bibliographical information on each.

21. Ball, John, ed. *The Mystery Story: An Appreciation.* San
     Diego: University Extension, University of California,
     1976. 390pp.

     A collection of articles described as a "retrospective
     look at the genre with comments on its conventions." The
     articles are annotated individually in the appropriate
     sections.

22. Barzun, Jacques, and Wendell Hertig Taylor. *A Book of*
     Prefaces to Fifty Classics of Crime Fiction, 1900-1950.
     New York: Garland Publishing, 1976. 112pp.

     Garland Publishing reprinted fifty classics of crime
     fiction with prefaces by Barzun and Taylor. In addition
     all fifty prefaces were printed together in this volume.
     Each is annotated separately.

23. Boileau-Narcejac [Pierre Boileau and Thomas Narcejac].
     Le Roman Policier. Paris: Petite Bibliothèque Payot,
     1964. 235pp.

     Although partly superseded by Narcejac (item 53), this
     concise survey of the police novel emphasizes French con-
     tributions to the genre between 1900 and 1939.

24. Boucher, Anthony. *Multiplying Villainies: Selected Mystery
     Criticism, 1942-1968.* Edited by Robert E. Briney and
     Francis M. Nevins, Jr. Boston: A. Bouchercon, 1973.

     Representative selection of Boucher's mystery criticism
     from *San Francisco Chronicle* and *New York Times*, plus book
     introductions and essays.

25. Butler, William Vivian. *The Durable Desperadoes.* London:
     Macmillan, 1973. 285pp.

     Focuses on a "particular thriller genre which was born
     in the second half of the 1920's, flourished throughout
     the thirties and to some extent has been flourishing ever
     since"--that of the "Gentleman Outlaw." Examines the crea-
     tion of such gentleman outlaws as Leslie Charteris's The
     Saint, John Creasey's The Toff, and Roderic Graeme's
     Blackshirt.

26. Caillois, Roger. *Le Roman Policier.* Buenos Aires: SUR,
     1941. Part reprinted (in English translation) *Chimera*
     5 (Summer 1947): 67-79.

     Argues that the detective story must have two elements:
     murder and investigation, and that it represents "the
     struggle between the element of organization and the ele-
     ment of turbulence."

27. Champigny, Robert. *What Will Have Happened: A Philosophical
     and Technical Essay on Mystery Stories.* Bloomington:
     Indiana University Press, 1977. 183pp.

     Argues that the mystery story may be characterized by the
     fact that "the narrated process is oriented toward a retro-
     active denouement that should transfigure the whole se-
     quence." Analyzes the "ludic" (playful) and aesthetic
     interest of the genre using many examples.

28. Depken, Friedrick. *Sherlock Holmes, Raffles, and Their
     Prototypes.* Chicago: Fanlight House, 1949. 89pp.

     Traces the history of the mystery and detection story
     from its beginning in the nineteenth century as an offshoot

of the criminal novel through Poe, Gaboriau, Conan Doyle,
and Hornung.

29. Dupuy, Josée. *Le Roman Policier*. Paris: Librairie Larousse,
     1974. 192pp.

     A concise history of the detective novel that classifies
     "narrative schemes" used in the genre and links it to such
     contemporary modern works as William Faulkner's *Sanctuary*.

30. Eames, Hugh. *Sleuths, Inc.: Studies of Problem Solvers:
     Doyle, Simenon, Hammett, Ambler, Chandler*. Philadelphia:
     J.B. Lippincott, 1978. 228pp.

     Consists of essays on each of the authors named in the
     sub-title. See the entries under each author.

31. Geherin, David J. *Sons of Sam Spade: The Private Eye Novel
     in the 70's*. New York: Frederick Ungar, 1980.

     Published too late for annotation, but according to
     Publishers Weekly it traces the background of the hard-
     boiled private eye, then examines three newcomers: Robert
     Parker, Roger Simon, and Andrew Bergman.

32. Gilbert, Michael F., ed. *Crime in Good Company: Essays
     on Criminals and Crime-Writing*. London: Constable, 1959.
     242pp.

     A collection of articles on real and fictional crime.
     The critical articles on crime fiction are annotated in-
     dividually.

33. Haining, Peter. *Mystery!: An Illustrated History of Crime
     and Detective Fiction*. London: Souvenir Press, 1977.
     176pp.

     Pictures from magazines (and some books) arranged with
     very little commentary to illustrate the "major develop-
     ments and important characters" in crime and detective
     fiction from Poe through the 1930s.

34. Harper, Ralph. *The World of the Thriller*. Cleveland, Ohio:
     Press of Case Western Reserve University, 1969. 139pp.

     Contends that literary competence is only a minor part
     of a thriller's ability to arouse strong feelings because
     such works "are written for the sake of and written about
     the interior life of man." The essential theme of the
     thriller, he argues, is modern man's search for identity
     and control.

35. Haycraft, Howard, ed. *The Art of the Mystery Story: A Collection of Critical Essays.* New York: Simon and Schuster, 1946. 545pp.

    A collection of essays; the critical articles on crime fiction are annotated separately in the appropriate sections.

36. Haycraft, Howard. *Murder for Pleasure: The Life and Times of the Detective Story.* New York: D. Appleton-Century, 1941. 409pp.

    Contends that "the essential theme of the detective story is the professional detection of crime" and surveys the writers who have most *influenced* the genre. States that there was a "sharply parallel development of the detective story and the democratic processes." The two main requirements of the detective story are, Haycraft argues, that it "play fair" and be readable.

37. Jones, Robert Kenneth. *The Shudder Pulps: A History of the Weird Menace Magazines of the 1930's.* West Linn, Ore.: Fax Collector's Editions, 1975. 238pp.

    Defines "weird menace" as "a form of mystery story in which the villain perpetrated seemingly supernatural deviltries, which were logically explained at the end." Surveys this field and notes that when there were detectives in such stories they were flawed in some way.

38. Keating, H.R.F. *Murder Must Appetize.* London: Lemon Tree Press, 1975. 64pp.

    Not available for annotation but described in the 1975 *Armchair Detective* bibliography as a survey of the classic years of the English detective story.

39. Lacassin, Francis. *Mythologie du Roman Policier.* Paris: Union Générale d'Editions, 1974. 2 vols.

    Contends that the detective novel is linked to, and important in, the development of the "serious" novel.

40. Lacombe, Alain. *Le Roman Noir Américain.* Paris: Union Générale d'Editions, 1975. 188pp.

    This structural and thematic study stresses the function of the "initiation" journey, the city, violence, and sex in the hard-boiled detective story.

41.   La Cour, Tage, and Harold Mogensen. *The Murder Book: An
      Illustrated History of the Detective Story.* New York:
      Herder and Herder, 1971. 192pp.

      A compilation of eighty-three short articles on various
      aspects of mystery fiction that emphasizes European sources
      but also includes major English-language works. (Originally
      published in Danish.)

42.   Lambert, Gavin. *The Dangerous Edge.* New York: Grossman
      Publishers, 1976. 272pp.

      In this treatment of eight crime novelists (and filmmaker
      Alfred Hitchcock) Lambert argues that to spend a lifetime
      conveying the experience of fear a person must have had
      a childhood trauma or experience of dread, and that "some
      kind of religious belief, or violent reaction against it,
      lies behind" all the works discussed. See annotations under
      Ambler, Buchan, Chandler, Chesterton, Collins, Conan Doyle,
      and Greene.

43.   Landrum, Larry N., Pat Browne, and Ray B. Browne, eds.
      Dimensions of Detective Fiction. Bowling Green, Ohio:
      Bowling Green University Popular Press, 1976. 290pp.

      A collection of essays, most previously unpublished.
      Each essay is separately annotated.

44.   Larmoth, Jeanine. *Murder on the Menu.* New York: Scribners,
      1972. 268pp.

      Surveys cooking and eating habits of fictional detectives.
      Includes recipes by Charlotte Turgeon.

45.   Madden, Cecil, ed. *Meet the Detective.* Harrisburg, Penn.:
      The Telegraph Press, 1935. 158pp.

      Transcriptions of BBC radio talks in which writers
      describe and discuss the detectives they have created.
      Annotated under each individual author: Bailey, Bentley,
      Charteris, Cole, Crofts, Freeman, Grayson, Grierson, Horler,
      McNeile, Mason, Rohmer, Soutar, and Wynne.

46.   Madden, David, ed. *Tough Guy Writers of the Thirties.*
      Carbondale: Southern Illinois University Press, 1968.
      247pp.

      Collection of original essays, some of which are on
      mystery and detective fiction and are annotated individually.

47. Marsch, Edgar. *Die Kriminalerzählung: Theorie, Geschichte, Analyses*. Munich: Winkler, 1972. 295pp.

    Analyzes the theory and history of the detective story from Poe and Wilkie Collins through Dürrenmatt. .

48. Mason, Bobbie Ann. *The Girl Sleuth: A Feminist Guide*. Old Westbury, N.Y.: Feminist Press, 1975. 144pp.

    Contends that it is important to understand the popularity of the girl detective with young girls (she provides a stimulating role model) because it mirrors hidden wishes and values as well as helps to mold them. Lists and analyzes some of the most popular series heroines, particularly Nancy Drew.

49. Merry, Bruce. *Anatomy of the Spy Thriller*. Dublin: Gill and Macmillan, 1977. 253pp.

    Argues that spy thrillers offer "an entertainment, a political confrontation and a refutation of normal values," and contends that the plots and the details in spy stories rarely correspond to what is known about real-life intelligence operations. Details the ingredients of the standard spy thriller, such as the use of simultaneous events on different continents to lead to the plot's climax.

50. Messac, Régis. *Le "Detective Novel" et l'Influence de la Pensée Scientifique*. Paris: H. Champion, 1929. Reissued Geneva: Slatkine Reprints, 1975. 698pp.

    Contends that the development of mystery fiction can be traced back to the seventeenth and eighteenth centuries and that the French and English Gothic novel can be linked to the genre. Stresses the influence of scientific thought on the detective novel as well as on fiction in general.

51. Murch, A.E. *The Development of the Detective Novel*. New York: Philosophical Library, 1958. 272pp.

    Contends that the purpose of a detective story is to puzzle the readers and make them think. Surveys the major and minor writers in the field but has very little on works after 1940.

52. Narcejac, Thomas. *Esthétique du Roman Policier*. Paris: Le Portulan, 1947. 199pp.

    Contends that the low esteem in which the police novel has been held is unmerited and that it is a work of the imagination that uses logic without being subservient to

it. The police novel is a genuine literary genre with its
own conventions, unities, and particular qualities.

53.   Narcejac, Thomas. *Une Machine à Lire: Le Roman Policier.*
      Paris: Denoël/Gonthier, 1975. 250pp.

      A study which covers such topics as the development of
      the genre, the fantastic, political, and religious elements
      in mystery fiction, and its moral implications.

54.   Nevins, Francis M., Jr., ed. *The Mystery Writer's Art.*
      Bowling Green, Ohio: Bowling Green University Popular
      Press, 1970. 338pp.

      A collection of essays on several writers as well as on
      various topics in the field of mystery and detection fic-
      tion. Each essay is individually annotated.

55.   Ousby, Ian. *Bloodhounds of Heaven: The Detective in English
      Fiction from Godwin to Doyle.* Cambridge, Mass.: Harvard
      University Press, 1976. 194pp.

      Argues that fictional detectives reflect social reality
      and begins with background explaining the ambivalence
      toward the police in eighteenth-century Britain. Also con-
      tends that World War I destroyed the world order which made
      Sherlock Holmes possible and that among the chief appeals
      of the genre are didacticism and fantastic adventure.

56.   Palmer, Jerry. *Thrillers: Genesis and Structure of a
      Popular Genre.* New York: St. Martin's Press, 1979. 226pp.

      Argues that the thriller formula is "competition and
      conspiracy" and describes several types of thrillers in-
      cluding the "negative thriller," which suggests that the
      world is not secure. Also provides the historical back-
      ground in the detective story and a "sociology of the
      thriller."

57.   Panek, LeRoy. *Watteau's Shepherds: The Detective Novel in
      Britain, 1914-1940.* Bowling Green, Ohio: Bowling Green
      University Popular Press, 1979. 240pp.

      Panek states that this book is not a "one thesis tract."
      Instead, he has treated each of his subjects in a slightly
      different manner. There are chapters on Bentley, Christie,
      Milne, Sayers, Cox, Allingham, Carr, and Marsh, each of
      which is annotated separately.

58. Pate, Janet. *The Book of Sleuths*. Chicago: Contemporary
     Books, 1977. 124pp.

     A series of short treatments of many fictional sleuths
     with the theme that the development of the detective novel
     is related to changes in society and technology. Lists film,
     television, and theater treatments of each sleuth as well
     as published texts.

59. Pearson, Edmund. *Dime Novels: Or Following an Old Trail
     in Popular Literature*. Boston: Little, Brown, 1929.
     280pp.

     Describes such detectives of the dime novel as Old Cap,
     an adventurer and master of disguise, and Old Sleuth,
     featured in stories described as "cunning and cowardly
     crime foiled and frustrated by vigorous and victorious
     virtue."

60. Penzler, Otto, ed. *The Great Detectives*. Boston: Little,
     Brown, 1978. 281pp.

     A collection of articles by famous detective story
     writers about their detectives. Each is annotated sepa-
     rately.

61. Penzler, Otto. *The Private Lives of Private Eyes, Spies,
     Crimefighters, and Other Good Guys*. New York: Grosset
     and Dunlap, 1977. 214pp.

     In-depth biographies of twenty-five great detectives,
     mostly garnered directly from the books in which they
     appear and supplemented with information from films, radio
     and television programs, and essays written by their
     creators.

62. Queen, Ellery. *In the Queens' Parlor and Other Leaves from
     the Editors' Notebook*. New York: Simon and Schuster,
     1957. 195pp.

     This is a collection of quite short pieces on the general
     theme of mystery and detective fiction. It includes ob-
     servations, anecdotes, and reminiscences.

63. Rodell, Marie F. *Mystery Fiction: Theory and Technique*.
     New York: Duell, Sloan and Pearce, 1943. 230pp.

     A handbook for would-be mystery/detection writers but
     also of some interest to readers of the genre. Outlines
     basic plots, various ways of adding complications, and
     other stratagems for writing mystery fiction.

64. Routley, Erik. *The Puritan Pleasures of the Detective Story: A Personal Monograph.* London: Gollancz, 1972. 253pp.

    Routley treats several detective story writers (chiefly British writers of the classical detective story) in detail and in his prologue argues that three conditions are necessary for the genre to flourish: (1) a tradition of police integrity, (2) a public willing to accept a hero who never fails, (3) a public eager "to take pleasure in the special activity of observation." In his final chapter, he connects the popularity of the detective story with "the puritan belief in the perfectibility of society."

65. Ruehlmann, William. *Saint with a Gun: The Unlawful American Private Eye.* New York: New York University Press, 1974. 155pp.

    Argues that the heroes of private-eye fiction in America are virtually always avengers.

66. Sandoe, James. *The Hard-Boiled Dick: A Personal Checklist.* Chicago: Arthur Lovell, 1952. 8pp.

    Sandoe's personal selection of essential works for a collection of hard-boiled detective fiction, with commentary on each author.

67. Schönhaar, Rainer. *Novelle und Kriminalschema: Ein Strukturmodell deutscher Erzählkunst um 1800.* Berlin: Verlag Gehlen, 1969. 220pp. [*Novella and the Structure of Criminal Stories: A Model of the Structure of German Narrative Prose Around 1800.*]

    Contends that early 19th-century German narrative prose has elements of the detective story structure.

68. Schulz-Buschhaus, Ulrich. *Formen und Ideologien des Kriminel-Romans: Ein gattiengsgeschichtlicher Essays.* Frankfurt: Athenaion, 1975.

    A history of the detective novel stressing both form and ideology.

69. Schwartz, Saul, ed. *The Detective Story: An Introduction to the Whodunit.* Skokie, Ill.: National Textbook Company, 1975. 442pp.

    A high school textbook which contains detective stories with very brief introductions and exercises for students.

70. Scott, Sutherland. *Blood in Their Ink: The March of the Modern Mystery Novel*. London: Stanley Paul, 1953. 200pp.

    Surveys the mystery genre, concentrating on the "years of plenty" (1925-1939). Also devotes chapters to such topics as techniques, "dos and don'ts," and the future of the mystery novel. In the "dos and don'ts" chapter he has thirty-three items, including injunctions to play fair with the reader, use an authentic background, and avoid sex. In the last chapter he predicts that the genre will continue to be "a means of relaxation and enjoyment."

71. Stevenson, W.B. *Detective Fiction: A Reader's Guide*. London: Cambridge University Press, 1949. 20pp.

    Basically a list of recommended mystery books with an introduction in which Stevenson traces the history of the detective story.

72. Stewart, R.F. *... And Always a Detective: Chapters on the History of Detective Fiction*. North Pomfret, Vt.: David and Charles, 1980. 352pp.

    Published too late for annotation, but the publisher states that the book concentrates on detective fiction before Arthur Conan Doyle.

73. Symons, Julian. *The Detective Story in Britain*. London: Longmans, Green, 1962. 48pp.

    Surveys the major British mystery/detection writers from Wilkie Collins and Conan Doyle through the World War II era. Emphasizes the "Great Detective" as the central figure of the genre, and argues that post-war writers have abandoned the Great Detective concept, which has resulted in a new form called "the crime novel."

74. Symons, Julian. *Mortal Consequences: A History--From the Detective Story to the Crime Novel*. [British title: *Bloody Murder*.] New York: Harper and Row, 1972. 209pp.

    Symons argues that any attempt to subdivide the crime/suspense story into distinct sub-genres creates more confusion than it resolves. He also notes that a typical story in the genre may have "almost no literary merit," but that "it may still be an ingenious, cunningly deceptive, and finely constructed piece of work." That said, he proceeds to conduct an extensive historical survey of the genre, from Poe and other progenitors to the contemporary spy novel.

75. Talburt, Nancy Ellen, and Lyna Lee Montgomery. *A Mystery Reader: Stories of Detection, Adventure, and Horror.* New York: Scribners, 1975. 458pp.

A textbook consisting of stories, study questions, and a few famous essays on the genre.

76. Thomas, Gilbert. *How to Enjoy Detective Fiction.* London: Rockliff, 1947. 108pp.

Maintains that the reader's enjoyment of detective fiction will be enhanced if he learns to recognize the various types of detective fiction. Thomas lists eight categories (with an example of each), such as a "solution arrived at by analysis of Material Evidence," and by "Analysis of Testimony." Most of the book is devoted to a history of detective fiction, the organization of Scotland Yard, and some famous real-life criminal cases.

77. Thomson, H. Douglas. *Masters of Mystery: A Study of the Detective Story.* London: W. Collins Sons, 1931. 288pp. [Reprinted by Dover in 1978.]

Argues that the primary interest of the detective story is not crime and that in such fiction moral standards "are healthily taken for granted." Maintains that the basic element of the genre is a puzzle to be solved by logical deduction, but there must be more than the puzzle, and the emotional elements are excitement, bewilderment, and surprise. Thomson then traces the history of the detective story.

78. Watson, Colin. *Snobbery with Violence: Crime Stories and Their Audience.* New York: St. Martin's Press, 1971. 256pp.

In addition to his opinions of many writers of mystery and detection fiction, Watson provides the social background of the genre, pointing out the increased availability of books and leisure time in the Victorian era and the snobbery in the British detective story between the wars as well as the xenophobia of the thriller of that period.

79. Wells, Carolyn. *The Technique of the Mystery Story.* Springfield, Mass.: Home Correspondence School, 1913. 336pp.

Although written mainly for writers of mystery and detective stories, this analysis of forms and techniques, with many quotations and examples, is quite useful to the reader and student of the genre also. Wells contends that the mystery story has "no deeper intent" than "to entertain, to interest, to amuse," and that the popularity of the genre is easy to understand because "inquisition into the curious is universal."

80. Winks, Robin W., ed. *Detective Fiction: A Collection of Critical Essays*. Englewood Cliffs, N.J.: Prentice-Hall, 1980.

   Published too late for annotation.

81. Winks, Robin W., ed. *The Historian as Detective: Essays on Evidence*. New York: Harper and Row, 1969. 543pp.

   Winks's introductions to the essays in this collection and his footnotes point out the parallels between the work of the historian and that of fictional detectives.

82. Winn, Dilys, ed. *Murder Ink: The Mystery Reader's Companion*. New York: Workman Publishing, 1977. 522pp.

   A collection of nearly three hundred brief miscellaneous items, virtually none of which are reprints, ranging from Ian Carmichael's account of his portrayal of Lord Peter Wimsey on television, through a list of abbreviations used by English police, to a short article on elderly maiden lady detectives.

83. Winn, Dilys, ed. *Murderess Ink: The Better Half of the Mystery*. New York: Workman Publishing, 1979. 304pp.

   A collection of approximately 200 miscellaneous items connected with women and crime or crime-writing, such as a short biographical sketch of Josephine Tey and a list of real-life female murderers.

84. Woelcken, Fritz. *Der literarische Mord*. Nürnberg: Nest, 1953. New York: Garland Publishing, 1979.

   A study first published in 1953 of the categories of English and American detective fiction as well as of many specific writers.

DISSERTATIONS

85.   Aisenberg, Nadya. "The Crime Novel: The Poetry of Justice."
      Ph.D. dissertation, University of Wisconsin, 1978.

      In this dissertation, Aisenberg examines a wide variety
      of crime fiction, arguing that it shares with folk tales
      and mythology many common themes--the Quest, poetic justice,
      identity and recognition, etc. The genre's use of these
      primal literary themes accounts for much of its continuing
      popularity.

86.   Ambrosetti, Ronald J. "A Study of the Spy Genre in Recent
      Popular Literature." Ph.D. dissertation, Bowling Green
      State University, 1973.

      Maintains that the achievement of the spy genre is its
      combination of traditions found in popular formula genres
      with classical myth and in its narrowing of the gap between
      "elitist" and popular literature. Also contends that the
      genre accurately reflects the cold war era.

87.   Brill, Amy. "Remembering Mysteries: The Nineteenth-Century
      Detective Story as a Modern Art of Memory." Ph.D. dis-
      sertation, Syracuse University, 1978.

      This dissertation is based on the ideas of Frances Yates,
      who states that "the art of memory" is composed of "spatial
      orientation toward the parts of a whole; grotesque or
      exaggerated imagery in the service of aiding memory;
      appreciation of means rather than ends," and "a multi-
      levelled interpretation." The elements of the detective
      story--discovery of the culprit's motives, means, and
      opportunity, plus the personality of the detective--"em-
      body the four components" of Yates's concept.

88.   Burton, Carl T. "The Hero as Detective." Ph.D. disserta-
      tion, Columbia University, 1973.

      Examines the manner in which nineteenth-century English
      writers used the figure of the detective, including chap-
      ters on Dickens's use of detectives in his fiction, Wilkie
      Collins's *The Moonstone*, and the Sherlock Holmes stories.

89.   Eisinger, Erica M. "The Adaptation of Detective Story
      Techniques in the French New Novel." Ph.D. dissertation,
      Yale University, 1973.

Contends that the French new novel shares certain assumptions and techniques with detective fiction: reality is mysterious, a search for the meaning of events, and an investigator/detective. Such elements as a confusion of identity and role, suppression of information, inversion (in which events are not presented in chronological order), and an unreliable narrator are common to both genres.

90. Fritz, Kathlyn Ann. "Patterns and Perceptions of Homicide in Detective Novels." Ph.D. dissertation, Yale University, 1975.

Maintains that detective fiction reflects the values of the culture that produces it and reads it, and that murder in detective novels can be seen as a symbol of deviance, but the character of the victim and the character of the murderer and his motive must be considered.

91. Grella, George J. "The Literature of the Thriller: A Critical Study." Ph.D. dissertation, University of Kansas, 1967.

In this dissertation, Grella applies the vocabulary and techniques of modern literary criticism to the thriller genre, arguing that there is valid literary merit in the form. He covers both the formal and hard-boiled detective genres, as well as both heroic and realistic spy fiction, identifying each genre as a form of "comedy of manners, romance, or the mythic and ironic modes, all masquerading as popular fiction."

92. Mooney, Joan. "The American Detective Story: A Study in Popular Fiction." Ph.D. dissertation, University of Minnesota, 1968. Reprinted as "Best-Selling American Detective Fiction." *Armchair Detective* 3 (January 1970): 97-114; 3 (April 1970): 141-160; 3 (July 1970): 215-239; 4 (October 1970): 12-29; 4 (January 1971): 87-103.

Contends that "mystery fiction can be studied as a valid reflection of actual society" from the viewpoint of "the society it presents in fictional form and the social factors which made certain authors extremely popular."

ARTICLES AND PORTIONS OF BOOKS

93.   Adams, Gail. "Double Jeopardy: Husband and Wife Teams in
      Detective Fiction." *Armchair Detective* 8 (August 1975):
      251-256.

      Examines several husband and wife detective teams--
      Christie's Beresfords, Hammett's Charleses, and the
      Lockridges' Norths--and concludes that wives in these
      teams generally "do not have courage but rather foolish-
      ness," that "their natural curiosity is really caused by
      boredom," and that their detection is really intuition.

94.   Adams, Sr. John. "Detective-Fiction Game." *Overland Monthly*
      90 (August 1932): 173-174, 181, 191-192.

      In an analysis of detective fiction from the writer's
      point of view, Adams argues that it is the function of
      the mystery writer to play a game with the reader. Using
      Sherlock Holmes and Dr. Watson as his models, he illus-
      trates how adroit writers dole out clues piecemeal, along
      with a red herring here and there, to keep the audience
      in suspense until the denouement.

95.   Adey, Robert C.S. "In Search of the 'Con Man.'" *Armchair
      Detective* 2 (July 1969): 259, 261.

      Contends that the term "con man" is difficult to define
      and lists ten stories which feature such a character.

96.   Adey, Robert C.S. Introduction to *Locked Room Murders and
      Other Impossible Crimes*. London: Ferret Fantasy, 1979.

      In this introduction to a listing of over twelve hundred
      locked room mysteries, Adey provides a history of the form
      and notes that it is now seldom seen in novels but still
      appears in short stories.

97.   Altick, Richard D. "Literature with a Sanguinary Cast."
      Victorian Studies in Scarlet. New York: W.W. Norton,
      1970, pp. 67-85.

      Observes that "murder was a staple" of nineteenth-century
      popular fiction and traces this interest from the Newgate
      novel of the 1830s and early 1840s through the novels of
      Dickens to its culmination in "the great vogue of the
      sensation novel" in the 1860s. Wilkie Collins's *The Woman
      in White* and Mary Elizabeth Braddon's *Lady Audley's Secret*
      were two of the greatest successes in this genre that tried

"to render murder and other crimes plausible in terms of the mid-Victorian reader's own familiar social environment." Contends that this is what lent "the sensation novel its irresistible fascination."

98. "An American View of English Detective Fiction." *Bookman* (London) 82 (July 1932): 191.

Maintains that English detective fiction is, in general, far superior to American in plot, suspense, and writing style.

99. Amis, Kingsley. "My Favorite Sleuths." *Playboy* 13 (December 1966): 145, 343-349. Slightly revised version printed as "Unreal Policemen." *What Became of Jane Austen? And Other Questions.* New York: Harcourt Brace Jovanovich, 1971, pp. 108-125.

Amis notes the dichotomy between mystery/detection stories involving real policemen and unreal, super-detectives like Sherlock Holmes. He argues that Holmes and three successors—Father Brown (Chesterton), Nero Wolfe (Stout), and Doctor Fell (Carr) are more memorable than the true-to-life sleuths.

100. "And Is It Ever True?" *Times Literary Supplement* 23 June 1961, p. v.

The author argues that the detective story is more false than true "if it is assessed in terms of its picture of criminal investigation." The genre does, however, teach us much about ourselves—our love of the mysterious, and the need for escape in modern society.

101. Aucott, Robert. "When *Was* the Golden Age, Anyway?" *Armchair Detective* 5 (July 1972): 207-208.

Surveys the dates various critics have given as the Golden Age of mystery/detective fiction and suggests 1930 as "The Golden Year," listing the twenty-three best books published in that year.

102. Auden, W.H. "The Guilty Vicarage: Notes on the Detective Story, by an Addict." *Harper's Magazine* 196 (May 1948): 406-412. Reprinted *The Dyer's Hand, and Other Essays.* New York: Random House, 1962, pp. 146-158.

Auden "confesses" his addiction to this frivolous genre, and offers his definition of the detective story. It must involve a murderer who is, by a rational process of elim-

ination of other suspects, brought to justice. He identifies the archetypal characters of the genre as The
Victim, The Murderer, The Suspects, and The Detective.

103.   Aydelotte, William O. "The Detective Story as a Histori-
        cal Source." *Yale Review* 39 (Autumn 1949): 76-95.
        Reprinted *The Popular Arts: A Critical Reader*. Edited
        by Irving Deer and Harriet A. Deer. New York: Scrib-
        ners, 1967, pp. 132-154. Also reprinted *The Mystery
        Writer's Art* (item 54), pp. 306-325. Also reprinted
        Dimensions of Detective Fiction (item 43), pp. 68-82.

        Though Aydelotte denies that the detective story
        portrays "an accurate picture of modern life" because
        of its undue emphasis on crime, he does argue that, by
        studying the reasons for the popularity of the genre, one
        can learn significant truths about society. He finds
        that society yearns for a world that is understandable;
        thus the solution to a fictional crime is particularly
        gratifying.

104.   Baird, Newton. "Aristotle's Operative, Or, The Case of
        the Classic Barzun." *Armchair Detective* 8 (November
        1974): 15-23.

        Contends that the detective story "imitates not only
        life, but its intellectual father, Aristotle."

105.   Ball, John. "The Ethnic Detective." *The Mystery Story*
        (item 21), pp. 143-160.

        Defines an ethnic detective in literature as "someone
        who appears as a minority representative in the eyes of
        the reader." Uses such examples as Charlie Chan, Judge
        Dee, Inspector Ghote, and Inspector Napoleon Bonaparte.
        Argues that these ethnic detectives probably resulted
        from the specialized knowledge or background of the
        authors and a search for novelty rather than a desire
        to comment on the plight of minorities.

106.   Ball, John. "Murder at Large." *The Mystery Story* (item
        21), pp. 1-26.

        To support his thesis that detective fiction is an
        important literary genre and worthy of serious study,
        briefly cites some of the outstanding detective writers,
        beginning with Poe, and their creations. Argues that its
        standards and quality have steadily improved.

107. Bander, Elaine. "The English Detective Novel Between the
      Wars: 1919-1939." *Armchair Detective* 11 (July 1978):
      262-273.

      Maintains that during this period the English detective
      novel evolved from a puzzle story in the 1920s into "the
      detective novel of manners of the 1930s, which explicitly
      advertised the author's value system," and that by the
      end of this period the "average reader of detective fic-
      tion was reading for manner, not matter."

108. Bandy, Eugene Franklin. "Jacques Barzun: A Critic Talks
      About Mystery Criticism." *Publishers Weekly* 213 (13
      March 1978): 68-69.

      In an interview Barzun observes that "criticism has
      played an important role in improving the genre" and does
      not think that the classic detective story, whose demise
      he had noted in 1965, will be revived.

109. Barzun, Jacques. "A Critical Vocabulary for Crime Fiction."
      Armchair Detective 4 (January 1971): 75-78.

      A commentary on, and listing of, words and phrases com-
      monly found in detective fiction in an attempt to stan-
      dardize and develop a terminology for analyzing and crit-
      ically discussing the genre. It was published here as a
      preview of the kind of terminology that would be used
      in the still to be published *Catalogue of Crime* (item 2).

110. Barzun, Jacques. "Detection and the Literary Art." *New
      Republic* 144 (24 April 1961): 17-20. Also printed *The
      Delights of Detection*. Edited by Jacques Barzun. New
      York: Criterion Books, 1961, pp. 9-23. Reprinted *The
      Mystery Writer's Art* (item 54), pp. 248-262.

      Barzun argues that the short story is the ideal form
      for detective fiction, and identifies five parts which
      are common to all good stories in the genre: the preamble,
      the predicament, the discourse on method, the action on
      the basis of deduction, and the explanation. He states
      that the supreme quality of the genre is "invention,
      which is to say imagination" and defends it as valid
      literature.

111. Barzun, Jacques. "Detection in Extremis." *Crime in Good
      Company* (item 32), pp. 134-145.

      Argues that such additions to the detective story as
      psychology and romance are spoiling it and that current

"serious" fiction has virtually nothing to offer the
mystery/detection genre.

112.   Barzun, Jacques. "The Detective Story." *Holiday* 24 (July
       1958): 6, 8-11, 138.

       Barzun laments what he perceives as the decline of the
       detective story. He argues that the attempt to introduce
       psychology into these stories has reduced or completely
       eliminated the possibility of heroism, thus rendering
       the genre boring.

113.   Barzun, Jacques. "From *Phedre* to Sherlock Holmes." *Energies
       of Art: Studies of Authors, Classic and Modern.* New
       York: Harper, 1956, pp. 303-323.

       Barzun mourns the demise of the detective story, argu-
       ing that it has gone the way of the madrigal and the
       heroic couplet. Barzun's chief interest in these stories
       is the "How"--the process by which the crime is solved.
       This element, he observes, is increasingly displaced
       in modern detective stories by an emphasis on psychology,
       which he regards as unfortunate.

114.   Barzun, Jacques. "The Illusion of the Real." *The World
       of Raymond Chandler* (item 676), pp. 159-163.

       Contends that Raymond Chandler's arguments in "The
       Simple Art of Murder" (item 156) against the classical
       detective story and in favor of the hard-boiled school
       are not valid. Particularly disputes the idea that the
       hard-boiled detective novel is more realistic than the
       classical, citing such examples as the physical indestruc-
       iblility of the usual hard-boiled detective.

115.   Barzun, Jacques. "Meditations on the Literature of Spying."
       American Scholar 34 (1965): 167-178.

       Barzun bemoans the drab world of Le Carré's spies,
       arguing that the spy story is valuable because it permits
       the reader to share the richness--both exalted and sor-
       did--of an exotic life.

116.   Barzun, Jacques. "Not 'Whodunit?' But 'How?'" *Saturday
       Review* 27 (4 November 1944): 9-11.

       In an attempt to define the parameters of the detective
       story, Barzun argues that such a story "is a narrative of
       which the chief interest lies in the palpable process of
       detection." It is the process--not the detective or the

criminal--that is at the heart of the genre. Barzun also
claims that most of the original detective plots have
been used up, and that the genre is dying out.

117. Barzun, Jacques. "The Novel Turns Tale." *Mosaic* 4 (1971):
33-40.

Barzun distinguishes between the novel--"a narrative
that professes to illuminate life by pretending to be
history"--and the tale, which is older, more studied,
less spontaneous, and which Barzun prefers. Analyzing
mystery stories in light of this distinction, he argues
that critics of the classical, or puzzle-oriented detective story are mistaken when they attack these stories
as unrealistic. The stories are tales, and thus not required to be absolutely realistic.

118. Barzun, Jacques. "Requiescat." *Chimera* 5 (Summer 1947):
59-66.

Argues that the core of a detective story is "curiosity
about material things and their behavior" and character
and human feelings are subordinate. Contends that Dorothy L.
Sayers's last detective novel is probably the end of the
genre.

119. Barzun, Jacques. "Suspense Suspended." *American Scholar*
27 (Autumn 1958): 496+.

Argues that detective fiction adapts the conventions
of the "serious" fiction being written at the same time
and has now "fallen on evil days ... because the contemporary fiction on which it rests is not adaptable to
its needs."

120. Barzun, Jacques, and Wendell Hertig Taylor. Introduction
to *Classic Stories of Crime and Detection.*
Edited by Jacques Barzun and Wendell Hertig Taylor.
New York: Garland Publishing, 1976. Also printed in
A Book of Prefaces (item 22), pp. 5-11.

Defines "classics of crime fiction" as stories that
have endured the test of time, which in turn implies they
have imagination, style, originality, and "elegance of
form." Traces the prejudice against mysteries to the
dominance of the novel, which concentrates on character
and social problems.

121. Basney, Lionel. "Corpses, Clues, and the Truth." *Christianity Today* 18 (30 August 1974): 16-17.

Argues that the detective story is moral because it
demands a real, specific offense, real, specific guilt,
and that the culprit never escapes.

122. Basney, Lionel. "Pornography of Moral Indignation."
      Christianity Today 20 (19 December 1975): 17-19.

The effect of the detective story is not moral because
the readers begin to see people outside their own class
or nationality as being sinners from which they must be
protected. Basney states that Chesterton and Simenon do
not inspire this attitude because their detectives work
through "imaginative sympathy" with the culprit.

123. Baudou, Jacques. "Les Petits-Maîtres du Roman Policier
      Français." *Europe* no. 571-572 (November-December 1976):
      150-154.

Argues that the golden age of the detective novel in
France (judged by the number of novels published) occurred
during the post-World War II period (1945-1950) and that
it began to decline in the sixties with the emergence
of the spy novel. Briefly surveys some of the forgotten
detective writers of this period.

124. Baunsgaard, Hilmar. "A Defense for Crime Fiction." *Arm-
      chair Detective* 10 (October 1977): 358-359.

The author, former Prime Minister of Denmark, argues
that the best detective stories are literature, as worth-
while as any good novel. Detective stories entertain and
follow the same rules as the novel--they must have accurate descriptions of characters and milieu and an exciting
plot. Cites many examples of Scandinavian contributions
to detective fiction.

125. Beattie, Anna B. "Whet Your Wits on a Clue." *Survey* 64
      (15 July 1930): 350-351.

Argues that reading detective stories is good for social
workers, primarily "as the best possible form of escape
literature" but also to acquire such useful "techniques"
as observation of detail and judging of character.

126. Becker, Jens Peter. "The Mean Streets of Europe: The In-
      fluence of the American 'Hard-Boiled School' on Euro-
      pean Detective Fiction." *Superculture: American Popular
      Culture and Europe*. Edited by Christopher W.E. Bigsby.
      Bowling Green, Ohio: Bowling Green University Popular
      Press, 1975, pp. 152-159.

Argues that European intellectuals and critics admired
and valued "hard-boiled" American detective fiction,
particulary the novels of Raymond Chandler, Dashiell
Hammett, and Ross Macdonald, and the short stories that
appeared in pulp magazines such as *Black Mask* in the
1920s and 1930s, before they were properly appreciated
in America. Concludes that it was "one of the achieve-
ments of the American hard-boiled school" to add social
criticism to "the melodramatic form of the detective
story."

127.   Benét, Stephen Vincent. "Bigger and Better Murders."
       Bookman 63 (May 1926): 291-296.

       Observes that detective fiction has developed from a
       literary sideline to be apologized for into a real indus-
       try. The genre continues to be popular because of great
       fictional detectives like Sherlock Holmes, the interest
       of intellectual, cultured people such as Woodrow Wilson,
       and, most significantly, the trend in the genre toward
       character and away from plot.

128.   Benét, William Rose. "Here's to Crime!" *Saturday Review*
       4 (18 February 1928): 605+.

       In a long preface to a review of some current detective
       novels, Benét argues that the vicarious thrill of the
       "atavistic" manhunt is one appeal of the genre; others
       are the desire to be frightened and then reassured and
       to solve a puzzle. Contends that murder is the best crime
       for such a story because it justifies a great amount of
       effort to solve it.

129.   Berkeley, Anthony. "To A.D. Peters." *The Second Shot.*
       New York: Doubleday, Doran, 1931, pp. 5-7.

       States his belief that the best efforts of contemporary
       detective writers are being directed to developing
       character and atmosphere, the direction in which he thinks
       the detective story should go. Argues that the "days of
       the crime puzzle pure and simple, relying entirely upon
       plot," are numbered.

130.   Blake, Nicholas. Introduction to *Murder for Pleasure:*
       The Life and Times of the Detective Story, by Howard
       Haycraft. London: Davies, 1942. [This introduction
       does not appear in the American edition.] Reprinted as
       "The Detective Story--Why?" *The Art of the Mystery*
       Story (item 35), pp. 398-405.

Contends that the detective story has attained its
popularity because it successfully blends fantasy with
reality. If an author puts unreal characters into realistic settings, he produces the *roman policier*; if he puts
realistic characters into unrealistic situations, he produces a novel of manners.

131.   Bleiler, Everett F. "Chinese Detectives in Poland." *Armchair Detective* 11 (October 1978): 343-345.

Translates the preface to *The Righteous Judgments of
Magistrate Pao* (Warsaw, 1960), by Polish sinologist
Tadeusz Zbikowski. The book presents "Polish translations
of twenty stories featuring the most famous of all Chinese
detectives," Pao Kung. Points out that "Zbikowski's introduction differs occasionally in fact and opinion from
the work of Van Gulik."

132.   Blom, K. Arne, and Jan Broberg. "Detective Fiction in
Sweden." *Armchair Detective* 9 (October 1976): 272-273,
333.

In a survey of detective fiction in Sweden, Blom and
Broberg contend that although some detective fiction was
written in Sweden in the 1890s, the first modern crime
novel in that country was *Doktor Glas*, published in 1905
by Söderberg. They list and comment on some outstanding
Swedish detective fiction writers.

133.   Blom, K. Arne, and Jan Broberg. "Panorama du Roman
Policier Suédois." *Europe* no. 571-572. (November-December 1976): 154-159.

Surveys the history of the detective novel in Sweden,
which the authors contend really began in 1838 with the
publication of Carl Jomas Love Almquist's *Skållnora Kvarn*.

134.   Bogan, Louise. "Time of the Assassins." *Nation* 158 (22
April 1944): 475-476, 478. Reprinted *Selected Criticism:
Prose, Poetry*. New York: Noonday, 1955, pp. 258-263.

Basing much of her analysis of the development of
detective fiction on Roger Caillois' *Le Roman Policier*
(item 26), Bogan concludes that detective fiction is
worthy of serious critical attention and should not be
isolated from the "mainstream of literature."

135.   Borowitz, Albert I. "New Gaslight on Jack the Ripper."
Armchair Detective 9 (June 1976): 175-177, 234.

In an article largely devoted to exploring theories
about the identity of Jack the Ripper, points out some

of the more interesting literary works concerning him, such as Marie Belloc Lowndes's *The Lodger*.

136.   Boucher, Anthony. "The Ethics of the Mystery Novel." *Tricolor* 2 (October 1944): 97-102. Reprinted *The Art of the Mystery Story* (item 35), pp. 384-389.

Notes the trend away from unquestioned conservatism in mystery/detection fiction. Argues that, in general, these stories reflect the mores of the time, the prejudices and preferences of the day.

137.   Boyd, Stuart. "Homicide in Fiction." *The Murderer and His Victim*. By John M. Macdonald. Springfield, Ill.: Charles C. Thomas, 1961, pp. 372-404.

In this chapter which he contributed to Macdonald's book, Boyd contends that most writers of mystery and detection fiction deal with murder "because they know it sells books" and that most use the solving of the puzzle to explain away the "vicarious interest in the bloody deed itself," but some, such as Mickey Spillane, make "no pretense in [their] appeal to hob-nailed emotions."

138.   Boynton, H.W. "Adventures and Riddles." *Bookman* 49 (May 1919): 321-327.

Along with brief observations on a number of mystery novels he is reviewing, Boynton observes that mystery fiction is "mechanical romance" because of its emphasis on plot and lack of emphasis on literary style.

139.   Boynton, H.W. "In Behalf of the Puzzle Novel." *Bookman* 58 (November 1923): 295-298.

Contends that "a writer of detective stories should have the tastes of a child and the mind of a chess player," both of which make sex and characterization irrelevant to this genre of fiction. The mystery or "puzzle" novel is a means of relaxation and escape that one does not have to be a fool to enjoy.

140.   Breen, Jon L. "Detective Fiction and the Turf." *Armchair Detective* 5 (October 1971): 24.

States that horse racing far outdistances all other sports as a background for detective stories and argues that two reasons are that race handicapping is like mystery reading and that the track has traditionally been associated with gambling and gangsters.

141. Breen, Jon L. "On the Passing of *Manhunt.*" *Armchair De-
      tective* 1 (April 1968): 89, 93.

      Notes the demise of *Manhunt*, in its day "the world's
      best selling crime fiction magazine." First issued in
      1953, it encouraged the hard-boiled school of detective
      fiction. This and its notable list of contributors made
      it, Breen contends, one of the most important detective
      magazines ever.

142. Bremner, Marjorie. "Crime Fiction for Intellectuals."
      Twentieth Century 156 (September 1954): 246-252.

      Maintains that the well-educated enjoy detective fic-
      tion for the variations within a convention or formula.

143. Briney, Robert E. "Death Rays, Demons, and Worms Unknown
      to Science: The Fantastic Element in Mystery Fiction."
      The Mystery Story (item 21), pp. 235-289.

      Defines the fantastic element as a "real or apparent
      departure from natural law or current knowledge" and
      cites examples from Wilkie Collins and Conan Doyle to
      Sax Rohmer and John Dickson Carr. Argues that this highly
      specialized subcategory of mystery fiction that features
      psychic or occult detectives is proof that the mystery
      story framework can support a wide variety of themes,
      backgrounds, and objectives.

144. Briney, Robert E. "*Mystery Book Magazine*: An Appreciation
      and Index." *Armchair Detective* 8 (August 1975): 245-
      250.

      Maintains that *Mystery Book Magazine* (1945-1951) was a
      small magazine but worthy of attention because of its
      "intelligent editorship" and large number of high quality
      stories. In contrast to *Ellery Queen's Mystery Magazine*,
      which featured short stories, it emphasized complete
      novels. An index to the fiction appearing in it is
      appended.

145. Brophy, Brigid. "Detective Fiction: A Modern Myth of
      Violence?" *Hudson Review* 18 (Spring 1965): 11-30. Re-
      printed in *Don't Never Forget: Collected Views and
      Reviews*. New York: Holt, Rinehart and Winston, 1967,
      pp. 121-142.

      Argues that, although the detective story is not a
      myth in the strictest sense of an anonymous timeless
      story supposedly true, it does follow patterns and for-
      mulas as myths do. After discussing ancient Greek and

Christian myths concludes that the modern age does not have many myths and the ones that do exist are found in modern popular fiction. Contends that the detective story hero is closely akin to the Greek heroes of myth.

146. Broun, Heywood. "Sherlock Holmes and the Pygmies." *Woman's Home Companion* 57 (November 1930): 21, 124, 126.

Contends that Conan Doyle, by creating Sherlock Holmes, and Woodrow Wilson, by stating that he enjoyed mystery stories, created the "present vogue of mystery stories in America." Also contends that humor is a defect in a detective story and that all writers in the genre since Conan Doyle have been under his influence.

147. Byrd, Max. "The Detective Detected: From Sophocles to Ross Macdonald." *Yale Review* 64 (Autumn 1974): 72-83.

Byrd posits three types of "detective stories": the "detective" finds that he is himself the criminal (e.g., Sophocles, Conrad); the detective finds the one guilty person and thus establishes the innocence of everyone else (e.g., Conan Doyle); the detective believes the world is corrupt and only he is innocent (e.g., Hammett and Chandler).

148. Carlisle, Charles R. "Strangers Within, Enemies Without: Alienation in Popular Mafia Fiction." *Dimensions of Detective Fiction* (item 43), pp. 194-202.

Contends that Mafia fiction, although written primarily as escapist literature, is permeated by the theme of alienation, portraying the *mafioso* as alienated not only from society but from his own kind and sometimes even from his own family in such novels as Mario Puzo's *The Godfather*.

149. Carr, John Dickson. "The Grandest Game in the World." *Ellery Queen's Mystery Magazine* 41 (March 1963): 53-68. Reprinted *The Mystery Writer's Art* (item 54), pp. 227-247.

Contends that masterpieces of detection fiction are more than realistic crime stories. Their authors are adept at "the game"--providing clues to the reader without revealing the ultimate resolution of the mystery until the end of the story.

150. Cawelti, John G. *Adventure, Mystery, and Romance: Formula
      Stories as Art and Popular Culture*. Chicago: University
      of Chicago Press, 1976, pp. 80-191.

      In his four chapters on the detective story Cawelti
      argues that the "classical or ratiocinative" tale has,
      since World War II, largely given way to other types,
      such as the hard-boiled, in which adventure or melodrama
      are stressed and that the detective story in some measure
      reflects its historical period. Cawelti describes the
      hard-boiled detective as a "man of virtue in an amoral
      and corrupt world."

151. Cawelti, John G. "The Gunfighter and the Hard-Boiled
      Dick: Some Ruminations on American Fantasies of Heroism."
      American Studies 16 (1975): 49-64.

      Cawelti notes the similarities between the cowboy and
      the private eye--they are both professional men of vio-
      lence, but they are reluctant to use violence unless
      provoked. He argues that the popularity of the private
      eye, an "isolated hero in a pervasively corrupt society,"
      reflects a strain of pessimism in the American tradition.

152. Cawelti, John G. "The New Mythology of Crime." *Boundary
      2* 3 (Winter 1975): 325-357.

      In this article largely concerned with non-mystery/de-
      tection works, Cawelti describes an enforcer as ruthless
      and professional and gives John D. MacDonald's Travis
      McGee as a prime example.

153. Cawelti, John G. "Trends in Recent American Genre Fiction."
      Kansas Quarterly 10 (Fall 1978): 5-18.

      In an essay largely devoted to fantasy Cawelti contends
      that science fiction and the international intrigue
      thriller are flourishing "at the expense of the tradi-
      tional detective story."

154. Chandler, Frank Wadleigh. "The Literature of Crime-Detec-
      tion." *The Literature of Roguery*, Volume 2. New York:
      Burt Franklin, 1958, pp. 524-549.

      Contends that detective literature differs from the
      literature of roguery in its positive emphasis on the
      detective rather than the criminal and in its compara-
      tively modern origins. In a historical survey briefly
      notes the contributions of Gaboriau, Poe, Dickens, and
      Conan Doyle.

155. Chandler, Raymond. "Casual Notes on the Mystery Novel."
     Raymond Chandler Speaking (item 675), pp. 63-70. Re-
     printed *Writer* 76 (July 1963): 13-16, 46. Also reprinted
     Writing Detective and Mystery Fiction. Edited by A.S.
     Burack. Boston: Writer, 1967, pp. 81-89.

     Chandler discusses ten "rules" for the writing of
     mystery fiction, such as the necessity for credible
     motivation and technically sound methods of murder and
     detection. His premier rule is that the mystery novel
     "must be reasonably honest with the reader." (This article
     was written in 1949 but not published until after
     Chandler's death.)

156. Chandler, Raymond. "The Simple Art of Murder." *Atlantic
     Monthly* 174 (December 1944): 53-59. Revised version
     printed in *The Art of the Mystery Story* (item 35), pp.
     222-237. Reprinted *The Simple Art of Murder*. Boston:
     Houghton Mifflin, 1950, pp. 519-532.

     Argues that the classical detective story is successful
     neither as an intellectual problem nor "artistically as
     fiction." It is not about real murders or real life.
     Dashiell Hammett, he contends, "gave murder back to the
     kind of people that commit it for reasons," and he "put
     these people down on paper as they were" and "demonstrated
     that the detective story can be important writing." "The
     realist in murder," Chandler continues, writes of a
     corrupt world, "but down these mean streets a man must
     go who is not himself mean, who is neither tarnished nor
     afraid. The detective in this kind of story must be such
     a man."

157. Chandler, Raymond. "The Simple Art of Murder." *Saturday
     Review* 33 (15 April 1950): 13-14. Revised version
     printed in *The Simple Art of Murder*. Boston: Houghton
     Mifflin, 1950, pp. viii-x.

     In this essay, which is entirely different from item
     156, Chandler offers his appraisal of the mysteries (in-
     cluding his own early stories) published in the pulp
     magazines. In these stories, he contends, one could
     "recognize the authentic power of a kind of writing that
     even at its most mannered and artificial made most of
     the fiction of the time taste like a cup of lukewarm
     consommé at a spinsterish tearoom," and that in them the
     mystery became "hard and cynical about motive and
     character." He concludes that there are no classics of
     crime and detection because no one has exhausted the
     possibilities of the form.

158.   Charney, Hanna. "Pourquoi le 'Nouveau Roman' Policier?"
       French Review 46 (October 1972): 17-23.

       Examines the crime fiction of writers connected with
       the *nouveau roman* and the conflict between the latter
       and the rationalism of the traditional detective story.

159.   Chastaing, Maxime. "Le Roman Policier Classique." *Europe*
       no. 571-572 (November-December 1976): 26-50.

       Overview of the rules and structures of the classic
       detection novel.

160.   Chesterton, Cecil. "Art and the Detective." *Temple Bar*
       (London) 134 (10 October 1906): 322. Reprinted *Living
       Age* 251 (24 November 1906): 505-510.

       Deplores the "indiscriminate condemnation of detective
       fiction" and by citing the work of Gaboriau, Wilkie
       Collins, Poe, and Conan Doyle, argues against this un-
       deserved criticism.

161.   Chesterton, G.K. "About Shockers." *As I Was Saying*. New
       York: Dodd, Mead, 1936, pp. 200-210.

       Argues that the suspects in detective fiction ought to
       be good, respectable people, instead of criminals and
       shady characters. Otherwise, there is no shock when the
       real culprit is revealed.

162.   Chesterton, G.K. "A Defence of Detective Stories." *The
       Defendant*. London: R.B. Johnson, 1901, pp. 118-123.
       Reprinted *The Art of the Mystery Story* (item 35), pp.
       3-6.

       Defends the detective story as "the earliest and only
       form of popular literature in which is expressed some
       sense of the poetry of modern life." It also restores the
       sense of excitement to doing what is right--i.e., to
       apprehending criminals.

163.   Chesterton, G.K. "The Domesticity of Detectives." *The
       Uses of Diversity: A Book of Essays*. New York: Dodd,
       Mead, 1921, pp. 34-42.

       Contends that a good detective story is one that deals
       with "small" events. The genre is properly concerned with
       "a plan or problem set within certain defined limits";
       when it attempts to include broader social or political
       concerns, it loses its impact.

164.   Chesterton, G.K. "How to Write a Detective Story." *The
       Spice of Life and Other Essays*. Edited by Dorothy
       Collins. Philadelphia: Dufour, 1966, pp. 15-21.

       Maintains that to the extent the detective story is
       "literary craftsmanship, constructive rather than cre-
       ative," it can be taught. He gives five basic principles
       of the genre, such as the "story is written for the moment
       when the reader does understand" as well as for the moments
       when he does not.

165.   Chesterton, G.K. "On Detective Novels." *Generally Speak-
       ing*. London: Methuen, 1937, pp. 1-7. Reprinted *Readings
       on the Modern Essay*. Edited by Edward S. Noyes. Boston:
       Houghton Mifflin, 1933, pp. 471-475. Reprinted *The Man
       Who Was Chesterton*. Edited by R.T. Bond. New York: Dodd,
       1937, pp. 79-93.

       Contends that the whole point of the detective story
       is the moment of surprise, wherein the secret of the plot
       is revealed; advocates keeping these denouements brief
       and to the point.

166.   Chesterton, G.K. Preface to *The Wrong Letter*, by Walter
       S. Masterman. New York: E.P. Dutton, 1926, pp. v-ix.
       Reprinted as "Detective Stories." *G. K. C. as M. C.:
       Being a Collection of Thirty-Seven Introductions*.
       London: Methuen, 1929, pp. 173-177.

       Contends that the desire to be deceived--"to be stupider
       than the man who wrote the story"--is basic to the ap-
       preciation of mystery/detection fiction.

167.   "Chinese Apathy Toward Crime Detection." *Literary Digest*
       116 (23 September 1933): 14.

       Quotes at length from an article by a Chinese writer
       (identified only as T. K. C.) which argues that detective
       fiction is not popular with the Chinese because "it can
       never flourish in any country where the criminal procedure
       is arrest, torture, confession and death," the Chinese
       mind is "unequal to the task of sustained and close
       reasoning," Chinese are not curious, and "human life is
       worthless" in China.

168.   Christopher, Joe R. "The Case of the Vanishing Locomotives,
       or a Hell of a Way to Run a Railroad." *Armchair Detec-
       tive* 1 (January 1968): 56-58.

Plot summaries of three mystery stories in which a train disappears: "The Lost Special" by Conan Doyle, "The Adventure of the Lost Locomotive" by August Derleth, and "Snowball in July" by Ellery Queen.

169.   Christopher, Joe R. "Detective Fiction in the Wade Collection." *Armchair Detective* 9 (October 1976): 274-275.

Observes that the Marion E. Wade Collection at Wheaton College, Wheaton, Illinois, reputedly has the best G.K. Chesterton collection in the United States and the best Dorothy L. Sayers collection in the world.

170.   Christopher, Joe R. "*The Marble Faun*: A Whydunit." *Armchair Detective* 11 (January 1978): 78.

Points out that Nathaniel Hawthorne's *The Marble Faun* (1860) is "not a murder mystery, but it is a mystery and it *does* involve murder."

171.   Christopher, Joe R. "Murder at the Crossroads: or, Oedipus the Detective." *Armchair Detective* 2 (July 1969): 225-226.

Argues that Sophocles's *Oedipus the King* can be regarded as a murder mystery: there is a murder which Oedipus, as detective, investigates, and several clues are given as to the murderer's identity.

172.   Christopher, Joe R. "The Rites of a Mystery Cult." *Armchair Detective* 5 (April 1972): 152-153.

Agrees with Brigid Brophy's essay on detective fiction (see item 145) that such stories are modern myths and are a reaction to the French Revolution but does not agree with her idea that the stories offer absolution of guilt. Christopher contends that the reader identifies with the detective and nearly every detective "is revealing his own guilt in discovering a murderer."

173.   Chung, Sue Fawn. "From Fu Manchu, Evil Genius, to James Lee Wong, Popular Hero: A Study of the Chinese-American in Popular Periodical Fiction from 1920-40." *Journal of Popular Culture* 10 (Winter 1976): 534-547.

Contends that positive stereotypes of Chinese-Americans in popular periodical fiction began to appear in the mid-1920s with Charlie Chan. His success led to the introduction in the mid-1930s of James Lee Wong, State Department Secret Agent, completing the transition from evil genius (Dr. Fu Manchu) to popular hero.

174.   Cohen, Ralph. "Private Eyes and Public Critics." *Partisan
       Review* 24 (Spring 1957): 235-243.

       Cohen argues that a parallel exists between literary
       criticism and the private-eye novel--both of which are
       concerned with getting to the heart of a mystery--thus
       perhaps accounting for the rising critical popularity of
       the genre.

175.   Colbron, Grace I. "The Detective Story in Germany and
       Scandinavia." *Bookman* 30 (December 1909): 407-412.

       Surveys the German and Scandinavian detective story,
       briefly commenting on the outstanding writers. Concludes
       that there are few detective stories written in these
       countries because the need for cheap literature is sup-
       plied by translations of French or English works.

176.   Comber, Leon. "An Introduction to the World of Magistrate
       Pao." *The Strange Cases of Magistrate Pao: Chinese Tales
       of Crime and Detection*. Rutland, Vt.: Charles E. Tuttle,
       1964, pp. 9-31.

       In a historical survey of how Magistrate Pao's cases
       were collected and translated, points out some of the
       peculiarly Chinese features of the tales and of all
       Chinese detective stories such as the element of the
       supernatural, and the use of torture (various methods
       that could be used, both legal and illegal are described
       in some detail).

177.   Cone, Edward T. "Three Ways of Reading a Detective Story--
       Or a Brahms Intermezzo." *Georgia Review* 31 (1977):
       554-574.

       Using various Sherlock Holmes stories as examples, Cone
       demonstrates the three levels of interest that the detec-
       tive genre can produce. The first is the simplest--a
       curiosity about the outcome of the plot. The second, which
       comes during a rereading of the story, is analytical;
       and the third, when the reader is thoroughly familiar
       with the work, is a satisfying combination of the first
       two.

178.   Connolly, Cyril. "Deductions from Detectives." *New States-
       man and Nation* 2 (5 December 1931): vii-viii.

       Contends that the great virtues of the detective story
       are three: every detail (including brand names) must be
       right; it has a passion for the countryside, and it is
       the closest that current literature gets to a pure form.

179. "Conversations with a Psychoanalyst: Janet A. Kennedy,
      M.D." *The Mystery and Detection Annual 1972* (item 16),
      pp. 191-197.

      In this interview Kennedy argues that the interest in
      crime is greater than the interest in a puzzle and its
      solution for the reader of mystery and detection fiction
      and that such fiction offers an acceptable method of
      channelling aggressions. Also states that people today
      do not want mysteries explained.

180. "Cops and Novels: The Sleuth in Fact and Fancy." *Times
      Literary Supplement* 25 February 1955, p. v.

      Analyzes several popular fictional detectives from
      Dupin to Ellery Queen, concluding that, despite their
      eccentricities, many share the following characteristics
      with their real life counterparts: they are hard working,
      intelligent, and dedicated to their job.

181. Corbett, James. "The Art of Writing Thrillers." *Contem-
      porary Review* 182 (October 1952): 240-243.

      Describes his method of writing thrillers and maintains
      that the thriller writer must have a gift for evolving
      plots in addition to a "vivid imagination ... infinite
      resource, ingenuity, and the capacity for taking pains."

182. Cox, J. Randolph. "Detection in the Guilt-Age." *Armchair
      Detective* 8 (February 1975): 111-120.

      Surveys the landmarks in detective fiction from Poe to
      the present and maintains that the function of the genre
      can fruitfully be studied by studying its audience.

183. Cox, J. Randolph. "That Mysterious Aide to the Forces
      of Law and Order." *Armchair Detective* 4 (July 1971):
      221-229.

      After a brief survey of the masked avenger in detective
      fiction, concentrates on The Shadow, contending that he
      and the pulp magazines died out because the "spirit and
      substance of the [post-World War II] world was different"
      and because "the proper medium for the stories was now
      a visual one."

184. Creasey, John. "Mystery the World Over." *Rotarian* 91
      (December 1957): 14-16.

      Contends that people read mysteries because they want
      to find a place, even in fantasy, where "the best man
      always wins."

185. Creasey, John. "The Social Consequences of Crime-Writing."
     Armchair Detective 4 (October 1970): 38-40.

     Contends "that thrillers, at their best, are the moral-
     ity plays of our age," which can also portray the future
     and whose detective heroes have the same qualities as the
     heroes of folklore.

186. "Crime and the Reader." *Nation* 86 (13 February 1908):
     143-144.

     The popularity of detective fiction can be traced to
     the potential detective in everyone—the love of an ex-
     citing game.

187. "Crime Fiction." *The Concise Encyclopedia of Crime and
     Criminals*. Edited by Sir Harold Scott. London: Andre
     Deutsch, 1961, pp. 84-87.

     Contends that the common qualities of "excitement,
     action, violence and suspense" make crime fiction appeal
     to a wide public. Surveys the history of the genre and
     states that it reflects the society of the decade before
     the one in which it was written.

188. "Crime in Current Literature." *Westminster Review* 147
     (April 1897): 429.

     In a consideration of crime in all types of literature
     the author maintains that the popularity of detective
     fiction is dangerous to both the "minds and morals" of
     the readers as well as to "the character of our English
     literature." Excepts only "clever writers like Conan
     Doyle."

189. "Crime in Fiction." *Blackwood's Edinburgh Magazine* 148
     (August 1890): 172-189.

     Argues that crime in fiction leaves the reader morally
     degraded and that the novelists have exhausted their
     ingenuity in inventing new crimes and sensations. Con-
     cludes that the reading public will become satiated with
     this type of fiction. Much of the article is devoted to
     a survey of crime fiction, particularly by French writers,
     whom the author considers the masters of the genre.

190. "Crime Should be Credible." *Saturday Review* (London)
     154 (8 October 1932): 365.

     Two fundamentals of a good crime story are that "the
     circumstances of the crime must be possible" and the mo-

tives of the criminal and the behaviors of the investigators must be logical."

191.   Cruse, Amy. "Crime Fiction." *After the Victorians*. London:
       George Allen and Unwin, 1938, pp. 138-148.

       Argues that the Victorians regarded crime as an evil
       not to be dealt with lightly. Not until Wilkie Collins's
       The Woman in White (1860) was crime fiction treated as a
       fit subject for comedy. The appearance of *The Mystery of
       a Hansom Cab* (1887) by Fergus Hume and *A Study in Scarlet*
       (1887) by Conan Doyle marked an important turning point
       in the history of crime fiction: the shift of emphasis
       from the criminal to the crime and the subordination of
       the characters to the plot.

192.   Cuff, Sergeant. "Chacun à son Mystère." *Saturday Review*
       36 (24 January 1953): 19-20.

       States that the most common weakness of mystery stories
       is a skimpy plot and that current writers in the genre
       "don't devote enough time and thought to detection."

193.   Cuff, Sergeant. "The Toughie Submerged." *Saturday Review*
       38 (24 December 1955): 14-15.

       Observes that the "toughie" detective story has de-
       clined during the year, an encouraging trend. A list of
       what he considers to be good mysteries published during
       the year is appended.

194.   Cummings, J.C. "Detective Stories." *Bookman* 30 (January
       1910): 499-500.

       Argues for a step-by-step method of solving crimes in
       detective fiction--just as a real life detective would
       do it.

195.   Cushing, Charles Phelps. "Who Writes These Mystery Yarns?"
       Independent 118 (9 April 1927): 382-388.

       Argues that mystery stories appeal to educated people
       because most of them are written by such professional
       people as doctors, lawyers, and critics. Gives many
       examples. Also states that the intellectual activity
       of solving a puzzle is the essence of the genre.

196.   Dane, Clemence. "The Best Detective Story in the World."
       Bookman 75 (October 1932): 539-541.

Maintains that the Biblical story of Susannah, who was
saved by Daniel's examination of both the evidence and
the witnesses, is the best detective story because it was
the first time the detective story formula was used and
because it has never been surpassed.

197. Davey, Jocelyn. "Mysteryland Revisited." *Reporter* 20
        (16 April 1959): 37-38.

Argues that the classical detective story is like Plato's
Dialogues and the modern type like Greek drama: "Man
struggling with the blind forces of fate."

198. Davis, Dorothy Salisbury. "View from the Middle Window."
        Publishers Weekly 213 (13 March 1978): 46-57.

Admits that she does not like "the ultrarealism" of
some contemporary mystery novels and deplores "the ex-
ploitation of the mystery novel as a vehicle for pornography, the pornography of violence as well as sex and of
sexual violence."

199. Denbie, Roger. "A Mystery Story Writer Replies to Pro-
        fessor Waite." *Scribner's Magazine* 95 (April 1934):
        22 [*sic*].

Denbie, whose book *Death on the Limited* was used by
Waite (item 501) as a prime example of a detective novel
written in ignorance of the law, defends himself by
quoting references to search warrants in the book, by
stating that he consulted police detectives before writing
the book, and by stating that an author has no responsibility to have his police follow rules that are "commonly
and persistently" ignored by real police.

200. "The Detection Club." *Commonweal* 16 (17 August 1932): 380.

Deprecates the decline in the quality of detective
fiction and applauds the formation of the Detection Club,
an organization with the aim of returning detective fiction to its original traditions.

201. "Detective Stories." *Atlantic Monthly* 81 (April 1898):
        573-574.

Contends that most detective stories are not analytic,
as Poe recommended, but rather "purely synthetic or con-
structive" because the author already knows the solution
to the mystery before he begins to write.

202. "'Detectiveness' in Fiction." *Nation* 95 (15 August 1912):
      141-142.

      Maintains that reading a detective story is "a stirring
      mental exercise, with just enough of the complex back-
      ground of life to distinguish it from a problem in mathe-
      matics."

203. "Detectives in Fiction: A Study of Literary Fashions."
      Times Literary Supplement 12 August 1926, pp. 529-530.
      Reprinted *Living Age* 330 (18 September 1926): 638-643.
      Also reprinted *Men and Books*. Edited by Malcolm S.
      MacLean and Elisabeth K. Holmes. New York: Ray Long
      and Richard R. Smith, 1932, pp. 334-343.

      Contends that the detective story is a contemporary
      creation and that its technique is still developing, with
      unconventional features appearing that give the author
      more freedom of action. Concludes that the English de-
      tective story has grown in stature since the time of Poe
      and Conan Doyle.

204. DeVoto, Bernard. "Easy Chair." *Harper's* 190 (December
      1944): 36-37.

      In a reply to Edmund Wilson's attack on mystery fiction
      (item 515), DeVoto argues that one should not apply an
      inappropriate set of critical criteria to the genre and
      concludes that mysteries are popular because they are
      "the only current form of fiction that is pure story."

205. Dickson, Carl Byron. "Edmund Wilson and the Detective
      Story." *Armchair Detective* 9 (June 1976): 189-190.

      In a reply to Wilson's essay "Who Cares Who Killed
      Roger Ackroyd?" (item 515), observes that Wilson's con-
      clusions are "ludicrous" and that "taste is personal and
      we are all prejudiced where it is concerned."

206. DiManno, Yves. "Roman Policier et Société." *Europe* no.
      571-572 (November-December 1976): 117-125.

      Contends that, unlike older detective fiction writers,
      recent French writers in the genre tend to attack the
      established political system.

207. Donald, Miles. "Popular Fiction." *The American Novel in
      the Twentieth Century*. New York: Barnes and Noble,
      1978, pp. 176-195.

There are two types of detective stories: "the tightly
composed puzzle and the atmosphere-creating thriller."
The formula is so important in the genre that the stories
often have the air of a product. Makes brief comments on
many writers of detective fiction.

208. Donotor, Tekla, Elizabeth Tucker, and Antony Hellenberg.
"Folklore and the Detective Story." *Folklore Forum* 8
(1975): 13/335-21/343.

Using the detective novels of Mickey Spillane, Ian
Fleming, John D. MacDonald, Agatha Christie, and others
as a basis for their study, the authors contend that all
major folktale heroes are found in detective fiction and
that like *Valhamarchen* it "usually represents a naive
view of the world in which good triumphs over evil and
the moral order of the universe is affirmed in the happy
ending."

209. Donovan, Frank P. "Mystery Rides the Rails." *Armchair
Detective* 1 (July 1968): 124-128; 2 (October 1968):
46-48; 2 (January 1969): 103-107; 2 (April 1969): 176-
179.

The train is not so popular with American mystery writers
as with English. Lists and comments on several American
and English mystery novels and short stories in which
trains play a part. Lists many more without comments.

210. Dove, George N. "Intruder in the Rose Garden." *Armchair
Detective* 9 (October 1976): 278-280.

Argues that the attitude of classic detective fiction
toward the private eye is based on "social snobbery."
Examines four stories in which "the private detective is
lower on the social scale than the sleuth-protagonist."

211. Dove, George N. "The Police Procedural." *Armchair Detective* 10 (April 1977): 133-137; 10 (July 1977): 241-
243; 10 (October 1977): 320-323; 11 (January 1978):
74-77; 11 (April 1978): 150-152; 11 (July 1978): 249-
251.

Traces the development of the police procedural through
its thirty-year history and identifies some of its themes
that are not found in older forms of detective fiction:
for example, the hostile public, interservice rivalry,
overworked police force, and policemen with family problems.

212. Dove, George N. "'Shades of Dupin.': Fictional Detectives
      on Detective Fiction." *Armchair Detective* 8 (November
      1974): 12–14.

      Maintains that "references by people in detective
      stories to other people in other detective stories have
      been made so frequently that they constitute at least a
      minor convention of the genre."

213. Durham, Philip. "The *Black Mask* School." *Tough Guy Writers
      of the Thirties* (item 46), pp. 51–79. Reprinted *The
      Mystery Writer's Art* (item 54), pp. 197–226.

      Contends that in the pulp magazine *Black Mask*, the
      hard-boiled private detective hero emerged as did a unique
      attitude toward violence that "provided both an ethical
      and an aesthetic justification" for its use.

214. Edmiston, Susan. "The Nine Most Devilish Murders."
      Esquire 84 (August 1975): 66–67, 136.

      Contrary to the dictum that the simplest methods of
      fictional murder are the best, Edmiston maintains that
      the best remembered mystery stories are the ones in which
      the murder is committed in an ingenious or bizarre way.
      She comments briefly on nine mysteries that satisfy this
      criterion, including Dorothy L. Sayers's *The Nine Tailors*
      and Poe's *The Murders in the Rue Morgue*.

215. Eisinger, Erica M. "Detective Story Aspects of the
      Nouveau Roman." *Armchair Detective* 12 (Fall 1979):
      362–365.

      Contends that the French *nouveau roman* often derives
      both its form and content from detective fiction. Also
      argues that both genres share the assumption that "reality
      is mysterious" and also share the viewpoint of the in-
      vestigator. Cites examples from the novels of Alain Robbe-
      Grillet, among others.

216. Ellin, Stanley. "The Crime Short Story: An American View."
      Crime in Good Company (item 32), pp. 163–177.

      Contends that "the crime-story magazines today offer
      a writer the greatest possible freedom to express himself
      in any way he desires."

217. Elwin, Malcolm. "Psychology of the Thriller." *Saturday
      Review* (London) 156 (26 August 1933): 230.

Maintains that the thriller fulfills the same function as the crossword puzzle, but it must play upon the emotions.

218. "Entertaining Inquiry: The Nature of the Detective Story." *Times Literary Supplement* 25 February 1955, p. iv.

Argues that "a high degree of public security" is necessary for the enjoyment of stories about murder and that one of the chief attractions of the detective story is "the perennially fascinating situation of pursuit."

219. Evans, Verda. "Mystery as Mind-Stretcher." *English Journal* 61 (April 1972): 495-503.

Maintains that teachers of English should pay more attention to mystery stories and divides the genre into six categories: classical, police procedural, situational, Gothic, espionage, and social comment.

220. Fadiman, Clifton. "On Reading Mysteries." *Good Housekeeping* 116 (February 1943): 30, 79.

Argues that the mystery story satisfies our sense of order and our sense of morality.

221. Farrar, John. "Have You a Detective in Your Home?: Today's Craze for Crime in Fiction, and Its Causes." *Century* 96 (May 1929): 84-89.

Contends that the popularity of crime fiction has three chief causes: weariness with realism, love of a puzzle, and snobbery. Farrar then surveys the genre and divides it into six categories: horror, puzzle, mystery, fantastic pursuit, underworld, and murder.

222. Fiedler, Leslie. *Love and Death in the American Novel.* New York: Dell, 1969, pp. 503-513.

In a discussion of three popular literary genres--the ghost story, science fiction, and the detective story--Fiedler contends that the last performs "for the middlebrow reader the function of evoking and purging terror" but that the "pseudo-scientific novel of detection is nearly dead in the United States." As the popularity of Hammett, Chandler, and Spillane has faded, their former audience "has turned to science fiction."

223. Field, Louise Maunsell. "Philo Vance & Co., Benefactors." *North American Review* 235 (March 1933): 254-260.

Notes that people are greatly interested in murder
stories and traces this interest back through Greek
tragedy and Shakespeare. Contends that this popularity
comes from the fact that everyone has at some time wanted
to murder someone. Argues that the detective story gives
the reader a vicarious release for this desire and is
also a deterrent because in detective stories the murderer
is always discovered.

224.   Filstrup, Jane Merrill. "Cats in Mysteries." *Armchair
       Detective* 11 (January 1978): 59-62; 11 (April 1978):
       134-138.

Points out that cats have played all three roles in
mystery fiction--criminal, victim, and detective. Lists
mystery novels in which cats have played a part and
briefly comments on them.

225.   Filstrup, Jane Merrill. "The Shattered Calm: Libraries
       in Detective Fiction." *Wilson Library Bulletin* 53
       (December 1978): 320-327; 53 (January 1979): 392-398.

Surveys a great number of detective stories in which a
library, private or public, is involved. Notes that when
a librarian is a character in such a story she is likely
to be female and a victim of the crime rather than the
sleuth or criminal. Filstrup does, however, describe
a number of stories in which a librarian is a sleuth.

226.   Fiscalini, Janet. "Elementary, My Dear Watson." *Common-
       weal* 75 (27 October 1961): 116-118.

Maintains that the conventions and rules of the detective story define a "fantasy" because real crimes are not
solved by these rules. "This logically fantastic world
implied its fantastically logical hero," and thus detectives like Sherlock Holmes were created.

227.   Fisher, Peter, and Hans Daiber. "Der Kriminalroman--
       Entwicklungen, Aspecte." *Merkur* 23 (September 1969):
       846-866.

The detective novel today often tends to be overin-
tellectual. Also, it faces the problem that criminality
is not so easily defined as it once was.

228.   Fisher, Steve. "Pulp Literature: Subculture Revolution
       in the Late 1930s." *Armchair Detective* 5 (January
       1972): 91-92, 95.

Contends that the dominant school in pulp magazine
writing changed in the late 1930s from objective to sub-
jective.

229. Flanagan, Thomas. "'Amid the Wild Lights and Shadows':
The Life and Early Death of the Detective Story."
Columbia University Forum 1 (Winter 1957): 7-10. Reprinted *The Columbia University Forum Anthology*. Edited
by Peter Spackman and Lee Ambrose. New York: Atheneum,
1968, pp. 3-8.

Argues that the classical detective story, in which a
puzzle is constructed and solved in an orderly fashion,
is too often only a diversion. It should be, he contends,
a "splendid and impressive form of romance, with a subject as well as a method," each appropriate to the other.
All the great detective stories partake of this romance.

230. Fletcher, Connie. "The Case of the Missing Criminal: Crime
Fiction's Unpaid Debt to its Ne'er-Do-Well." *Armchair
Detective* 10 (January 1977): 17-20.

Contends that by studying the criminal in fiction much
can be learned about the past and about ourselves because
the presentation of the criminal "changes as popular
attitudes change." Traces the portrayal of the criminal
from the eighteenth century to modern times.

231. Forbes, Elizabeth. "Fairies and Sleuths." *Opera* 20
(December 1969): 1021-1025.

Surveys, with summaries, detective stories which have
used opera as part of the plot or setting and comments
on the correctness of the musical detail in each.

232. Frank, Waldo. "The Mystery Tale." *New Republic* 48 (13
October 1926): 220-221.

Maintains that good mystery fiction should "arouse
emotions of terror, mystery," amazement, and the excitement of the hunt. Cites J.S. Fletcher as his example of
the current mystery writer who best meets all these requirements.

233. Freeman, R. Austin. "Art of the Detective Story." *Nineteenth Century* 95 (May 1924): 713-721. Reprinted *Dr.
Thorndyke's Crime File*, by R. Austin Freeman. Edited
by P.M. Stone. New York: Dodd, Mead, 1941, pp. 3-16.
Also reprinted *The Art of the Mystery Story* (item 35),
pp. 7-17.

Argues that while style, setting, and characterization are important to the detective genre, they are "secondary and subordinate" to the intellectual, puzzle-solving aspects of the story. Thus an author must plot his story carefully, making sure that it is free from "fallacies of reasoning." Also contends that detective fiction is a valid literary genre, arguing that its critics always attack the worst examples of the form instead of investigating the best.

234.   Gadney, Reg. "Criminal Tendencies." *London Magazine* 12 (June–July 1972): 110–122.

Using the works of Patricia Highsmith and Ross Macdonald as examples, argues that crime fiction no longer stresses a struggle between good and evil: both authors instead stress menace and uncertainty.

235.   Gardiner, Harold C. "The Barbarians Are Within the Gates." *In All Conscience: Reflections on Books and Culture.* Garden City, N.Y.: Hanover House, 1959, pp. 21–25.

In this article, written in response to a piece by Ben Ray Redman (item 417), Gardiner concurs with Redman's conclusion that detection is now almost non-existent in "detective fiction," while crime is dominant. Both Gardiner and Redman cite Mickey Spillane as the leading exponent of the brutality and sadism rampant in detective fiction. Gardiner concludes that "if this type of book were not degenerate and foul, it would still be vulgar and crude."

236.   Gardner, Erle Stanley. "The Case of the Early Beginning." *The Art of the Mystery Story* (item 35), pp. 203–207.

Traces the history of the hard-boiled private eye through the *Black Mask* era, and contends that the "air of authenticity" in the genre has bred a shrewder, more knowledgeable readership.

237.   **Garfield, Brian. "The State of the Art: A Symposium Conducted by Brian Garfield."** *Publishers Weekly* 213 (13 March 1978): 50–51.

Contains the responses of several major American and European mystery writers to the question: "Do you perceive any important recent changes in crime-detective-suspense-mystery writing or publishing?"

238. Gass, Sherlock Bronson. "Desipere in Loco." *The Criers of the Shops*. Boston: Marshall Jones, 1925, pp. 335-351.

    Argues that detective fiction is not a literary genre at all but a game with certain rules and conventions. The paramount convention is that the detective must bring reason and intellect to the game.

239. Gayot, Paul. "Sur la Littérature Policière Potentielle." *Europe* no. 571-572 (November-December 1976): 164-166.

    Surveys the history and goals of OULIPOPOL (Ouvroir de Littérature Policière Potentielle): to analyze fiction not written as detective novels in order to reveal their basic mystery fiction structures.

240. Geherin, David J. "The Hard-Boiled Detective Hero in the 1970's: Some New Candidates." *Armchair Detective* 11 (January 1978): 49-51.

    Points out that three current writers have different approaches to the hard-boiled detective fiction of Hammett and Chandler: Robert B. Parker, who imitates, Roger L. Simon, who updates, and Andrew Bergman, who parodies. They also demonstrate in their novels that the hard-boiled detective novel can "adapt to the changing times while remaining faithful to the spirit of the form."

241. Gerber, Richard. "Name as Symbol: On Sherlock Holmes and the Nature of the Detective Story." *Armchair Detective* 8 (August 1975): 280-287.

    Gerber justifies this exhaustive semantic and psychological analysis of the name "Sherlock Holmes" by stating that the name is a "signalling" name, one that is expressive in a concealed or subliminal manner, and that analyzing the name is a way to obtain "insight into otherwise concealed depths." Since Holmes "also represents *the* hero of the detective novel," insight into his character also means obtaining insight into "the basic psychic structure of the detective novel."

242. Gerould, Katharine Fullerton. "Murder for Pastime." *Saturday Review* 12 (3 August 1935): 3-4, 14.

    Contends that English detective stories are better than American ones because English writers write better, do not resort to sensationalism, and because American writers have not completely accepted the "purely intellectual nature" of the genre.

243.   Gilbert, Elliot L. "The Detective as Metaphor in the
       Nineteenth Century." *Journal of Popular Culture* 1
       (Winter 1967): 256-262. Reprinted *The Mystery Writer's
       Art* (item 54), pp. 285-294.

       Argues that detective stories can show both the possi-
       bilities and limitations of reason. Uses such writers as
       Poe, Conan Doyle, Dickens, Hammett, and Chandler to ex-
       plain his thesis.

244.   Gilbert, Elliot L. "McWatters' Law: The Best Kept Secret
       of the Secret Service." *Dimensions of Detective Fiction*
       (item 43), pp. 22-36.

       Contends that in the 19th century the fictional detec-
       tive hero represented a criticism of, and growing disil-
       lusionment with, a rationalistic approach to solving human
       problems and that the detective as a failure was just as
       popular in the 19th century as the detective as a success.

245.   Gilbert, Michael. "The Moment of Violence." *Crime in Good
       Company* (Item 32), pp. 105-125.

       Contends that "a thriller is more difficult to write
       than a detective story," partly because it is not such a
       rigid form. Most important, he maintains, is the way the
       writer builds up to and describes the moment of violence.

246.   Gilbert, Michael. "The Spy in Fact and Fiction." *The
       Mystery Story* (item 21), pp. 205-232.

       Traces the history of the spy novel, beginning with
       John Buchan in the thirties, through Eric Ambler, Ian
       Fleming, and Len Deighton. Cites examples from the work
       of each to illustrate the changing concept of the spy
       in fiction from "chivalrous espionage" to the basically
       more realistic.

247.   Gottschalk, Jane. "The Games of Detective Fiction."
       Armchair Detective 10 (January 1977): 74-76.

       Contends that it is "the art of the writing that makes
       it at all possible to play the detective games, from
       identifying with the hero to using clues to solve the
       problem."

248.   Gottschalk, Jane. "Mystery, Murder, and Academe." *Armchair
       Detective* 11 (April 1978): 159-169.

       In a survey of detective fiction that has an academic
       setting, Gottschalk contends that such stories usually

fall into one of three categories: (1) famous detectives who temporarily become involved in academe, (2) unknown detectives who discover violence in academe, (3) amateur detectives who are members of academe and who "sometimes go beyond the confines of their world to assist in restoring order in other 'worlds.'"

249. Goulart, Ron. "Dime Detectives." *Cheap Thrills: An Informal History of the Pulp Magazines*. New Rochelle, N.Y.: Arlington House, 1972, pp. 113-133.

Argues that it was in the 1920s and in *Black Mask* magazine that the private eye "first became an important American hero." The magazine during these years published Dashiell Hammett, Raymond Chandler, and many other detective writers who were, or were to become, notable.

250. Goulart, Ron. Introduction to *The Hardboiled Dicks: An Anthology and Study of Pulp Detective Fiction*. Edited by Ron Goulart. London: T.V. Boardman, 1967, pp. vii-xiv.

Argues that *Black Mask* "contributed most to the creation of the hardboiled detective" and that the first hardboiled detective was Race Williams, created by Carroll John Daly in the early 1920s. Comments on the characteristics of the stories (an urban setting and lots of action) as well as the characteristics of the detectives themselves ("straight forward and single-minded").

251. Graves, Robert. "After a Century, Will Anyone Care Whodunit?" *New York Times Book Review* 25 August 1957, pp. 5, 24.

Answers the question in the title with a negative, excepting Hammett and Simenon, because writers of detective stories tend to write for unimportant reasons, like money or fame, rather than because a story forced itself on them as writers of "real" books do.

252. Graves, Robert, and Alan Hodge. *The Long Weekend: A Social History of Great Britain 1918-1939*. New York: Macmillan, 1941, pp. 289-291.

The authors note that in the 1930s "lowbrow reading" was dominated by detective novels and "not one in a thousand had any verisimilitude." Only Dashiell Hammett had both writing ability and experience with crime, but he was not widely read in England. A detective novel, they maintain, is not meant to be realistic but instead a fantastic puzzle.

253.   Green, Anna Katharine. "Why Human Beings are Interested
       in Crime." *American Magazine* 87 (February 1919): 38+.

       Observes that detective stories are popular because
       people like to solve a puzzle and that murder is the most
       interesting crime because it is irrevocable and involves
       two people.

254.   Greene, Suzanne Ellery. "The Whodunits: Escape and
       Realism." *Books for Pleasure: Popular Fiction, 1914-
       1945*. Bowling Green, Ohio: Bowling Green University
       Popular Press, 1974, pp. 94-115.

       In this consideration of best selling mysteries from
       1926 through 1941, Greene observes that they are shorter
       and contain more action than most best sellers of the
       period. She also argues that they show a responsibility
       of the strong for the weak as well as suggesting that
       official law must be supplemented by "private just men."

255.   Grella, George. "The Gangster Novel: The Urban Pastoral."
       Tough Guy Writers of the Thirties (item 46), pp. 186-
       198.

       Grella argues that the gangster in literature is the
       contemporary equivalent of the cowboy--individualistic,
       instinctive, and violent. The appeal of the gangster
       novel lies in its simplicity: "the gangster's world is
       full of violent contrasts and easy distinctions."

256.   Grella, George. "Murder and Manners: The Formal Detective
       Novel." *Dimensions of Detective Fiction* (item 43), pp.
       37-57.

       Contends that the formal detective novel has retained
       its popularity--not because of the solving of a puzzle
       or the reader matching his wits against the detective's--
       but because it is a "comedy of manners in fiction." The
       conventions of the form represent a stylized, virtually
       changeless world to which a reader can turn for a sense
       of familiarity, stability, and security.

257.   Grella, George. "Murder and the Mean Streets: The Hard-
       Boiled Detective." *Contempora* 1 (March 1970): 6-15.
       Reprinted *Armchair Detective* 5 (October 1971): 1-10.

       Argues that the hard-boiled detective novel reflects
       American society just as the classical one reflects
       English society. The hard-boiled story combines "romance
       themes and structures" with a realistic surface.

258. Grenander, M.E. "Heritage of Cain: Crime in American
      Fiction." *Annals of the American Academy* 423 (January
      1976): 47-66.

      Devotes virtually all the article to "serious" fiction
      because "the detective story must share, not challenge,
      its readers' assumptions; otherwise they will not care
      about the solution of its puzzle."

259. Groff, Mary. "Bloody but Readable." *Armchair Detective*
      11 (July 1978): 234-236.

      Against the background of World War I traces the tastes
      of the mystery reading public during this period, point-
      ing out that many mystery novels dealt with domestic or
      civilian crime, perhaps to provide the illusion of a
      safer, saner atmosphere than that of the war.

260. Groff, Mary. "Friday, February 25, 1955." *Armchair Detec-
      tive* 10 (July 1977): 232-234.

      Notes that the London *Times Literary Supplement* pub-
      lished a detective fiction special number on this date
      and briefly describes each article.

261. Groff, Mary. "It's a Novel World." *Armchair Detective* 9
      (October 1976): 314-315.

      A survey of mystery fiction from 1878 through 1961,
      interspersed with important events throughout the world
      to relate mystery literary landmarks to happenings in
      the real world.

262. Groff, Mary. "The Last Year." *Armchair Detective* 11
      (April 1978): 145-149.

      Contends that 1939 was the last year of The Golden
      Age of Detective Fiction, a period in which detective
      novels were characterized by numerous servants, English
      country houses, stables, and assured incomes.

263. Gruber, Frank. "The Life and Times of the Pulp Story."
      Brass Knuckles. Los Angeles: Sherbourne Press, 1966,
      pp. 7-46. This introductory article was expanded and
      published as *The Pulp Jungle*. Los Angeles: Sherbourne
      Press, 1967. 189pp.

      The bulk of this work is Gruber's story of his career
      as a writer of pulp stories, but near the end he does
      list and explain the eleven key elements of the "fool-
      proof" mystery plot formula.

264. Guymon, E.T., Jr. "Why Do We Read This Stuff?" *The Mystery Story* (item 21), pp. 361-363.

Argues that mystery fiction is the "greatest escape literature of all time" and briefly comments on the difficulties of acquiring out of print and rare classics.

265. Haines, Helen E. "The Lure of Crime." *What's in a Novel?* New York: Columbia University Press, 1942, pp. 218-238.

Maintains that there are many reasons for the popularity of the mystery novel, such as distracting without oppressing and offering a temporary escape from reality, but its primary appeal "lies in the universal allure of a mystery."

266. Hallett, Charles A. "The Retrospective Technique and Its Implications for Tragedy." *Comparative Drama* 12 (Spring 1978): 3-21.

In the larger context of analyzing how "structural elements can play a determining role ... in the way a work of art renders experience," particularly in drama, argues that in its structure "retrospective drama closely resembles the archetypal detective story": there is a mystery and a search into the past to solve the mystery. Cites examples from such plays as *A Doll's House* and *Oedipus Rex* to illustrate this point.

267. Hamill, Pete. "We Tell Stories: A Talk Given at a Monthly MWA Meeting in New York." *Armchair Detective* 12 (January 1979): 3-5.

Contends that the main object of the novel is to tell a story, and that mystery writers, at a time when "two kinds of novels are being written: those to be read, and those to be reviewed," prefer to write novels "that are meant to be read."

268. Hamilton, Cicely. "The Detective in Fiction." *The English Spirit*. Edited by Anthony Weymouth [pseudonym of Ivo G. Cobb]. London: George Allen and Unwin, 1942, pp. 130-135.

Maintains that with Sherlock Holmes "the reign of the detective in fiction" began. Agrees with Dorothy L. Sayers' contention that there is a link between the "English skill in the detective story and the traditional English respect for law and order" that partly explains why practitioners of the detective story do not flourish in totalitarian states.

269. Hankiss, Jean. "Littérature 'Populaire' et Roman-Policier."
      Revue de Littérature Comparée 8 (July 1928): 556-563.

      Argues that the detective novel is a complex literary
      genre the appeal of which is due to such characteristics
      as the mysterious settings, the excitement of a crime,
      the triumph of the scientific spirit in everyday life
      through the use of close observation and logical deduc-
      tion.

270. Hardy, Thomas J. "The Romance of Crime." *Books on the
      Shelf*. London: Philip Allan, 1934, pp. 219-235.

      Argues that crime stories are popular because they make
      the reader feel that the ordinary could at any moment
      become the extraordinary. Differentiates between escapist
      novels, which take the reader out of his surroundings,
      and the "romance of crime," which reconciles the reader
      to his surroundings.

271. Hare, Cyril. "The Classic Form." *Crime in Good Company*
      (item 32), pp. 55-84.

      In addition to a lengthy analysis of the structure of
      detective fiction, Hare contends that such fiction "is
      written for amusement. It presents a purely imaginary
      world into which the reader is invited to enter for the
      pleasure and mental stimulation he finds there."

272. Hart, James D. *The Popular Book: A History of America's
      Literary Taste*. New York: Oxford University Press,
      1950, pp. 257-261.

      Argues that the popularity of detective stories in the
      1930s had three main causes: (1) they achieved "social
      decency" in the writings of Van Dine, Christie, and Sayers
      as well as from the "myth" that professors endorsed them;
      (2) they gave the reader the relaxation of "concentrating
      on a problem removed from their daily lives"; (3) the
      growth of rental libraries.

273. Hartman, Geoffrey. "Literature High and Low: The Case of
      the Mystery Story." *The Fate of Reading and Other
      Essays*. Chicago: University of Chicago Press, 1975,
      pp. 203-222.

      Using terms derived from Aristotle's *Poetics*, Hartman
      argues that a "heart of darkness" scene is the focus of
      detective fiction and that "recognition" and "reversal"
      are paths toward it. Uses examples chiefly from Ross
      Macdonald and Raymond Chandler.

274. Hartman, Geoffrey. "The Mystery of Mysteries." *New York Review of Books* 18 (18 May 1972): 31-34.

In the context of a review of Ross Macdonald's *The Underground Man* argues that the mystery story is a case of "arrested development" and that its popularity is related to its image of society.

275. Harwood, H.C. "Detective Stories." *Outlook* (London) 59 (1 January 1927): 7-8.

Maintains that the detective story must present a puzzle which is neither obvious nor impossible and that the detective examines the evidence as the representative of the reader.

276. Hawthorne, Julian. "Riddle Stories." *Library of the World's Best Mystery and Detective Stories: American.* Edited by Julian Hawthorne. New York: Review of Reviews, 1907, pp. 9-19.

Points out that in riddle stories the unraveling or weaving of the puzzle or riddle is paramount, not the character of the detective, although in really outstanding riddle stories character and plot may be used to enhance each other.

277. Haycraft, Howard. "Dictators, Democrats, and Detectives." *Saturday Review* 20 (7 October 1939): 8. Reprinted *Spectator* 163 (17 November 1939): 676-677.

Upon the occasion of some detective novels being banned in Fascist Italy, observes that detective fiction flourishes in a democratic, free society that encourages the use of reason.

278. Haycraft, Howard. "Evolution of the Whodunit in the Years of World War II." *New York Times Book Review* 12 August 1945, pp. 7, 29. Reprinted as "The Whodunit in World War II and After." *The Art of the Mystery Story* (item 35), pp. 536-542.

Contends that during the war years the level of technical and literary craftmanship was high but there were few exciting discoveries. The best writers of the period continued the chief development of the 1930s: "The movement away from the mechanical formula whodunit and toward the novel of manners and character with a crime motif." Haycraft also notes an increased "awareness of personal peril" in the genre and also lists the critics who have taken notice of detective fiction. He divides them into four categories: viewers with alarm, seekers after truth, clockstoppers, and non-fencers-in.

279. Hays, R.W. "Chess in the Detective Story." *Armchair Detective* 5 (October 1971): 19-23; 7 (May 1974): 203-204.

    An informal survey of mystery and detective fiction which uses chess in some way.

280. Hays, R.W. "The Clue of the Dying Message." *Armchair Detective* 7 (1973): 1-3.

    A systematic but not comprehensive examination of the "dying message clue" in detective fiction, this article covers only cases "in which the dying message is given by a murder victim and in which the investigator's purpose is to use the message as a clue to some important factor in the murder."

281. Hays, R.W. "More 'Shades of Dupin!'" *Armchair Detective* 8 (August 1975): 288-289.

    Suggested by George N. Dove's article "Shades of Dupin!" (item 212), this article notes such "insider" references as an Agatha Christie character who impersonates other fictional detectives and a John Dickson Carr character who says, "We're in a detective story."

282. Hays, R.W. "Religion and the Detective Story." *Armchair Detective* 8 (November 1974): 24-26.

    Surveys detective fiction in which religion or religious characters are important.

283. Hedman, Iwan. "Mystery Fiction in Scandinavia." *Armchair Detective* 3 (April 1970): 173-175.

    A survey of mystery fiction in Scandinavia beginning with World War I (when it reached a peak in readership).

284. Heidenry, John. "Bad Days on the Rue Morgue." *Commonweal* 96 (28 July 1972): 412.

    "Detective novels are for people who hate style," states Heidenry. "They have no moral worth, philosophical ambition, or nobility of style." Some good detective stories have been written, he says, but current attempts to call works such as Ross Macdonald's *The Underground Man* literature are "lies."

285.   Highet, Gilbert. "The Case of the Disappearing Detectives."
       People, Places and Books. New York: Oxford University
       Press, 1953, pp. 256-264.

       Argues that one of the main reasons why mystery fiction
       is not treated as serious literature is that while it
       tries to be realistic, the character of the detective is
       often unrealistic, citing as examples Poe's Auguste Dupin,
       Dorothy L. Sayers's Peter Wimsey, and Hammett's Sam Spade
       and Nick Charles. Argues also that most of the writing
       in mystery stories is bad and that mystery writers are
       too preoccupied with the "mechanics of their puzzle."
       Concludes that the only mystery and detective stories
       which are literature are those which "embody the tragedy
       that accompanies crime."

286.   Hill, Lew. "The Hero in Criminal Literature." *Pacific
       Quarterly: An International Review of Arts and Ideas*
       3 (January 1978): 33-41.

       Argues that the various types of heroes in mystery and
       detective fiction are analogous to the types of heroes
       in "straight" fiction.

287.   Hobsbawm, Eric. "The Criminal as Hero and Myth." *Times
       Literary Supplement* 23 June 1961, p. vi.

       Traces the changing attitudes toward the criminal and
       his changing role in society through history, observing
       that the popularity of English detective fiction--a middle-
       class creation--is a reflection of the insecurity of that
       class and of a desire to maintain the established order.

288.   Hoch, Edward H. "A Mirror to Our Crimes." *Armchair Detec-
       tive* 12 (Summer 1979): 280-285.

       Mystery writers often use their art as a means to
       illuminate real crime. Points out some outstanding ex-
       amples of this, from Vidocq's fictionalized *Memoirs* (1828)
       through works by Julian Symons and Michael Gilbert.

289.   Hoffman, Nancy Y. "The Doctor and the Detective Story."
       Journal of the American Medical Association 224 (2 April
       1973): 74-77.

       Points out that there is a "huge mass of crime litera-
       ture in which doctors appear variously as detectives,
       villains, victims, expert witnesses or authors," and that
       "diagnosis is the fine art of medical sleuthing." Comments
       on crime fiction written by and about doctors, particularly

works by Conan Doyle, R. Austin Freeman, and Josephine Bell.

290. Hoffman, Nancy Y. "Mistresses of Malfeasance." *Dimensions of Detective Fiction* (item 43), pp. 97-101.

Surveys some women writers of the genre from Anna Katharine Green (1878) to Jean Dodds Freeman (1971).

291. Holman, C. Hugh. "Detective Fiction as American Realism." *Popular Literature in America*. Edited by James C. Austin and Donald A. Koch. Bowling Green, Ohio: Bowling Green University Popular Press, 1972, pp. 30-41.

Contends that the American detective story became a popular literary force in the last quarter of the nineteenth century primarily because of the development of the physical sciences, the scientific method, and "local color" writing.

292. Holquist, Michael J. "Whodunit and Other Questions: Metaphysical Detective Stories in Post-War Fiction." *New Literary History* 3 (Autumn 1971): 135-156.

Holquist contends that the detective story is to such writers as Robbe-Grillet, Borges, and Nabokov "what the structural and philosophical presuppositions of myth and depth psychology" were to such writers as Mann, Joyce, and Woolf.

293. Hoppin, Hector. "Notes on Primitive Modes of Detection." *Chimera* 5 (Summer 1947): 39-48.

After describing "detection" in primitive societies (which often requires the investigator to identify with the victim's soul), Hoppin contends that readers of detective fiction identify, not with the victim, but with the detective *and* the murderer, representatives of both the moral and the anti-social sides of their personalities.

294. Howe, Sir Ronald. "A Personal Reaction." *Times Literary Supplement* 25 February 1955, p. xii.

Howe, Deputy Commissioner at Scotland Yard, states that he enjoys reading detective novels but contends that their writers are too preoccupied with murder and that they undervalue the importance of dull, routine work and the legal restrictions on the activities of the police.

295. Hubin, Allen J. "Patterns in Mystery Fiction: The Durable Series Character." *The Mystery Story* (item 21), pp. 291-318.

As a preface to a nineteen-page list of series characters in mystery fiction, argues that a series character
offers an author a chance to explore character and background in depth and contends that the listing of the most
lasting may be useful in displaying trends and changes
in public taste.

296.   Huet, Marie-Hélène. "Enquête et Représentation dans le
       Roman Policier." *Europe* no. 571-572 (November-December
       1976): 98-104.

       Contends that the detective novel is distinguished from
       the traditional novel by two main factors: (1) it does
       not present an orderly chronological series of events;
       (2) it extends an invitation to the reader to participate
       in the game of matching wits with the detective.

297.   Hugo, Grant. "The Political Influence of the Thriller."
       Contemporary Review 221 (December 1972): 284-289.

       Contends that the thriller is a "natural medium" for
       the "modern propagandist" to use in reaching an audience
       because it can appeal to "emotion, prejudices and cravings"
       that are often unconscious.

298.   Hutchinson, Horace G. "Detective Fiction." *Quarterly Re-
       view* (London) 253 (July 1929): 148-160.

       Maintains that there is a clear literary distinction to
       be made between detective stories and adventure stories.
       A detective story poses a problem at or near the beginning,
       the solution of which occupies the rest of the book. An
       adventure story is a series of adventures that keep
       building until the end and in which there may be one or
       more detectives.

299.   Hutter, Albert D. "Dreams, Transformations, and Literature:
       The Implications of Detective Fiction." *Victorian
       Studies* 19 (December 1975): 181-210.

       Contends that detective fiction recreates a previous
       happening through subjective narrative and that the pro-
       cess of discovery, rather than the particular event dis-
       covered, is central to detective fiction just as it is
       to dreaming and to *Oedipus Rex*.

300.   Ilyina, Natalia, and Arkadi Adamov. "Detective Novels:
       A Game and Life." *Soviet Literature* no. 3 (1975): 142-
       150.

Cast in the form of a dialog between the two authors, the article contends that the main difference between Soviet and Western detective novels is that Soviet detective fiction tries to add psychological and social content to the genre rather than first emphasizing the solving of a puzzle as Western detective writers do.

301. "In the Best Tradition: Mystification and Art." *Times Literary Supplement* 25 February 1955, p. viii.

Argues that a crime novel which is to survive must be written by someone who is both a talented novelist and has the ability to "mystify and astonish." Uses examples by Christie, Iles, Hammett, and Bardin to support the thesis.

302. Inge, William Ralph. "Crime Stories." *A Pacifist in Trouble*. London: Putnam, 1939, pp. 290-295.

Inge "supposes" that peaceful citizens like to escape in their imaginations to a world in which their moral code does not apply and that there is the additional pleasure of solving a puzzle. Argues that the detective novel should have more characteristics of a "serious" novel.

303. Innes, Michael. "Death as a Game." *Esquire* 63 (January 1965): 55-56.

Argues that "nothing *real* must be allowed in" the detective story. "Let your guilt and misery, for instance, be real and you crack the mold of the form."

304. Jinka, Katsuo. "Mystery Stories in Japan." *Armchair Detective* 9 (February 1976): 112-113.

Observes that prior to World War II Japanese mystery stories "were generally considered lowbrow and designed for kids, and almost all ... were simply shockers." Briefly comments on both pre-war and contemporary outstanding Japanese mystery writers.

305. Johnston, Charles. "The Detective Story's Origin." *Harper's Weekly* 54 (12 February 1910): 16-17, 34.

Maintains that the first detective story written in modern Europe is Voltaire's *Zadig*, which is an imitation of the *Arabian Nights* in atmosphere, incident, and "mischievous joy." Zadig is similar to Sherlock Holmes in his ability to make deductions from faint clues. Gives extended plot summary of *Zadig* and a tale from the *Arabian Nights* to demonstrate their similarity.

306.   Johnston, Charles. "A Web of World-Old Oriental Tales."
       Library of the World's Best Mystery and Detective Stories: Oriental. Edited by Julian Hawthorne. New York: Review of Reviews, 1908, pp. 11-14.

       Observes that there is a "treasure-house" of oriental tales as old as civilization and that many of the best tales of deduction come from *The Thousand and One Nights*.

307.   Jones, Archie H. "Cops, Robbers, Heroes and Anti-Heroines: The American Need to Create." *Journal of Popular Culture* 1 (Fall 1967): 114-127.

       Argues that the detective as hero in popular culture was a response to the urbanization of the country which made the Western hero somewhat out of date (though still popular).

308.   Kelly, R. Gordon. "Explaining the Detective Story." *Armchair Detective* 5 (July 1972): 214-215.

       Contends that various attempts to "explain" the detective story fail to make an essential inquiry: what is the difference between people who read detective fiction and those who do not? Kelly admits this would be difficult.

309.   Kennedy, Foster. "From Whodunits to Poetry." *Saturday Review* 24 (18 October 1941): 34.

       Maintains that "part of the value of great poetry is in its ability to embrace many of the elements of the truly great detective story": both must be carefully constructed according to strict conventions.

310.   Kermode, Frank. "Novel and Narrative." *The Theory of the Novel: New Essays*. Edited by John Halperin. New York: Oxford University Press, 1974, pp. 155-174.

       Devotes part of a general article on narrative in the novel to the detective story, arguing that it is a "good example of the overdevelopment of one element of narrative at the expense of others." The story is told in such a manner that the "principal object of the reader is to discover, by an interpretation of clues, the answer to a problem posed at the outset." Uses specific examples from E.C. Bentley's *Trent's Last Case* to illustrate his point.

311. Kittredge, William, and Steven M. Krauzer. "The Evolution of the Great American Detective: The Reader as Detective Hero." *Armchair Detective* 11 (October 1978): 318-330. A reprint of the introduction to their *Great American Detective*. New York: New American Library, 1978, pp. x-xxxiv.

     Maintains that the most "distinctive quality" of the American private detective is his role as defender of social order and justice.

312. Knox, Ronald A. Introduction to *The Best English Detective Stories of 1928*. Edited by Ronald A. Knox and H. Harrington. New York: Horace Liveright, 1929, pp. 9-23. Revised version printed as "Detective Stories." *Literary Distractions*. New York: Sheed and Ward, 1958, pp. 180-198.

     We like detective stories because they allow us to escape to problems which are more baffling than our own but nevertheless have an answer. The action takes place at the beginning of the story and the plot consists of the unraveling. Knox also describes several "rules" of the detective story.

313. Krouse, Agate Nesaule, and Margot Peters. "Murder in Academe." *Southwest Review* 62 (Autumn 1977): 371-378.

     Academe has long been a frequent setting for detective novels. Until the past two decades the university was treated as an Eden, but recently some detective novels set in academe reflect a disillusionment with the academic world.

314. Krutch, Joseph Wood. "Only a Detective Story." *Nation* 159 (25 November 1944): 647-648, 652. Reprinted *The Art of the Mystery Story* (item 35), pp. 178-185.

     Argues that detective stories are popular because their authors seek the classical, elementary virtues of fiction. Things proceed logically to a comprehensible end, unlike "serious fiction," which is often deliberately incomprehensible.

315. LaBorde, Charles. "Dicks on Stage: Form and Formulas in Detective Drama." *Armchair Detective* 11 (July 1978): 214-229; 11 (October 1978): 348-356; 12 (January 1979): 83-88; 12 (Spring 1979): 158-164; 12 (Summer 1979): 246-254; 12 (Fall 1979): 341-347.

In this detailed examination of mystery drama, LaBorde
identifies several categories of mystery plays--police
procedural, murder-house, psychological thrillers--and
analyzes each type, using numerous examples to illustrate
his comments.

316.   Lachman, Marvin. "The American Regional Mystery." *Armchair
       Detective* 9 (November 1975): 11-13; 9 (October 1976):
       260-266; 10 (October 1977): 294-306.

Consists of short comments on mystery novels which are
set in the western and mountain states, including Alaska
and Hawaii.

317.   Lachman, Marvin. "Sports and the Mystery Story." *Armchair
       Detective* 6 (October 1972): 1-6; 6 (February 1973):
       83-85; 6 (August 1973): 243-245; 7 (May 1974): 195-197;
       7 (August 1974): 261-262, 269; 8 (February 1975): 108-
       110. [Tennis section originally published as "Tennis
       and the Mystery Story." *World Tennis*, January-February
       1972.]

Surveys mystery stories which use the following sports
as background: tennis, prizefighting, bullfighting, base-
ball, basketball, football, golf, and cricket. Points out
the clichés, the errors, and the successes in the handling
of each sport.

318.   Lachman, Marvin. "Virgil Tibbs and the American Negro in
       Mystery Fiction." *Armchair Detective* 1 (April 1968):
       86-89.

Contends that World War II marked a turning point in
the treatment of Blacks in mystery fiction and concludes
that by the beginning of the 1950s "important mystery
writers were beginning to treat Negroes in a sympathetic
(or at least balanced) light as secondary characters."

319.   Landrum, Larry N., Pat Browne, and Ray B. Browne. Intro-
       duction to *Dimensions of Detective Fiction* (item 43),
       pp. 1-10.

Contends that the adventure story and Gothic and domestic fiction, as well as Poe, were important in forming
detective fiction. The detective is an outsider, they
also point out, and "the description of manners is one
of the most important aspects of the formal detective
story."

320. Lauterbach, Edward. "Our Heroes in Motley." *Armchair Detective* 9 (June 1976): 178-179.

    Citing Sherlock Holmes, Fu Manchu, and The Shadow as outstanding examples of famous fictional characters who have become "folklore heroes," points out that jokes, puns, and epigrams attributed to them have reversed the more usual process of oral to written.

321. Lauterbach, Edward, and Karen Lauterbach. "The Crossword Puzzle Metaphor and Some Crossword Puzzle Mysteries." *Armchair Detective* 10 (April 1977): 167-174.

    States that "since there have been so many comparisons of the mystery story with crossword puzzles, it is not surprising that there are detective stories which incorporate actual crossword puzzles as a specific feature of their plot." Lists some examples of these stories and comments on them.

322. Lawrence, Hilda. "Domesticating the Murderer." *Saturday Review* 28 (17 February 1945): 16-18.

    Maintains that the current trend in detective fiction toward situations and people that seem ordinary or familiar is a positive one.

323. "A Lawyer and a Mystery Writer Trade Blows." *Literary Digest* 103 (26 October 1929): 47-49.

    Lawyer John Waite had attacked the detective story (item 502), and this article reports S.S. Van Dine's reply in the *New York World Magazine*. Van Dine argued that the writer need only convince the reader, not a court of law and that real detectives often do use the illegal means to which Waite objected.

324. Lejeune, Anthony. "Age of the Great Detective." *Times Literary Supplement* 23 June 1961, p. vii.

    Argues that the Great Detective grew to fame in "a world of assured values," but that world has been shaken, and the Great Detective is disappearing.

325. **Leonard, John. "I Care Who Killed Roger Ackroyd."** *Esquire* 84 (August 1975): 60-61, 120.

    Argues that detective novels need no more justification than that they are good *stories*.

326. Lerner, Max. "Politics Makes Strange Dead Fellows."
      Esquire 80 (December 1973): 158-160.

      Admits that he no longer likes to read mystery/detective
      fiction, which he considers to be "mechanical puzzles,"
      but prefers instead espionage or spy fiction largely
      because it is a "branch of the political novel" with
      power as the ultimate goal.

327. "Line of Heroes: Some Detectives of Character." *Times
      Literary Supplement* 25 February 1955, p. ix.

      Denies that the plot is the only point of interest in
      mystery/detection fiction. Defends the genre against
      charges of neglecting the development of its characters
      by citing several memorable protagonists, from Dupin and
      Holmes to 20th-century sleuths.

328. Lochte, Richard S., II. "The Private Eye: Enduring as a
      $1.29 Steak." *Chicago Daily News* 10 June 1967. Reprinted
      Armchair Detective 3 (January 1970): 117-119.

      Contends that after a hiatus of ten years the private
      detective is once again proving to be the most lasting
      creation in modern fiction. Briefly surveys the develop-
      ment of the private detective beginning with *Black Mask*
      (a pulp magazine) through the detectives of Hammett,
      Chandler, and Ross Macdonald.

329. Lochte, Richard S., II. "Rogue's Gallery." *Armchair Detec-
      tive* 2 (April 1969): 158-160.

      Argues that the debonair literary rogue may be a
      vanishing breed and discusses some of the most famous,
      concentrating on E.W. Hornung's Raffles, Maurice LeBlanc's
      Lupin, and Leslie Charteris's The Saint.

330. "Long Way After Poe." *Nation* 85 (19 September 1907): 251-
      252.

      Maintains that rules and conventions for writing detec-
      tive fiction can be traced back to Poe, who "knew the
      art of mystifying without resorting to the concealment
      of clues."

331. Lucas, E.V. "Search in Fiction." *Living Age* 251 (8 Decem-
      ber 1906): 632-634.

      Argues that the search is the essence of the detective
      story and that neither blood nor a crime should be neces-
      sary.

332. McAleer, John. "The Game's Afoot: Detective Fiction in the Present Day." *Kansas Quarterly* 10 (Fall 1978): 21-38.

Surveys the genre today including such topics as courses taught in colleges, the collecting of detective novels, important books and reviewers in the field, and current writers and trends in detective fiction.

333. McCarthy, Mary. "Murder and Karl Marx." *Nation* 142 (25 March 1936): 381-383.

Contends that the contemporary mystery story is becoming increasingly "class-conscious," largely because "the possibilities of the puzzle ... are all but exhausted." Observes that American class-conscious mystery writers form "a virtually united front against any form of social innovation."

334. McCleary, G.F. "The Popularity of Detective Fiction." *Fortnightly* 161 (January 1947): 61-67. Reprinted *On Detective Fiction and Other Things*. London: Hollis and Carter, 1960, pp. 11-18.

Argues that the popularity of the detective story has three main causes: it has a happy ending, its problem furnishes a not too exacting mental activity, and events rather than thoughts are stressed.

335. McCloy, Helen. "Whodunits—Still a Stepchild." *New Republic* 133 (31 October 1955): 29.

Observes two trends in the mysteries of 1955: the "increasing internationalism" in scenes and characters, and a "blurring of all distinctions between detective stories, mystery stories and suspense novels, and, what is more important, a blurring of the distinction between the suspense novel and the so-called straight novel."

336. McCourt, Edward A. "Home on the Range." *Saturday Review* 29 (2 November 1946): 23.

Maintains that no one with any literary judgment can take seriously the detective story's claims to be significant literature and that the Western has just as good a claim to be considered significant.

337. McDade, T.M. "True or Fact Crime." *Publishers Weekly* 213 (13 March 1978): 48.

Argues that portraying true crime in fiction requires
no less skill than inventing stories. Surveys the development of fictionalized true crime from the 1930s through
the 1970s.

338. Macdonald, Ross. "The Writer as Detective Hero." *On Crime
      Writing.* Santa Barbara, Calif.: Capra Press, 1973, pp.
      9-24. Reprinted *The Mystery Writer's Art* (item 54), pp.
      295-305. Also reprinted *The Capra Chapbook Anthology.*
      Edited by Noel Young. Santa Barbara, Calif.: Capra Press,
      1979, pp. 75-90.

      Contends that the detective has always "represented his
      creator and carried his values into action in society"
      and that his own main contribution to the development of
      detective fiction has been the creation of a narrator-hero,
      "as the mind of the novel."

339. Macdonald, Ross. "Writing *The Galton Case.*" *On Crime
      Writing.* Santa Barbara, Calif." Capra Press, 1973, pp.
      25-45. Reprinted *The Capra Chapbook Anthology.* Edited
      by Noel Young. Santa Barbara, Calif.: Capra Press,
      1979, pp. 91-111.

      Argues that the "convention of the detective novel"
      can be a "means of knowing oneself and saying the unsay-
      able," and that the "characters are in varying degrees
      versions of the author."

340. McGill, V.J. "Henry James: Master Detective." *Bookman*
      72 (November 1930): 251-256.

      Contends that in the works of Henry James "we shall
      find our fill of subtle mysteries and fine-spun solutions,
      all enacted intricately in the minds of incredibly clever
      people." McGill then uses Willard Huntington Wright's
      exposition of the characteristics of the detective novel
      (item 522) to demonstrate that the novels and tales of
      James are excellent detective stories.

341. Macgowan, Kenneth. Introduction to *Sleuths: Twenty-Three
      Great Detectives of Fiction and Their Best Stories.*
      Edited by Kenneth Macgowan. New York: Harcourt, Brace,
      1931, pp. ix-xv.

      Argues that fictional detectives "seem to live more
      vividly than any other group of men outside the finest
      of serious fiction," but that full characterization of
      other characters in a detective story usually detracts
      from its quality. Also contends that the methods of real

police and detectives are quite unlike those of the best
detective fiction.

342. McLuhan, Marshall. "Footprints in the Sands of Crime."
      Sewanee Review 54 (October 1946): 617-634.

      Argues that the sleuth in popular detective fiction
      is "the degenerate heir of Renaissance megalomania."

343. McSherry, Frank D., Jr. "The Amateurs' Hour." *Armchair
      Detective* 3 (October 1969): 14-22.

      Surveys a number of series characters who have "acted
      as amateurs in crime and detection" and finds that they
      do not perform as well as professional fictional detec-
      tives.

344. McSherry, Frank D., Jr. "Avant-Garde Writing in the
      Detective Story." *Armchair Detective* 3 (January 1970):
      96.

      States that he is aware of only two experimental stories
      that have been published in mass circulation magazines
      and both are detective stories that appeared in *Ellery
      Queen's Mystery Magazine*: "The Man in the Velvet Hat"
      (1944) and "The Finger Man" (1945) by Jerome and Harold
      Prince. The two stories use a technique closely akin to
      stream-of-consciousness and are an outstanding combination
      of mystery and horror.

345. McSherry, Frank D., Jr. "The Golden Road to Samarkand:
      The Arabian Nights in Detective Fiction." *Armchair
      Detective* 7 (February 1974): 77-94; 7 (August 1974):
      264-282.

      Argues that using the Far East as a location in mystery
      stories gives them the added appeal of romance and adven-
      ture.

346. McSherry, Frank D., Jr. "Judge Crater and His Fellow
      Travellers." *Armchair Detective* 4 (July 1971): 195-218;
      8 (February 1975): 99-103.

      States that fiction about "vanishers" is usually based
      on actual cases and examines many fictional and factual
      vanishers.

347. McSherry, Frank D., Jr. "Lady in a Straightjacket."
      Armchair Detective 9 (June 1976): 201-202.

Points out that *Mystery Book Magazine* had a regular
feature that was unique: a very short, short story combined with a crossword puzzle. "Words were left blank
in the story and solution of the mystery required solution
of the puzzle" by the reader.

348.   McSherry, Frank D., Jr. "A New Category of the Mystery
       Story." *Armchair Detective* 2 (October 1968): 23-24.
       Revised version printed as "The Janus Resolution."
       The Mystery Writer's Art (item 54), pp. 263-271.

       States that a new kind of mystery story has appeared.
       He labels it the Double Mystery and defines it as a mys-
       tery in which the criminal elements can be explained in
       two different but equally probable ways, "one mundane
       and the other supernatural." Argues that this type belongs
       both to the mystery/detection and fantasy genres and cites
       numerous examples of stories which fit into both genres.

349.   McSherry, Frank D., Jr. "The Shape of Crimes to Come."
       The Mystery Writer's Art (item 54), pp. 326-338.

       Argues that detection/crime stories are not bound by
       temporal concerns. Thus stories set in the future, as
       well as those set in the present or past, may legitimately
       be considered mystery/detection fiction. Analyzes several
       science fiction stories in this context.

350.   McSherry, Frank D., Jr. "The Smallest Sub-Genre." *Arm-
       chair Detective* 10 (July 1977): 267-269.

       Points out that the smallest sub-genre of detective
       fiction is that in which the reader is the detective.
       Identifies and briefly mentions five stories that qualify
       for this sub-genre. Speculates that the small number is
       perhaps due to the difficulty of writing such a story.

351.   McSherry, Frank D., Jr. "Under Two Flags: The Detective
       Story in Science Fiction." *Armchair Detective* 2 (April
       1969): 171-173.

       Discusses several novels which were published and re-
       viewed as science fiction but which are legitimate detec-
       tive stories by any definition. Because they are set in
       the future they are classified as science fiction rather
       than detective fiction.

352.   McSherry, Frank D., Jr. "Who-Really-Dun-It?: Two Sub-
       Branches of the Detective Story." *Armchair Detective*
       2 (January 1969): 88-93.

Defines two sub-groups of detective fiction in which a possible solution to a real life unsolved crime is presented. In the first type the writer "solves" the case, and in the second type the writer uses his fictional detective to do so. McSherry lists and discusses novels of both types.

353. Maloney, Martin. "A Grammar of Assassination." *ETC.: A Review of General Semantics* 11 (Winter 1954): 83–95. Reprinted *Our Language and Our World*. Edited by S.I. Hayakawa. New York: Harper and Brothers, 1959, pp. 256–271.

Contends that popular arts differ from fine arts in using formulas instead of insights and that detective novels use the two universal themes of pursuit and guilt. Suggests that such recent developments in the genre as the works of Hammett and Spillane are "an echo, a reflection, of the inner world" in which many of us live.

354. Margolies, Edward. "The American Detective Thriller and the Idea of Society." *Dimensions of Detective Fiction* (item 43), pp. 83–87.

Argues that American hard-boiled detective fiction is based on a code of morality unique to American society rather than being completely amoral as George Orwell has suggested.

355. Marion, Denis. "Detective Novel." *Living Age* 357 (November 1939): 283–285. [Translated from *Nouvelle Revue Française*.]

Argues that the detective story is in decline and states that its best hope is in greater depth of characterization such as is found in F.W. Crofts, Dorothy L. Sayers, and Anthony Berkeley.

356. Marsh, Ngaio. "Starting with People." *Mystery and Detection Annual 1973* (item 17), pp. 209–210.

Marsh defends the non-traditional detective story--including her own--against the criticism that it ignores "real emotional problems" and concentrates instead on the mechanics of police work. She argues that this is an almost inevitable result of attempting to introduce fully rounded characters into a genre that puts a premium on solving puzzles.

357. Mason, A.E.W. "Detective Novels." *Nation and Athenaeum*
      36 (7 February 1925): 645-646.

      Maintains that "one touch of fairyland" ruins a detec-
      tive story completely and that such a story should be
      written so that the reader will not guess the solution
      during the first reading but on the second reading will
      see that the truth was set out to see.

358. Matthew, Christopher. "Guilty of Concealing Criminals."
      Critic 34 (Winter 1975): 66-71.

      Very short interviews with, and commentary on, several
      contemporary crime writers with a statement by Julian
      Symons as the theme: "The detective story, in which puzzle
      and plot were all, has been pretty well replaced now by
      the crime novel, in which it is the character and back-
      ground that count."

359. Matthews, Brander. "Poe and the Detective Story." *Scrib-
      ner's Magazine* 42 (September 1907): 287-293.

      Maintains that it is usually difficult to discover the
      origins of a literary form and that the early examples
      tend to be feeble, but that the detective story began
      at a definite time with a masterpiece, "The Murders in
      the Rue Morgue." The true interest in a detective story,
      Matthew contends, is not the mystery but the process of
      solving the problem.

360. Maugham, W. Somerset. "The Defense of Who Done-Its."
      Senior Scholastic 46 (2 April 1945): 15. [Originally
      published in the *New York Post*.]

      Argues that detective stories are read because, unlike
      contemporary serious fiction, they tell stories.

361. Maugham, W. Somerset. "Give Me a Murder." *Saturday Evening
      Post* 213 (28 December 1940): 27, 46-49. Summary printed
      in *Saturday Review* 23 (4 January 1941): 24. Whole arti-
      cle reprinted as "The Decline and Fall of the Detective
      Story." *The Vagrant Mood: Six Essays*. Garden City, N.Y.:
      Doubleday, 1953, pp. 101-132.

      After admitting his predilection for a good detective
      story, Maugham argues that a good detective story should
      not have romance, humor, literary style, or erudition.
      Also argues that the reasons for the popularity of the
      genre are directness, brevity, and action.

362. Maugham, W. Somerset. Preface to *Ashenden or: The British Agent*, by W. Somerset Maugham. Garden City, N.Y.: Doubleday, Doran, 1941, pp. vii-xiii.

Maintains that the main goal of fiction should be to entertain and makes further observations which apply to espionage fiction as well as to other types of fiction: a novel should have a plot with a beginning, middle, and an end, and the novelist should not try to imitate life but should keep close enough to reality not to outrage the reader's credulity.

363. Maurice, Arthur Bartlett. "The Detective in Fiction." *Bookman* 15 (May 1902): 231-236.

Contends that there are no contemporary dime novel detectives, such as Old Sleuth, who inspire the imagination. Maintains that there is a direct link between such juvenile likes and an appreciation of Gaboriau's Lecoq or Conan Doyle's Sherlock Holmes, the best of modern detectives.

364. May, Clifford D. "Whatever Happened to Sam Spade? The Private Eye in Fact and Fiction." *Atlantic Monthly* 236 (August 1975): 27-35.

Most of the article compares and contrasts real life private investigators with fictional ones. Comments by such detective fiction writers as Ross Macdonald and Rex Stout on their work are included.

365. Melvin, David Skene. "The Secret Eye: The Spy in Literature; The Evolution of Espionage Literature: A Survey of the History and Development of the Spy and Espionage Novel." *Pacific Quarterly: An International Review of Arts and Ideas* 3 (January 1978): 11-26.

Surveys the espionage novel and some of the public attitudes toward the spy which affected the fiction. Divides recent spy fiction into romantic (e.g., Fleming) and realistic (e.g., Le Carré).

366. Merry, Bruce. "The Spy Thriller" *London Magazine* 16 (April/May 1976): 8-27.

A short exposition of the thesis of his book *Anatomy of the Spy Thriller* (item 49), concluding with nine requirements for writing a best-selling spy thriller.

367.   Mertz, Stephen. "Captain Shaw's Hard-Boiled Boys."
        Armchair Detective 12 (Summer 1979): 264-265.

        The Hard-Boiled Omnibus, edited by Joseph Shaw, is an
        anthology of stories originally published in *Black Mask*
        magazine during his editorship. Shaw "was proud of the
        magazine's place in the development not only of detective
        fiction but also of American fiction in general." Includes
        Shaw's comments on some of the writers who were published
        in *Black Mask*.

368.   Milne, A.A. "Books and Writers." *Spectator* 186 (6 April
        1951): 452.

        Contends that the natural medium for a tale of mystery
        and detection is the short story, and therefore a detec-
        tive novel is either a "short story expanded" or a "short
        story delayed."

369.   Milne, A.A. "Introducing Crime." *By Way of Introduction*.
        New York: E.P. Dutton, 1929, pp. 47-51.

        States that he prefers detective stories to be well-
        written, to have no romantic interest, and to have an
        amateur detective.

370.   Mochrie, Margaret. "They Make Crime Pay." *Delineator* 130
        (February 1937): 28-29.

        Consists of brief remarks on six women mystery story
        writers: Wells, Sayers, Rinehart, Taylor, Eberhart, and
        Christie.

371.   Monblatt, Bruce L. "The Detective Story: Pertinent?"
        Armchair Detective 4 (April 1971): 170-171.

        Argues that the "mystery novel is important in depict-
        ing the type of society in which we live" and that mystery
        criticism should eschew trivia and be more relevant to
        larger themes in American life and literature.

372.   Montesinos, José F. "Imperfect Myths." *Chimera* 5 (Summer
        1947): 2-11.

        This Spanish critic argues that the Anglo-Saxon's
        "direct and simple" style is most appropriate to the de-
        tective story, but it is difficult for the writer of Latin
        descent "to tell a tale in which the ingenuity and sub-
        tlety resides in the plot itself and not in the expression."

373. Morton, Charles W. "Accent on Living." *Atlantic Monthly* 199 (May 1957): 89-90.

   Observes that the average mystery story's object is attained by "techniques of repetition and delay" that make one wonder why anyone ever reads these stories.

374. Moskowitz, Sam. "The Challenge of the Detective Pulps." *Under the Moons of Mars: A History and Anthology of "The Scientific Romance" in the Munsey Magazines, 1912-1920*. New York: Holt, Rinehart and Winston, 1970, pp. 386-392.

   Singles out the publication of *Detection Story Magazine* (1915) as the first "specialized fiction" magazine. Also contends that the publication was a significant "step in the transition from the dime novels to the pulps." Comments briefly on other pulp magazines devoted to detective stories.

375. Moskowitz, Sam. "Crime: From Sherlock to Spaceships." *Strange Horizons*. New York: Scribners, 1976, pp. 122-159.

   Maintains that the popularity of the Sherlock Holmes stories helped effect a transition between the detective story and science fiction that would eventually result in "a valid detective story that was at the same time a true science fiction story." Traces this gradual development, citing numerous examples of practitioners of the detective story in science fiction.

376. Mott, Frank Luther. "Case of the Best Seller Mystery." *Golden Multitudes: The Story of Best Sellers in the United States*. New York: Macmillan, 1947, pp. 262-268.

   Argues that neither escapism nor preoccupation with crime are valid objections to the mystery story and traces the popularity of the genre in the United States.

377. Muhlen, Norbert. "The Thinker and the Tough Guy." *Commonweal* 51 (25 November 1949): 216-217.

   Maintains that the traditional detective story has undergone a change that perhaps reflects "a change in the views of contemporary society." Instead of reason, the tough detective uses violence as a weapon to fight crime and derives his pleasure from his "love of violence and money."

378.   Murdoch, Derrick. "The Case of the Vanishing Hero."
       *Pacific Quarterly: An International Review of Arts and
       Ideas* 3 (January 1978): 42-49.

       Surveys various definitions of the classic detective
       story and the reasons readers like it. Suggests that "the
       uncertainty characterizing every aspect of this age" may
       be antithetical to that form.

379.   Murdoch, Walter. "On Bloodstains." *Collected Essays*.
       London: Angus and Robertson, 1945, pp. 244-247.

       Observes that the detective story has become critically
       respectable because Oxford University Press has devoted
       two volumes of its prestigious World's Classics series
       to *Stories of Crime and Detection*. Concludes that the
       detective story may be "the most purely intellectual of
       all forms of fiction."

380.   Nevins, Francis M., Jr. "Name Games: Mystery Writers and
       Their Pseudonyms." *The Mystery Story* (item 21), pp.
       343-358.

       Contends that the economics of book publishing force
       prolific mystery writers to use pseudonyms because hard-
       cover publishers want to publish only a few books a year
       by the same author. Other writers use pseudonyms because
       the genre they are writing in demands it (e.g., gothics,
       hard-boiled) or to divide their "popular" from their
       "serious" work. Concludes that much can be learned about
       the mystery story through studying why certain writers
       chose to use pseudonyms.

381.   Nevins, Francis M., Jr. "Pulp Tradition in Mystery Fiction:
       A Panel Discussion." *Armchair Detective* 6 (May 1973):
       133-150.

       In a wide-ranging panel discussion chaired by Nevins,
       the participants (Donald A. Yates and George Grella with
       John Cawelti contributing from the audience) comment on
       the "American pulp tradition in mystery fiction: how it
       originated, how it differed from the dominant tradition
       that grew up parallel to it; the classic British tradition,
       and some of the directions in which it went after it be-
       came established."

382.   Nevins, Francis M., Jr. "Social and Political Images in
       American Crime Fiction." *Armchair Detective* 5 (January
       1972): 61-78.

A transcript of a panel discussion (which includes questions and comments from the audience) on crime fiction by Nevins and Donald A. Yates, Robert E. Washer, Norman Donaldson, and Allen J. Hubin at the 1971 meeting of the Popular Culture Association.

383. Nicolson, Marjorie. "The Professor and the Detective." *Atlantic Monthly* 143 (April 1929): 483-493. Reprinted *Men and Books*. Edited by Malcolm S. MacLean and Elisabeth K. Holmes. New York: Ray Long and Richard R. Smith, 1932, pp. 315-333. Also reprinted *The Art of the Mystery Story* (item 35), pp. 110-127.

Contends that detective fiction is popular with academics partly because it represents an escape, not from life but from formless "psychological" literature and concludes that scholars are "detectives of thoughts" who use essentially the same methods that their favorite detectives use.

384. "Noble Art of Mystery." *Nation* 125 (14 September 1927): 242.

Argues that a mystery writer "is not a novelist and should not be judged as one, or compared with one, or declared inferior to one because he does something else."

385. Nourissier, François. "Pox on Vacuity." *Atlas* 10 (August 1965): 117-119.

Nourissier notes the growing acceptance among intellectuals of such sub-literatures as detective stories and science fiction. He believes that this growing "Pop Art mentality" shows dissatisfaction with vague abstractions and a desire for more reality. Also states that "we have returned to primitive forms of expression, to childhood: that is, to folly."

386. Nye, Russel. "The Dime Novel Tradition." *The Unembarrassed Muse: The Popular Arts in America.* New York: Dial Press, 1970, pp. 200-215.

States that there were two basic formulas in the dime novel: the western and the detective story. "The dime-novel detective story was not a mystery, but a cops-and-robbers story, intended to excite and entertain." It flourished between the late 1880s and the mid-1930s and featured such heroes as Old Sleuth, Nick Carter, and the Shadow.

387. Nye, Russel. "Murderers and Detectives." *The Unembarrassed
      Muse: The Popular Arts in America*. New York: Dial Press,
      1970, pp. 244-268.

      Contends that "detective-mystery stories are ideally
      fitted to a popular market that wants the excitement of
      fiction without the sophistication and complexities of
      the formalized, higher-level novel." Traces the history
      of the detective story from Poe through Mickey Spillane
      and Ian Fleming.

388. O'Faolain, Sean. "Give Us Back Bill Sikes." *Spectator*
      154 (15 February 1935): 242-243.

      Argues that the main weakness of the detective story is
      that it says the least about the most interesting charac-
      ter, the criminal.

389. "On Intellectual Thrillers." *Bookman* 76 (March 1933):
      253-254.

      Defines the requirements for intellectual thrillers or
      shockers: good plot, supernatural elements, and a satis-
      fying conclusion that does not give a "prosaic explanation
      for mysterious occurrences."

390. "On the Floor of His Library." *Nation* 103 (5 October
      1916): 317-318.

      Points out that the only books in which one can escape
      the war are detective stories. Also notes that most mur-
      ders in such stories seem to take place in private li-
      braries in the London suburb of Hampstead.

391. Orel, Harold. "The American Detective-Hero." *Journal of
      Popular Culture* 2 (Winter 1968): 395-403.

      Argues that the American detective-hero began as an
      intellectual observer in the stories of Poe and gradually
      developed into the *acting* detective of Dashiell Hammett
      and Raymond Chandler.

392. Ousby, Ian. "Vidocq Translated." *Bloodhounds of Heaven*
      (item 55), pp. 43-75.

      The fictionalized memoirs of Eugène-François Vidocq
      (published in Paris in 1828-1829) helped to effect an
      important transition (between Godwin and Dickens) in the
      literary development of the detective hero: he "emerges
      as a defined literary stereotype" and finally becomes a
      middle-class hero "whose values reflect those of the
      writer and his audience."

393. "Out of the Ordinary: The Novel of Pursuit and Suspense."
     Times Literary Supplement 25 February 1955, p. vi-vii.

     After a survey of the novel of pursuit and suspense
     concludes that it deserves more critical attention, par-
     ticularly at a time when "serious" fiction "has become
     a vehicle for ponderous philosophical or sociological
     theory."

394. Parrinder, Patrick. "George Orwell and the Detective
     Story." *Journal of Popular Culture* 6 (Spring 1973):
     692-697. Reprinted *Dimensions of Detective Fiction*
     (item 43), pp. 64-67.

     States that Orwell's essay "Grandeur et Décadence des
     roman policier anglais" is an important examination of
     the mystery story as an "intellectual exercise" as opposed
     to the "crime thriller," two categories which Orwell
     contends are quite clear-cut. Orwell cites examples from
     the work of Conan Doyle, Ernest Bramah, and R. Austin
     Freeman to support his arguments.

395. Paterson, John. "A Cosmic View of the Private Eye."
     Saturday Review 36 (22 August 1953): 7-8, 31-33.

     Paterson argues that the private-eye story is more than
     mere escapism. The rise of the hard-boiled detective in
     the 1920s and 1930s, he asserts, accurately reflected a
     profound change in the nature of American society.

396. Patrick, Q., Patrick Quentin, and Jonathan Stagge [all
     pseudonyms of Richard Wilson Webb]. "Who'd Do It?: An
     Apologia for Mystery Novelists." *Chimera* 5 (Summer 1947):
     12-17.

     Argues that detective fiction is in "a clumsy, amphib-
     ious phase"--half literature and half puzzle.

397. Paul, Elliot. "Whodunit." *Atlantic Monthly* 168 (July 1941):
     36-40.

     Defines a "whodunit" as a "murder story, with suspects
     who are innocent" and a culprit who is caught in the end.
     Observes that "it must be interesting and well written.
     The detective must be the only character who turns out
     exactly as he seems."

398. Peck, Harry Thurston. "The Detective Story." *Studies in
     Several Literatures.* New York: Dodd, Mead, 1909, pp.
     257-278.

Maintains that the true interest of an excellent detective story is largely intellectual. It is "a battle of wits, a mental duel, involving close logic, a certain amount of applied psychology, and also a high degree of daring" on the part of both the criminal and the detective. Cites as examples Voltaire's *Zadig*, Poe's detective stories, Gaboriau's *Monsieur Lecoq*, and the Sherlock Holmes stories of Conan Doyle.

399.   Pederson-Krag, Geraldine. "Detective Stories and the Primal Scene." *Psychoanalytic Quarterly* 18 (1949):207-214. Reprinted *Dimensions of Detective Fiction* (item 43), pp. 58-63.

Argues that the mystery story reader tries actively to "relive and master traumatic infantile experiences he once had to endure passively."

400.   Penzler, Otto. "The Amateur Detectives." *The Mystery Story* (item 21), pp. 83-109.

Although he cites examples of popular amateur detectives, Penzler argues that the trend in contemporary fiction is toward professionals.

401.   Penzler, Otto. "The Great Crooks." *The Mystery Story* (item 21), pp. 321-341.

Argues that the criminal is more important to the mystery story than the detective because, although the crook can exist independently, the detective must have a crime and a criminal to detect. Categorizes fictional criminals as good guys and bad guys, citing examples of each. Concludes there are few great fictional criminals today because in real life crime is so prevalent that the public is unsympathetic to criminals.

402.   Philmore, R., and J. Yudkin. "Inquest on Detective Stories." *Discovery* 1 (April 1938): 28-32.

Maintains that the "age of the scientific detective story" began with Agatha Christie's *Mysterious Affair at Styles* (1920), in which a plausible, scientific method of poisoning was used. Surveys the different ways detective fiction writers use to plausibly commit murder and points out that Dorothy L. Sayers's *Unnatural Death* uses an ingenious but implausible method of murder.

403.   Philmore, R. "Second Inquest on Detective Stories." *Discovery* 1 (September 1938): 296-299.

Observes that for writers of detective fiction the
standard motives for murder--greed, passion, or jealousy--
have certain disadvantages, the principal one being the
difficulty the writer has concealing the identity of the
murderer. Contends that the best murders in detective
fiction are committed because of some event in the past.

404. Portugal, Eustace. "Death to the Detectives!" *Bookman*
      (London) 84 (April 1933): 28.

States that "Sherlock Holmes is almost the only detective who is also a lasting contribution to literature."
When he surveys the current fictional detectives, Portugal
is able to be truly enthusiastic about only two: Chesterton's Father Brown and Rufus King's Lieutenant Valcour.
(For an answer see item 480).

405. Portuondo, José Antonio. "Whodunits in Spanish." *Américas*
      6 (August 1954): 13-16, 26-27.

States that translations (chiefly from English) of
detective fiction are very popular in Spanish America,
but few such works are written there. Surveys Spanish-
American writers who have worked in the genre and notes
that they tend to imitate foreign authors.

406. Powers, Richard Gid. "J. Edgar Hoover and the Detective
      Hero." *Journal of Popular Culture* 9 (Fall 1975): 257-
      278. Reprinted *Dimensions of Detective Fiction* (item
      43), pp. 203-227.

Argues that Hoover modeled himself on the popular detective hero of the pulp magazines and that the public's
identification of him and the F.B.I. with the fictional
detective hero was an important element in "Hoover's
success in imposing the ritualistic view of crime in
American public opinion."

407. Priestley, J.B. "Detective Stories in Bed." *Delight*. New
      York: Harper, 1949, pp. 4-7.

States that he likes to read detective stories before
going to sleep because they offer entertaining puzzles
with tidy solutions and allow him to escape from the
insoluble problems of the world.

408. Priestley, J.B. "On Holiday with the Bodies." *Saturday
      Review* (London) 142 (3 July 1926): 8-10.

Argues that detective fiction, unlike all other types
of fiction, need not be "decent literature" to be readable.

409.   Pronzini, Bill. "The Saga of the Phoenix That Probably
        Should Never Have Arisen." *Armchair Detective* 10 (April
        1977): 106-111.

        Maintains that Phoenix Press, a hardcover publisher
        of mystery fiction from 1935 to 1952, published very low
        quality mystery fiction. Most of the article is a list
        of some of their titles with comments to illustrate his
        point.

410.   Queen, Ellery. Introduction to *101 Years' Entertainment:
        The Great Detective Stories, 1841-1941*. Edited by
        Ellery Queen. Boston: Little, Brown, 1941, pp. v-xviii.

        Contends that the true form of detective fiction is the
        short story and that a detective novel is simply a padded
        short story. Also surveys the types of detective short
        stories.

411.   Queen, Ellery. "Leaves from the Editor's Notebook." *The
        Art of the Mystery Story* (item 35), pp. 406-414.

        A collection of seven short "critical commentaries"
        from *Ellery Queen's Mystery Magazine* on such topics as
        detective trademarks and detectives' names.

412.   Quincunx. "In General: Cult of Detective Stories." *Satur-
        day Review* (London) 150 (6 December 1930): 746.

        Contends that reading detective stories is a mind-
        dulling habit because of the repetition of formula in
        the genre.

413.   Ramsey, G.C. "Criticism and the Detective Story." *Armchair
        Detective* 1 (April 1968): 90-93.

        Maintains that detective fiction's lack of critical
        respectability is attributable partly to its mass popular-
        ity and academic jealousy by scholars whose specialties
        are not popular, but even more importantly to its struc-
        ture that must be built around a puzzle.

414.   Rausch, G. Jay, and Diane K. Rausch. "Developments in
        Espionage Fiction." *Kansas Quarterly* 10 (Fall 1978):
        71-82.

        Contends there are three general "streams" of spy fic-
        tion. The most recent is the "heroic professional agent,

or Bond stream." The other two are "the amateur spy and the anti-heroic professional agent." Predicts "a falling off in the number and quality of espionage novels in the years immediately ahead."

415. Raynor, Henry. "The Decline and Fall of the Detective Story." *Fortnightly* 173 (February 1953): 125-133.

Contends that Conan Doyle's Sherlock Holmes stories represent the classical detective story at its best. Since then, the emphasis on exploration of motive, secondary characters, and "fantastication" at the expense of human reason has led to its decline.

416. Redman, Ben Ray. "The Ansbacher Incarnate." *Saturday Review* 36 (18 July 1953): 11-12.

In the context of a review of Eric Ambler's *The Schirmer Inheritance* Redman briefly traces the history of the thriller from the *Golden Ass* through chivalric romances and the picaresque novel. The current appeal of this type of book, he suggests, comes from its reflection of our "present human predicament," surrounded "by unknown perils and unspeakable possibilities."

417. Redman, Ben Ray. "The Decline and Fall of the Whodunit." *Saturday Review* 35 (31 May 1952), 8-9, 31-32.

Redman surveys the detective story since 1914. "For a good many years the detective story advanced steadily on two fronts: it became increasingly ingenious and it became increasingly well written." With Hammett in 1929, however, sex and violence came into the genre as never before, and Chandler began where Hammett left off. But with Mickey Spillane the genre is "debased." Detection is almost absent; all that is left is brutality, sex, and murder.

418. Reeve, Arthur B. "In Defense of the Detective Story." *Independent* 75 (10 July 1913): 91-94.

Contends that it is not the crime but other elements that fascinate the reader of the detective story.

419. Reilly, John M. "Classic and Hard-Boiled Detective Fiction." *Armchair Detective* 9 (October 1976): 289-291, 334.

Contends that the labels "classic" and "hard-boiled" detective fiction are useful distinctions in critical analysis of the genre because they tend to emphasize that

differences in detective fiction "occur largely in the
author's choice of milieu and stress in characterization."

420.   Reilly, John M. "On Reading Detective Fiction." *Armchair
       Detective* 12 (January 1979): 64-65.

       Maintains that the conventions in detective fiction
       serve to distance the crime from the reader's immediate
       experience as well as promising eventual restoration of
       law and order through the resolution of the crime.

421.   Reilly, John M. "The Politics of Tough Guy Mysteries."
       University of Dayton Review 10 (1973): 25-31.

       The ideology of the Tough Guy Mysteries (Hammett,
       Chandler *et al.*) is not Marxist but "disillusioned popul-
       ism," in which reality is a "struggle of naked power" and
       motives are regarded cynically and individualism is cham-
       pioned.

422.   Revzin, I.I. "Notes on the Semiotic Analysis of Detective
       Novels: With Examples from the Novels of Agatha Christie."
       New Literary History 9 (Winter 1978): 385-388.

       In this short article Revzin applies the methodology of
       semiotics to some novels of Agatha Christie (and by exten-
       sion to detective fiction in general), but his purpose
       is a trial of the methodology more than an illumination
       of the mystery/detection genre.

423.   Rhodes, Henry T.F. "The Detective in Fiction--and in
       Fact." *Cornhill Magazine* 157 (January 1938): 53-67.

       Argues that the chief differences between fictional and
       real detection are that in the latter the amateur does
       not solve the crime which has baffled the police and
       scientific methods of detection are not infallible. Praises
       Freeman Wills Crofts and those he has inspired for writing
       realistic detective stories.

424.   Rice, Craig. "Murder Makes Merry." *The Art of the Mystery
       Story* (item 35), pp. 238-244.

       Contends that there is a place for humor in the detec-
       tive story; cites such examples as the wisecracking pri-
       vate eye and the bumbling cop.

425.   Richardson, Maurice. "It's All Been Done Before." *Times
       Literary Supplement* 8 December 1966, pp. 1144-1145.

Richardson reviews the history of violence and sadism in 19th-century fiction, and argues that there is a link between this theme and the evolution of detective fiction. He notes the close, almost symbiotic, relationship between the detective and the criminal and analyzes the work of Conan Doyle, John Buchan, and Sax Rohmer in this light.

426. Rinehart, Mary Roberts. "Repute of the Crime Story." *Publishers Weekly* 117 (1 February 1930): 563-566.

Points out that practically all recent Presidents have read detective stories and contends that such reading relaxes by "substituting one form of mental activity for another," by concerning oneself with a problem which is not one's own. States that the present vogue for crime stories is a result of their improved quality and the post-war "emotional slump," which made readers demand more engrossing books.

427. Rivière, François. "Fascination de la Réalité Travestie." *Europe* no. 571-572 (November–December 1976): 104-117.

Makes an analogy between the author/reader and the victim/criminal/detective relationships in detective fiction.

428. Rivière, François. "La Fiction Policière ou le Meurtre du Roman." *Europe* no. 571-572 (November–December 1976): 8-25.

Argues that detective fiction should be considered an important novelistic genre that "explores signs of the ultimate reality, the one perceived in the mirror of the unconscious."

429. Robbins, L.H. "They Get Away with Murder." *New York Times Magazine* 17 November 1940, pp. 8, 23.

Contends that the contemporary mystery story "has grown up and became an all-round novel" with a mystery in it.

430. Roberts, Kenneth. "For Authors Only." *Saturday Evening Post* 205 (24 September 1932): 14-15, 46-48. Reprinted *For Authors Only and Other Gloomy Essays*. Garden City, N.Y.: Doubleday, Doran, 1936, pp. 3-26. Reprinted as **"British Mysteries."** *The Kenneth Roberts Reader*. Garden City, N.Y.: Doubleday, Doran, 1945, pp. 186-195.

Contends that heroines of British detective novels are usually "mental deficients" and that in such novels an

American is introduced whose dialog is completely unrealistic.

431.   Rogers, Cameron. "We Dare You to Read the First Three
        Pages." *World's Work* 49 (January 1925): 335-339.

        Surveys the genre of detective fiction from Poe to the
        time of writing and states that it has "grown cosmopolitan
        and not a little distinguished."

432.   Rolo, Charles J. "Simenon and Spillane." *New World Writing:
        First Mentor Selection*. New York: New American Library,
        1952, pp. 234-245. Reprinted *Mass Culture: The Popular
        Arts in America*. Edited by Bernard Rosenberg and David
        Manning White. Glencoe, Ill.: Free Press, 1957, pp.
        165-175.

        Argues that the murder mystery presents "the problem of
        Evil" and that popular detectives reflect the times in
        which they are created. Sherlock Holmes is scientific,
        Hercule Poirot represents pure reason, Mike Hammer wrath-
        ful vengeance, and Maigret understanding.

433.   Ruhm, Herbert. Introduction to *The Hard-Boiled Detective:
        Stories From Black Mask Magazine, 1920-1951*. Edited by
        Herbert Ruhm. New York: Random House, 1977, pp. viii-
        xviii.

        Maintains that it was in *Black Mask* that the American
        detective story developed. Its stories depicted an irra-
        tional, disorderly world where "violence was the means
        to all ends" and the language used was slangy and tough.
        Much of Dashiell Hammett's work and Raymond Chandler's
        first six stories appeared in it, helping to make it
        famous.

434.   Sandoe, James. "Criminal Clef: Tales and Plays Based on
        Real Crimes." *Wilson Library Bulletin* 21 (December
        1946): 299-307.

        An annotated bibliography of mystery/detection stories
        that are based on real crimes.

435.   Sandoe, James. "Dagger of the Mind." *Poetry* 68 (June
        1948): 146-163. Reprinted *The Art of the Mystery Story*
        (item 35), pp. 250-262.

        In an analysis of the persistent attraction of the
        horror story, examines a number of twentieth-century
        examples, arguing that they all ultimately derive their
        power from "the horror of man's inhumanity to man."

436. Sandoe, James. "The Detective Story and Academe." *Wilson Library Bulletin* 18 (April 1944): 619-623.

   An annotated bibliography of mystery/detection fiction set on college campuses.

437. Sandoe, James. "The Private Eye." *The Mystery Story* (item 21), pp. 111-123.

   Contends that a private eye must have integrity, a sense of imminent violence and evil, a need for money, and must work alone. Sandoe includes an annotated list of novels in which he believes the private eye is pre-eminent.

438. Sarjeant, William A.S. "Detectives and Geology." *Armchair Detective* 11 (July 1978): 294-297.

   Contends that geology as a profession for a detective hero provides ample opportunity for travel, "involvement in potentially explosive political and monetary situations," and the creation of an eccentric personality. Cites numerous examples of geology in mystery fiction ranging from Conan Doyle to Arthur Upfield.

439. Sauder, Rae Norden. "They Kill and Tell." *Independent Woman* 21 (October 1942): 303, 317-318.

   In an interview Isabelle Taylor, editor-in-chief of Doubleday, Doran's Crime Club, attributes the huge wartime growth in the popularity of mystery novels to the public's wish to escape from personal problems and the war as well as to their liking for a puzzle. Taylor maintains that "women have the edge on men in writing ... because the hard-boiled school is on the wane, and they have a knack for full-bodied detective stories that stand up as novels." Most of the article is devoted to brief comments on some successful women mystery writers, such as Agatha Christie and Mary Roberts Rinehart.

440. Sayers, Dorothy L. "Aristotle on Detective Fiction." *Unpopular Opinions: Twenty-One Essays*. New York: Harcourt, Brace, 1947, pp. 222-236.

   Contends that many of Aristotle's statements about writing and composition can be applied to the detective story, particularly his comments on the three necessary elements of a plot: reversal of fortune, discovery, and suffering.

441. Sayers, Dorothy L. Introduction to *Great Short Stories
      of Detection, Mystery and Horror*. Edited by Dorothy L.
      Sayers. London: Victor Gollancz, 1928. [Published in
      the U.S. as *The Omnibus of Crime*. New York: Payson and
      Clarke, 1929.] Reprinted *The Art of the Mystery Story*
      (item 35), pp. 71-109. Reprinted as "Detective Fiction:
      Origins and Development." *Writing Detective and Mystery
      Fiction*. Edited by A.S. Burack. Boston: Writer, 1967,
      pp. 3-48. Shortened version printed as "Sport of Noble
      Minds." *Saturday Review* 6 (3 August 1929): 22-23.

      Contends that "the general principles of the detective
      story were laid down forever" in five tales by Edgar Allan
      Poe and traces the evolution of the genre through Wilkie
      Collins and Conan Doyle to the "Modern 'Fair-Play' Method,"
      in which the reader is given all the "clues and discoveries"
      that the detective knows. Concludes that there are signs
      that the formula may be becoming exhausted but speculates
      that a new formula may be developed which is less rigid
      and brings the detective story closer to the novel of
      manners.

442. Sayers, Dorothy L. Introduction to *Great Short Stories
      of Detection, Mystery and Horror--Second Series*. Edited
      by Dorothy L. Sayers. London: Victor Gollancz, 1931.
      [Published in the U.S. as *The Second Omnibus of Crime*.
      New York: Coward-McCann, 1932.]

      States that the creation of a detective story begins
      with a central idea (such as "an ingenious method of con-
      structing an alibi") and then plot and characters must
      be fashioned to plausibly embody that idea. In recent
      years, Sayers contends, the detective story tends to have
      "a more elaborate and realistic psychology than was once
      thought necessary or desirable," and many a work has been
      written which is "rather a novel with a detective interest
      than a detective-story pure and simple." Argues that the
      detective short story is in difficult circumstances be-
      cause it can develop very little plot or characterization
      and "must be summed up in a single surprise." The reader
      of detective fiction plays an important part. He or she
      must be "alert and amiable": it is nearly impossible to
      win over the determinedly hostile reader.

443. Sayers, Dorothy L. Introduction to *Great Short Stories of
      Detection, Mystery and Horror--Third Series*. Edited by
      Dorothy L. Sayers. London: Victor Gollancz, 1934. [Pub-
      lished in the U.S. as *The Third Omnibus of Crime*. New
      York: Coward-McCann, 1935.]

Contends that the technique of the short story has
greatly influenced the detective novel so that it often
has the shape of a short story and that the "best detective short stories are those which are concerned with a
single, not too complicated, twist or trick." Also states
that the plain unpretentious style of the detective story
stands out in contrast to the suggestive, more pretentious
literary style of the horror story.

444. Sayers, Dorothy L. "Other People's Great Detectives."
Illustrated 1 (29 April 1939): 18-19.

Singles out Wilkie Collins's Sergeant Cuff, Conan
Doyle's Sherlock Holmes, and G.K. Chesterton's Father
Brown as detective characters which will "pass the test
of time."

445. Sayers, Dorothy L. "The Present Status of the Mystery
Story." *London Mercury* 23 (November 1930): 47-52.

The mystery story, Sayers argues, is becoming more highbrow and "is in great danger of losing touch with the
common man."

446. Scott, Mark. "An Introduction to the Private Eye Novel."
Cunning Exiles: Studies of Modern Prose Writers. Edited
by Don Anderson and Stephen Knight. London: Angus and
Robertson, 1974, pp. 198-217.

Observes that the term "hard-boiled" is "no more than a
critical convenience" that was "coined in the 1930's to
characterize the hero of the novels and his stance towards
the world in general." Comments on the detective heroes
of Hammett, Chandler, and Ross Macdonald.

447. Scott-James, R.A. "Detective Novels." *London Mercury* 39
(February 1939): 377-379.

Contends that detective novels are generally only a
diversion and cannot be considered fine art. Detective
novels do not give the reader any aesthetic statisfaction,
only relaxation.

448. Scrutton, Mary. "Addiction to Fiction." *Twentieth Century*
159 (April 1956): 363-373.

In an article on the popularity of novels in general,
Scrutton observes that detective novels seem to gratify
a desire for "completeness," neatness, and limited investigation that she identifies as being reasons for reading
all novels.

449.   Seaborne, Edward R. Introduction to *The Detective in
       Fiction: A Posse of Eight*. Edited by Edward A. Seaborne.
       London: George Bell and Sons, 1938, pp. 1-36.

       After a brief historical survey of detective fiction
       observes that in order to flourish the genre needs an
       "intellectual and legally minded community" and that a
       successful detective story inspires the reader's sympathy
       with the detective.

450.   "The Secret Attraction." *Times Literary Supplement* 25
       February 1955, pp. i-ii.

       Argues that the detective story can satisfy both the
       urge for excitement and for justice: "we can commit a
       murder in the morning and catch ourselves out in the
       afternoon." Contends that recent writers of detective
       fiction, in search of fresh material, have turned to pure
       sensationalism and "desperado prose."

451.   Seelye, John. "Buckskin and Ballistics: William Leggett
       and the American Detective Story." *Journal of Popular
       Culture* 1 (Summer 1967): 52-57.

       Contends that Leggett--an American radical critic, edi-
       tor, and writer of the 1830s--should be studied by anyone
       interested in the development of the detective story be-
       cause several of his stories depend on simple acts of
       detection and because he created the first amateur detec-
       tive.

452.   Seldes, Gilbert. "Diplomatic Delight." *Bookman* 66 (Septem-
       ber 1927): 91-93.

       In a survey of current mystery fiction Seldes maintains
       that "the best detective stories are the best written
       detective stories," although good writing does not auto-
       matically make such a story good.

453.   Shaffer, Anthony. "Death of a Bloodsport." *Harper's
       Bazaar* 104 (November 1970): 122-123.

       Maintains that the classic English detective story,
       called the "most popular of modern bloodsports" by Nicholas
       Blake (C. Day Lewis), is dead, "first outlawed by Raymond
       Chandler and Dashiell Hammett and then polished off by
       Ian Fleming and his lackluster imitators."

454.   Sherlock Holmes and After." *Saturday Review* 6 (19 July
       1930): 1201.

Argues that the detective story is a popular escape
because it is real enough to be interesting but is not
close enough to the reader's personal experience to arouse
anxiety.

455. "Shifting the Apology." *Saturday Review* 3 (11 September
      1926): 97.

      Observes that detective fiction is "a literature of
      escape" that is "sufficiently removed from the routine
      of existence to give it the glamour of the unknown."

456. Shrapnel, Norman. "The Literature of Violence and Pursuit."
      Times Literary Supplement 23 June 1961, pp. i-ii.

      Argues that mystery and detective fiction have much to
      offer other fiction: "natural dynamic," scope for generat-
      ing and using atmosphere, and "relevance ... to the real-
      life myth and fantasy of the day."

457. "The Silver Age: Crime Fiction from Its Heyday Until Now."
      Times Literary Supplement 25 February 1955, pp. xi-xii.

      The silver age of crime fiction dates from the post-
      World War I era. It is characterized by technical expert-
      ise, but also by self-consciousness. Two of its contribu-
      tions to the genre of crime fiction are the hard-boiled
      private eye and the spy thriller.

458. Simpson, Helen. "Down Among the Dead Men." *Bookman* (London)
      87 (December 1934): 145-146.

      In introducing her review of several recent works of
      detective fiction, Simpson argues that the eccentricities
      of fictional detectives are necessary to individualize
      them because their methods are basically the same.

459. Sisk, John P. "Crime and Criticism." *Commonweal* 64 (20
      April 1956): 72-74.

      Observes that the mystery story needs "a sustaining
      body of criticism to give it stature" and specifically
      cites Ben Ray Redman's article (item 417) as an example
      of criticism that deals with the genre. Also states sev-
      eral reasons why people read mystery stories: to relax,
      to unravel a puzzle, and to satisfy a "fascination with
      death" as well as to satisfy the desire to confront death
      in some way.

460.   Slung, Michele B. Introduction to *Crime on Her Mind:*
        Fifteen Stories of Female Sleuths from the Victorian
        Era to the Forties. Edited by Michele B. Slung. New
        York: Pantheon Books, 1975, pp. xvi-xxx.

        States that between 1867 and 1901 at least twenty women
        detectives appeared who could all be called "ladylike,"
        and cites examples to illustrate her thesis. Argues that
        few important women detectives appeared during the Golden
        Age of detective fiction (roughly 1918-1930) but in the
        following period they became an accepted part of the
        genre.

461.   Slung, Michele B. "Women in Detective Fiction." *The*
        Mystery Story (item 21), pp. 125-140.

        After an admittedly subjective survey of women's con-
        tribution to the field of mystery and detective fiction
        concludes that, while women have always been important
        contributors to this genre, the heightened feminism of
        the 1970s should produce a corresponding increase in
        novels that feature women as well as men as intelligent
        detectives.

462.   Smith, Harrison. "New Detectives." *Good Housekeeping* 125
        (September 1947): 26-27, 100, 102-105.

        Contends that the crime wave during prohibition made
        the "lily-fingered amateur detective" nearly obsolete
        but that the characters and plot of the hard-boiled
        stories have become stereotyped. States that something
        new will emerge.

463.   Smith, Susan Harris. "The Case of the Corpse in the
        Classroom." *CEA Critic* 38 (1976): 18-22.

        Smith defends detective fiction as an appropriate sub-
        ject for classroom study. She also summarizes the develop-
        ment of the genre and of the literary criticism it has
        inspired.

464.   Snow, C.P. "The Classical Detective Story." *From Parnassus:*
        Essays in Honor of Jacques Barzun. Edited by Dora B.
        Weiner and William B. Keylor. New York: Harper and Row,
        1976, pp. 16-22.

        In an analysis of Barzun's criticism of the genre, Snow
        distinguishes between the private eye-oriented tales and
        the older, "classical," or puzzle solving stories. States
        that Barzun's criticism indicates a preference for the
        classical detective story.

465. Snyder, John R. "The Spy Story as Modern Tragedy."
      Literature/Film Quarterly 5 (1977): 216-234.

      In tracing the history of the spy story--both British
      and American--Snyder argues that the genre differs from
      the related mystery/detection genre in that the real
      world--history and politics--is an integral part of the
      spy story, but peripheral to mystery/detection. The spy
      story, with its alienated, often passive anti-hero, is
      an accurate reflection of the malaise of the modern world.

466. Spanos, William V. "The Detective and the Boundary: Some
      Notes on the Postmodern Literary Imagination." *Boundary
      2* 1 (Fall 1972): 147-168.

      In examining works of such writers as Beckett and
      Robbe-Grillet, Spanos contends that it is "no accident
      that the paradigmatic archetype of the postmodern literary
      imagination is the anti-detective story." He uses works
      of Conan Doyle for most of his examples of the workings
      of the detective story.

467. Stange, G. Robert. "The Detective Story Mystery." *Chimera*
      5 (Summer 1947): 31-38.

      Argues that the core of the main line of detective
      fiction is a faith in reason and science, but its failing
      is that it lulls us rather than awakening our perceptions.

468. Starrett, Vincent. "From Poe to Poirot." *Books Alive: A
      Profane Chronicle of Literary Endeavor and Literary
      Misdemeanor*. New York: Random House, 1970, pp. 184-210.

      Argues that the reader of detective fiction derives
      pleasure from identifying with both the criminal and the
      detective and the fact that virtue always wins. Surveys
      the history of the genre from Poe to the late 1930s.

469. Starrett, Vincent. "Of Detective Literature." *Fourteen
      Great Detective Stories*. Edited by Vincent Starrett.
      New York: Modern Library, 1928, pp. ix-xv.

      Maintains that the popularity of mystery fiction is
      unique and universal and speculates that some of the
      reasons may be that it is "sexless," appeals to all ages,
      and contains the lure of the mysterious.

470. Starrett, Vincent. "Some Chinese Detective Stories."
      *Bookman's Holiday: The Private Satisfactions of an
      Incurable Collector*. New York: Random House, 1942, pp.
      3-26.

States that the fairly rigid conventions of the Imperial
Chinese detective story, particularly its reliance on the
supernatural and the revelation of the criminal's identity
at the beginning of the story, make it doubtful that
Western readers would enjoy these stories. Cites examples
from several Chinese detective novels, particularly those
featuring the judges Pao Kung and Di Jen-djieh to support
his contentions.

471. Steeves, Harrison R. "A Sober Word on the Detective Story."
      Harper's 182 (April 1941): 485-492. Reprinted *The Art
      of the Mystery Story* (item 35), pp. 513-526.

Argues that the detective story remains popular because
it reinforces the concept of justice triumphant while
testing the wits of its readers.

472. Stein, Aaron Marc. "The Detective Story—How and Why."
      Princeton University Library Chronicle 36 (Autumn 1974):
      19-46.

In this survey of the detective story and such pre-de-
tective crime stories as *Oedipus Rex* and *Hamlet*, Stein
argues that the detective story can thrive only in a society with a legal system based on the Anglo-Saxon idea
that a person is innocent until proven guilty. A belief
in science and reason are also important, he maintains.

473. Stein, Aaron Marc. "The Mystery Story in Cultural Per-
      spective." *The Mystery Story* (item 21), pp. 29-59.

Argues that detective fiction's 19th-century beginnings
reflect that century's faith in reason and argues that
crucial cultural changes such as the disappearance of
torture and appearance of organized police forces influenced the conception and acceptance of detective fiction.

474. Stéphane, Nelly. "Mais où Sont les Lupins d'Antan?" *Europe*
      no. 604-605 (August-September 1979): 84-89.

Identifies three different types of detective novels:
the one that focuses on the criminal (Arsène Lupin), the
one that focuses on the detective (Sherlock Holmes, James
Bond), and the spy novel in which the hero pretends to
be a traitor in order to unmask his adversary.

475. Sterling, Stewart. "Strictly Phoney." *Publishers Weekly*
      141 (21 March 1942): 1172-1174.

This article is an argument (in the form of a fictional dialog with a real police detective) that "real cops and real detective techniques are more interesting and exciting than tales of the amateur with a love of artichokes, a prodigious memory and an Alsatian rabbit retriever."

476. Stern, Philip Van Doren. "The Case of the Corpse in the Blind Alley." *Virginia Quarterly Review* 17 (April 1941): 227-236. Reprinted *The Art of the Mystery Story* (item 35), pp. 527-535.

Argues that the detective story reached its peak at its inception in the works of Edgar Allan Poe. Contemporary examples of the genre lack literary value; they are merely puzzles.

477. Stevens, George. "Death by Misadventure." *Saturday Review* 24 (18 October 1941): 6-7, 34-36.

On the one hundredth anniversary of the publication of "The Murders in the Rue Morgue," observes that detective fiction criticism is largely "pseudo-scholarly." Cites as a positive exception to this Howard Haycraft's *Murder for Pleasure*. Maintains that it is in the "rereadability of a detective novel that its chances for survival inhere."

478. Stevenson, Burton Egbert. "Supreme Moments in Detective Fiction." *Bookman* 37 (March 1913): 49-54.

Maintains that the interest of a detective story is "intellectual and not emotional." There are only four classic detectives: Dupin, Tabaret, LeCoq, and Sherlock Holmes. Describes what he considers to be the supreme moment of each.

479. Stewart, Lawrence D. "Gertrude Stein and the Vital Dead." *The Mystery and Detection Annual 1972* (item 16), pp. 102-123.

Stewart examines Stein's comments related to the detective story.

480. Stone P.M. "Long Life: To Some Detectives." *Bookman* (London) 84 (June 1933): 150-151.

In this reply to Eustace Portugal (item 404), Stone argues that the virtues of such detectives as Lord Peter Wimsey and Philo Vance outweigh their sometimes irritating eccentricities, and states that Portugal's omission of Dr. John Thorndyke and Inspector Joseph French from his

article is inexcusable because they are the current
"luminaries" in the genre.

481. Storr, Anthony. "A Black-and-White World." *Times Literary
      Supplement* 23 June 1961, p. ii.

      Contends that "in the crime story both our antisocial
      impulses and our consciences can find satisfaction."

482. Stout, Rex. "Grim Fairy Tales." *Saturday Review* 32 (2
      April 1949): 7-8, 34. Reprinted as "Crime in Fiction."
      Writing for Love or Money. Edited by Norman Cousins.
      New York: Longmans, Green, 1949, pp. 118-126.

      Contends that the essence of the detective story is
      reason and that the writer of such stories must create
      an interesting detective and an exciting story without
      violating that principle.

483. Stout, Rex. "The Mystery Novel." *The Writer's Book.* Edited
      by Helen Hull. New York: Harper and Brothers, 1950, pp.
      62-67.

      Writing about the conventions of the classical detective
      story, Stout contends that many of the dicta promulgated
      about writing it, such as "you must play fair with the
      reader," are "nonsense." Contends that it is the "excel-
      lence of writing or invention of a new twist or brilliance
      of performance by the detective" that is most important.

484. Stout, Rex. "These Grapes Need Sugar." *Vogue's First
      Reader.* New York: Julian Messner, 1942, pp. 421-425.

      Argues that women crime writers have made murder too
      genteel.

485. Strachey, John. "The Golden Age of English Detection."
      Saturday Review 19 (7 January 1939): 12-14.

      Surveys English fiction in the 1930s and argues that
      only in detective fiction are there "characteristic
      signs of vigor and achievement." Cites Sayers, Christie,
      Crofts, Allingham, Innes, and Blake.

486. Strong, L.A.G. "The Crime Short Story: An English View."
      Crime in Good Company (item 32), pp. 149-162.

      Argues that in the mystery detective short story "the
      length can be exactly matched to the energy of the idea"
      without the padding which is too often seen in the crime
      novel. Also maintains that the emphasis will be on struc-
      ture rather than characterization in a short story.

487. Strunsky, Simeon. "Cold Chills of 1928." *Essays for Discussion*. Edited by Anita P. Forbes. New York: Harper and Brothers, 1931, pp. 185-190.

     Maintains that the detective story is a "powerful force for righteousness and law and order" because in it the criminal is always caught, the judicial system operates efficiently, and "disintegrating forces that threaten society" seldom appear.

488. Symons, Julian. "An End to Spying, Or, From Pipe Dreams to Farce." *Times Literary Supplement* 12 December 1968, pp. 1411-1412.

     Symons traces the development of the British spy novel from Ambler to Fleming, Le Carré, and Deighton. He argues that the film versions of the Bond stories threaten to turn the entire genre into gimmicky farce.

489. Symons, Julian. "The Face in the Mirror." *Crime in Good Company* (item 32), pp. 129-133. Reprinted *Critical Occasions*. London: Hamish Hamilton, 1966, pp. 149-153.

     Argues that crime stories need not be as constricted by formula as they usually are: "The crime novel at its best is something more serious and more interesting than a parlour game, ... its author's business will always be to investigate, with all the freedom that the medium permits him, the springs of violence."

490. Symons, Julian. "The Great Detective." *Saturday Book 14*. Edited by John Hadfield. New York: Macmillan, 1954, pp. 47-53.

     Symons discerns the following character traits in Sherlock Holmes, Philo Vance, Ellery Queen, and other "Great Detectives": he knows everything; he is eccentric and usually egotistical; and he is above the law.

491. Symons, Julian. "New Paths in Crime Fiction." *Times Saturday Review* (London) 19 February 1972, p. 6.

     States that the greatest change in crime fiction is in the detective, who now may be of either sex, any race, and any sexual persuasion but is no longer an omniscient amateur. Distinguishes between the detective story, in which the puzzle is the first concern, and the crime novel, in which the psychology of the characters is more important.

492. Symons, Julian, and Edmund Crispin. "Is the Detective
      Story Dead?" *Times Literary Supplement* 23 June 1961,
      pp. iv–v.

      A recorded dialog between the two authors which covers
      many more topics than are indicated in the title.

493. "Throw Out the Detective." *Saturday Review* 56 (1 December
      1928): 421–422.

      Argues that only one in ten detective stories are worth
      reading and contends that writers could escape the tired
      old formulas if they wrote mystery stories without detec-
      tives in them.

494. Todd, Ruthven. "A Trinity of 'Tecs: From Where to Where?"
      Chimera 5 (Summer 1947): 49–58.

      States that there have been three kinds of detectives
      in detective fiction: the professional, the eccentric
      amateur, and the hard-boiled. The first, he contends, has
      nearly disappeared.

495. Todorov, Tzvetan. "The Typology of Detective Fiction."
      The Poetics of Prose. Ithaca, N.Y.: Cornell University
      Press, 1977, pp. 42–52.

      Argues that "the masterpiece of popular literature is
      precisely the book which best fits its genre," rather than
      the one which transcends it. Todorov then divides the
      detective story into three types: classical, thriller,
      suspense.

496. "Tram Cars or 'Dodgems': Detection, Thrills and Horror."
      Times Literary Supplement 25 February 1955, p. ii.

      Argues that the detective story is a restricted form
      in contrast to the flexibility of the thriller.

497. Ulanov, Barry. "The Mystery Story." *The Two Worlds of
      American Art: The Private and the Popular*. New York:
      Macmillan, 1965, pp. 284–297.

      Contends that the popularity of the mystery story is
      largely due to its orderly presentation of a problem
      that is then solved. Agrees with Chesterton's dictum
      that "simplicity and brevity are of the essence of the
      detective story" and that its model is "the short story
      and not the novel."

498. Van Gulik, Robert. "Translator's Preface." *Celebrated Cases of Judge Dee (Dee Goong An): An Authentic Eighteenth-Century Chinese Detective Novel*. New York: Dover, 1976, pp. i-xxiii.

     States that detective stories have been popular in China for more than a thousand years, reaching the height of development in the 18th and 19th centuries. States that Chinese detective stories have five important features that make them different: (1) little suspense; (2) supernatural elements preferred to realism; (3) long, detailed narratives filled with digressions; (4) large number of characters (often more than 100); (5) a full description of the criminal's punishment.

499. Van Meter, Jan R. "Sophocles and the Rest of the Boys in the Pulps: Myth and the Detective Novel." *Dimensions of Detective Fiction* (item 43), pp. 12-21.

     Argues that the detective story is one of the most ancient literary genres and in order "to understand both its nature and its appeal we must first understand it as a variety of myth which is central to our culture."

500. Vickers, Roy. "Crime on the Stage: The Criminological Illusion." *Crime in Good Company* (item 32), pp. 178-191.

     Argues that "crime drama owes virtually nothing to the real-life criminal."

501. Waite, John Barker. "If Judges Wrote Detective Stories." *Scribner's Magazine* 95 (April 1934): 275-277.

     Waite, a professor of law, contends that "rulings of judges make actual crimes more difficult to solve than the fiction writers realize." He states that detectives and police in fiction tend to use illegal detention of suspects and witnesses as well as illegal methods of ·obtaining evidence. (See item 199 for reply.)

502. Waite, John Barker, and Miles W. Kimball. "The Lawyer Looks at Detective Fiction." *Bookman* 69 (August 1929): 616-621. Reprinted *The Art of the Mystery Story* (item 35), pp. 436-446.

     Argues that in much detective fiction the detective uses illegal means to obtain evidence or determines guilt on the basis of evidence that "would make him a laughing-stock if introduced into an actual court of

justice." Uses many detailed examples to illustrate the
point.

503. Walters, Margaret. "English Whodunits: Where Are They
      Now?" New Republic 170 (20 April 1974): 21-23.

      Predicts a resurgence of the classic English mystery
      story, "a fairy tale for the educated man, glamorizing
      the class structure and his place in it." When times are
      bad and "class tensions surface again," the English return
      to the "comforting, conservative, comic" English mystery
      story.

504. Waugh, Hillary. "The Mystery Versus the Novel." The
      Mystery Story (item 21), pp. 61-80.

      States that the mystery is to the novel what the sonnet
      is to poetry: a stylized form with rigid rules which pro-
      vides a disciplined training ground for the novel. Con-
      cludes that the "ultimate distinction between the mystery
      and the novel [is] motive." If the author's motive is
      mystery, the work is a mystery.

505. Waugh, Hillary. "The Police Procedural." The Mystery Story
      (item 21), pp. 163-187.

      Argues that the police procedural represents a major
      new type of mystery story. States that the classical
      detective story presents a puzzle, but the police pro-
      cedural presents social problems.

506. Whipple, Leon. "Nirvana for Two Dollars." Survey 62 (1
      May 1929): 191-192.

      Contends that detective stories are read by people
      who want to escape their world of "labor and tension"
      and find "serious" literature too concerned with sociol-
      ogy and psychology to be a real escape and that the dead
      people in detective tales are "symbols pure as algebra."

507. Whiteside, Thomas. "Murder a Minute." Colliers 123 (5
      February 1949): 28-29, 68-70.

      States that few mystery writers have any experience
      with actual crime and notes some common errors in crime
      fiction, such as picking up a gun with a handkerchief to
      preserve fingerprints. Reports that Richard H. Hoffmann,
      a psychiatrist, maintains that reading murder mysteries
      enables people to get rid of aggressions harmlessly and
      to solve problems not their own.

508. "Who Done It--As Dickens Did It." *Colliers* 131 (14 March 1953): 74.

     This editorial maintains that the current "crusade against whodunits by intellectual professors" will fail. Article states that it agrees with the *New York Daily News* in maintaining that some of the best writing today comes from mystery writers.

509. Williams, H.L. "The Germ of the Detective Novel." *Book Buyer* 21 (November 1900): 268-274.

     Contends that the French created the police hero, and "the English made the conception more concrete."

510. Williams, Valentine. "Crime Fiction According to Hoyle." *Saturday Evening Post* 204 (11 July 1931): 33, 108-109.

     Maintains that "pace, plausibility, suspense, surprise" are the "essential ingredients" of detective fiction.

511. Williams, Valentine. "Detective Fiction." *Bookman* 67 (July 1928): 521-524.

     Distinguishes between the "shocker" or "thriller" and the detective story. The latter must be a mystery story and is of comparatively recent origin. Observes that technique, more than characterization, is important in writing good detective stories.

512. Williams, Valentine. "The Detective in Fiction." *Fortnightly Review* 128 (September 1930): 381-392.

     Contends that Poe invented the detective story and Conan Doyle made it respectable. Also contends that Vidocq inspired Poe, who in turn inspired Gaboriau.

513. Williams, Valentine. "On Crime Fiction." *What Is a Book?: Thoughts About Writing*. Edited by Dale Warren. Boston: Houghton Mifflin, 1935, pp. 119-129. Reprinted *Writing Detective and Mystery Fiction*. Edited by A.S. Burack. Boston: Writer, 1967, pp. 271-280.

     Argues that plot and plausibility are the key ingredients in crime fiction.

514. Williams, Valentine. "Putting the Shocks into 'Shockers.'" *Bookman* 66 (November 1927): 270-272.

     Maintains that construction is all important in writing a good shocker and cites classic examples of the genre.

515. Wilson, Edmund. "Who Cares Who Killed Roger Ackroyd?:
      Second Report on Detective Fiction." *New Yorker* 20
      (20 January 1945): 52-54, 57-58. Reprinted *Classics
      and Commercials: A Literary Chronicle of the Forties*.
      New York: Farrar, Straus, 1950, pp. 257-265. Also
      reprinted *A Literary Chronicle: 1920-1950*. Garden City,
      N.Y.: Doubleday, 1956, pp. 338-345. Also reprinted *The
      Art of the Mystery Story* (item 35), pp. 390-397. Also
      reprinted *Mass Culture: The Popular Arts in America*.
      Edited by Bernard Rosenberg and David Manning White.
      Glencoe, Ill.: Free Press, 1957, pp. 149-153.

      In this famous article, which is a response to reaction
      to his criticism of the genre in "Why Do People Read
      Detective Stories?" (item 516), Wilson finds detective
      novels generally extremely deficient in writing style,
      characterization, and human interest, and he is unable
      to ignore the demands of his "imagination and literary
      taste" to take the novels as intellectual problems. "With
      so many fine books to be read ... there is no need to
      bore ourselves with this rubbish."

516. Wilson, Edmund. "Why Do People Read Detective Stories?"
      New Yorker 20 (14 October 1944): 73-74, 76. Reprinted
      *Classics and Commercials: A Literary Chronicle of the
      Forties*. New York: Farrar, Straus, 1950, pp. 231-237.
      Also reprinted *A Literary Chronicle: 1920-1950*. Garden
      City, N.Y.: Doubleday, 1956, pp. 323-328.

      Contends that the detective story as a type of imagina-
      tive writing looks "completely dead" but explains its
      popularity as lying in the appeal of the "omniscient
      detective" who discovers the crime and its perpetrator,
      an appeal even more obvious in the atmosphere of fear,
      guilt, and hopelessness (of not knowing whom to blame)
      that characterized the period between the First and
      Second World Wars. (See also item 515.)

517. Wingate, Nancy. "Getting Away with Murder: An Analysis."
      Journal of Popular Culture 12 (Spring 1979): 581-603.

      Examines a small group of detective novels in which
      the murderer escapes justice and argues that "the satis-
      faction of the traditional mystery comes not from the
      reader's certainty of the immanence of justice but from
      his certainty of the immanence of truth."

518. Woods, Katharine Pearson. "The Renaissance of Wonder."
      Bookman 10 (December 1899): 340-343.

Observes that it is natural for man to wonder about
and investigate the unknown. Since detective stories,
therefore, appeal to such a "fundamental need of the
human mind" they should be considered a respectable
literary form.

519. "The World of the Detective Story." *Times Literary Supple-*
      ment 17 September 1954, p. xxxviii. Reprinted *American*
      Writing Today: Its Independence and Vigor. Edited by
      Allan Angoff. New York: New York University Press,
      1957, pp. 171-176.

      States that "American detective stories in particular
      exemplify the well-known American liking for violence
      and often reveal a sadistic or masochistic streak." The
      author also contends that, "at a deeper level," detective
      story readers seek a safe world that makes sense.

520. Wright, Lee. "Command Performance." *The Art of the Mystery*
      Story (item 35), pp. 287-291.

      Argues that the mystery genre is subject to the law of
      supply and demand. Changes in the genre depend upon the
      presence of a receptive audience for those changes.

521. Wright, Lee. Murder is My Business--Sort Of." *McCall's*
      96 (April 1969): 97-98, 185.

      Wright suggests that there are so many good women
      writers of mystery and detective fiction because fictional
      homicide provides "a sublimation of the irritations
      built up in any homemaker's day."

522. Wright, Willard Huntington. "The Detective Novel."
      Scribner's Magazine 80 (November 1926): 532-539. Re-
      printed as Introduction to *The Great Detective Stories*.
      Compiled and edited by Willard Huntington Wright. New
      York: Scribners, 1927, pp. 3-37. Reprinted as "The
      Great Detective Stories." *The Art of the Mystery Story*
      (item 35), pp. 33-70.

      Argues that the detective novel is not fiction in the
      usual sense but "a complicated and extended puzzle cast
      in fictional form." It must, however, have a sense of
      reality to keep the puzzle from being trivialized. Surveys
      the genre from Poe to the present.

523. Wright, Willard Huntington [under the pseudonym S.S. Van
      Dine]. "Twenty Rules for Writing Detective Stories."
      American Magazine 106 (September 1928): 14+. Reprinted

Philo Vance Murder Cases. New York: Scribners, 1936,
pp. 74-81. Reprinted *The Art of the Mystery Story* (item
35), pp. 189-193.

Contends that the detective story is an "intellectual
game" that should follow such "rules" as determining the
culprit by logical deductions and having no love interest.

524.   Wrong, Edward Murray. Introduction to *Crime and Detection.*
New York: Oxford University Press, 1926, pp. ix-xxx.
Reprinted *The Art of the Mystery Story* (item 35), pp.
18-32.

Argues that the detective story is a respectable genre.
Cites examples from Biblical and Greek antiquities and
summarizes the history of the form, with emphasis on
British contributions.

525.   Wyndham, Horace. "Lure of the Crime Book." *Saturday Review*
(London) 156 (8 July 1933): 41.

States that crime books of all kinds are always popular
because "crime is necessarily dramatic." Recommends the
government's *Criminal Statistics for the Year* as the best
crime book on the market.

526.   Yates, Donald A. "The Detective Literature of the Americas."
Armchair Detective 4 (October 1970): 5-9.

Contends that Latin American countries have created
detective literature and briefly surveys the contributions
of several countries to determine the influence of national
temperaments on the genre.

527.   Yates, Donald A. Introduction to *Latin Blood: The Best
Crime and Detective Stories of South America.* Edited
by Donald A. Yates. New York: Herder and Herder, 1972,
pp. xi-xv.

Points out that most detective fiction published in
Latin America is translated from English-language originals but its great popularity has encouraged native
authors, particularly in metropolitan areas of Argentina,
Mexico, and Chile. Most Latin American detective story
writers use pseudonyms and American or English backgrounds
because that is what the reading public expects.

528.   Yates, Donald A. "The Locked Room." *Michigan Alumnus
Quarterly Review* 73 (1957): 218-225. Revised version
printed as "The Locked House: An Essay on Locked Rooms."

Armchair Detective 3 (January 1970): 81-84. Reprinted
as "An Essay on Locked Rooms." *The Mystery Writer's Art*
(item 54), pp. 272-284.

Argues that the "locked room" mystery attracts mystery
writers because it allows them the greatest challenge to
their cleverness and ingenuity. Surveys the form from
Poe to the present.

529. Yates, Donald A. "Locked Rooms and Puzzles: A Critical
Memoir." *The Mystery Story* (item 21), pp. 189-203.

Defining the detective story as essentially a puzzle
story, Yates argues that the "locked room" puzzle is the
oldest of this type of story and owes its popularity to
the public liking for a crime requiring a solution,
methodical and relevant evidence, and a solution compatible
with the facts as presented.

530. Zegel, Sylvain. "Whodunit--Soviet Style." *Atlas* 9 (May
1965): 309-310. [Originally published in *Le Figaro
Litteraire*.]

States that the detective story flourishes in Russia
and provides a surprisingly candid view of contemporary
Soviet life.

Section Two
Individual Authors

ADAMS, CLEVE F. (1895-1949). Pseudonym: John Spain

531. Nevins, Francis M., Jr. "The World of Cleve F. Adams."
      Armchair Detective 8 (May 1975): 195-200.

      Adams's private eyes are usually just as tough, brutal,
      and rotten as the people they pursue, and his plots com-
      bine the "most familiar hardboiled elements." His con-
      cept of the private detective was more cynical than
      Chandler's.

ADAMS, HARRIET L. See CAROLYN KEENE

ALDRICH, THOMAS BAILEY (1836-1907)

532. Samuels, Charles E. *Thomas Bailey Aldrich*. New York:
      Twayne, 1965, pp. 97-99.

      Argues that *The Stillwater Tragedy* is "an unfortunate
      combination of detective and labor novel" written in a
      deliberate attempt to win critical favor.

533. Tanasoca, Donald. "*Stillwater Tragedy*: A Socio-Detective
      Novel." *American Notes and Queries* 1 (1963): 148-150.

      Although Aldrich had a good grasp of the fundamentals
      of detective story construction even in the early days
      of the genre, Tanasoca argues, the mystery/detection ele-
      ments of his story are out of place in this otherwise
      straightforward social novel which examines nineteenth-
      century capital-labor problems.

ALLINGHAM, MARGERY (1904-1966). Series character: Albert Campion

534. Allingham, Margery. "The Art of Writing Mysteries."
      Holiday 34 (September 1963): 11-15.

      Allingham contends that "the mystery is an art form,"
      the discipline of which requires conventions that give

it a prescribed form. She describes her early efforts at
writing mysteries and the creation of her detective hero,
Albert Campion. The success of that character she attributes to her realization that he could change and grow.

535.   Barzun, Jacques, and Wendell Hertig Taylor. Preface to
        Dancers in Mourning, by Margery Allingham. New York:
        Garland Publishing, 1976. Also printed in *A Book of*
        Prefaces (item 22), pp. 15-16.

        Maintains that Allingham skillfully manipulates a varied
        cast of characters while maintaining suspense and tension
        and eventually reducing a bizarre set of incidents to a
        satisfactory conclusion.

*   Panek, LeRoy. "Margery Allingham." *Watteau's Shepherds*
        (item 57), pp. 126-144.

        Points out that until the early 1930s Allingham wrote
        thrillers that featured swiftly paced plots with plenty
        of action and surprises and good and bad characters easily
        recognizable. Then she was influenced by the traditional
        detective story and her novels conformed more and more
        to this genre. Numerous examples of both kinds of novels
        are given.

536.   Peters, Margot, and Agate Nesaule Krouse. "Women and
        Crime: Sexism in Allingham, Sayers, and Christie."
        Southwest Review 59 (Spring 1974): 144-152.

        Peters and Krouse argue that the British detective novel
        is a conservative genre, as reflected in the attitudes of
        the three female authors examined here. Allingham's
        women--even her intelligent women--are unquestionably
        subservient to their men, assert the authors, as the
        relationship between Lady Amanda Fitton and Albert Campion
        illustrates.

537.   Pike, Barry. "Margery Allingham's Albert Campion: A
        Chronological Examination of the Novels in Which He
        Appears." *Armchair Detective* 9 (November 1975): 1-6;
        9 (February 1976): 95-101; 10 (January 1977): 25-29, 84;
        10 (April 1977): 117-125; 10 (July 1977): 244-248; 10
        (October 1977): 324-335; 11 (January 1978): 34-44; 11
        (April 1978): 177-185; 11 (July 1978): 274-280; 11
        (October 1978): 372-388; 12 (January 1979): 34-39; 12
        (Spring 1979): 168-173; 12 (Fall 1979): 348-352.

        Examines in some detail the Albert Campion novels,
        pointing out (among other things) that his physical ap-

pearance and his character become more serious in the
later novels.

*   Routley, Erik. *The Puritan Pleasures of the Detective
        Story* (item 64), pp. 149-156.

        Maintains that Allingham ranks above Ngaio Marsh or
        Dorothy Sayers as a detective story writer because she
        has brought the form to a new peak of maturity. In her
        more evocative stories there is a "sense of brooding
        evil, as opposed to irrational and self-indulgent terror."

AMBLER, ERIC (1909-   ). Also wrote with Charles Rodda (1891-   )
   under the pseudonym Eliot Reed

538.   Ambrosetti, Ronald. "The World of Eric Ambler: From Detec-
       tive to Spy." *Dimensions of Detective Fiction* (item 43),
       pp. 102-109.

       Ambrosetti argues that Ambler's novels represent the
       transition from the detective tale to the spy story.

539.   Davis, Paxton. "The World We Live In: The Novels of Eric
       Ambler." *Hollins Critic* 8 (1971): 1-11.

       Davis surveys Ambler's career and argues that his "dis-
       tinctive contribution to 20th-century fiction" was that
       he discarded the conventional well-bred, glamorous hero,
       and established "a believable world, shabby, gritty,
       devious, threatening but compellingly interesting, to re-
       place them." He further contends that *The Intercom Con-
       spiracy*, a fairly late work, is the capstone of Ambler's
       career.

*   Eames, Hugh. "Eric Ambler." *Sleuths, Inc.* (item 30), pp.
        148-184.

        Quotes Ambler's statement that he was greatly influenced
        by Sherlock Holmes. Eames contends that Ambler was "the
        first thriller writer to attack capitalism." His books
        feature unheroic protagonists and interesting criminals.
        Includes long summaries of and commentaries on Ambler's
        major books.

540.   Hopkins, Joel. "Interview with Eric Ambler." *Journal of
       Popular Culture* 9 (Fall 1975): 285-293.

       Ambler traces his career as a writer of mystery/espionage
       fiction. He analyzes the leftist politics in his early

novels, his disinclination to research his work, and his
belief that his stories are effective because of "the
technique of gradual revelation"--tension built by an
accumulation of small details.

*   Lambert, Gavin. *The Dangerous Edge* (item 42), pp. 104-131.

Ambler's work, Lambert contends, mirrored his life. He
argues that Ambler's novels, from *The Dark Frontier* to
The Intercom Conspiracy, reflect their author's psychological development.

541.   Rausch, George J., Jr. "The Works of Eric Ambler." *Armchair Detective* 2 (July 1969): 260-261.

Rausch argues that Ambler's stories show great attention
to both locale and psychology and that they feature decent
but non-heroic protagonists.

542.   Symons, Julian. "Confidential Agents." *London Times* 5 July
1956, p. 13. Reprinted *Critical Occasions*. London:
Hamish Hamilton, 1966, pp. 168-173.

In the context of a review of *The Night-Comers*, Symons
points out that Ambler's strengths are "seemingly realistic,
yet curiously exotic," descriptions of settings and technical skill in controlling "the tenuous threads of his
stories" so that he maintains interest throughout the book.

*   Symons, Julian. *Mortal Consequences* (item 74), pp. 228-230.

Symons argues that the six espionage novels that Ambler
wrote before the outbreak of World War II are superior
to those that were written after the war. Though the later
novels show the same "mastery of construction," Ambler's
disillusionment with the Soviet Union in the postwar era
was reflected in a perceptible lessening of enthusiasm
and hope in these works.

ANTONY, PETER. Pseudonym of Peter Shaffer (1926-   ) and Anthony
Shaffer (1926-   )

543.   Glenn, Jules. "Anthony and Peter Shaffer's Plays: The Influence of Twinship on Creativity." *American Imago* 31
(1974): 270-292.

In a discussion of *The Public Eye*, Glenn argues that
the protagonists exhibit the psychological characteristics
of twins. He particularly emphasizes the close, non-verbal

relationship between the two characters and suggests that Shaffer is sensitive to such characteristics because he himself is a twin.

544. Glenn, Jules. "Twins in Disguise: A Psychoanalytical Essay on *Sleuth* and *The Royal Hunt of the Sun*." *Psycho-analytic Quarterly* 43 (1974): 288-302.

In an extended discussion of *Sleuth*, Glenn argues that the two characters of the play exhibit twin-like behavior, such as affection/aggression and sexual rivalry. He suggests that Shaffer is sensitive to these characteristics because he is a twin.

545. Kennedy, Veronica M.S. "A Possible Source for the Opening of *Sleuth*." *Armchair Detective* 7 (May 1974): 175.

Suggests that the opening of *Sleuth* was inspired by "The Footprint in the Sky" by Carter Dickson (John Dickson Carr).

ARLEN, MICHAEL (1895-1956)

546. Keyishian, Harry. *Michael Arlen*. Boston: Twayne, 1975. 150pp.

In his comprehensive, chronological survey of Arlen's career, Keyishian argues that *Hell! Said the Duchess* is a minor work; that *Flying Dutchman* is not well thought out; but that *The Crooked Coronet* contains well-written stories. Keyishian also provides plot summaries and character analyses for Arlen's works as well as a discussion of their critical reception.

ASHE, GORDON. See JOHN CREASEY

AUBREY-FLETCHER, HENRY LANCELOT. See HENRY WADE

AVALLONE, Michael (1924-   )

547. Nevins, Francis M., Jr. "Murder at Noon." *New Republic* 179 (22 July 1978): 26-28.

Maintains that Avallone has a very personal viewpoint and style that remains the same from novel to novel. Analyzes his cycle of approximately thirty novels dealing

with Detective Ed Noon, citing numerous examples of
Avallone's outlandish, fantastic style and characters.

BAGBY, GEORGE. Pseudonym of Aaron Marc Stein (1906-   )

548. Bagby, George. "Inspector Schmidt." *The Great Detectives*
      (item 60), pp. 193-204.

      Bagby points out that Inspector Schmidt has one major
      physical weakness, his feet, and that he is "a man of
      sensibility" but not sentimental and that he is adept at
      the "affectionate insult."

BAGLEY, DESMOND (1923-   )

549. Harvey, Deryck. "A Word with Desmond Bagley." *Armchair
      Detective* 7 (August 1974): 258-260.

      In a wide-ranging interview, Bagley states that he does
      not write mystery novels. "There's usually a crime element
      in it, but they aren't detective stories in the sense that
      there's a mystery to be solved." He classifies his books
      as action or adventure novels.

BAILEY, H.C. (1878-1961)

550. Bailey, H.C. "Meet Mr. Fortune." *Meet the Detective* (item
      45), pp. 90-97.

      States that Fortune is not modelled on a particular
      person but on various people that Bailey has met.

551. Barzun, Jacques, and Wendell Hertig Taylor. Preface to
      Mr. Fortune: Eight of His Adventures, by H.C. Bailey.
      New York: Garland Publishing, 1976. Also printed in *A
      Book of Prefaces* (item 22), pp. 17-18.

      Contends that Bailey is most successful in his short
      stories and that his detective, Reggie Fortune, can be
      classified as "intuitive" but that he also values facts
      as well as imagination and hypothesis.

*   Haycraft, Howard. *Murder for Pleasure* (item 36), pp. 125-
      128.

      Observes that Bailey's writing style is like G.K. Chester-
      ton's style in that both often "stretch characterization
      to the point of caricature."

*   Routley, Erik. *The Puritan Pleasures of the Detective Story* (item 64), pp. 81-88.

Maintains that Bailey's detective, Reggie Fortune, is a "rebel disciple" of Sherlock Holmes because for Fortune it is not "the solution that is the thing" but the "redressing of injustice."

*   Thomson, H. Douglas. *Masters of Mystery* (item 77), pp. 253-254.

Argues that Bailey's character, Mr. Fortune, belongs to the old school of detectives, the "infallible intuitionalists."

BAKER, ASA. See BRETT HALLIDAY

BALL, JOHN (1911-   )

552.   Ball, John. "Virgil Tibbs." *The Great Detectives* (item 60), pp. 227-234.

Cast in the form of a dialog between Ball and Tibbs, the article stresses the importance of dignity to the character.

553.   Lachman, Marvin. "Virgil Tibbs and the American Negro in Mystery Fiction." *Armchair Detective* 1 (April 1968): 86-89.

After a brief survey of blacks in mystery fiction, Lachman contends that John Ball's black detective, Virgil Tibbs, exemplifies many of the characteristics of the great fictional detectives.

BALLARD, W.T. (1903-   ). Pseudonyms: Neil MacNeil, John Shepherd

554.   Mertz, Stephen. "W.T. Ballard: An Interview." *Armchair Detective* 12 (January 1979): 14-19.

Ballard, one of the original contributors to *Black Mask* magazine in the 1930s, helped pioneer the hard-boiled school of detective fiction. He created Bill Lennox, the first hard-boiled detective in a series to work exclusively with the movie industry as a background.

BALZAC, HONORÉ DE (1799-1850)

*   Murch, A.E. *The Development of the Detective Novel* (item
       51), pp. 51-59.

       Contends that Balzac coordinates "the elements of de-
       tective interest" in Ann Radcliffe and James Fenimore
       Cooper. In *Maître Cornelius* (1831) and *Une Ténébreuse
       Affaire* (1841), Balzac was "the first really great novel-
       ist to devote serious attention to the working out of
       detective themes in fiction."

555.   Saintsbury, George. Introduction to *The Works of Honoré
       de Balzac*, Volume 30. New York: University Society
       Publishers, 1898, pp. ix-xi.

       Contends that Balzac "begat Poe," who fathered the crime
       novel.

*   Symons, Julian. *Mortal Consequences* (item 74), pp. 30-31.

       Argues that Balzac's primary interest in crime "is as
       a single element in the social fabric that orders human
       personality." Though his books deal with crime, they are
       not crime novels.

BENNETT, ARNOLD (1867-1931)

556.   Davis, Oswald H. *The Master: A Study of Arnold Bennett.*
       London: Johnson, 1966. 206pp.

       In a chapter entitled "The Improper Fantasias," Davis
       defends Bennett's mystery fiction as exhilarating. *The
       Ghost*, he argues, is well written and witty, and all of
       these works are full of the spirit of youthful excitement.

557.   Drabble, Margaret. *Arnold Bennett: A Biography.* London:
       Weidenfeld & Nicolson, 1974. 397pp.

       In the context of a biography of Bennett, Drabble takes
       passing note of his mystery/detection work--what she calls
       "sensational fiction"--noting that Bennett's critical
       reputation is based on his more serious work.

558.   Lafourcade, Georges. *Arnold Bennett: A Study.* New York:
       Haskell House, 1971. 299pp.

       In a chapter entitled "Farce and Melodrama," Lafourcade
       analyzes Bennett's mystery/detection writing, defending
       it against the scorn of orthodox Bennett critics. These

stories were, he argues, written with "zest and gusto," and it was in these books that Bennett worked out many of the ideas that made his serious fiction a critical success.

559. Lucas, John. *Arnold Bennett: A Study of His Fiction*. London: Methuen, 1974. 235pp.

Lucas spends little time on Bennett's mystery fiction, although he does pause to examine *The Grand Babylon Hotel* in some detail and brand it a poor imitation of Conan Doyle and Elinor Glyn.

560. Ravenscroft, N.C. "Arnold Bennett as a Writer of Crime Fiction." *Armchair Detective* 10 (April 1977): 182.

Describes a juvenile crime-detection novel, *Sydney Yorke's Friend*, written by Bennett in 1893 and calls it "a simple enough tale."

561. Young, Kenneth. *Arnold Bennett*. London: Longman, 1975. 54pp.

Young argues that although *The Grand Babylon Hotel* is "thin stuff," it did give Bennett an opportunity to develop the luxury hotel theme that he was to use later in his serious novels. He identifies "The Death of Simon Fuge" as the best of Bennett's mystery work.

BENNETT, JAY (1912-). Pseudonym: Steve Rand

562. Janeczko, Paul B. "An Interview with Jay Bennett." *English Journal* 65 (May 1976): 86-88. Expanded version printed *Armchair Detective* 10 (October 1977): 342-346.

In this interview Bennett comments on a number of subjects related to his mystery fiction and the genre in general. Among other things, Bennett contends that a good mystery story is closer to "literature in general" than most people realize and that the genre deserves more serious attention.

BENTLEY, E.C. (1875-1956)

563. Barzun, Jacques, and Wendell Hertig Taylor. Preface to *Trent's Last Case*, by E.C. Bentley. New York: Garland Publishing, 1976. Also printed in *A Book of Prefaces* (item 22), pp. 19-20.

Argues that the book is a classic because of its successful blending of accurate deduction from clues, sustained psychological and emotional scenes that arise
naturally from the plot, "the subtle use of 'point of
view' in detection, the self-depreciatory manner of the
artist-sleuth," and "the well-bred tone of the prose."

564.   Bentley, E.C. "Meet Trent." *Meet the Detective* (item 45),
       pp. 98-105.

While acknowledging his admiration of and debt to Conan
Doyle, Bentley observes that he deliberately made Trent,
his own protagonist, frivolous and light-hearted to contrast with the Victorian seriousness of Sherlock Holmes.

565.   Bentley, E.C. "*Trent's Last Case.*" *Those Days.* London:
       Constable, 1940, pp. 249-261.

In this chapter of his autobiography, Bentley states
that he conceived his detective as a reaction against the
ostentatious eccentricities and seriousness of Sherlock
Holmes. He decided, after thinking about the plot, to
make the hero's "obviously correct solution of the mystery
turn out to be completely wrong," partly to "show up the
infallibility of the Holmesian method."

566.   Haycraft, Howard. "*Trent's Last Case* Reopened." *New York
       Times Book Review* 15 December 1963, pp. 18-19. Reprinted
       Trent's Last Case, by E.C. Bentley. San Diego: University
       Extension, University of California, 1977, pp. 266-268.

In his reassessment of the novel upon its re-issue in
1963, Haycraft maintains that "Bentley's chief contributions to the genre are his easy naturalism and quiet
humor." Haycraft also notes Bentley's use of character as
a means of detection; "often imitated, it has rarely been
surpassed."

*   Panek, LeRoy. "E.C. Bentley." *Watteau's Shepherds* (item
       57), pp. 29-37.

Maintains that Bentley combined the serious (imitation)
and comic (parody) reactions to Sherlock Holmes in *Trent's
Last Case.*

567.   Redman, Ben Ray. Introduction to *Trent's Case Book*, by
       E.C. Bentley. New York: Alfred A. Knopf, 1964, pp. v-
       xii.

Maintains that Bentley did not believe that the solution was everything in a detective novel but also wanted to provide some light-hearted entertainment along the way.

*   Routley, Erik. *The Puritan Pleasures of the Detective Story* (item 64), pp. 119-123.

Contends that *Trent's Last Case* is "the first real detective novel" and that it is pleasure to read because of its "literary craftsmanship." Quotes Bentley as saying that the book "is not so much a detective story as an exposure of detective stories."

567a.   Sayers, Dorothy L. Introduction to *Trent's Last Case*, by E.C. Bentley. New York: Perennial Library, 1978, pp. x-xiii.

Sayers contends that *Trent's Last Case* ranks with *The Moonstone* and the Sherlock Holmes stories "as a classic of detective fiction," largely because of its style and vivid characterizations.

568.   Stein, Aaron Marc. Introduction to *Trent's Last Case*, by E.C. Bentley. San Diego: University Extension, University of California, 1977, pp. ix-xxv.

Maintains that the strengths of the book are its wit, its stylish prose, the intellectual enjoyment of its intricate plot, and its charming characters. Its weaknesses are its lack of suspense and menacing atmosphere and its characters' tendencies to make speeches rather than conversation.

*   Thomson, H. Douglas. "Mr. E.C. Bentley's *Trent's Last Case*." *Masters of Mystery* (item 77), pp. 147-155.

Contends that "never have the virtues of the genre been quite so elegantly displayed" as in *Trent's Last Case*: "the formal problem intertwined with the character problems; the sincerity of the character study ... the naturalness of the 'motivation'; the tenseness and also the humor of the situation," and above all, "that supreme climax."

BERKELEY, ANTHONY. Pseudonym of Anthony Berkeley Cox (1893-1970)

*   Panek, LeRoy. "Anthony Berkeley Cox." *Watteau's Shepherds* (item 57), pp. 111-125.

Observes that although in many ways Cox epitomizes the
Golden Age detective story writer (inventive methods of
murder, original characters, ingenious plots) he is almost forgotten today. This neglect is probably because he
seldom featured sympathetic characters in his stories
and that his plots, though clever, tended to follow a
standard pattern.

BEYNON, JANE LEWIS. See LANGE LEWIS

BIERCE, AMBROSE (b. 1842--disappeared in 1914). Pseudonym: Dod
Grile

569. Berkove, Lawrence I. "Ambrose Bierce's Concern with Mind
      and Man." Ph.D. dissertation, University of Pennsylvania,
      1962.

      In this dissertation, Berkove analyzes the underlying
      philosophical premises in Bierce's short stories, finding
      skepticism and stoicism at their base. With this founda-
      tion, Berkove argues that Bierce's stories are not mere
      thrillers, but are "skillful literary creations," designed
      to persuade the reader of the futility of existence.

570. Bleiler, E.F. Introduction to *Ghost and Horror Stories
      of Ambrose Bierce*. New York: Dover, 1964, pp. v-xx.

      Bleiler observes that Bierce's ghost stories are
      unusual in that they are written in a very stylized manner
      and yet convey such intense personal feelings. He argues
      that Bierce's supernatural stories were metaphors of his
      own childhood, written for cathartic effect.

571. Davidson, Cathy N. "Literary Semantics and the Fiction
      of Ambrose Bierce." *ETC.: A Review of General Semantics*
      31 (1974): 263-271.

      Davidson observes that Bierce's stories work because of
      his disruption of linear plotlines, and argues that his
      goal was "to reveal graphically the dangers of semantic
      sloppiness" by showing the reader how a misread clue can
      lead to disaster.

572. Davidson, Cathy N. "The Poetics of Perception: A Semantic
      Analysis of the Short Fiction of Ambrose Bierce." Ph.D.
      dissertation, State University of New York at Bingham-
      ton, 1974.

In this dissertation, Davidson analyzes Bierce's narrative styles. She argues that he uses four basic techniques: linear progression, flashbacks, dual point of view narratives, and multiple point of view narratives. Each style influences the reader slightly differently, according to Bierce's intent.

573. Fadiman, Clifton. "Ambrose Bierce: Portrait of a Misanthrope." *The Collected Writings of Ambrose Bierce*. New York: Citadel Press, 1946, pp. xi-xix.

Fadiman argues that Bierce's nihilism was genuine and pervasive, indeed, that it was the source of his inspiration. "Bierce's morbidity was exceptionally fertile."

574. Grenander, M.E. *Ambrose Bierce*. New York: Twayne, 1971. 193pp.

Grenander argues that Bierce's tales can be divided into didactic tales, mimetic tales of passion, mimetic tales of moral choices, and mimetic tales of action. Grenander selects several stories of each type for extended analysis. He places Bierce's supernatural stories in the first two categories.

575. Grenander, M.E. "Bierce's Turn of the Screw: Tales of Ironical Terror." *Western Humanities Review* 11 (1957): 257-264.

Grenander argues that, although he was influenced by Poe, Bierce was no mere imitator. Bierce's tales differ from those of Poe in that they add a twist of irony to the horror.

576. Hill, Larry L. "Style in the Tales of Ambrose Bierce." Ph.D. dissertation, University of Wisconsin, 1973.

In this dissertation, Hill addresses himself to the manner in which Bierce conveys his "pitiless realism" and "perverse wit" in his stories. He finds that Bierce uses formal language, a cold, ironic tone, and intense imagery to impart a high degree of realism to his tales.

577. Josephson, Matthew. *Portrait of the Artist as American*. New York: Octagon Books, 1964, pp. 178-198.

Josephson argues that Bierce's tales of the supernatural are not inconsequential. *The Death of Halpin Frayser* "is two generations ahead of its time" in terms of its psychological insights.

578. Kenton, Edna. "Ambrose Bierce and 'Moxon's Master.'"
      Bookman 62 (September 1925): 77-79.

      Kenton argues that "Moxon's Master," rather than more
      famous tales, best illustrates Bierce's conception of man:
      "man is a machine set in motion by fear."

579. Knight, Grant C. *The Critical Period in American Literature*.
      Chapel Hill: University of North Carolina Press, 1951,
      pp. 38-42.

      Knight argues that Bierce's concept of horror differs
      from that of Poe in that, where Poe's use of horror is
      basically unrealistic, Bierce's is quite rational, and
      thus all the more terrifying.

580. McLean, Robert C. "The Deaths in Ambrose Bierce's 'Halpin
      Frayser.'" *Papers on Language and Literature* 10 (1974):
      394-402.

      McLean opposes the traditional critical view that
      Frayser was murdered by an other-worldly agent. He argues
      instead that Bierce has left clues throughout the story
      to suggest that Frayser's father was the killer. Thus, he
      asserts, Bierce's tale is representative of the American,
      rather than the European, Gothic style.

581. McWilliams, Carey. *Ambrose Bierce: A Biography*. Hamden,
      Conn.: Archon, 1967. 358pp.

      McWilliams argues against the general critical assumption
      that Bierce's supernatural tales were, like Poe's, the
      product of a disordered mind, and that, further, Bierce
      did not copy Poe's style. Bierce worked in the tradition
      of the "terror-romance" that dates back to Walpole's *The
      Castle of Otranto* in the eighteenth century.

582. Miller, Arthur. "The Influence of Edgar Allan Poe on
      Ambrose Bierce." *American Literature* 4 (May 1932):
      130-150.

      Miller examines the criticism comparing Bierce to Poe
      and marshals considerable evidence, by juxtaposing two
      texts side by side on a page, indicating Bierce's debt
      to Poe.

583. Pattee, Fred Lewis. *The Development of the American Short
      Story*. New York: Harper, 1923, pp. 302-306, 308.

Pattee argues that Bierce was an impressionist rather
than a realist. Bierce's tales are haunting but basically
mechanical, "lacking the human element."

584. Rubens, Philip M. "The Literary Gothic and the Fiction of
     Ambrose Gwinett Bierce." Ph.D. dissertation, Northern
     Illinois University, 1976.

     In this dissertation, Rubens examines Bierce's fiction
     for its Gothic characteristics. He argues that more than
     half of Bierce's tales can be considered Gothic, since
     they deal in such various staples of the genre as the
     doppelgänger, the experimenter, ghosts, and haunted houses.

585. Snell, George. "Poe Redivivus." *Arizona Quarterly* 1
     (Summer 1945): 49-57.

     Snell argues that Bierce and Lafcadio Hearn were much
     indebted to Poe. Bierce "modelled his form and his subject
     matter directly upon Poe, though he lacked Poe's depth."

586. Stein, William B. "Bierce's 'The Death of Halpin Frayser':
     The Poetics of Gothic Consciousness." *Emerson Society
     Quarterly* 47 (1972): 115-122.

     Stein argues that 'Halpin Frayser' is an "attempt to
     capture all the associations and dissociations of thought
     that merge into a single perception of what is called
     reality." He accomplishes this by an ambiguous narrative
     and by dangling puns and red herrings before his readers,
     not resolving their questions until the end of the story.

587. Wiggins, Robert A. *Ambrose Bierce*. Minneapolis: University
     of Minnesota Press, 1964. 48pp.

     Wiggins considers Bierce "a master of the *outré*." In a
     survey of Bierce's life and works, he argues that the tales
     of the supernatural are symbolic projections of real
     terror.

588. Wiggins, Robert A. "Ambrose Bierce: A Romantic in an Age
     of Realism." *American Literary Realism, 1870-1910* 4
     (1971): 1-10.

     Wiggins argues that critical evaluation of Bierce as a
     realist is possible only by ignoring his tales of mystery.
     Despite living and writing in the Age of Realism, Bierce's
     best work, and also his personal life, mark him as a
     Romantic.

589. Woodruff, Stuart C. "The Short Stories of Ambrose Bierce:
      A Critical Study." Ph.D. dissertation, University of
      Connecticut, 1962.

      In this dissertation, Woodruff argues that Bierce's
      thriller stories are "conventional in manner" and are
      aimed more at diversion than at art. They are, he feels,
      inferior to Bierce's military stories, which are more
      deeply felt.

590. Woodruff, Stuart C. *The Short Stories of Ambrose Bierce:*
      A Study in Polarity. Pittsburgh: University of Pittsburgh
      Press, 1965, pp. 116-152.

      Woodruff asserts that in Bierce's short stories, the
      "characteristic theme is the inscrutable universe itself,
      whose mechanisms checkmate man's every attempt to assert
      his will or live his dream." Woodruff's analysis con-
      centrates on *Tales of Soldiers and Civilians,* which he
      considers superior to the stories of the supernatural that
      often depend upon sadistic violence for their effect.

BIGGERS, EARL DERR (1884-1933)

591. Breen, Jon L. "Murder Number One: Earl Derr Biggers."
      New Republic 177 (30 July 1977): 38-39.

      Points out that although Biggers's detective, Charlie
      Chan, is now regarded as an "ethnic stereotype," at the
      time of his creation "he represented a deliberate cor-
      rective" to such sinister Oriental villains as Fu Manchu.
      Contends that "Biggers's strengths as a writer were his
      gently humorous style and his ability to bring his
      characters to life within the limits of commercial fiction."
      Despite the weakness of his plotting, Biggers managed to
      create "one of the immortal fictional detectives."

592. Ellman, Neil. "Charlie Chan Carries On." *Armchair Detective*
      10 (April 1977): 183-184.

      States that the title of the fourth novel in the series
      of six Charlie Chan stories written in the 1920s and
      early 1930s, *Charlie Chan Carries On,* has a double meaning
      because Chan's popularity has endured and "outlived the
      memory of his creator," Earl Derr Biggers. Maintains that
      Chan was the first "domestic" detective in fiction: he
      was married and had a family. Biggers modified the Western
      stereotype of Orientals by making Chan kindly rather than
      sinister and by placing him on the side of law and order
      rather than portraying him as a villain.

BLACKMORE, RICHARD DODDRIDGE (1825-1900)

593. Jiggens, Clifford. "Inspector Bucket's Rival." *Armchair Detective* 12 (Summer 1979): 270-271.

States that though Blackmore is remembered today for one book, *Lorna Doone*, he wrote a dozen or more novels. One of them was a mystery story, *Clara Vaughan*, which included the character Inspector Cutting, who along with Dickens's Inspector Bucket, has "the distinction of being the first English police detective to be featured in a work of fiction."

BLACKWOOD, ALGERNON (1869-1951)

594. Letson, Russell F., Jr. "The Approaches to Mystery: The Fantasies of Arthur Machen and Algernon Blackwood." Ph.D. dissertation, Southern Illinois University, 1975.

In this dissertation, Letson investigates the relationship between the works of Blackwood and Machen. They share, he argues, "more than surface similarities," though Blackwood is the more optimistic of the two writers. He examines fourteen of Blackwood's short stories, finding in them all a possibility of renewal, or a return to Eden before the Fall.

BLAKE, NICHOLAS. Pseudonym of Cecil Day Lewis (1904-1972)

595. Barzun, Jacques, and Wendell Hertig Taylor. Preface to *Minute For Murder*, by Nicholas Blake. New York: Garland Publishing, 1976. Also printed in *A Book of Prefaces* (item 22), pp. 21-22.

Contends that Blake skillfully maintains tension while gradually removing suspicion from a "large cast of characters" until, in a "dramatic, protracted confrontation scene" the conclusion is reached.

BLANC, SUZANNE

596. Kearns, Winn. "Traveler with Crime: Suzanne Blanc." *Armchair Detective* 8 (May 1975): 194.

In an interview, Blanc states that each of her mystery novels--which feature an American Indian detective, Inspector Mendenes--"contains an Indian joke" and "a philosophy about life."

BLOOD, MATTHEW. See BRETT HALLIDAY

BONNER, MARGERIE (1905-)

597.   Grace, Sherrill. "Margerie Bonner's Three Forgotten
       Novels." *Journal of Modern Literature* 6 (April 1977):
       321-324.

       Bonner, chiefly known as Malcolm Lowry's wife and editor,
       wrote two mystery novels, *The Last Twist of the Knife* and
       The Shapes that Creep, both published in 1946. They are
       well plotted and effectively use descriptive detail.

BORGES, JORGE LUIS (1899-)

598.   Gillespie, Robert. "Detections: Borges and Father Brown."
       Novel 7 (Spring 1974): 220-230.

       Borges has suggested that Chesterton's Father Brown
       stories have influenced him, and Gillespie states that
       both authors "play with similar notions of contradiction,
       necessity, circular time, and transcendental reality."

BOX, EDGAR. Pseudonym of Gore Vidal (1925-)

599.   Dick, Bernard F. *Apostate Angel: A Critical Study of Gore
       Vidal.* New York: Random House, 1974, pp. 78-79.

       States that Vidal temporarily traded his usual writing
       for "faster loot in penning hit whodunits" to compensate
       for the financial failures of *Judgment of Paris* and
       Messiah.

BRADDON, MARY ELIZABETH (1837-1915)

600.   Booth, Bradford A. "Trollope's *Orley Farm*: Artistry Manque."
       Victorian Literature: Modern Essays in Criticism. Edited
       by Austin Wright. New York: Oxford University Press,
       1961, pp. 358-359.

       Argues that *Lady Audley's Secret* is nothing more than a
       sensation novel with its only interest in the solving of
       the mystery.

601.   Donaldson, Norman. Introduction to *Lady Audley's Secret*,
       by Mary Elizabeth Braddon. New York: Dover Publications,
       1974, pp. v-xiv.

Points out that Braddon's idea for the book came from Wilkie Collins's *The Woman in White* (1860). Maintains that the story is skillfully constructed and that the book's chief strength is "its sheer readability."

602. Gerould, Gordon Hall. *The Patterns of English and American Fiction.* Boston: Little, Brown, 1942, p. 400.

Observes that *Lady Audley's Secret* was successful not because it was original, but because it combined all the elements which were popular with readers at that time: crime, mystery, romantic love, and sentimentality.

603. James, Henry. "Miss Braddon." *Notes and Reviews: A Series of Twenty-Five Papers Hitherto Unpublished in Book Form.* Cambridge, Mass.: Dunster House, 1921, pp. 108-116.

States that Braddon resorted to "extreme measures" to write her first successful novel. Her use of melodramatic style and mysterious atmosphere created the first "sensation" novel, *Lady Audley's Secret.*

604. "*Lady Audley's Secret.*" *Nation* 100 (11 February 1915): 161-162.

States that the reality of Braddon's work was achieved through use of simple characterizations and subtle use of psychology.

* Murch, A.E. *The Development of the Detective Novel* (item 51), pp. 155-157.

Points out that Braddon devised an original method for presenting *Lady Audley's Secret*--from the start the reader is aware of Lady Audley's character and the suspense centers around whether she will be found out.

605. Nyberg, Benjamin M. "The Novels of Mary Elizabeth Braddon (1837-1915): A Reappraisal of the Author of *Lady Audley's Secret.*" Ph.D. dissertation, University of Colorado, 1965.

Although Braddon was an author of great versatility and talent, her fame rests on an early "sensational" novel, *Lady Audley's Secret.* Includes a critical discussion of her other novels.

606. "Old-Time Thrillers." *Literary Digest* 45 (17 August 1912): 262-263.

States that Braddon and Wilkie Collins founded the
English school of sensational novels and thus "revived
the mysterious and sensational element in fiction."

* Ousby, Ian. *Bloodhounds of Heaven* (item 55), pp. 135-136.

Observes that Braddon's preference for upper-class
society created a milieu in which professional policemen
would have seemed vulgar. Therefore, she created a detective hero who was a "gentleman of pleasure" transformed
into a dutiful citizen.

607. "Queen of Circulating Libraries." *Critic* 16 (31 October
      1891): 239.

      States that the quality of Braddon's work decreased
      as her output increased and blames her publisher for
      stressing quantity over quality.

608. Wolff, Robert Lee. *Sensational Victorian: The Life and
      Fiction of Mary Elizabeth Braddon.* New York: Garland
      Publishing, 1979. 529pp.

      Published too late for annotation but according to
      the publisher the book "brings vividly to life the Vic-
      torian stage, the Victorian publishing industry, and a
      brilliant and undeservedly forgotten woman's triumphs
      over Victorian society."

BRAMAH, ERNEST. Pseudonym of Ernest Bramah Smith (1868-1942)

609. Barzun, Jacques, and Wendell Hertig Taylor. Preface to
      Max Carrados, by Ernest Bramah. New York: Garland
      Publishing, 1976. Also printed in *A Book of Prefaces*
      (item 22), pp. 23-24.

      Argues that it is the satirical tone of the Carrados
      stories that makes them seem so fresh and undated.

610. Belloc, Hilaire. Preface to *Kai Lung's Golden Hours.* New
      York: George H. Doran Company, 1923, pp. 1-6.

      States that the lack of public and critical appreciation
      of Bramah's works was due, in part, to the lack of commu-
      nication between "those who desire to find good stuff and
      those who can produce it." Nevertheless, Belloc feels
      that popularity is only a matter of chance: "It matters
      little whether strong permanent work finds a thousand or
      fifty thousand or a million of readers. Rock stands and
      mud washes away."

611. "Died. Ernest Bramah Smith." *Time* 40 (6 July 1942): 80.

    Short obituary notice that mentions the extreme sense
    of privacy that Smith cultivated regarding his professional,
    as well as personal, life.

612. Field, Louise Maunsell. "Ernest Bramah and His Blind
    Detective." *Literary Digest International Book Review*
    2 (May 1924): 464-465.

    Bramah's detective, Max Carrados, though blind, has
    trained himself to use his other senses to solve cases
    in the most extraordinary methods.

*   Routley, Erik. *The Puritan Pleasures of the Detective
    Story* (item 64), pp. 73-80.

    Contends that Bramah's "The Eastern Mystery" demonstrates
    the strong "link between the English puritan tradition
    and the detective story" because of Bramah's rejection
    of one of that tradition's basic assumptions: there is no
    such thing as "blind faith" because that is a response
    made by supernatural or demonic forces. "Faith may be
    implicit, but it is not blind."

613. Squire, J.C. *Life and Letters*. London: Heinemann, 1917,
    pp. 40-46.

    States that Bramah embellishes his plots with melodra-
    matic details, making them "ceremonial to the point of
    absurdity."

614. White, William. "Ernest Bramah on China: An Important
    Letter." *PMLA* 87 (May 1972): 511-513.

    When Ernest Bramah Smith wrote his Kai Lung stories, he
    created a China which seemed so real that many reviewers
    and readers debated whether or not he had ever lived in
    China. This article includes correspondence with Smith,
    who describes his sources of inspiration for the Kai Lung
    stories and his process of writing.

615. White, William. "Kai Lung in America: The Critical Per-
    ception of Ernest Bramah." *American Book Collector* 9
    (June 1959): 15-19.

    States that although Bramah's stories were written with
    great style and wit, they were unfairly ignored by re-
    viewers who probably did not regard detective stories as
    worthwhile literature.

BRAND, CHRISTIANNA. Pseudonym of Mary Christianna Milne Lewis
   (1907-)

616.   Brand, Christianna. "Inspector Cockrill." *The Great Detectives* (item 60), pp. 57-66.

       Brand singles out Inspector Cockrill's "acute powers of observation," considerable understanding of human nature, and "total integrity and commitment" as the reasons for his success.

BRAND, MAX. See FREDERICK FAUST

BROCK, ROSE. See JOSEPH HANSEN

BROWN, FREDRIC (1906-1972)

617.   Baird, Newton. "Paradox and Plot: The Fiction of Fredric Brown." *Armchair Detective* 9 (October 1976): 282-288; 10 (January 1977): 33-38, 85-87; 10 (April 1977): 151-159.

       Argues that Brown emphasized character development, but he did not neglect his plots, which were notable for their ingenuity. His best work "concentrates on the intangibles of psychological truth without neglecting material evidence."

BROWN, ZENITH JONES. See LESLIE FORD

BROWNE, HOWARD (1908-). Pseudonym: John Evans

618.   Lewis, Caleb A. "Interview with Howard Browne." *Armchair Detective* 11 (April 1978): 172-176.

       Although he was influenced by Mark Twain and James M. Cain, Browne states that it was his admiration for Raymond Chandler that inspired him to try writing a mystery novel. Admits that in his first novel, *Halo in Blood*, he tried "to capture the essence" of Chandler's style and that his detective, Paul Pine, was an imitation of Chandler's Philip Marlowe. Later, Browne developed a style more his own.

BUCHAN, JOHN (1875-1940)

*   Cawelti, John G. *Adventure, Mystery, and Romance* (item
        150), pp. 31-32.

        Maintains that Buchan's thrillers reflected the social
        assumptions of his time, such as the threat of "racial
        subversion" of the white British Empire. Cawelti contends
        that Buchan's current upopoularity is an indication of
        changing social assumptions.

619.   Daniell, David. *The Interpreter's House*. London: Nelson,
        1975. 226pp.

        Contends that Buchan was a serious novelist who was
        influenced by Scott and Stevenson; though his mysteries
        were full of romance and adventure, his novels demanded
        a "maturity" in his readers.

620.   Dukeshire, Theodore P. "John Buchan." *Armchair Detective*
        7 (May 1974): 198-203.

        Argues that the two principal influences on Buchan's
        writing were Sir Walter Scott and Robert Louis Stevenson.
        Also details how Buchan used incidents from the lives of
        his friends and himself in his works. Checklist of his
        books and short stories is included.

621.   Green, Benny. "Buchan a Hundred Years On." *Spectator* 235
        (30 August 1975): 282-283.

        Maintains that Buchan's novels all follow the classic
        formula of the quest.

622.   Greene, Graham. "The Last Buchan." *Spectator* 166 (18 May
        1941): 430, 432. Reprinted *The Lost Childhood and
        Other Essays*. New York: Viking, 1952, pp. 104-105.

        States that the remarkable quality of Buchan's novels
        is the "completeness" of the worlds they describe; Buchan
        knew the dramatic value of adventure in familiar, real-
        istic settings.

623.   **Hartley, Anthony. "Scottish Romantic." *Spectator* 196**
        (25 May 1956): 731-733.

        Points out that there are only two classes of society
        in Buchan's novels, the aristocracy and the very poor.
        Also observes that since Buchan did not portray the middle
        class, there is unreality in his portrayal of English
        society.

624.   Hodge, David. "Literary Career." *Living Age* 292 (20
       January 1917): 171-175.

       Maintains that Buchan's greatest virtue was his versa-
       tility: he wrote histories and journalism as well as
       thrillers.

*   Lambert, Gavin. *The Dangerous Edge* (item 42), pp. 79-104.

       Contends that Buchan had a horror of "suburbanism"
       and the mediocrity of middle-class values; therefore,
       he always placed his heroes in dangerous situations,
       "preferring the cult of the last chance."

625.   Pritchett, V.S. "The Man from the Manse." *New Statesman*
       70 (17 September 1965): 400-401.

       States that Buchan used Scottish folklore as a basis
       for his early novels, but when he wrote his thrillers he
       adopted an English conception of international conspir-
       acies.

626.   Raymond, John. "The Roman from the Gorbals." *New States-
       man* 51 (2 June 1956): 630-631.

       Argues that what makes Buchan's thrillers exciting is
       the fact that they are "genuine fantasies, the day-dreams
       of an exceptionally gifted man."

627.   Schubert, Leland. "Almost Real Reality: John Buchan's
       Visible World." *Serif* 2 (September 1965): 5-14.

       Observes that all of Buchan's novels and short stories
       are adventures that center around pursuit of one of the
       characters. Also points out the importance of geography
       in Buchan's plots.

*   Symons, Julian. *Mortal Consequences* (item 74), pp. 235-
       236.

       States that although Buchan combined imagination with
       material based on his own experiences as Director of
       Intelligence during World War I, his novels are notable
       for their scenery rather than their plots.

628.   Turnbaugh, Roy. "Images of Empire: George Alfred Henty
       and John Buchan." *Journal of Popular Culture* 9 (Winter
       1975): 734-740.

       Argues that both Henty and Buchan were "quintessential
       imperialist authors," but their works show a difference

of style, emphasis, and value that reflected different views of the British empire during mid- and late Victorian periods.

629. Usborne, Richard. "John Buchan." *Clubland Heroes: A Nostalgic Study of Some Recurrent Characters in the Romantic Fiction of Dornford Yates, John Buchan and Sapper.* London: Constable, 1953, pp. 83-139.

Maintains that Buchan's plots are exciting and his narrative style casual and unassuming but that he fails to create memorable characters. Examines such Buchan heroes as Richard Hannay, Sandy Arbuthnot, and Edward Leithen.

630. Vorhees, Richard J. "Flashman and Richard Hannay." *Dalhousie Review* 53 (1973): 113-120.

States that George MacDonald Fraser's *Flashman Papers* is very similar to Buchan's *The Thirty-Nine Steps.* Compares the characters Flashman and Richard Hannay and concludes that they both have a special type of innocence found in traditional adventure stories.

BULLETT, GERALD (1894-1958). Pseudonym: Sebastian Fox

631. Barzun, Jacques, and Wendell Hertig Taylor. Preface to *The Jury,* by Gerald Bullett. New York: Garland Publishing, 1976. Also printed in *A Book of Prefáces* (item 22), pp. 25-26.

After pointing out other mystery novels in which the jury plays an important role, concludes that Bullett's novel has not been excelled in this area.

BURKE, THOMAS (1886-1945)

632. Bjorkman, Edwin. "Thomas Burke." *Bookman* 64 (January 1927): 561-567.

States that the novelty of the sordid atmosphere attracted and held Burke's readers and gave them excursions into areas which were normally forbidden to them.

633. "New Master of the Mystery and Romance of London's Underworld." *Current Opinion* 63 (November 1917): 337.

Observes that Burke writes with romance and poetry about London's slums though he often resorts to the use of "thrilling abnormal incidents" to conceal the melodrama of the plots.

634.   Seldes, Gilbert. "Rediscovery and Romance." *Dial* 63 (19 July 1917): 65-67.

States that Burke's stories have too much romance; they are not realistic and are "purposeless and lacking in social direction."

BURTON, MILES. Pseudonym of Cecil John Charles Street (1884-1961)

635.   Barzun, Jacques, and Wendell Hertig Taylor. Preface to *The Secret of High Eldersham*, by Miles Burton. New York: Garland Publishing, 1976. Also printed in *A Book of Prefaces* (item 22), pp. 27-28.

Maintains that Burton's novel is one of the first of modern mystery stories to use witchcraft as an important element of the plot.

BUTLER, WALTER C. See FREDERICK FAUST

BUTOR, MICHEL (1926-   )

636.   O'Donnell, Thomas D. "Michel Butor's *Passing Time* and the Detective Hero." *The Mystery and Detection Annual 1973* (item 17), pp. 211-220.

Butor uses a detective novel within a novel as a means of pointing out parallels between the detective and the artist.

CAIN, JAMES M. (1892-1977)

637.   Adams, Jay. "Another Toughie by Mr. Cain." *Saturday Review* 29 (1 June 1946): 10-11.

Maintains that Cain's talent is as a storyteller rather than as a novelist. His novels are about "cheap little people caught up by events they can neither understand nor control," and his pages reflect excitement rather than life.

638. Frohock, W.M. "The Tabloid Tragedy of James M. Cain."
      Southwest Review 34 (1949): 380-386. Reprinted *Novel
      of Violence in America*. London: Arthur Barker, 1957,
      pp. 13-22.

      Argues that Cain calculated his effect on his readers
      and used various tricks to exploit their fascination
      and morbid curiosity about the savage, tawdry side of
      human nature. States that nothing Cain wrote was outside
      the realm of trash and that he was "sure-handed in the
      manipulation of materials."

639. Macdonald, Ross. "Cain X3." *New York Times Book Review*
      2 March 1969, pp. 1, 49-51.

      States that Cain's use of the vernacular was his source
      of "imaginative strength" and analyzes his effective use
      of "vulgar language" in *The Postman Always Rings Twice*,
      Mildred Pierce, and *Double Indemnity*.

640. Madden, David. *James M. Cain*. New York: Twayne, 1970.
      200pp.

      Examines Cain's work as a phenomenon of popular culture
      and supports his "hard-boiled" novels as minor, though
      valid, contributions to world literature. Madden argues
      against critics who charge that Cain has written nothing
      but trash by stating that Cain's writing style allows
      his novels to become sources of "nonthematic or pure
      experiences."

641. Madden, David. "James M. Cain and the Tough Guy Novelists
      of the 30's." *The Thirties: Fiction, Poetry, Drama*.
      Edited by Warren French. Deland, Fla.: Everett/Edwards,
      1976, pp. 63-71.

      Observes that Cain realized that in spite of a pretense
      of refinement through "civilization" Americans have a
      large appetite for violence which has become evident in
      our popular culture. Cain established a "tough-guy" style
      of writing which is blunt and devoid of ideology. Using
      this "purity of vision" he breaks through established
      attitudes and morals to show the nightmares underneath.

642. Madden, David. "James M. Cain: Twenty-Minute Egg of the
      Hard-Boiled School." *Journal of Popular Culture* 1
      (Winter 1967): 178-192.

      States that the tough guy novel began as an impersonal
      vision of America during the Depression. Cain and the

other hard-boiled writers wrote *about* and *to* the masses,
"giving violent impetus to their forbidden dreams, drama-
tizing their darkest temptations and their basic physical
drives." Cain was the quintessence of this type of writer
and was more interested in action suggesting explanations
of crime than in presenting a solution.

643. Madden, David. "James M. Cain's *The Postman Always Rings
      Twice* and Albert Camus's *L'Etranger.*" *Papers in Language
      and Literature* 6 (Fall 1970): 407-419.

      States that Camus based his writing style for *L'Etranger*
      on the hard-boiled style of writing of Cain and Hammett.
      Madden also states that "characteristics of literature
      of revolt, as exemplified by Camus, apply as well to
      American tough fiction," especially the emphasis on con-
      crete situations and facts rather than abstract attitudes.
      Madden compares the two authors' works and finds that
      both novels are based on the idea of the absurdity of
      life and man's existence.

644. Madden, David. "Morris' *Cannibals*, Cain's *Serenade*: The
      Dynamics of Style and Technique." *Journal of Popular
      Culture* 8 (Summer 1974): 59-70.

      Maintains that the study of a popular novel (Cain's)
      can enhance the study of a serious novel (Morris') since
      many times, "the aesthetic experience can best be under-
      stood by considering simple rather than complex examples."
      Further points out that Cain achieved an "aesthetic
      distance" from his work due to his obsessively objective
      and dispassionate attitude toward the basic elements of
      his novels.

645. Madden, David. "The 'Pure' Novel and James Cain."
      University Review 30 (March 1964): 235-239.

      Points out that Cain believed that illusion in a novel
      arises from the impersonality of the work. Cain's lack
      of personal involvement in moral considerations not only
      allowed him to achieve this impersonality, but also
      moved the serious reader to an almost complete emotional
      commitment to the experiences of the novel.

646. Oates, Joyce Carol. "Man Under Sentence of Death: The
      Novels of James M. Cain." *Tough Guy Writers of the
      Thirties* (item 46), pp. 110-128.

Examines the relation between Cain and his reader.
States that Cain's novels catered to an American desire
for simple justice: one who dares too much ultimately
becomes trapped by his own actions. This created a small,
unrealistic world, in which "accidental encounters have
the force of destiny behind them," but in Cain's novels
it is not the "why" but the "how" that is important.

647. Starr, Kevin. "It's Chinatown." *New Republic* 173 (26
      July 1975): 31-32.

States that of all the tough guy writers (Hammett,
Chandler, McCoy), Cain possessed the most brutal, pessi-
mistic view of human nature. By using only the bare
essentials in his writing style, Cain forces the reader
into an "act of imaginative cooperation," the reader
visualizing the details of the story.

648. Van Nostrand, Albert D. *The Denatured Novel.* Indianapolis:
      Bobbs-Merrill, 1960, pp. 126-132.

Maintains that Cain wrote his novels as if they were
movie scenarios, with chapters made up of scenes and
groups of lines approximating camera shots. This style
of writing reduces plot complexities to mere conflicts,
without an attitude or theme toward its subject. Cain
does not give justification for the protagonists' actions,
and thus his novels emphasize the "what" and "how," not
the "why."

649. Wilson, Edmund. "The Boys in the Back Room: 1. James M.
      Cain." *Classics and Commercials: A Literary Chronicle
      of the Forties.* New York: Farrar, 1950, pp. 19-22.

Cain's protagonists are usually doomed to a fate fore-
cast from the start of the novel. Wilson observes that
Cain is ingenious as he traces the tangles his characters
get themselves into, and even has "brilliant moments of
insight" but regrets the use of such "conventions of
Hollywood" as coincidences and reversals of fortune.
This, Wilson states, makes Cain's works the "Devil's
parody of the movies" and reduces the author to a "writer
for the studios."

CAIN, PAUL. Pseudonym of George Sims (1902-1966)

650. Hagemann, E.R. "Introducing Paul Cain and His *Fast One*:
      A Forgotten Hard-Boiled Writer, a Forgotten Gangster
      Novel." *Armchair Detective* 12 (January 1979): 72-76.

Argues that Cain's *Fast One*, first serialized in *Black
Mask* magazine in 1932 and published as a book in 1933,
is the best gangster novel "ever to appear." Speculates
that it was quickly forgotten because the public was
satiated by gangsters in books or on the screen by 1933.

CANADAY, JOHN EDWIN. See MATTHEW HEAD

CARR, JOHN DICKSON (1905-1977). Pseudonyms: Carr Dickson,
   Carter Dickson, Roger Fairbairn

*   Cawelti, John G. *Adventure, Mystery, and Romance* (item
       150), pp. 140-141.

       States that an important aspect of the "hard-boiled"
       detective story is its use of the modern city as a
       background; points out that Carr transforms the city
       into a "place of enchantment and mystery."

651.   Dueren, Fred. "Henri Bencolin." *Armchair Detective* 8
       (February 1975): 98, 123.

       A description of one of Carr's characters who charac-
       terizes himself by saying, "I can tamper with the law
       when, where, and how I like."

652.   Greene, Douglas G. "John Dickson Carr, Alias Roger
       Fairbairn, and the Historical Novel." *Armchair Detec-
       tive* 11 (October 1978): 339-341.

       Contends that "one of Carr's greatest innovations
       during the 1930's was a detective novel with a historical
       setting"--*Devil Kinsmere*, which he published under the
       pseudonym of Roger Fairbairn. Gives several examples
       from the book that emphasize its detective elements.

653.   Herzel, Roger. "John Dickson Carr." *Minor American
       Novelists*. Edited by Charles Alva Hoyt. Carbondale:
       Southern Illinois University Press, 1970, pp. 67-80.

       States that Carr's most important contribution to de-
       tective literature was the "locked-room mystery."
       Also observes that Carr uses conflict between the common-
       sense world and the "miraculous," but since the detective's
       function is to destroy the miraculous by explaining the
       "impossible solution," Carr builds with one hand while
       destroying with the other.

654. Levin, Bernard. "Murder? Bluntly It Is Not Worth It." *London Times* 15 March 1977, p. 16.

States that Carr was one of the most ingenious of mystery writers. A specialist of impossible situations (murder committed in a locked room) he was a master of the "howdunit."

* Murch, A.E. *The Development of the Detective Novel* (item 51), pp. 234-235.

Maintains that Carr often experimented with the building of mystery and suspense by the introduction of supernatural elements.

* Panek, LeRoy. "John Dickson Carr." *Watteau's Shepherds* (item 57), pp. 145-184.

Maintains that "Carr's novels (with the exception of *The Burning Court*) were constructed as puzzles" and that one of his favorite motifs is the relationship between magic and murder. Analyzes Carr's detectives, including his first one, Henri Bencolin.

* Symons, Julian. *Mortal Consequences* (item 74), pp. 119-121.

Observes that Carr is unique among mystery writers in his mastery of the "locked-room" mystery. States, however, that the use of this device means that everything else becomes subservient to the formula.

655. Taylor, Robert Lewis. "Two Authors in an Attic." *New Yorker* 27 (8 September 1951): 39-48; 27 (15 September 1951): 36-51.

An admiring profile of Carr that provides an overview of Carr's career and working habits, along with a brief analysis of his work.

CASPARY, VERA (1904-   )

656. Caspary, Vera. "Mark McPherson." *The Great Detectives* (item 60), pp. 141-146.

McPherson appears in only one book, *Laura*, and his creator states that in the first drafts of the novel he was merely a lifeless device, but he gradually took over the story, "asserting his personality in a way never contemplated in early drafts and outlines."

CASSELLS, JOHN. See W. MURDOCH DUNCAN

CHANDLER, RAYMOND (1888-1959). Series character: Philip Marlowe

657.   Abrahams, Etta C. "Visions and Values in the Action
       Detective Novel: A Study of the Works of Raymond
       Chandler, Kenneth Millar, and John D. MacDonald."
       Ph.D. dissertation, Michigan State University, 1973.

       Argues that Marlowe is, as an outsider, a social critic
       but that the works of Chandler (as well as those of the
       other two writers studied) reinforce the values of
       society at large.

658.   Abrahams, Etta C. "Where Have All the Values Gone? The
       Private Eye's Vision of America in the Novels of Ray-
       mond Chandler and Ross Macdonald." *Armchair Detective*
       9 (February 1976): 128-131.

       Argues that Marlowe is a social critic and that his
       sharpest criticism is centered on Hollywood.

659.   Barzun, Jacques, and Wendell Hertig Taylor. Preface to
       The Lady in the Lake, by Raymond Chandler. New York:
       Garland Publishing, 1976. Also printed in *A Book of
       Prefaces* (item 22), pp. 29-30.

       Contends that the novel is a classic Chandler work
       because it demonstrates careful craftmanship in the
       balancing of plot and subplot.

660.   Becker, Jens P. "Murder Considered as One of the Fine
       Arts." *Literatur in Wissenschaft und Unteraicht* 6
       (March 1973): 31-42.

       Uses Chandler's short story "I'll be Waiting" to work
       out some of the essential characteristics of Chandler
       and other writers for *Black Mask* magazine.

661.   Beekman, E.M. "Raymond Chandler and an American Genre."
       Massachusetts Review 14 (1973): 149-173.

       Argues that Raymond Chandler's works are not merely
       detective stories but are novels which use elements of
       the tradition of detective fiction and "either amplify
       or destroy established constrictions" through Chandler's
       "superior artistic imagination." Gives many examples of
       Chandler's sharp figurative language.

662. Binyon, T.J. "A Lasting Influence?" *The World of Raymond Chandler* (item 676), pp. 171-183.

      Contends that Chandler's influence on most of the writers of "hard-boiled" detective fiction is surprisingly "minimal, even non-existent." Surveys a great number of these writers and finds Chandler has most influenced Ross Macdonald and John D. MacDonald.

663. Bruccoli, Matthew J. *Raymond Chandler: A Checklist*. Kent, Ohio: Kent State University Press, 1968. 35pp.

      Primary bibliography.

664. Bruccoli, Matthew J. *Raymond Chandler: A Descriptive Bibliography*. Pittsburgh: University of Pittsburgh Press, 1979. 149pp.

      Primary bibliography. Includes reproductions of title pages and dust jackets.

*   Cawelti, John G. "Hammett, Chandler, and Spillane." *Adventure, Mystery, and Romance* (item 150), pp. 174-182.

      Argues that Chandler's use of the "hard-boiled detective formula" to deal with such serious themes as "romantic illusion" and "destructive innocence" gives his characters a complexity and depth lacking in most writers in the genre.

*   Chandler, Raymond. "The Simple Art of Murder" (item 156).

      Argues that the classical detective story is successful neither as an intellectual problem nor "artistically as fiction." It is not about real murders or real life. Dashiell Hammett, he contends, "gave murder back to the kind of people that commit it for reasons," and he "put these people down on paper as they were" and "demonstrated that the detective story can be important writing." "The realist in murder," Chandler continues, writes of a corrupt world, "but down these mean streets a man must go who is not himself mean, who is neither tarnished nor afraid. The detective in this kind of story must be such a man."

*   Chandler, Raymond. "The Simple Art of Murder" (item 157).

      In this essay, which is entirely different from item 156, Chandler offers his appraisal of the mysteries (including his own early stories) published in the pulp

magazines. In these stories, he contends, one could
"recognize the authentic power of a kind of writing that
even at its most mannered and artificial made most of
the fiction of the time taste like a cup of lukewarm
consommé at a spinsterish tearoom," and that in them
the mystery became "hard and cynical about motive and
character." He concludes that there are no classics of
crime and detection because no one has exhausted the
possibilities of the form.

About his own stories he says that of course he wishes
they were better, but because of the requirements of
the mystery formula, "if they had been much better they
would not have been published," and that his dream was
to "exceed the limits of a formula without destroying
it."

665.   Conrad, Peter. "The Private Dick as Dandy." *Times Literary
       Supplement* 20 January 1978, p. 60.

       Ostensibly a review of *The World of Raymond Chandler*
       and *The Notebooks and English Summer* by Chandler, this
       article argues that "Chandler turns slang into a poetic
       diction, just as he turns down-at-the-heels sleuthing
       into a chivalric quest."

666.   Crider, Allen B. "The Private-Eye Hero: A Study of the
       Novels of Dashiell Hammett, Raymond Chandler, and Ross
       Macdonald." Ph.D. dissertation, University of Texas
       at Austin, 1972.

       Argues that, like Hammett's detectives, Chandler's
       Marlowe "lives in an absurd world," but unlike Hammett's
       detectives Marlowe becomes involved with his clients.
       The real story in Chandler's novels is "his hero's
       search for truth."

667.   Davies, Russell. "Omnes Me Impune Lacessant." *The World
       of Raymond Chandler* (item 676), pp. 31-42.

       Argues that "the secret of Chandler's success" is the
       element of self-mockery in the narration.

668.   "Dead Men Do Talk." *Newsweek* 25 (14 May 1945): 95-97.

       Chandler's characters are "realistically nasty, sordid,
       and mean," but they are three dimensional. Marlowe is
       cynical but a man of virtue. Quotes Chandler as saying
       he has tried to take murder away from the upper classes,
       "the vicar's rose garden, and back to the people who are
       really good at it."

669. Dove, George N. "The Complex Art of Raymond Chandler." *Armchair Detective* 8 (August 1975): 271-274.

   Argues that Chandler "was a master in the craft of construction."

670. Durham, Philip. *Down These Mean Streets a Man Must Go: Raymond Chandler's Knight.* Chapel Hill: University of North Carolina Press, 1963. 173pp.

   Contends that Chandler's Marlowe is an Arthurian hero combined with the American Western tradition and that he "went among the people in the language of the people."

671. Durham, Philip. Introduction to *Killer in the Rain*, by Raymond Chandler. Harmondsworth, England: Penguin Books, 1966, pp. 7-12.

   In this introduction to a group of Chandler's short stories, Durham details how Chandler, with superb crafts-manship, formed novels out of his short stories and contends that the theme of his novels--the "compelling necessity" of the detective to correct social wrongs--was developed in the short stories.

*   Eames, Hugh. "Philip Marlowe--Raymond Chandler." *Sleuths, Inc.* (item 30), pp. 185-221.

   Argues that as a problem solver Marlowe is handicapped by his honesty and sensitivity but that he does solve problems for people who "have suddenly been overwhelmed by an emergency."

672. Elliott, George P. "Country Full of Blondes." *Nation* 190 (23 April 1960): 354-356, 358-360.

   Chandler looked at the world "in the expectation that good and evil are all mixed together." Dialog is "fast, glittering, and tough," but some of his descriptions are more romantic than tough. No writer better conveyed the feel of Los Angeles in the thirties, forties, and early fifties.

673. Finch, G.A. **"From Spade to Marlowe to Archer: An Essay."** *Armchair Detective* 4 (January 1971): 107-110.

   After outlining the Hammett hero and style, Finch con-tends that Chandler differs from Hammett in his use of "the diversionary encounter and multiple plot movements" as well as in taking the leisure to reflect on various topics which did not directly advance the action.

674. Finch, G.A. "Marlowe's Long Goodbye." *Armchair Detective*
      6 (October 1972): 7-11.

      Chandler circumvented rather than manipulated the
      formulas of detective fiction and changed the center of
      interest from the course of the action to the consequences
      of the action.

675. Gardiner, Dorothy, and Kathrine Sorley Walker, eds.
      Raymond Chandler Speaking. Boston: Houghton Mifflin,
      1962. 271pp.

      A collection of Chandler's correspondence arranged by
      subject matter and two previously unpublished works: a
      short story and a fragment of a novel.

676. Gross, Miriam, ed. *The World of Raymond Chandler*. New
      York: A & W Publishers, 1977. 190pp.

      A collection of essays, many of which are personal
      reminiscences. The ones which treat Chandler's writing
      are annotated individually.

677. Highsmith, Patricia. Introduction to *The World of Raymond
      Chandler* (item 676), pp. 1-6.

      Highsmith tries to find connections between Chandler's
      life and work but finally concludes "his life doesn't
      fit in with what he wrote," except for Marlowe's sense
      of decency. Contends that his abundance of similies gives
      his writing humor and vigor.

678. Holden, Jonathan. "The Case for Raymond Chandler's Fiction
      as Romance." *Kansas Quarterly* 10 (Fall 1978): 41-47.

      Notes that Philip Durham in *Down These Mean Streets
      a Man Must Go* and George Grella in "Murder and the
      Mean Streets" (items 670 and 257) point out the parallel
      between Chandler's works and chivalric romance. Holden
      explains this parallel further with summaries of parts
      of the books and quotations from critics on chivalric
      romance.

679. Homberger, Eric. "The Man of Letters (1908-12)." *The
      World of Raymond Chandler* (item 676), pp. 9-18.

      Notes that Chandler was an essayist, poet, and reviewer
      in London between 1908 and 1912, describes that world
      (though little is known of Chandler's life of that time),
      and points out some literary references which appear in
      Chandler's detective stories, which were written over two
      decades later.

680. Howard, Leon. "Raymond Chandler's Not-So-Great Gatsby."
      Mystery and Detection Annual 1973 (item 17), pp. 1-15.

      Details a large number of parallels between F. Scott
      Fitzgerald's *The Great Gatsby* (1925) and Chandler's
      The Long Goodbye (1953) and states that it is uncertain
      how conscious this might be, but contends that--in any
      case--when compared to Fitzgerald's book Chandler's is
      "tougher on crooks, tougher on the rich, tougher in his
      insistence that people be responsible for their actions."

681. James, Clive. "The Country Behind the Hill." *The World
      of Raymond Chandler* (item 676), pp. 115-126.

      Argues that his style is the most enduring feature of
      Chandler's work and that "even at its most explicit, what
      he wrote was full of implication."

682. Jameson, Fredric. "On Raymond Chandler." *Southern Review*
      6 (1970): 624-650.

      Chandler's fifteen years as an oil executive in Los
      Angeles (before he started writing) enabled him to have
      special insight into the atmosphere and power structure
      of the city. That he spent his boyhood in England made
      the American language to some extent an adopted one for
      him and forced him to be a stylist. In addition, there
      takes place in Chandler's novels "a de-mystification of
      violent death."

*   Lambert, Gavin. "A Private Eye: Raymond Chandler." *The
      Dangerous Edge* (item 42), pp. 210-234.

      Contends that Chandler's conventional, unexciting life
      increased his fascination with sex, violence, and greed
      that resulted in the creation of Marlowe, "an exaggeration
      of the possible," who becomes the mouthpiece for Chand-
      ler's own beliefs and fears. Examples from the novels
      are given to illustrate this thesis.

683. Legman, G. *Love and Death: A Study in Censorship.* New
      York: Hacker Art Books, 1963, pp. 68-70.

      Contends that Chandler's Marlowe is "clearly homo-
      sexual."

684. Lid, R.W. "Philip Marlowe Speaking." *Kenyon Review* 31
      (1969): 153-178.

      Chandler was "an extraordinary cultural historian" in
      his detailing of the Los Angeles of the thirties and

forties and the "schizoid aspects of American culture."
He saw America as "criminally obsessed with the dollar."
Marlowe's speech is an "authentic American voice" although
Chandler spent his boyhood in England and remained to
some extent an outsider in America.

685.   McShane, Frank. *The Life of Raymond Chandler*. New York:
       Dutton, 1976. 306pp.

       Argues that Chandler was "one of the most important
       writers of his time as well as one of the most delightful"
       and attempts to show how his life affected his work.
       Contends that his half-American, half-English background
       gave him "exceptional insight."

686.   Mason, Michael. "Deadlier Than the Male." *Times Literary
       Supplement* 17 September 1976, p. 1147.

       Mason notes Chandler's ambivalence toward sexuality--the
       more tempting the woman in his novels, the more likely
       it is that she is a killer--and that sex becomes more
       and more the overt concern of his later novels. *The Blue
       Dahlia*, however, is an exception to this trend.

687.   Mason, Michael. "Marlowe, Men and Women." *The World of
       Raymond Chandler* (item 676), pp. 89-101.

       Argues that Chandler's novels have "a strongly homo-
       sexual cast." Cites such items as "misogyny, a relish
       for certain male characters, and femininity in the hero."

688.   Orel, Harold. "Raymond Chandler's Last Novel: Some Ob-
       servations on the 'Private Eye' Tradition." *Journal
       of the Central Mississippi Valley American Studies
       Association* 2 (Spring 1961): 59-63.

       Playback is a caricature of Chandler's earlier work
       because Marlowe is out of date.

*   Palmer, Jerry. "The Negative Thriller." *Thrillers* (item
       56), pp. 40-52.

       Using Chandler's *The Long Goodbye* as an example of
       the negative thriller Palmer concludes that the chief
       difference between the positive and the negative thriller
       is the latter's "sense of bleakness and unfulfillment."

689.   Parker, Robert B. "The Violent Hero, Wilderness Heritage
       and Urban Reality: A Study of the Private Eye in the
       Novels of Dashiell Hammett, Raymond Chandler and Ross
       Macdonald." Ph.D. dissertation, Boston University, 1971.

Argues that the private eye in the novels of Chandler (and Hammett and Macdonald) takes frontier values into the city.

690. Parsons, Luke. "On the Novels of Raymond Chandler." *Fortnightly* 175 (May 1954): 346-351.

Chandler uses the conventions of the tough school: "violence, alcoholism, promiscuity, and moral nihilism" but he "infuses a small glow of humanity" into that world.

691. Parsons, Luke. "Simenon and Chandler." *Contemporary Review* 197 (January 1960): 56-58.

Because of their "serious purpose and relationship to life" the detective stories of Simenon and Chandler are literature. Chandler's women do, however, tend to be cardboard "symbols of the sickness of society."

692. Pollock, Wilson. "Man with a Toy Gun." *New Republic* 146 (7 May 1962): 21-22.

In this review of *Raymond Chandler Speaking*, Pollock argues that Chandler was not an intellectual and his novels have no political conscience; he believed society corrupt and that one could do little about it. Also states that he knew the language of the underworld well.

693. Powell, Lawrence Clark. Foreword to *The Raymond Chandler Omnibus*. New York: Alfred A. Knopf, 1964, pp. v-viii.

Argues that of all the hundreds of novels written about Los Angeles, Chandler's are the closest to the truth of the city. States that style is the word which explains the high quality of his books.

694. Reck, Tom S. "Raymond Chandler's Los Angeles." *Nation* 221 (20 December 1975): 661-663.

Contends that Chandler brings Los Angeles into focus with descriptions of vegetation and architecture that "represent the internal sickness" of the city. Other details suggest its "chaos," "evil," and "rottenness."

*   Ruehlmann, William. *Saint with a Gun* (item 65), pp. 76-90.

Argues that Chandler gave his detective, Philip Marlowe, the "quality of redemption," the one quality that Chandler felt Dashiell Hammett lacked. Ruehlmann cites numerous examples from the novels that emphasize Marlowe's integrity and sensitivity.

695. Ruhm, Herbert. "Raymond Chandler: From Bloomsbury to
      the Jungle--and Beyond." *Tough Guy Writers of the
      Thirties* (item 46), pp. 171-185.

      Argues that Chandler continually experimented with
      the mystery genre. His hero Marlowe is all-knowing,
      competent, good, and defends essentially conservative
      values.

696. Russell, D.C. "Chandler Books." *Atlantic Monthly* 175
      (March 1945): 123-124.

      Argues that Chandler's "artistry of craftsmanship" and
      realism are as good as that of many famous novelists.
      Gives many examples to show his talent for imagery. States
      that Chandler uses characteristic American speech and
      humor.

697. Schickel, Richard. "Raymond Chandler's Private Eye."
      Commentary 35 (February 1963): 158-161.

      In this article, which is ostensibly a review of *Ray-
      mond Chandler Speaking*, Schickel argues that Chandler's
      great theme was that the moral man must suffer loneliness
      because he "refused to play the game of life in a con-
      ventionally immoral or amoral way." Chandler's hero does
      not have a life of continual excitement; he sets out "to
      record the experience of urban loneliness."

698. Sissman, L.E. "Raymond Chandler Thirteen Years After."
      New Yorker 48 (11 March 1972): 123-125.

      Contends that Hammett is overrated but that Chandler
      has a "magic" which is the result of his "placing an
      ordinary but incorruptible man in a city that is ripely
      and palpably corrupt" and sending him on a quest for
      truth. Sissman also calls Chandler an early reporter of
      the failure of our cities and praises his skill with
      words, but states that the pulp fiction formula was his
      "worst enemy."

699. Symons, Julian. "An Aesthete Discovers the Pulps." *The
      World of Raymond Chandler* (item 676), pp. 19-29.

      Argues that Chandler's detective stories "carried over
      into an alien field the literary aestheticism of his
      youth."

700. Symons, Julian. "The Case of Raymond Chandler." *New York
      Times Magazine* 23 December 1973, pp. 12+.

Contends that Marlowe is, in his own way, almost as
incredible as Philo Vance or Lord Peter Wimsey and quotes
Chandler calling Marlowe "a creature of fantasy." The
qualities of Chandler's novels, Symons contends, are
"crackling dialogue, shaky plotting ... tremendous pace
and excitement," and Marlowe.

701.   Symons, Julian. "Marlowe's Victim." *Times Literary
       Supplement* 23 March 1962, p. 200. Reprinted *Critical
       Occasions*. London: Hamish Hamilton, 1966, pp. 174-180.

In this article Symons argues that the character of
Marlowe is "a disastrous piece of self-indulgence" for
Chandler.

*   Symons, Julian. *Mortal Consequences* (item 74), pp. 142-
       144.

Argues that Chandler should be read primarily for his
style and secondarily for "the California background,
the jokes, the social observation, the character of
Marlowe."

702.   Thomson, James. "Murder with Honor." *New Republic* 179
       (22 July 1978): 28-31.

In Chandler's third person stories the protagonist
tends to be vicious and his thoughts are not explained,
but in the first person novels (the first fully-realized
one is *The Big Sleep*, 1939) the protagonist is "clearly
the most honest man in a thoroughly corrupt world."

703.   Thomson, James. "The Slumming Angel: The Voice and Vision
       of Raymond Chandler." Ph.D. dissertation, University
       of Pennsylvania, 1977.

Analyzes not only Chandler's detective fiction but also
his early writing as a young man in England to show that
the dominant theme in Chandler is the man "who seeks
truth in a world of falsehood."

704.   Wells, Walter. "Grey Knight in the Great Wrong Place."
       *Tycoons and Locusts: A Regional Look at Hollywood Fic-
       tion of the 1930's.* Carbondale: Southern Illinois
       University Press, 1973, pp. 71-85.

Contends that Chandler uses the Southern California
region "as a living, heterogeneous entity" that "helps
to shape the Chandler aesthetic" and analyzes *Farewell
My Lovely* (1940) to show the "effects of regional involvement in his fiction."

CHARTERIS, LESLIE (1907-   ). Name originally: Leslie Charles
Bowyer Yin. Series character: Simon Templar (The Saint)

Butler, William Vivian. *The Durable Desperadoes* (item 25).

> Devotes many pages to Charteris and argues that,
> being Anglo-Chinese, Charteris both loved England and
> was exasperated by it. "The love created The Saint: the
> exasperation gave a remarkably sharp edge to The Saint's
> repartee."

705.   Charteris, Leslie. "Meet The Saint." *Meet the Detective*
       (item 45): pp. 51-60.

> States that he regards The Saint as "the personifica-
> tion of an attitude of mind." This makes it possible to
> regard him in a very personal way but with a certain
> detachment.

706.   Lofts, W.O.G., and Derek Adley. *The Saint and Leslie
       Charteris*. Bowling Green, Ohio: Bowling Green University
       Popular Press, 1972. 135pp.

> Observes that the character of The Saint was built on
> the "successful formula of a gentleman crook who took
> justice into his own hands." Nearly half of the book is
> a list of the publications of Charteris.

CHASE, JAMES HADLEY. Pseudonym of René Brabazon Raymond (1906-   )

707.   Dukeshire, Theodore P. "The Caper Novels of James Hadley
       Chase." *Armchair Detective* 10 (April 1977): 128-129.

> Maintains that Chase's novels fit into the sub-genre
> of the "caper novel" and gives examples from various
> novels to illustrate his contention.

708.   Dukeshire, Theodore P. "James Hadley Chase." *Armchair
       Detective* 5 (October 1971): 32-34.

> Chase presents a world in which innocent men are
> electrocuted while killers go free, and a private eye
> chooses love over duty. Includes checklist.

709.   Orwell, George. "Raffles and Miss Blandish." *Dickens,
       Dali, and Others: Studies in Popular Culture*. New York:
       Reynal and Hitchcock, 1946, pp. 202-221. Reprinted *The
       Collected Essays, Journalism and Letters of George Or-
       well*, Volume 3. Edited by Sonia Orwell and Ian Angus.

New York: Harcourt, Brace, 1968, pp. 212-224. Also re-printed *Mass Culture: The Popular Arts in America.* Edited by Bernard Rosenberg and David Manning White. Glencoe, Illinois: Free Press, 1957, pp. 154-164. Also reprinted *The Art of the Essay.* Edited by Leslie A. Fiedler. New York: Thomas Y. Crowell, 1958, pp. 465-476.

Argues that Hornung's *Raffles* and James Hadley Chase's *No Orchids for Miss Blandish* can be compared sociologically because both concentrate on the criminal rather than the detective and both are "morally equivocal."

*   Palmer, Jerry. *Thrillers* (item 56), pp. 41-43.

States that Chase's novel *Just Another Sucker* is an example of a "Negative Thriller," a form in which the hero succeeds but the reader is left with "a sense of unease."

710.   Smith, Susan Harris. "No Orchids for George Orwell." *Armchair Detective* 9 (February 1976): 114-115.

Smith contends that the criticism of Chase by George Orwell in "Raffles and Miss Blandish" (item 709) is wrong and that "Chase's premise is that in a corrupt society the only possible moral force resides in the individual."

CHESTER, GEORGE RANDOLPH (1869-1924)

711.   Borowitz, Albert. "The Many Rises and Falls of J. Rufus Wallingford." *Armchair Detective* 12 (January 1979): 28-29.

Chester was fascinated by the line that separates trickery and business cleverness and stated that it was where the lines intersected that "the most dramatic business stories will be found." He therefore created Get-Rich-Quick Wallingford, a comic confidence man whose name has become part of American folklore.

CHESTERTON, G.K. (1874-1936). Series character: Father Brown

712.   Barker, Dudley. *G.K. Chesterton: A Biography.* New York: Stein and Day, 1973, pp. 194-197.

Devotes only a few pages to Chesterton's detective
stories, mainly to note that the first was the best and
that the strain of devising new plots for Father Brown
soon showed.

713.   Barzun, Jacques, and Wendell Hertig Taylor. Preface to
       The Innocence of Father Brown, by G.K. Chesterton. New
       York: Garland Publishing, 1976. Also printed in *A Book
       of Prefaces* (item 22), pp. 31-32.

       Contends that Chesterton was better at "devising the
       crimes" than "producing their explanation," but to
       Chesterton the fantastic and supernatural were "no less
       real, and much more significant, than the drab appearance
       of daily things."

714.   Breen, Jon L. "The Invisible Man Revisited." *Armchair
       Detective* 4 (April 1971): 154.

       Contends that G.K. Chesterton's story "The Invisible
       Man" fails to convince the reader of his implausible
       premise or to make that premise believable even within
       the framework of the story.

715.   Gillespie, Robert. "Detections: Borges and Father Brown."
       Novel 7 (Spring 1974): 220-230.

       Borges has suggested that Chesterton's Father Brown
       stories have influenced him, and Gillespie states that
       both authors "play with similar notions of contradic-
       tion, necessity, circular time, and transcendental
       reality."

*   Haycraft, Howard. *Murder for Pleasure* (item 36), pp. 74-
       77.

       Contends that Chesterton is an important innovator in
       detective fiction, giving the genre prestige and respect-
       ability that it needs for survival and development. Con-
       cludes that although many of Chesterton's Father Brown
       stories do not meet the standards of good detective fic-
       tion, in creating Father Brown he gave the genre one of
       its most illustrious and lovable detective characters.

716.   Hays, R.W. "A Lesser Chesterton Detective: Mr. Pond."
       Armchair Detective 9 (February 1976): 125.

       Chesterton's detective stories featuring Mr. Pond have
       many of the same themes of his Father Brown series ex-
       cept the religious theme is not so important.

717. Hays, R.W. "The Private Life of Father Brown." *Armchair Detective* 4 (April 1971): 135-139.

After a speculative commentary on Father Brown's private life, analyzes and identifies recurrent themes in the stories, particularly Chesterton's use of religion.

718. Hollis, Christopher. *The Mind of Chesterton*. Coral Gables, Fla.: University of Miami Press, 1970. 303pp.

Hollis devotes only a few pages to the Father Brown stories. He states that they have the usual improbabilities of the genre except that they do not defy psychological probability.

719. Hunter, Lynette. *G.K. Chesterton: Explorations in Allegory*. New York: St. Martin's Press, 1979, pp. 140-158.

Maintains that "the Father Brown stories constitute both an interpretation and an expression of Chesterton's philosophy": they are "an allegory of life" in which man must realize the meaning of the clues he has been given and act upon them. This "is impossible without Christian reason," Hunter maintains. One of Chesterton's major concerns in the stories is the relationship between the detective/priest and the criminal. Cites many examples from the stories to support her contentions.

720. Knox, Ronald A. "Father Brown." *Literary Distractions*. New York: Sheed and Ward, 1958, pp. 170-179.

Argues that the chief virtues of Chesterton's detective stories are their ingenuity, Chesterton's "scene-painting," and the ability of his detective to solve crimes by being a shrewd judge of men. In some of the later stories his didactic purpose overshadows the detective interest.

721. Lachman, Marvin. "Religion and Detection: Sunday the Rabbi Met Father Brown." *Armchair Detective* 1 (October 1967): 19-24.

Using the format of a fictional conversation between Father Brown and Harry Kemelman's Rabbi Small to compare two detectives whose main vocation is religious, Lachman points out that Father Brown's method is to plan the murder himself so that he will then understand the mind of the murderer and then realize who the murderer must be.

*   Lambert, Gavin. "Final Problems 2: G.K. Chesterton."
      The Dangerous Edge (item 42), pp. 63-78.

      Argues that the Father Brown stories reveal Chesterton's
      obsession with melodrama. Using examples from several of
      the stories Lambert contends that they do not reflect a
      progressively profound exploration of life but a gradual
      decline of the creative and imaginative powers.

722. Lowndes, Robert A.W. "G.K. Chesterton's Father Brown."
      Startling Mystery Stories (Fall 1970). Reprinted *Arm-
      chair Detective* 9 (June 1976): 184-188, 235.

      Father Brown's method is to put himself "into the
      spiritual condition of the criminal. Thus, he knows how
      the crime was done, why, and by whom." His effectiveness
      also depends upon people thinking he is merely a "celibate
      simpleton."

*   Murch, A.E. *The Development of the Detective Novel* (item
      51), pp. 199-202.

      Contends that Chesterton's detective stories have a
      special importance not only because his Father Brown is
      one of the unforgettable heroes of detective fiction,
      but also because "the criminal ... is a human being with
      good as well as bad impulses," and because Father Brown
      was most interested in discovering the psychological
      causes that led the criminal to commit the crime.

723. Robson, W.W. "G.K. Chesterton's 'Father Brown' Stories."
      Southern Review 5 (Summer 1969): 611-629. Revised
      version published as "Father Brown and Others." *G.K.
      Chesterton: A Centenary Appraisal*. Edited by John
      Sullivan. New York: Barnes and Noble, 1974, pp. 58-72.

      Chesterton's detective stories "are without doubt the
      most ingenious" ever written and are, along with *The Man
      Who Was Thursday*, the best of his writings. The Father
      Brown stories can be regarded as variations on the theme
      of "The Purloined Letter" by Poe. Father Brown has no
      supernatural powers, but he is more observant than most
      people and he can identify with the murderer.

*   Routley, Erik. "The Fairy Tale and the Secret: Father
      Brown." *The Puritan Pleasures of the Detective Story*
      (item 64), pp. 104-116.

      Contends that the Father Brown stories are generally
      misunderstood because they are seen as moralistic but

they usually hinge on the detective writer's device of "misdirection" and the contrast between the familiar and the fantastic.

* Symons, Julian. *Mortal Consequences* (item 74), pp. 78-81.

   Argues that Chesterton's detective stories made reality "seem like fantasy" and usually "exemplify a witty paradox about the condition of society or the nature of man."

724. West, Julius. *G.K. Chesterton: A Critical Study*. London: Martin Secker, 1972 (originally published 1915). 191pp.

   In the four pages devoted to Chesterton's detective stories, West states that Chesterton may be said to have invented a new type of detective story: "the sort that has no crime, no criminal, and a detective whose processes are transcendental." He also argues that Father Brown is Chesterton's "completest and most human creation," but finds the Father Brown stories lacking because the criminals in them are lunatics and because there is a logical flaw in each story.

CHEYNEY, PETER (1896-1951)

725. Harrison, Michael. *Peter Cheyney: Prince of Hokum*. London: Neville Spearman, 1954. 303pp.

   In the "achievement" section of this biography, Harrison maintains that the popularity of Cheyney's Lemmy Caution stories was a result of their "readability" as well as the elements of sex, violence, and mystery in them.

726. Hedman, Iwan. "Peter Cheyney." *Armchair Detective* 4 (January 1971): 111-113.

   Brief commentary on Cheyney's fictional detectives, particularly Lemmy Caution whom he introduced in *This Man is Dangerous* (1936) and who has been called "the biggest and most human detective since the famous Sherlock Holmes." A checklist of Cheyney's novels is included.

CHILDERS, ERSKINE (1870-1922)

*   Symons, Julian. *Mortal Consequences* (item 74), pp. 233-
         234.

         Observes that *The Riddle of the Sands* was the first
         spy story with any literary pretensions. States that
         Childers wrote with great skill and an underlying ideal-
         ism "that takes for granted the way in which an honorable
         man must act."

CHRISTIE, AGATHA (1890-1976)

727.   Allingham, Margery. "Mysterious Fun for Millions of
         Innocent Escapists." *New York Times Book Review* 4 June
         1950, p. 3.

         States that Christie and Dorothy L. Sayers gave the detec-
         tive story "a concrete shape" and "both life and tradi-
         tion." Observes that Christie's appeal is made directly
         to the "honest human curiosity in all of us" and that
         her characters are basically recognizable, familiar
         types.

728.   Athanason, Arthur Nicholas. "*The Mousetrap* Phenomenon."
         Armchair Detective 12 (Spring 1979): 152-157.

         Maintains that *The Mousetrap* "asserts the triumph of
         a social order" and stability that have virtually vanished
         in "contemporary English life" and that is why it had
         such "nostalgic appeal for English middle-classs audiences
         of the 1950's."

729.   Bargainnier, E.F. "Agatha Christie's Other Detectives:
         Parker Pyne and Harley Quin." *Armchair Detective* 11
         (April 1978): 110-115.

         Pyne and Quin appear only in Christie's short stories
         of the 1920s and 1930s, but they represent important
         examples of Christie's experiments in adding narrative
         interest by using elements not usually considered com-
         patible with the detective story form. "In the Pyne stories
         she combines detection ... and the manipulation of human
         lives to achieve their happiness, while in the Quin
         stories she combines detection and fantasy."

730.   Barnard, Robert. *A Talent to Deceive: An Appreciation of
         Agatha Christie*. New York: Dodd, Mead, 1980.

Published too late for annotation, but according to *Publishers Weekly*, the book "examines the qualities that made Christie books the best sellers they have been and includes a study in depth of three Christie novels and an analysis of her detectives' characters."

731. Barnes, Daniel R. "A Note on *The Murder of Roger Ackroyd.*" *Mystery and Detection Annual 1972* (item 16), pp. 254-255.

Quotes Percy Lubbock in *The Craft of Fiction* (published five years before *Roger Ackroyd*) saying that in a murder mystery story the narrator cannot be the murderer. Suggests that Christie may have read this and accepted it as a challenge.

732. Barzun, Jacques, and Wendell Hertig Taylor. Preface to *The Murder of Roger Ackroyd*, by Agatha Christie. New York: Garland Publishing, 1976. Also printed in *A Book of Prefaces* (item 22), pp. 33-34.

Points out that the controversial ending of *Roger Ackroyd* still causes arguments and refers to Haycraft's dictum that "it is after all the reader's job to keep his wits about him and ... to suspect *everybody*."

733. Behre, Frank. *Get, Come and Go: Some Aspects of Situational Grammar.* (Gothenburg Studies in English, 28). Stockholm: Almquist, 1973. 174pp.

Studies the speech patterns and the use of the verbs "come" and "go" in Christie's novels. Behre states that Christie's characters are much more varied in their speech patterns than the characters of any other author.

734. Behre, Frank. *Studies in Agatha Christie's Writings: The Behavior of a Good (Great) Deal, A Lot, Lots, Much, Plenty, Many, A Good (Great) Many.* (Gothenburg Studies in English, 19). Stockholm: Almquist, 1967. 203pp.

States that Christie places greater importance on the use of dialogue than most other writers. Behre observes that "the main stream of events flows through the dialogue until it reaches open water, where the truth is unravelled."

735. Benedict, Stewart H. "Agatha Christie and Murder Most Unsportsman Like." *Claremont Quarterly* 9 (Winter 1962): 37-42.

States that Christie has developed a formula different
from other mystery writers: she constructs a totally implausible situation and introduces characters who react
realistically for realistic motives.

*   Cawelti, John G. *Adventure, Mystery, and Romance* (item
       150), pp. 111-119, 129-137.

       Cawelti attributes Christie's great success to her
       ability to skillfully balance detection and mystification
       and then to provide enough character and atmosphere to
       maintain, but not detract from, the all-important story
       line. Cawelti compares two Christie books--*An Overdose
       of Death* and *Third Girl*--and finds that the first is
       successful because it maintains balance, whereas the
       second story fails because it does not keep the balance
       between detection and mystification.

736.   Crispin, Edmund. "The Mistress of Simplicity." *Agatha
       Christie: First Lady of Crime* (item 743), pp. 39-48.

       Argues that Christie's success and popularity were due
       to the simplicity of her plots and writing style, achieved
       in part by omitting detailed descriptions of characters
       and locations.

737.   Dueren, Fred. "Hercule Poirot: The Private Life of a
       Private Eye." *Armchair Detective* 7 (February 1974):
       111-115.

       Gathers together from Christie's stories and novels
       the facts about Poirot's life, habits, and associates.

738.   Feinman, Jeffrey. *The Mysterious World of Agatha Christie.*
       New York: Award Books, 1975. 190pp.

       Points out that Christie's "Byzantine" plotting is one
       of her trademarks and observes that by using psychological
       methods of detection that are timeless, her detectives
       may "outlive even those of Poe and Conan Doyle in the
       public affection."

739.   Grant, Ellsworth. "A Tribute to Agatha Christie." *Horizon*
       18 (Autumn 1976): 106-109.

       States that the underlying philosophy of Christie's
       novels is a deep regard for morality. Her novels represent
       evil as omnipresent, always ready to surface.

740. Grossvogel, David I. "Agatha Christie: Containment of
      the Unknown." *Mystery and Its Fictions: From Oedipus
      to Agatha Christie.* Baltimore: Johns Hopkins Univer-
      sity Press, 1979, pp. 39-52.

      Speculates that Christie's "continued success is due
      to the illusion and nostalgia" she conveys of a secure,
      ordered society. Analyzes in depth her first detective
      novel, *The Mysterious Affair at Styles* (1920), to
      illustrate his contention.

741. Hamblen, Abigail Ann. "The Inheritance of the Meek: Two
      Novels by Agatha Christie and Henry James." *Discourse*
      12 (1969): 409-413.

      Observes that, although there is no question of in-
      fluence, the plots of Christie's *Endless Night* and
      James's *Wings of the Dove* are almost exactly the same.
      Examines how both authors dramatized psychological
      "truths."

*   Haycraft, Howard. *Murder for Pleasure* (item 36), pp.
      129-133.

      Maintains that "the only really serious grounds for
      criticism" of Christie's stories is her reliance on, and
      unfair use of, "the least-likely-person" device. Observes
      that Poirot "comes closer to symbolizing his profession
      in the popular mind" than any fictional detective since
      Sherlock Holmes.

742. Holquist, Michael. "Murder She Says." *New Republic* 173
      (26 July 1975): 26-28.

      Observes that Christie is both an industry and an art
      and that she should be compared to Lewis Carroll or P.G.
      Wodehouse, "other masters of making something out of
      nothing."

743. Keating, H.R.F., ed. *Agatha Christie: First Lady of
      Crime.* New York: Holt, 1977. 224pp.

      A collection of essays on Christie. Those which are
      critical essays on her writing are annotated separately.

744. Kitchin, C.H.B. "Five Writers in One: The Versatility
      of Agatha Christie." *Times Literary Supplement* 25
      February 1955, p. x.

      Examines Christie's multifaceted talents: she has been
      a seeker after literary thrills, a gentle philosopher,

a learned archeologist, an acute observer of English
middle-class life, and a cosmopolitan, worldly writer.

745. Kramer, Peter G. "Mistress of Mystery." *Newsweek* 87
      (26 January 1976): 69.

      States that Christie was the leader of the "cozy
      school" of mystery writers in which plot was more im-
      portant than characterization, bloodshed was kept to a
      minimum, and suspense was that of a puzzle, more cerebral
      than emotional.

746. Lathen, Emma. "Conquering Christie." *London Times* 23
      April 1977, p. 8.

      States that Christie has become a vernacular art form
      in her own right. Observes also that her novels are so
      quintessentially English they have taken a special dimen-
      sion and interest for American readers.

747. Lathen, Emma. "Cornwallis's Revenge." *Agatha Christie:
      First Lady of Crime* (item 743), pp. 79-94.

      Lathen attempts to explain Christie's great popularity
      in the United States. States that people respond to
      stories and Christie is a great storyteller with an "ab-
      solute mastery of puzzle."

748. Lejeune, Anthony. "The Secret of Agatha Christie."
      Spectator 225 (19 September 1970): 294.

      Maintains that Christie's books are popular because
      her style of writing is direct and uncomplicated with a
      "texture smooth and homely as cream."

749. Levin, Bernard. "Murder? Bluntly It Is Not Worth It."
      London Times 15 March 1977, p. 16.

      States that although Christie was ingenious with her
      plots and could generate a great deal of suspense, her
      writing style was one of "unredeemed badness."

750. Lowenthal, Max. "Agatha Christie, Creator of Poirot,
      Dies." *New York Times* 13 January 1976, pp. 1, 40.

      States that Christie's forte was "supremely adroit
      plotting and sharp, believable characterization." Ob-
      serves that her writing style was sound but not remark-
      able and that she was unsatisfactory when attempting
      expressive writing.

751. Milne, A.A. "Books and Writers." *Spectator* 184 (30 June 1950): 893.

Contends that the most important quality of *The Mysterious Affair at Styles* is that it does not have a romantic entanglement that would detract from the suspense of the plot.

752. Murdoch, Derrick. *The Agatha Christie Mystery*. Toronto: Pagurian Press, 1976. 192pp.

Observes that critics were unable to understand the reason for Christie's continuous popularity. Murdoch states that one of the most important reasons was her non-literary quality, a "low-brow" approach which appealed to her readers.

753. "Obituary: Dame Agatha Christie, A Subtle Narrative Gift." *London Times* 13 January 1976, p. 16.

Observes that although Christie was not a particularly good writer, her skillful use of narrative and characterization made her stories immensely readable.

*   Palmer, Jerry. *Thrillers* (item 56), pp. 96-98.

Argues that the red herrings in *Death on the Nile* introduce "irrelevancies" that deviate from the plot thus taking the reader away from the area of "central concern."

*   Panek, LeRoy. "Agatha Christie." *Watteau's Shepherds* (item 57), pp. 38-63.

Maintains that Christie has no literary style, that her characters are superficial, and that there is "hardly any scene setting or atmosphere" in her books. Speculates that her popularity is largely due to the "idiosyncratic character" of her detective, Hercule Poirot, and her swiftly paced plots. Analyzes some of her more important novels to illustrate these contentions.

*   Peters, Margot, and Agate Nesaule Krouse. "Women and Crime: Sexism in Allingham, Sayers, and Christie." (item 53).

Argues that Christie developed her characters with a prejudice against women. States that this sexism is apparent in the depiction of Christie's two detectives: Poirot is a mentally superior, rational male, but Miss Marple is only successful due to her intuition and nosiness.

754. Ramsey, G.C. *Agatha Christie, Mistress of Mystery*. New
      York: Dodd, Mead, 1967. 124pp.

      This biography of Christie traces the development of
      her novels. Ramsey observes that the primary reason for
      the novels' success is the use of a well-made plot that
      explains every detail by the final chapter.

755. Riley, Dick, and Pam McAllister, eds. *The Bedside, Bath-
      tub and Armchair Companion to Agatha Christie*. New
      York: Frederick Ungar, 1979. 330pp.

      This book consists of synopses of most of Christie's
      works (without the solutions) alternating with over
      thirty short articles on such subjects as the various
      methods of murder in her books, English wardrobe customs,
      and the making of the film of *Witness for the Prosecution*.

756. Robyns, Gwen. *The Mystery of Agatha Christie*. Garden City,
      N.Y.: Doubleday, 1978. 247pp.

      Although this biography concentrates more on the
      "enigma" of Christie herself, it mentions each of her
      novels and plays and devotes a whole chapter to the
      writing of *The Murder of Roger Ackroyd* and its success.

*   Routley, Erik. *The Puritan Pleasures of the Detective
      Story* (item 64), pp. 129-137.

      Maintains that the secret of Christie's success is
      that "she writes to amuse, not to involve" and that "she
      made the detective story an institution." Quotes an ex-
      tended section from *The Pale Horse* (1961) that shows
      her "methods of working and ... the limitations of which
      she is conscious."

757. Symons, Julian. "All Aboard with Poirot." *Times Literary
      Supplement* 6 December 1974, pp. 1367-1368.

      Observes that Christie offers her readers an "extra-
      ordinary ingenuity" of plot construction that no other
      mystery writer can approach. States that although she
      normally needs room to develop her deceptions, her short
      stories also have a "remarkable adroitness."

758. Symons, Julian. "Christie Mystery." *New York Review of
      Books* 25 (21 December 1978): 37-39.

      States that Christie's novels are set in a fairy tale
      world based upon the manners and morals of her Edwardian
      childhood.

759. Symons, Julian. "The Mistress of Complication." *Agatha Christie: First Lady of Crime* (item 743), pp. 25-38.

In this study of Christie's plotting Symons states that "it is as a constructor of plots that she stands supreme among modern crime writers" and adds that most of her plots are based upon a fairly simple situation that is then elaborated upon.

* Symons, Julian. *Mortal Consequences* (item 74), pp. 98-99, 106-107.

States that Christie's novels began the trend of the "puzzle" mysteries, in which the characters' fates become of secondary importance to the plot.

* Thomson, H. Douglas. "The Orthodox Detective Story." *Masters of Mystery* (item 77), pp. 193-211.

Maintains that *The Murder of Roger Ackroyd* is Christie's masterpiece and "one of the best half-dozen detective stories ever written." Also contends that Christie "is in many respects a paragon of orthodoxy," believing "in a clean, slick murder and plenty of swift, exciting, low-brow action."

760. Ulam, Adam. "Murder and Class." *New Republic* 175 (31 July 1976): 21-23.

Contends that Christie deserves praise for "the ingenuity of her plots and the high literary merit of her writing."

761. Vinson, James. *Contemporary Dramatists*. New York: St. Martin's Press, 1973, pp. 150-155.

Observes that even at her worst Christie excels at telling a story and that often a surprise ending saves her weaker novels.

762. Watson, Colin. "The Message of Mayhem Parva." *Agatha Christie: First Lady of Crime* (item 743), pp. 95-110.

States that Christie's novels were popular because they were written as pure entertainment that would allow the reader to escape his own problems. "There would exist for these people none of the sordid and intractable problems of the real world."

* Watson, Colin. *Snobbery with Violence* (item 78), pp. 165-175.

Argues that Christie's novels were popular because they offered relaxation and diversion, "an area of immense contentedness," rather than shock, violence, or reality.

763. Weaver, William. "Music and Mystery." *Times Literary Supplement* 22 April 1977, p. 493.

Weaver argues that "in general, the arts do not come off well" in Christie's novels. Music, of which she was known to be fond, occupies a minor role in her stories, mostly in the form of nursery rhymes, old songs, and opera. Weaver catalogs passing references to music and musicians in the Christie canon.

764. Wynne, Nancy Blue. *An Agatha Christie Chronology*. New York: Ace Books, 1976. 266pp.

Consists of short (one- to three-page) discussions of each novel by Christie as well as listings of her short stories.

CLARK, ALFRED ALEXANDER GORDON. See CYRIL HARE

CLAYTON, RICHARD HENRY MICHAEL. See WILLIAM HAGGARD

CLEMENS, NANCY. See VANCE RANDOLPH

CLEMENS, SAMUEL LANGHORNE. See MARK TWAIN

COE, TUCKER. See DONALD E. WESTLAKE

COLE, G.D.H. (1889-1959), and MARGARET COLE (1893-   )

765. Barzun, Jacques, and Wendell Hertig Taylor. Preface to *The Murder at Crome House*, by G.D.H. Cole and Margaret Cole. New York: Garland Publishing, 1976. Also printed in *A Book of Prefaces* (item 22), pp. 35-36.

Contends that the novel is an excellent example of the traditional lengthy detective story "as it was done in the 1920's" because of its careful craftsmanship in constructing the plot and maintaining interest right to the end.

766. Cole, G.D.H., and Margaret Cole. "Meet Superintendent
    Wilson." *Meet the Detective* (item 45), pp. 116-128.

    The authors contend that Wilson is intended to be the
    kind of detective with whom the reader can identify and
    not a superman who knows everything.

COLLINS, MAX

767. Randisi, Robert J. "An Interview with Max Collins."
    Armchair Detective 11 (July 1978): 300-304.

    In this interview Collins briefly discusses most of
    his novels and his working methods.

COLLINS, WILKIE (1824-1889)

768. Anderson, Patrick. "Detective Story." *Spectator* 217
    (23 December 1966): 820.

    Observes that the "technical primitiveness" in *The
    Moonstone* allows greater interest and participation for
    the reader. Characters each relate part of the narrative,
    thus adding to reality.

769. Ashley, Robert. *Wilkie Collins*. London: Arthur Barker,
    1952. 144pp.

    States that Collins did not intend to write detective
    fiction; rather, he was merely writing mid-Victorian
    melodramas and happened to use devices (such as personal
    narrative and mysterious atmosphere) which have become
    standard in detective stories.

770. Ashley, Robert. "Wilkie Collins and a Vermont Murder
    Trial." *New England Quarterly* 21 (September 1948):
    368-373.

    Observes that Collins based many of his plots on actual
    crimes and trials. Traces the influence of an American
    murder trial on Collins's novelette, *The Dead Alive*.

771. Ashley, Robert. "Wilkie Collins and the Detective Story."
    Nineteenth-Century Fiction 6 (June 1951): 47-60.

    Observes that although *The Moonstone* is acknowledged
    as the first full-length detective novel, Collins made
    other significant contributions that separate the mystery
    story from the detective story.

772.   Ashley, Robert. "Wilkie Collins Reconsidered." *Nineteenth-Century Fiction* 4 (March 1950): 265-273.

        Maintains that jealous supporters of Dickens critically attacked Collins and thus contributed to the decline of his popularity and critical stature in the early twentieth century.

773.   Booth, Bradford A. "Wilkie Collins and the Art of Fiction." *Nineteenth-Century Fiction* 6 (September 1951): 131-143.

        Observes that Collins's revival of popularity is based on the fact that he was a good storyteller. He provided "escape fiction," and that, Booth states, is the primary function of a novelist.

774.   Brightman, William L. "A Study of *The Woman in White*." Ph.D. dissertation, University of Washington, 1974.

        Maintains that in *The Woman in White* Collins "skillfully works and re-works his conventional devices"--"passive hero," "innocent victim," "pale heroine"--until he creates a new and illuminating drama "that can be contrasted with the Gothic tradition from which it evolves." Concludes that the novel is an outstanding example of "Victorian Gothic melodrama."

*   Cawelti, John G. *Adventure, Mystery, and Romance* (item 150), pp. 134-135.

        Observes that Collins assures the reader that the hero will be proven innocent, thus allowing the reader to concentrate on the "pleasures of detection and mystification" without spending emotional energy worrying about the hero's fate.

775.   Davis, Nuel Pharr. *The Life of Wilkie Collins*. Urbana: University of Illinois Press, 1956. 360pp.

        Maintains that Collins took a "grim pleasure in exploring crime as the unrecognized chink in society's armor" and that his novels often seemed calculated to shock his readers.

776.   de la Mare, Walter. "The Early Novels of Wilkie Collins." *The Eighteen-Sixties: Essays by Fellows of the Royal Society of Literature*. Edited by John Drinkwater. Cambridge: Cambridge University Press, 1932, pp. 51-101.

        Observes that little is known critically or personally about Collins. Attributes this to two reasons: first, his close friendship with Dickens meant that Collins was usually overshadowed by his friend; second, Collins used very little self-portraiture in his early novels.

777. Delmar, Paul J. "The Sensation Fiction of Wilkie Collins." Ph.D. dissertation, University of Illinois at Urbana-Champaign, 1978.

Contends that both the villains and the heroes in Collins's major novels are "split" figures, "composed of diametrically opposite traits."

778. Eliot, T.S. "Wilkie Collins and Dickens." *Times Literary Supplement* 4 August 1927, pp. 525-526. Reprinted as Introduction to *The Moonstone*, by Wilkie Collins. London: Oxford University Press, 1928, pp. v-xii. Also reprinted *Selected Essays*. New York: Harcourt, Brace, 1950, pp. 409-418. Also reprinted *The Victorian Novel: Modern Essays in Criticism*. Edited by Ian Watt. New York: Oxford University Press, 1971, pp. 133-141.

States that although Poe was an enormous influence on mystery writers, contemporary English detective literature is influenced by Collins. In fact, most of the English detective heroes (including to some extent, Sherlock Holmes) are fallible, like Sergeant Cuff in *The Moonstone*.

779. Ellis, Stewart Marsh. *Wilkie Collins, Le Fanu and Others*. London: Constable, 1931, pp. 1-53.

Observes that Collins's mysteries are heightened by superb atmosphere; states that Collins became a "theatrical scene-painter of literature."

780. Elwin, Malcolm. "Wilkie Collins: The Pioneer of the Thriller." *London Mercury* 23 (April 1931): 574-584. Slightly expanded version printed in *Victorian Wallflowers: A Panoramic Survey of the Popular Literary Periodicals*. Port Washington, N.Y.: Kennikat Press, 1966, pp. 203-227.

Maintains that although Collins was a writer of great originality and popularity, his critical reputation has suffered from indiscriminate comparison with his friend, Charles Dickens. Points out some of Collins's contributions to detective literature.

781. Gerould, Gordon Hall. *Patterns of English and American Fiction*. Boston: Little, 1942, pp. 397-399.

    States that Collins gave the writing of romantic fiction
a new direction with the use of contemporary scenes,
realistic behavior of characters, and by withholding as
many explanations as possible. Collins perfected a formula
for escapist fiction that provided excitement plus
appeal to the intellect.

782. Gregory, E.R. "Murder in Fact." *New Republic* 179 (22
      July 1978): 33-34.

    Observes that anyone interested in "good technique in
detective fiction" should read Collins's major novels.
Singles out *The Moonstone* as his greatest achievement
and the most technically brilliant of his novels. Gives
several examples to illustrate his argument.

783. Hardy, Thomas J. "The Romance of Crime." *Books on the
      Shelf*. London: Philip Allan, 1934, pp. 222-226.

    Maintains that Collins is supreme in melodrama "for
the balance he maintains between character and plot and
the sheer human interest of his people."

*   Haycraft, Howard. *Murder for Pleasure* (item 36), pp.
      36-42.

    Contends that *The Moonstone*, technically speaking,
is not a detective novel but falls "between the romance
of incident and the novel of character." Collins used
"detection as a central theme" but "stopped just short
of creating a really new form."

784. Heldman, James M., Jr. "Wilkie Collins and the Sensation
      Novel." Ph.D. dissertation, University of North Carolina,
      1967.

    The content of Collins's novels has two basic charac-
teristics: "it is unusual" and "it is grounded in veri-
fiable evidence." They are either mystery novels or
"novels of intrigue." The mystery novels "concern the
gradual relaxation of information about the past." Also
contends that Collins "made significant contributions
to both the critical basis and the writing of the sensation novel."

*   Hutter, Albert D. "Dreams, Transformations, and Litera-
      ture: The Implications of Detective Fiction" (item
      299).

Argues that detective fiction is closely related to
the psychoanalytic process since both are derived from
"common cultural sources and conflict and both express
similar underlying assumptions." Analyzes *The Moonstone*
to illustrate the implications of dream theories on
literary criticism.

785. Hyder, Clyde K. "Wilkie Collins and *The Woman in White*."
      PMLA 54 (March 1939): 297-303.

Maintains that a French criminal case was not only the
source of inspiration for *The Woman in White* but also
influenced its narrative, in which each character relates
only what he knows, much as a witness does in court.

786. Knoepflmacher, U.C. "The Counterworld of Victorian
      Fiction and *The Woman in White*." *The Worlds of Victorian
      Fiction*. Edited by Jerome H. Buckley. Cambridge, Mass.:
      Harvard University Press, 1975, pp. 353, 360-369.

States that *The Woman in White* is a unique instance of
a Victorian author openly describing an attractive
"asocial counterworld" that was opposed to a civilized
world of order and conventional beliefs.

*   Lambert, Gavin. "Enemy Country: Wilkie Collins." *The
      Dangerous Edge* (item 42), pp. 1-30.

Observes that Collins was the first author to place
emphasis not on "what happens" but on "what happens
next," thus mastering the art of logical shock.

787. Lang, Andrew. "Mr. Wilkie Collins's Novels." *Contemporary
      Review* (London) 57 (January 1890): 20-28.

States that Collins's greatest literary achievement
was the narration of the mystery by various characters,
thus allowing the reader to view the "same set of circumstances through different eyes."

788. Lawson, Lewis A. "Wilkie Collins and *The Moonstone*."
      American Imago 20 (Spring 1963): 61-79.

Observes that Collins was daring in his treatment of
sex in the Victorian novel by insinuating that women,
through their dreams, have sexual impulses.

789. Lonoff, Sue. *Wilkie Collins and His Victorian Readers*.
      New York: AMS Press, 1980.

Published too late for annotation, but according to the publisher the book argues that Collins had an interest in technique, structure, and language that went beyond Victorian elements.

790. Lonoff, Sue. "Wilkie Collins and His Victorian Readers: A Study in the Rhetoric of Authorship." Ph.D. dissertation, City University of New York, 1978.

Contends that Collins's desire to appeal to a "middlebrow, middle-class" public affected every aspect of his fiction but did not prevent him from challenging or even shocking his readers.

791. McCleary, G.F. "A Victorian Classic." *Fortnightly* 160 (August 1946): 137-141. Reprinted as "A Victorian Masterpiece: *The Moonstone.*" *On Detective Fiction and Other Things.* London: Hollis and Carter, 1960, pp. 19-25.

Many critics consider *The Moonstone* to be the finest detective novel ever written. McCleary argues that the chief virtue of the book is its characterization, and that its detective "is probably the most life-like sleuth in the whole of mystery fiction."

792. Marshall, William H. *Wilkie Collins.* New York: Twayne, 1970. 159pp.

Observes that Collins was successful when writing about the Victorian world he knew but failed in his attempt to become "relevant" with his heavy-handed social reform novels.

793. Milley, Henry James Wye. "*The Eustace Diamonds* and *The Moonstone.*" *Studies in Philology* 36 (October 1939): 651-663.

Compares *The Moonstone* and Trollope's *The Eustace Diamonds* and concludes that the similarity of plot, characters, and narrative style was not accidental; Trollope was satirizing Collins's methods and was ridiculing methods of literary deduction.

794. Milne, A.A. "Books and Writers." *Spectator* 86 (6 April 1951): 452.

Argues that the greatest mystery of *The Moonstone* is the necessity for the detective, Sergeant Cuff, who fails to detect anything.

*   Murch, A.E. *The Development of the Detective Novel* (item
        51), pp. 102-114.

        States that Collins was the first author to use the
        "fair-play convention" and "gave new literary dignity
        to the detective novel."

795.   "Old-Time Thrillers." *Literary Digest* 45 (17 August
        1912): 262-263.

        Maintains that Collins and M.E. Braddon founded the
        English school of sensational novels and thus "revived
        the mysterious and sensational element in fiction."

*   Ousby, Ian. *Bloodhounds of Heaven* (item 55), pp. 117-128.

        States that with *The Moonstone* Collins abandoned the
        popular device of multiple plotting and concentrated on
        a single event, the theft of a diamond. Thus, for the
        first time in English literature, the reader finds that
        all the details in the narrative contribute directly to
        the final solution of the mystery.

*   Palmer, Jerry. *Thrillers* (item 56), pp. 112-114.

        States that Collins considered the theme of detection
        subordinate to the interplay of characters. Points out
        that Collins's narrative structure was based on legal
        proceedings and the characters who related the tale
        were like a series of witnesses.

796.   Pritchett, V.S. "The Roots of Detection." *Books in
        General*. New York: Harcourt, 1953, pp. 179-184.

        Argues that *The Moonstone* was the first and last of
        the great detective novels since Collins's style of
        writing was free of symbolism and double meanings,
        allowing the mystery to remain "pure."

797.   Reed, John R. "English Imperialism and the Unacknowledged
        Crime of *The Moonstone*." *Clio* 2 (June 1973): 281-290.

        Argues that *The Moonstone* is both a classic detective
        tale and "a novel of serious social criticism." The
        main "representatives of ordinary society are not
        favorably presented," and Sergeant Cuff apparently demon-
        strates Collins's idea that society's means "for the
        detection of crime is miserably ineffective." Reed con-
        cludes that "it is a national not a personal guilt that
        is in question in this novel."

798. "Review of *The Moonstone.*" *Athenaeum* 25 July 1868.
      Reprinted *The Art of the Mystery Story* (item 35), pp.
      379-380.

      This contemporary review selected by Howard Haycraft
      commends "the carefully elaborate workmanship, and the
      wonderful construction of the story." States that the
      beautiful epilogue "redeems that somewhat sordid detec-
      tive element."

799. Richardson, Maurice. Introduction to *Novels of Mystery
      from the Victorian Age*. Edited by Maurice Richardson
      and U.C. Knoepflmacher. London: Pilot Press, 1945,
      pp. vii-xvi.

      After commenting on Collins's reputation and literary
      career, focuses on *The Woman in White*, contending that
      in this novel Collins "writes at the top of his form,
      weaving his tortuous, melodramatic plot" with a light
      touch and creating "live, idiosyncratic characters" and
      "excruciatingly sustained suspense."

800. Robinson, Kenneth. *Wilkie Collins: A Biography*. Westport,
      Conn.: Greenwood Press, 1972. 348pp.

      States that Collins elevated the sensation novel to
      the level of serious fiction by removing its "gothic
      trappings" and relating it to the everyday Victorian
      world, thereby making it more credible and more fearful.

801. Rycroft, Charles. "The Analysis of a Detective Story."
      *Imagination and Reality: Psycho-Analytical Essays,
      1951-1961*. London: Hogarth Press and the Institute of
      Psycho-Analysis, 1968, pp. 114-128.

      This psychoanalytical interpretation of *The Moonstone*
      is based upon three assumptions about Collins: he was
      unconsciously compelled "to give symbolic expression"
      to the primal scene in his writings; he used such defenses
      as idealization to overcome anxiety; and "he was pre-
      occupied with virginity." Rycroft contends that the crime
      in *The Moonstone* "obviously represents a sexual inter-
      course" but does not necessarily justify the assumption
      "that the intercourse in question is the primal scene."
      This interpretation confirms part of Pedersen-Krag's
      hypothesis in "Detective Stories and the Primal Scene"
      (item 399)--that the popularity of detective stories
      is due to "their ability to reawaken the interest and
      curiosity originally aroused by observation of the primal
      scene."

802. Sayers, Dorothy L. Introduction to *The Moonstone*, by
Wilkie Collins. London: J.M. Dent, 1944, pp. v-xi.

Argues that Collins set a standard seldom equalled in
the next seventy years of the development of the genre.
He followed the "fair play" rule long before it was for-
mulated, and his "medical, legal, and police details"
are all exact. Sayers also praises Collins's treatment
of women as "human individuals in their own right" and
states that, though his style is "sober and pedestrian,"
he has "the power to invent a spacious world populated
with interesting and entertaining people."

803. Starrett, Vincent. Introduction to *The Moonstone*, by
Wilkie Collins. New York: Heritage Press, 1959, pp.
vii-xvi.

Observes that *The Moonstone* is "the first and longest
English detective novel" and that in it Collins "antici-
pated ... much that is now familiar to detective story
readers."

804. Starrett, Vincent. Introduction to *The Woman in White*,
by Wilkie Collins. New York: Heritage Press, 1964,
pp. v-xii.

Observes that "Collins' gift for creating atmosphere
is as important as his unusual plots" and that his "use
of atmosphere, of pictorial suggestion, is outstanding
in *The Woman in White*."

805. Sucksmith, Harvey Peter. Introduction to *The Woman in
White*, by Wilkie Collins. New York: Oxford University
Press, 1975, pp. vii-xxii.

Maintains that *The Woman in White* "as a total achievement is ... the greatest melodrama ever written" and
that it is not just an excellent mystery, "it is also a
novel of a very high order which chooses the world of
crime and mystery as its legitimate domain."

806. Swinburne, Algernon Charles. "Wilkie Collins." *Fortnightly
Review* 52 (1 November 1889): 589-599. Reprinted *The
Complete Works of Algernon Charles Swinburne*, Volume
15. Edited by Edmund Gosse and Thomas James Wise. New
York: Gabriel Wells, 1926, pp. 289-306.

States that Collins sacrificed his characters for the
ingenuity of his intricate plots.

807.   Symons, Julian. Introduction to *The Woman in White*, by
       Wilkie Collins. Harmondsworth, England: Penguin Books,
       1974, pp. 7-21.

       Observes that "the book is full of memorable characters"
       skillfully introduced. Equally expert is Collins's varia-
       tions of tone and style for the different narrators that
       enable him to maintain suspense throughout.

*   Symons, Julian. *Mortal Consequences* (item 74), pp. 43-
       46, 49-50.

       Argues that Collins has been unfairly criticized for
       being a writer of melodramas; points out that the differ-
       ences between Victorian mysteries and modern detective
       stories reflect changes in the nature and perceptions
       of society, not a lack of individual talent.

808.   Tillotson, Geoffrey. "Wilkie Collins's *No Name*." *Criticism
       and the Nineteenth-Century*. New York: Barnes and Noble,
       1951, pp. 231-243.

       Points out that *No Name* exhibits many characteristics
       of the "thriller," such as the interplay of "two sorts
       of detail, the accidental and the willed" and that plot,
       more than in-depth characterization, is its strength.

809.   Wagenknecht, Edward Charles. *Cavalcade of the English
       Novel*. New York: Holt, 1954, pp. 236-243.

       States that the real reason for the success of Collins's
       novels is his gift for creating an atmosphere of "thrills
       and chills," accomplished by withholding facts from the
       readers, who used their own imaginations to fill in the
       mental images.

810.   Waugh, Arthur. "Wilkie Collins and His Mantle." *Living
       Age* 233 (31 May 1902): 566-569.

       Maintains that although Conan Doyle is the best of
       Wilkie Collins's successors, Collins is still preeminent.
       Cites specific scenes to explain his preference for *The
       Moonstone* over *The Hound of the Baskervilles*.

811.   "Wilkie Collins, the Romanticist of Science." *Review of
       Reviews* 46 (August 1912): 232-234.

       States that Collins's greatest literary achievement
       was the subtle use of dramatic effect; he would excite
       the reader not by what he wrote, but by what he did not
       write, thus forcing the reader to fill in details with
       his own imagination.

812. Wolfe, Peter. "Point of View and Characterization in Wilkie Collins's *The Moonstone.*" *Forum* 4 (Summer 1965): 27-29.

Calls *The Moonstone* Collins's "most typical" and most technically interesting novel and points out as its three chief virtues the expert manipulation of the characters of Sergeant Cuff and Rachel Verinder, the control of the plot to maintain suspense, and the "admirable construction" of the novel as a whole.

CONAN DOYLE, ARTHUR. See DOYLE, ARTHUR CONAN

CONRAD, JOSEPH (1857-1924)

813. Baird, Newton. "Conrad's Probe to Absolute Zero." *Armchair Detective* 9 (November 1975): 43-49.

Argues that Conrad's *The Secret Agent* is somewhat like the later spy thriller except for its "intricate structure and levels of meaning."

814. Walton, James. "Conrad, Dickens, and the Detective Novel." *Nineteenth-Century Fiction* 23 (March 1969): 446-462.

Walton treats the influence of Dickens on Conrad's *The Secret Agent*, one portion of which is the use of the detective motif "to implement a comprehensive and intricate social satire."

CORNWELL, DAVID JOHN MOORE. See JOHN Le CARRÉ

COX, ANTHONY BERKELEY. See ANTHONY BERKELEY

COXE, GEORGE HARMON (1901-   )

815. Cox, J. Randolph. "Myster Master: A Survey and Appreciation of the Fiction of George Harmon Coxe." *Armchair Detective* 6 (February 1973): 63-74; 6 (May 1973): 160-166; 6 (August 1973): 232-241; 7 (1973): 11-24.

States that Coxe "writes of people caught up in webs of their own spinning, their stories told in a deceptively formal style." Surveys his work and concludes with a chronological list of his writings.

816. Coxe, George Harmon. "Flash Casey." *The Great Detectives*
      (item 60), pp. 37-46.

      Coxe points out that his detective, Flash Casey, was
      a press photographer who usually became involved in
      violence because of some personal reason--usually inter-
      ference with him or his equipment. He adds that the
      character was based on many people he met as a reporter.

CREASEY, JOHN (1908-1973). Principal mystery pseudonyms:
   Gordon Ashe, Robert Caine Frazer, Norman Deane, Michael
   Halliday, Kyle Hunt, J.J. Marric, Anthony Morton, Jeremy
   York

817. Boyles, John. "A Word for John Creasey: J.J. Marric's
      Gideon's Risk." *Armchair Detective* 11 (Summer 1978):
      282-283.

      Contends the Marric books are the best series that
      Creasey has ever done. Creasey develops with considerable
      skill a series that follows the investigation of crimes
      from the point of view of the police, using strong
      characterizations and competently linked subplots.

818. Brean, Herbert. "Man of More Than 400 Mysteries." *Life*
      52 (27 April 1962): 21-22.

      States that Creasey's output has surpassed that of
      Edgar Wallace and Georges Simenon. Observes that Creasey's
      quality is higher in those works written under the
      pseudonyms J.J. Marric and Gordon Ashe.

819. Creasey, John. "John Creasey--Fact or Fiction? A Candid
      Commentary in Third Person." *Armchair Detective* 2
      (October 1968): 1-5.

      Creasey describes his early life and way of working
      and makes a few comments on his own work such as, "His
      mammoth total ... proves also an impressive testament
      to his penetrating observation and understanding of
      human nature."

820. "Flow." *New Yorker* 36 (16 July 1960): 25-26.

      Contends the quality of Creasey's writing is not equal
      to that of Georges Simenon. Based on a short interview
      with Creasey, the article also states that Creasey's
      main object is quantity (ten to fifteen books a year),
      but "he is determined never to let his work fall below
      a certain level of workaday competence."

821. Harvey, Deryck. "The Best of John Creasey." *Armchair Detective* 7 (1973): 42-43.

Surveys a few highlights among Creasey's more than 560 books.

CRISPIN, EDMUND. Pseudonym of Robert Bruce Montgomery (1921-1978)

822. Barzun, Jacques. "In Memorium: Edmund Crispin, 1921-1978." *Armchair Detective* 12 (Winter 1979): 13.

Argues that Crispin's writing ability never allowed him to write "an unreadable sentence" and that he could never be dull.

823. Barzun, Jacques, and Wendell Hertig Taylor. Preface to *Buried for Pleasure*, by Edmund Crispin. New York: Garland Publishing, 1976. Also printed in *A Book of Prefaces* (item 22), pp. 37-38.

Singles out this novel as an excellent example of a book that has "so managed the classic elements of the crime tale as to make it serve the purposes of satirical comedy."

824. Critchley, Julian. "Fen's Creator." *Illustrated London News* Christmas Issue 1979, p. 47.

Points out that Crispin's books should not be taken seriously as realistic crime stories.

825. Montgomery, Robert Bruce. "Edmund Crispin." *Armchair Detective* 12 (Spring 1979): 183-185.

An autobiographical sketch written by Crispin for his publishing company under his real name, Robert Bruce Montgomery, in which he observes he does not particularly like spy stories or the "so-called 'realistic' type of crime story." Maintains that "crime stories in general and detective stories in particular should be essentially imaginative and artificial in order to make their best effect."

*   Routley, Erik. *The Puritan Pleasures of the Detective Story* (item 64), pp. 162-164.

Observes that Crispin has a similar style and "bent" to Michael Innes but that no detective writer is "so

boldly topical as Crispin in introducing ... real places
and real people."

CROFTS, FREEMAN WILLS (1879-1957)

826.   Barzun, Jacques, and Wendell Hertig Taylor. Preface to
       The Box Office Murder, by Freeman Wills Crofts. New
       York: Garland Publishing, 1976. Also printed in *A Book
       of Prefaces* (item 22), pp. 39-40.

       Observes that Croft's novels are "distinguished by
       intricate but sound plot construction."

827.   Crofts, Freeman Wills. "Meet Chief-Inspector French."
       Meet the Detective (item 45), pp. 80-89.

       States that he decided to make French an ordinary
       personality because there were already many brilliant
       eccentric detectives and because "striking characteristics,
       consistently depicted, are very hard to do."

*   Haycraft, Howard. *Murder for Pleasure* (item 36), pp.
       122-124.

       States that Crofts was the first to use the idea of
       step-by-step methods of police procedures in his mystery
       stories.

828.   Keddie, James, Jr. "Freeman Wills Crofts." *Armchair
       Detective* 2 (April 1969): 137-142.

       States that Crofts was one of the "pure detective fic-
       tion writers," and his work "is a great monument to
       wonderful writing." Includes a checklist of his writing.

*   Routley, Erik. *The Puritan Pleasures of the Detective
       Story* (item 64), pp. 124-127.

       Maintains that Crofts created "the first great police-
       man" in detective fiction, Inspector French, who succeeds
       "by plain puritan hard work."

*   Thomson, H. Douglas. "The Realistic Detective Story: Mr.
       Freeman Wills Crofts." *Masters of Mystery* (item 77),
       pp. 176-192.

       Contends that the two greatest writing assets of
       Crofts are his use of the unbreakable alibi and his
       precise narrative, but these are sometimes overshadowed

by his two weaknesses, the use of clichés in dialog and meticulous details in narrative.

CULVER, TIMOTHY J. See DONALD E. WESTLAKE

CURTISS, URSULA (1923-)

829. Waldron, Ann. "An Interview with Ursula Curtiss." *Armchair Detective* 4 (April 1971): 140-144.

In a wide-ranging interview, Curtiss explains why she began writing fiction and her method of plotting.

DALLAS, JOHN. See W. MURDOCH DUNCAN

DALY, CARROLL JOHN (1889-1958). Series character: Race Williams

830. Crider, Allen B. "Race Williams--Private Investigator." *Dimensions of Detective Fiction* (item 43), pp. 110-113.

Points out that virtually all the elements of the hard-boiled detective story are present in the work of Daly, although his style, pacing, and characterization are extremely poor.

831. Durham, Philip. "The *Black Mask* School." *The Mystery Writer's Art* (item 54), pp. 198-205.

Argues that Daly "was a careless writer and a muddy thinker who created the hard-boiled detective, the prototype for numberless writers," in Race Williams.

832. Nolan, William F. "Carroll John Daly: The Forgotten Pioneer of the Private Eye." *Armchair Detective* 4 (October 1970): 1-4.

Daly's private detective, Race Williams--who first appeared in *Black Mask* in 1922--is often credited as being the first of the hard-boiled private eyes, but Daly's awkward, repetitious writing style, and his inability to create three-dimensional characters, limited his popularity and quickly dated him.

DALY, ELIZABETH (1879-1967)

833. Waldron, Ann. "The Golden Years of Elizabeth Daly."
      Armchair Detective 7 (1973): 25-28.

      Contends that her detective "is surely the most urbane
      and charming--and the most unassuming." Quotes Daly as
      saying she tried always to "be literate, not literary."

DANIEL, ROLAND (1880-1969)

834. Lofts, W.O.G. "Roland Daniel--Prolific Mystery Writer."
      Armchair Detective 6 (August 1973): 242, 245.

      Daniel was a very popular and prolific mystery writer
      who wrote thrillers featuring a Chinese detective, Wu
      Fang, "purely because of his great love of the Far East,
      and especially anything Chinese."

DANNAY, FREDERIC. See ELLERY QUEEN

DAVIOT, GORDON. See JOSEPHINE TEY

DAVIS, GORDON. See E. HOWARD HUNT

DEANE, NORMAN. See JOHN CREASEY

DEBRETT, HAL. See BRETT HALLIDAY

DeFOREST, JOHN WILLIAM (1826-1906)

835. Davidson, James. "J.W. DeForest and His Contemporaries:
      The Birth of American Realism." Ph.D. dissertation,
      New York University, 1962.

      Contends that a theme of realism consistently runs
      through the plot of *The Wetheral Affair*. This theme
      deals with then current current events, politics, and
      how the individual is corrupted.

836. Ford, Philip H. "The Techniques of John William DeForest,
      Transitional Novelist." Ph.D. dissertation, Ohio State
      University, 1959.

States that *The Wetheral Affair* is one of the best examples of DeForest's comedy of manners in which the "comic spirit ranges" constantly over the main action and in which his characters are static individuals with no personalities.

837. Gargano, James W. "John W. DeForest: A Critical Study of His Novels." Ph.D. dissertation, Cornell University, 1955.

Points out how DeForest's critics reacted to the publication of *The Wetheral Affair* and briefly analyzes its main themes, its characters, and its value as a work of literary art.

838. Light, James F. *John William DeForest*. New York: Twayne, 1965, pp. 129-138.

Observes through detailed analysis of DeForest's main characters in *The Wetheral Affair* that he liked to endlessly repeat character oddities throughout his plot, resulting in no character development.

DEIGHTON, LEN (1929-   )

839. Erisman, Fred. "Romantic Reality in the Spy Stories of Len Deighton." *Armchair Detective* 10 (April 1977): 101-105.

States that "the world of Deighton's spy is a fragmented, evanescent one, in which nothing is permanent and little is trustworthy."

840. Fitzgibbon, Constantine. "Len Deighton's Cold New View." *Spectator* 228 (8 April 1972): 546.

Observes that Deighton, in his espionage novels, makes no attempt to change reality into fantasy, as in the James Bond series.

841. Moffett, Hugh. "Hot Spy Writer on the Lam." *Life* 60 (25 March 1966): 84+.

Argues that Deighton "was pioneering a new realism with a fictional documentary approach." He tries to bring the tragic element of espionage to his novels.

DE LA TORRE, LILLIAN (1902-   )

842.   De La Torre, Lillian. "The Pleasures of Histo-Detection."
       Armchair Detective 7 (May 1974): 155-162.

       Describes her method of writing what she terms "histo-
       detection" novels (solving mysteries in history): all
       are written in classic detective story form—first the
       puzzle, then the evidence, and then the solution. Histo-
       detection differs from a detective novel in that it is
       real: it is all based on historical sources—the conversa-
       tions, the acts, the evidence, and the real answer. Used
       Dr. Samuel Johnson and Boswell as her detectives.

843.   Hoch, Edward. "A Mirror to Our Crimes." *Armchair Detec-
       tive* 12 (Summer 1979): 282-283.

       Observes that De La Torre can produce popular mystery
       stories without the lure of a sensational murder.

844.   Wallace, Frances J. "Lillian De La Torre." *Wilson Library
       Bulletin* 23 (January 1949): 350.

       States that De La Torre's "rational temper" led her
       to combine literary research on the eighteenth century
       with mystery fiction.

DENNIS, RALPH

845.   Finch, G.A. "Have You Met Hardman?" *Armchair Detective*
       8 (August 1975): 275, 270 [*sic*].

       Observes that Dennis's detective fiction is "natural-
       istic" (relying on "exact pieces of information") and
       that his detective, Hardman, is not a member of the "totall
       invincible school" of detective heroes.

846.   Garner, Phil. "Mind If I Kill You Off in Chapter Three?"
       Atlanta Journal and Constitution 30 June 1974. Reprinted
       Authors in the News, Volume 1. Edited by Barbara
       Nykoruk. Detroit: Gale Research, 1976, pp. 130-131.

       Points out that all of Dennis's novels featuring his
       detective, Hardman, have Atlanta, Georgia, backgrounds
       that use "real streets and real landmarks." After the
       first book in the series, Dennis began loosely basing
       each of his plots on an actual event.

DENT, LESTER (1905-1959). Pseudonym: Kenneth Robeson, which was also used by Ron Goulart

847. Blosser, Fred. "The Man from Miami: Lester Dent's Oscar Sail." *Armchair Detective* 5 (January 1972): 93.

Florida has become a common setting for tough guy heroes, but Dent's Oscar Sail was one of the first to operate in that state.

848. Farmer, Philip José. *Doc Savage: His Apocalyptic Life.* New York: Doubleday, 1973. 226pp.

Contends that Dent is as good an "apocalyptic" novelist as Henry Miller or William Burroughs and constructs a "biography" of Dent's character Doc Savage.

849. Goulart, Ron. "Doc Savage and His Circle." *Cheap Thrills: An Informal History of the Pulp Magazines.* New Rochelle, N.Y.: Arlington House, 1972, pp. 75-84.

The publisher Street and Smith conceived the idea of the Doc Savage series and assigned Lester Dent to write them (Kenneth Robeson). All his humor is intentional, his openings abrupt, and his style choppy.

DERLETH, AUGUST (1909-1971)

850. Derleth, August. *A Praed Street Dossier.* Sauk City, Wis.: Mycroft and Moran, 1968. 108pp.

In two chapters detailing the creation and background of his character, Solar Pons, Derleth observes that Pons "came into being out of Sherlock Holmes." He also points out that "without exception, the Solar Pons stories have been written around titles. None of the stories was ever conceived without the prior challenge of a title." Also included in the volume are two Solar Pons stories, and chapters on Dr. Parker's background and Derleth's favorite pastiches.

DICKENS, CHARLES (1812-1870)

This bibliography contains more citations on Charles Dickens than on any other author, including Sir Arthur Conan Doyle. Since Dickens is not normally thought of as a mystery/detection writer, a word of explanation may be in order. Two of Dickens's novels--Bleak House and The Mystery of Edwin Drood--*contain elements of mystery/detection. In* Bleak House, *this element is perhaps secondary; in* Edwin Drood, *however, it is at the heart of the novel. Dickens is, of course, a titanic figure in nineteenth-century English literature, and his work, even the secondary aspects of it, has naturally drawn a great deal of critical attention.*

The situation is compounded by the fact that Dickens died before he finished writing Edwin Drood, *leaving that mystery forever unsolved. Scores of dedicated Dickensians have combed the extant portion of the story for clues as to how Dickens would have resolved the novel. Their commentary and speculation comprise a substantial portion of the citations below.*

851. Augburn, Gerald R. "The Function of Death in the Novels of Charles Dickens." Ph.D. dissertation, Columbia University, 1968.

Contends that Dickens's novels depict a struggle for life in a moribund world that threatens its inhabitants with death. *Edwin Drood* is primarily concerned with "a dead world and with the death-in-life existence of its hero, both of which are imaged by the decaying cathedral."

852. Aylmer, Felix. *The Drood Case.* London: R. Hart-Davis, 1964. 218pp.

A close examination of *Edwin Drood*, both as published and in manuscript, as well as Dickens's notebooks. Concludes that Jasper did not murder Drood, although he did inadvertently kill Datchery. Drood escapes to Egypt but returns to absolve Jasper, who reenacts the Datchery killing and then conveniently dies.

853. Aylmer, Felix. "First-Aid for the 'Drood' Audience." *Dickensian* 47 (1950/1951): 133-139.

Contends that Drood escaped safely from his would-be killer. Jasper is innocent of the assault on Drood, and is, in fact, Drood's half-brother.

854. Baker, Richard M. "The Datchery Assumption: Reply." *Nineteenth-Century Fiction* 4 (1949): 77-81.

In response to H.M. MacVicar (item 916), Baker defends his contention that Datchery is Hiram Grewgious in disguise.

855. Baker, Richard M. *The Drood Murder Case: Five Studies
      in Dickens' Edwin Drood.* Berkeley: University of
      California Press, 1951. 195pp.

      Five articles originally published between 1948 and
      1950. They were published in book form at the suggestion
      of Vincent Starrett. Each is annotated separately.

856. Baker, Richard M. "The Genesis of *Edwin Drood.*"
      Trollopian 3 (March 1949): 281-295; *Nineteenth-Century
      Fiction* 4 (June 1949): 37-50. Reprinted *The Drood
      Murder Case* (item 855), pp. 91-119.

      Points out several possible literary influences on
      the plot development of *Edwin Drood*, but concludes that
      more important than these was the "creative genius of
      Charles Dickens."

857. Baker, Richard M. "John Jasper--Murderer." *Trollopian*
      3 (September 1948): 99-118; 3 (December 1948): 177-
      199. Reprinted *The Drood Murder Case* (item 855), pp.
      42-90.

      Contends that "in its psychological implications"
      Dickens's portrayal of John Jasper as a potential mur-
      derer went "far beyond any of a similar nature he had
      previously made." Underlines the character's psychological
      complexity by tracing his actions in the novel.

858. Baker, Richard M. "Was Edwin Drood Murdered?" *Nineteenth-
      Century Fiction* 4 (September 1949): 111-128; 4 (Decem-
      ber 1949): 221-236. Reprinted *The Drood Murder Case*
      (item 855), pp. 120-153.

      Reviews the critical dispute over whether or not
      Edwin Drood survived the attack on his person. Concludes
      that Drood *was* murdered and that John Jasper was the
      culprit.

859. Baker, Richard M. "What Might Have Been: A Study for
      Droodians." *Nineteenth-Century Fiction* 4 (1950): 275-
      297; 5 (1950): 47-65. Reprinted *The Drood Murder Case*
      (item 855), pp. 154-195.

      Reviews the critical theories on how *Edwin Drood* would
      have ended had Dickens lived to finish the novel. Specu-
      lates that Jasper murdered Drood and Landless; that
      Datchery would have solved the mystery; that Jasper would
      have been tried, convicted, and executed; and that Rosa
      would have married Tartar.

860. Baker, Richard M. "Who Was Dick Datchery?" *Nineteenth-Century Fiction* 2 (1948): 201-222; 3 (1948): 35-53. Reprinted *The Drood Murder Case* (item 855), pp. 1-41.

Contends that the key to understanding *Edwin Drood* is the true identity of Dick Datchery. Reviews previous critical speculation on the matter, and concludes that Datchery was Hiram Grewgious in disguise.

861. Bengis, Nathan L. "John Jasper's Devotion." *Armchair Detective* 8 (May 1975): 165-178; 9 (November 1975): 25-40.

Argues that "Edwin Drood escaped and reappeared as Datchery." Includes bibliography and refutation of other critical theories.

862. Bilham, D.M. "*Edwin Drood*--To Resolve a Mystery?" *Dickensian* 62 (1966): 181-183.

Contends that an offhand and overlooked remark by Durdles indicates that Drood was buried in his father's tomb. Princess Puffer is Drood's mother and Jasper's sister. The revelation of her identity, had Dickens lived to finish the novel, would have provided the story's denouement.

863. Blakeney, T.S. "Problems of *Edwin Drood*." *Dickensian* 51 (1954/1955): 182-185.

Attacks Bleifuss's "Re-Examination" (item 864). Drood was killed--otherwise there is little point to the story.

864. Bleifuss, William W. "A Re-Examination of *Edwin Drood*." *Dickensian* 50 (1953/1954): 110-115, 176-186; 51 (1954/1955): 24-29.

Argues that Drood was not murdered, that such a development makes little sense in the context of the rest of the Dickens canon. *Drood* is a study of good and evil in the mainstream of other works by the mature Dickens and attempts to fabricate endings for the novel lose sight of this basic point.

865. Borowitz, Albert I. "The Mystery of Edwin Drood." *Armchair Detective* 10 (January 1977): 14-16, 82.

Surveys the commentaries on *Edwin Drood* and concludes that it "would have been one of Dickens's greatest novels" had it been completed.

866. Borowitz, Albert I. "*The Mystery of Edwin Drood*."
      Innocence and Arsenic: Studies in Crime and Literature.
      New York: Harper and Row, 1977, pp. 53–62.

      Reviews the history of *Drood* criticism, analyzing the
      consensus, where one exists, on the solution to the many
      puzzles in Dickens's unfinished story. Argues that the
      real mystery is not in the fate of Edwin Drood, "but in
      the psychology of Jasper and his eventual confrontation
      of his own misdeed."

867. Bort, Barry D. "A Study of Dickens' Heroes from Oliver
      Twist to John Jasper." Ph.D. dissertation, Brown
      University, 1960.

      Contends that Dickens's heroes developed in complexity
      as his career progressed. In contrast to the early
      novels, in which an innocent hero is thrust into the
      world and put through trials from which he emerges tri-
      umphant, John Jasper in *Edwin Drood* is a protagonist
      "whose desires are constrained by too narrowly defined
      social limitations." Jasper is doomed.

868. Boyd, Aubrey. *A New Angle on the Drood Mystery*. (Washing-
      ton University Studies 9, Humanistic Series No. 1)
      St. Louis: Washington University, 1921.

      Contends that Jasper is a mesmerist, using hypnotism
      on Neville Landless, Drood, and Rosa. In writing *Drood*,
      Dickens was influenced more by Poe than by Wilkie Collins.

869. Brend, Gavin. "Edwin Drood and the Four Witnesses."
      Dickensian 52 (1955/1956): 20–24.

      John Forster, Sir Luke Fildes, Charles Dickens, Jr.,
      and Charles Collins--Dickens's contemporaries--all claim
      to have been told by Dickens that Drood had been mur-
      dered. Brend argues that their testimony is inconsistent
      and unreliable. Contends that Dickens would have resur-
      rected Drood had he lived to complete the novel.

870. Brown, Arthur Washburn. *Sexual Analysis of Dickens's
      Heroes*. New York: Emerson Books, 1971, pp. 92–96.

      In a psychoanalytic approach to Dickens's work, Brown
      contends that John Jasper's split personality induced
      by his drug habit is the key to the resolution of *Edwin
      Drood*. Jasper would ultimately "accuse himself of the
      crime of murdering his nephew."

871. Butt, John. "*Bleak House* in the Context of 1851." *Nine-teenth-Century Fiction* 10 (June 1955): 1-21.

Points out that the focus of the book is a chancery case and that this reflects the interest the public was "taking in chancery that year." The character of Inspector Bucket was probably inspired by Dickens's interest in the recently formed detective branch of the Metropolitan Police force.

872. Caldwell, Margaret. Introduction to *The Mystery of Edwin Drood*, by Charles Dickens. Oxford: Clarendon Press, 1972, pp. xii-1.

Detailed analysis of the process by which Dickens wrote and published *Edwin Drood*, as well as its subsequent publishing history.

873. Carolan, Katherine. "Dickens' Last Christmases." *Dalhousie Review* 52 (1972): 373-383.

Contends that Dickens's use of Christmas in *Edwin Drood*--Drood is murdered on Christmas Eve--indicates how disillusioned Dickens had become with "the heartlessness and hypocrisy of Victorian society" in the decades since *A Christmas Carol*.

874. Chesterton, G.K. *Charles Dickens, the Last of the Great Men*. New York: Press of the Readers Club, 1942, pp. 169-172.

Likens *Drood* to the last performance of a master magician. The novel was a departure for Dickens--it represented a concerted attempt to concentrate on the plot of his story.

875. Clipper, Lawrence J. "Crime and Criminals in the Novels of Charles Dickens." Ph.D. dissertation, University of North Carolina, 1963.

Notes the fact that Dickens's treatment of police was generally unsympathetic. Contends that "even Inspector Bucket in *Bleak House* is a less sympathetic portrayal than is generally assumed, since he is the embodiment" of the dehumanizing forces in Victorian society.

876. Cohen, Jane Rabb. "Dickens' Artists and Artistry in *The Mystery of Edwin Drood*." *Dickens Studies* 3 (1967): 126-145.

In *Drood*, "Dickens endows all his characters with artistic gifts which delineate them and prove essential to the plot." Contends that Dickens's own powers parallel those of John Jasper, and that Dickens may have been attempting to achieve a personal catharsis through his art.

877. Collins, Philip. *Dickens and Crime*. Bloomington: Indiana University Press, 1968. 371pp.

In an extended analysis of John Jasper's character, argues that Jasper is obviously the murderer of Edwin Drood. Also notes the similarities between Inspector Bucket of *Bleak House* and the Inspector Field or Wield of the articles in Dickens's *Household Words* magazine.

878. Coolidge, Archibald C., Jr. *Charles Dickens as Serial Novelist*. Ames: Iowa State University, 1967. 256pp.

Examines the serial nature of Dickens's work. Contends that the murder mysteries in *Bleak House, Edwin Drood,* and three other novels "were used to give a kind of general goal to the slowly advancing and unraveling plots" of his novels.

879. Cox, Arthur J. "The *Drood* Remains." *Dickens Studies* 2 (1966): 33-44.

Notes Dickens's editorial revisions in the text of *Drood*. Argues that an examination of the Dickens manuscript indicates that Dickens knew at all times the direction his novel was taking.

880. Cox, Arthur J. "'If I Hide My Watch--.'" *Dickens Studies* 3 (1967): 22-37.

Notes the general critical agreement on the fact that Jasper was a mesmerist. Contends that previous critics have misunderstood Dickens's conception of animal magnetism. Dickens's philosophy owed much to David Hume, who emphasized "sympathy or moral accordance," rather than something grossly mechanical.

881. Cox, Arthur J. "The Morals of *Edwin Drood*." *Dickensian* 58 (1962): 32-42.

Agreeing that Jasper is a member of the Thuggee cult of ritual murderers, contends that Jasper murdered Drood, not "for the sake of any practical object, but to achieve what might be called 'a state of grace.'"

882. Crotch, W. Walter. *The Secret of Dickens*. New York:
      Haskell House, 1972, pp. 211-226.

      Contends that Inspector Bucket was "the fictional
      father of practically all the sleuths of the modern
      novel." Bucket is an intelligent observer who solves
      crimes by the strength of his inductive reasoning.

883. Davis, Earle. *The Flint and the Flame: The Artistry of
      Charles Dickens*. Columbia: University of Missouri
      Press, 1963, pp. 197-214, 283-303.

      Observes that the well-developed mystery in *Bleak
      House* succeeds in weaving together a large number of
      characters, each of whom "represents some part of Dickens'
      diagnosis" of the ills of Victorian England. *Edwin
      Drood* is a shorter work, with the mystery as the end
      rather than as the means. Notes the similarities between
      Drood and *The Moonstone*, by Dickens's friend Wilkie
      Collins, and suggests that these similarities may provide
      the key to the missing portion of Dickens's novel.

884. Duffield, Howard. "John Jasper--Strangler." *Bookman* 71
      (February 1930): 581-588.

      Argues that John Jasper was a member of the Thuggee
      sect, a group of ritual murderers.

885. Dunstan, J. Leslie. "The Ministers in Dickens." *Dickensian*
      56 (1960): 103-113.

      Observes that the Reverend Septimus Crisparkle is
      thoroughly atypical of Dickens's ministers. He is "a
      real man, a serious-minded clergyman, and one thoroughly
      involved in constructive fashion in the affairs of his
      fellow man."

886. Dyson, A.E. "*Bleak House*: Esther Better Not Born?"
      Dickens, Bleak House: A Casebook. Edited by A.E.
      Dyson. London: Macmillan, 1969, pp. 254-259.

      Contends that Inspector Bucket poses ethical problems
      for Dickens. Bucket is deceitful in the service of a
      higher truth, and he takes pleasure from his deceptions
      and from his victims' fear. At bottom, Bucket may be
      like Tulkinghorn.

887. Dyson, A.E. "*Edwin Drood*: A Horrible Wonder Apart."
      Critical Quarterly 11 (1969): 138-157.

Argues that *Edwin Drood*, though superficially a Gothic romance, is actually quite modern. Dickens's portrayal of John Jasper's divided self is prophetic. "His final novel is his most striking picture of the human situation in its starkest relationship to good and evil."

888. Dyson, A.E. *The Inimitable Dickens: A Reading of the Novels*. London: Macmillan, 1970, pp. 154-182, 267-293.

Points out that *Bleak House* "is a tale of detection and crime" in which closer attention must be paid to "Dickens's tone and structure ... as well as to his intentionally transparent hints" than in any other of his novels except *Edwin Drood*. Dyson also contends that the themes of *Edwin Drood* are "people watching and spying; people seeking to dominate and perhaps destroy others [and] devious paths converging for some still unknown end."

889. Everett, Edward S. "The Cloisterham Murder Case." *The Fred Newton Scott Anniversary Papers*. Chicago: University of Chicago Press, 1929, pp. 157-174.

Argues that John Jasper, in an opium-induced fog, murders Bazzard instead of Drood.

890. Ford, George H. "Dickens' Notebook and 'Edwin Drood.'" *Nineteenth-Century Fiction* 6 (1952): 275-280.

Cites parallels between Dickens's notebook and the finished portions of *Edwin Drood* to support his contention that Dickens wrote his last novel incorporating ideas and episodes written down earlier in the notebook.

891. Forster, John. *The Life of Charles Dickens,* Volume 2. London: Dent, 1966, pp. 365-375.

Dickens's biographer and contemporary claims to have been told by Dickens himself how *Edwin Drood* was to end. Jasper murdered Drood and Tartar was to apprehend Jasper and marry Rosa Bud.

892. Franklin, Stephen L. "Dickens and Time: The Clock Without Hands." *Dickens Studies Annual* 4 (1975): 1-35.

In a study of the temporal metaphors in Dickens's work, contends that *Bleak House* depicts "a whole society in moral peril and at odds with itself for want of a clear view of time and change." *Edwin Drood*, though a departure from the norm in its villain-protagonist and detective

novel format, is consistent with Dickens's view on
time--a disavowal of mindless tradition.

893.   Fraser, W.A. "Last Words on the *Drood* Mystery." *Dickensian*
       4 (1908): 99-100.

       Disputes J. Cuming Walters's contention that Helena
       Landless is Datchery (item 940). Argues that Bazzard
       is a more likely identity for the mysterious Datchery.

894.   Gomme, A.H. *Dickens*. London: Evans Brother, 1971, pp.
       93-98.

       Contends that Dickens's use of mystery in *Bleak House*
       and other novels tends to be stagey and contrived. The
       resultant melodrama gets in the way of the truth.

895.   Gottschalk, Paul. "Time in *Edwin Drood*." *Dickens Studies
       Annual* 1 (1970): 265-272.

       Contends that time is a major leitmotif in *Drood*.
       Cloisterham is a place of "shifting history," but "with
       an underlying permanence." Jasper, the protagonist, is
       both in time (as choirmaster) and out of time (in his
       opium reveries). Notes several references to the resolu-
       tion of problems "in the fulness of time."

896.   Greenhalgh, Mollie. "*Edwin Drood*: The Twilight of a God."
       Dickensian 55 (1959): 68-75.

       Contends that *Drood* is a departure for Dickens ("like
       a Brahms Symphony after a jazz session") when compared
       to *Pickwick Papers*. Dickens's weakened physical condition
       at the end of his life somehow led him to write a work
       "more relaxed and unselfconscious than anything he had
       written before."

897.   Hark, Ina Rae. "Marriage in the Symbolic Framework of
       The Mystery of Edwin Drood." *Studies in the Novel* 9
       (1977): 154-168.

       Notes Dickens's prediliction for ending his novels with
       a marriage. Suggests the implications of various alterna-
       tive matches for Rosa Bud. Contends that of all the
       possibilities, only marriage to Neville or to a resurrected
       Edwin (or remaining unmarried) would be thematically
       consistent with the first half of the novel.

*   Haycraft, Howard. *Murder for Pleasure* (item 36), pp.
       42-44.

Contends that Dickens's *Bleak House* and *Edwin Drood* had very little impact on the development of detective fiction. Concedes that, had Dickens lived to finish *Drood*, this might have been different.

898. Hill, T.W. "Drood Time in Cloisterham." *Dickensian* 40 (1943/1944): 113-117.

Contends that, though some critics have suggested that *Drood* takes place in 1842, evidence from the text and illustrations is contradictory and makes it impossible to determine the temporal setting of the novel.

899. Hill, T.W. "Notes on *The Mystery of Edwin Drood.*" *Dickensian* 40 (1943/1944): 198-204; 41 (1944/1945): 30-37.

Notes toward an annotated *Drood*; a series of commentaries on words or phrases in the novel.

900. Hirsch, Gordon D. "The Mysteries in *Bleak House*: A Psychoanalytic Study." *Dickens Studies Annual* 4 (1975): 132-152.

Contends that Freudian psychological theory can explain the obsession with mysteries of the key characters--Esther, Richard, Tulkinghorn, and Bucket. "The prototype for all curiosity and investigation of mysteries is the infantile sexual research that occurs at the Oedipal phase of development."

901. Holdsworth, William S. *Charles Dickens as a Legal Historian*. New Haven, Conn.: Yale University Press, 1929, pp. 79-115.

In a close analysis of the trial in *Bleak House*, observes that one of Dickens's primary intents was to catalog the abuses in the procedure of the Court of Chancery.

902. Hollington, Michael A. "Dickens and the Double." Ph.D. dissertation, University of Illinois, 1967.

Observes that the double in the nineteenth century is "a metaphor of schizophrenia." Contends that John Jasper of *Edwin Drood* is Dickens's finest schizophrenic portrait. Jasper's underlying motive for killing Drood is his own self-destruction.

903.   Hornback, Bert G. *"Noah's Arkitecture"*: *A Study of
        Dickens' Mythology*. Athens: Ohio University Press,
        1972, pp. 83-99.

        Contends that the mysteries and secrets that abound
        in *Bleak House* are metaphors for the failures of Vic-
        torian society. Dickens's solution, both for his charac-
        ters and for society, is to expose all the secrets.

904.   Hutter, Albert D. "The High Tower of His Mind: Psycho-
        analysis and the Reader of *Bleak House*." *Criticism*
        19 (Fall 1977): 296-316.

        By taking a psycholanalytic approach to the novel that
        concentrates on Dickens's "double narrative ... and his
        creation of a synthesizing detective figure," Hutter
        shows that "Dickens manipulates the inherent suspense
        of language and exploits crime, mystery, and its ultimate
        solution" in order to build "on every reader's experi-
        ence of transforming, from infancy, a mysterious and
        alien world into something integrated, whole, and
        ultimately, internalized."

905.   [Jackson, Henry]. *About Edwin Drood*. Cambridge: Cambridge
        University Press, 1911. 90pp.

        A close analysis of *Drood*, reviewing the various
        critical theories on the outcome of the story. Concludes
        that Jasper murdered Drood. Agrees with J. Cuming Walters
        (item 940) that Datchery was Helena Landless in disguise.

906.   Jacobson, Wendy S. "John Jasper and Thuggee." *Modern
        Language Review* 72 (1977): 526-537.

        Argues that the contention that Jasper was a member
        of the Indian Thuggee murder sect, while plausible, is
        not likely.

907.   Johnson, Edgar. *Charles Dickens: His Tragedy and Triumph*,
        Volume 2. New York: Simon and Schuster, 1952, pp. 1115-
        1126.

        Observes that, although in some respects *Edwin Drood*
        displays Dickens at the height of his powers, its atmo-
        sphere is autumnal.

908.   Kaplan, Fred. *Dickens and Mesmerism: The Hidden Springs
        of Fiction*. Princeton, N.J.: Princeton University
        Press, 1975, pp. 139-164.

Observes that Dickens uses mesmerism imagery in *Bleak House*, *Edwin Drood*, and other works to illumine his characters' recollections of the past.

909. Kavanagh, Mary. *A New Solution of the Mystery of Edwin Drood.* London: John Long, 1919. 32pp.

Contends that Drood survived Jasper's attack and assumed the identity of Lieutenant Tartar.

910. Kostelnick, Charles. "Dickens' Quarrel with the Gothic: Ruskin, Durdles, and *Edwin Drood.*" *Dickens Studies Newsletter* 8 (1977): 104-109.

Dickens's quarrel with the Gothic revival was not with the architecture itself, but with the "social and cultural context of these aesthetics." Contends that Durdles is "a satiric caricature of Ruskin's Gothic workman."

911. Kylander, Ellen C. "The Fate of Dickens' *Edwin Drood*: A Century of Commentary and Criticism." Ph.D. dissertation, University of Illinois at Urbana-Champaign, 1977.

Surveys the criticism of Dickens's unfinished novel, and observes that *Drood* "is indeed a work which rewards investigation."

912. Lane, Lauriat, Jr. "Dickens and Melville: Our Mutual Friends." *Dalhousie Review* 51 (1971): 315-331.

Cites thematic parallels between Dickens and Melville. *Billy Budd*, like *Edwin Drood*, portrays a struggle between good and evil, with the aim of revealing the truth, redeeming the falsely accused, confounding the wicked, and preserving the innocent.

913. Lane, Lauriat, Jr. "Dickens and the Double." *Dickensian* 55 (1959): 47-55.

In an analysis of Dickens's murderers, observes that Jasper is a split personality—choirmaster and opium addict. He loves Drood, his nephew, but is driven to kill him.

914. Lang, Andrew. *The Puzzle of Dickens' Last Plot.* London: Chapman and Hall, 1905. 100pp.

Contends that the most logical ending for *Drood* is that Jasper bungles Drood's murder. Drood then disguises himself as Datchery and hunts his assailant down.

915.   Leacock, Stephen. *Charles Dickens: His Life and Work.*
       Garden City, N.Y.: Doubleday, Doran, 1934, pp. 278-
       301.

       Reviews the unsolved problems in *Drood*, along with the
       history of critical speculation on the outcome of the
       novel. Contends that, despite persuasive evidence to
       the contrary, Drood escaped his would-be killer.

916.   MacVicar, H.M. "The Datchery Assumption: Expostulation."
       Nineteenth-Century Fiction 4 (1949): 75-79.

       In response to Richard M. Baker (item 860), MacVicar
       denies that Dick Datchery is Hiram Grewgious in disguise.
       (See item 854 for Baker's response.)

917.   Matchett, Willoughby. "Last Words on the *Drood* Mystery."
       Dickensian 4 (1908): 98-99.

       Disputes J. Cuming Walters's contention (item 940)
       that Helena Landless was Datchery in disguise.

918.   Matchett, Willoughby. "Mr. Datchery." *Dickensian* 4
       (1908): 17-21.

       Contends that Bazzard was Datchery.

919.   Mitchell, Charles. "*The Mystery of Edwin Drood*: The In-
       terior and Exterior of Self." *ELH: Journal of English
       Literary History* 33 (1966): 228-246.

       Argues that *Edwin Drood* is another example of Dickens's
       concern with "the dualism which constitutes the human
       entity: the relation between the inner and outer man."
       It is John Jasper's split personality that is the unify-
       ing "conceptual perspective" of the novel.

920.   Monod, Sylvère. *Dickens the Novelist.* Norman: University
       of Oklahoma Press, 1968, pp. 384-431, 488-502.

       Observes that *Bleak House* is a transitional work.
       Its detective characteristics have little in common
       with the traditional Dickensian works like *Pickwick
       Papers* or *Nicholas Nickleby*. *Edwin Drood* is remarkable
       for its fine characterizations and well-constructed
       story. Contends that Dickens himself may not have known
       how it would end.

*   Murch, A.E. *The Development of the Detective Novel*
       (item 51), pp. 92-114.

Traces detective themes in Dickens's work. Though many of his novels contain aspects of mystery and detection, only *Edwin Drood* was written for the purpose of propounding and solving a mystery.

921. Nicoll, Sir William Robertson. *The Problem of "Edwin Drood": A Study in the Method of Dickens.* London: Hodder and Stoughton, 1912. 212pp.

A close analysis of the *Drood* fragment. Concludes that Drood was murdered by Jasper. Agrees with J. Cuming Walters (item 940) that Datchery was Helena Landless in disguise. Includes bibliography.

922. Ousby, Ian. "The Broken Glass: Vision and Comprehension in *Bleak House.*" *Nineteenth-Century Fiction* 29 (1975): 381-392.

Contends that Inspector Bucket, more than any other character in *Bleak House*, sees things clearly. He is not confused by the "variegated spectacle" that disorients most of the other characters in the novel.

*   Ousby, Ian. "Charles Dickens." *Bloodhounds of Heaven* (item 55), pp. 99-110.

Contends that Dickens made an important contribution to the stereotype of the detective, culminating in *Bleak House*'s Inspector Bucket.

923. Pakenham, Pansy. "The Memorandum Book, Forster and *Edwin Drood.*" *Dickensian* 51 (1954/1955): 117-121.

Reviews the speculation by Dickens's contemporaries and confidants on the outcome of *Edwin Drood.* Includes a letter from Charles Collins, Dickens's son-in-law, claiming that Drood was indeed murdered, and that Rosa would likely have married Tartar.

924. Parker, Dorothy. "Allegory and the Extension of Mr. Bucket's Forefinger." *English Language Notes* 12 (1974): 31-35.

Analyzes Bucket's characteristic gestures. The movements of his hand--"holding, pointing, tapping"--become metaphors for Bucket's activities as a detective--"investigating, accusing, apprehending."

925. Proctor, Richard A. *Watched by the Dead: A Loving Study of Charles Dickens' Half Told Tale.* London: W.H. Allen, 1887. 166pp.

Lengthy analysis of *Edwin Drood* and speculation as to its likely conclusion. Contends that Drood escapes Jasper's murder attempt and returns, disguised as Datchery, to hunt down his assailant.

926. Quirk, Eugene F. "Dickens' Men of Law: Dickens' Changing Vision of English Legal Practice." Ph.D. dissertation, University of Illinois at Urbana-Champaign, 1972.

Observes that, in contrast to his characterizations in earlier works, Dickens has created in Hiram Grewgious of *Edwin Drood* "a legal figure ... elevated to the role of a principal force for good."

927. Roazen, Deborah Heller. "A Peculiar Attraction: *Bleak House*, *Der Prozess*, and the Law." *Essays in Literature* 5 (1978): 251-266.

Notes the similarities between Dickens's treatment of the legal process and that of Franz Kafka. Contends that Kafka was familiar with, and influenced by, *Bleak House*.

928. Robison, Roselee. "Time, Death and the River in Dickens' Novels." *English Studies* 53 (1972): 436-454.

Observes that Dickens's use of the river and water as images in *Edwin Drood* reinforces the theme of the "mysterious affinity between life and death."

929. Roussel, Roy. "The Completed Story of *The Mystery of Edwin Drood*." *Criticism* 20 (1978): 383-402.

Argues that the central question of *Drood* is "the possibility of its characters completing or fulfilling their lives." Neither Jasper nor Rosa will find this fulfillment.

930. Saunders, Montagu. *The Mystery in the Drood Family*. Cambridge: Cambridge University Press, 1914. 159pp.

Argues that Jasper, a split personality owing to his use of opium, would, in attempting to solve the murder of Edwin Drood, have tracked himself down. Identifies Dick Datchery with Hiram Grewgious.

931. Scott, P.J.M. *Reality and Comic Confidence in Charles Dickens*. London: Macmillan, 1979, pp. 69-71.

Notes the ambiguity of Inspector Bucket's motives in *Bleak House*. Draws a parallel between Bucket's toying with Dedlock and Dickens's toying with his readers.

932. Spilka, Mark. *Dickens and Kafka: A Mutual Interpretation.*
Bloomington: Indiana University Press, 1963, pp. 198–
240.

Cites parallels between *Bleak House* and *The Trial.*
Asserts that Dickens influenced Kafka. "Both writers
fashioned oddly religious Courts, and used them to
exemplify the adult world."

933. Starrett, Vincent. Introduction to *The Mystery of Edwin
Drood*, by Charles Dickens. New York: Heritage Press,
1941, pp. xiii–xxxi.

Surveys the history of Drood criticism and speculation.
Contends that there is strong evidence in the novel that
Drood was murdered. Some questions regarding the work
are unanswerable.

934. Steig, Michael, and F.A.C. Wilson. "Hortense Versus
Bucket: The Ambiguity of Order in *Bleak House.*"
Modern Language Quarterly 33 (1972): 289–298.

Notes Inspector Bucket's transformation from a repres-
sive force to a benevolent one in Chapter 53. Contends
that this results from Bucket's subjugation of Hortense.
Dickens found Hortense's "destructive virulence" so
disturbing that the man who could stop her is portrayed
in a different light thereafter.

935. Studley, Francis. "Last Words on the *Drood* Mystery."
Dickensian 4 (1908): 100–101.

Contends that Dickens's aim in *Drood* was to show the
effect of opium on an evil mind, just as DeQuincey showed
its effects on a good man.

936. Suddaby, John. "Was Dickens a Christmas Renegade?"
Dickensian 14 (1918): 285–288, 326–330.

Contends that Edwin Drood was never murdered. Such a
turn would have spoiled the plot; and, in any case, it
would have been inconsistent for Dickens, whose career
is inextricably bound up with the warmth of Christmas,
to have written of a murder on Christmas Eve.

937. Symons, Julian. *Charles Dickens.* New York: Haskell House,
1974. 94pp.

Contends that, although "Dickens has as good a title
as Edgar Allan Poe to be called the father of the modern
detective story," he was interested in literary puzzles

not for their own sake, but as a "medium for conveying
the melodrama that chiefly concerned him."

938. Thurley, Geoffrey. *The Dickens Myth: Its Genesis and
      Structure.* London: Routledge and Kegan Paul, 1976, pp.
      178-202, 329-350.

      Denies that Dickens is a mindless optimist. *Bleak
      House* is a critique of "Dickensian expectations, their
      ultimate illusoriness and destructive power." It is in
      Edwin Drood, however, that Dickens reaches "the nadir
      of weariness."

939. Van Hall, Sharon. "The Foe in the Mirror: The Self-De-
      structive Characters in Charles Dickens' Novels."
      Ph.D. dissertation, University of Illinois at Urbana-
      Champaign, 1975.

      Contends that by the time he created John Jasper in
      Edwin Drood, Dickens realized that "in art and in life
      good and evil are not distinct and separable qualities,
      that they are held in delicate balance within each of
      us." Argues that Dickens's own life is similar in many
      ways to those of his self-destructive characters.

940. Walters, J. Cuming. *Clues to Dickens' "Mystery of Edwin
      Drood."* New York: Haskell House, 1970. 116pp.

      Originally published in 1912, this book concludes
      that, had Dickens finished *Drood*, he would have revealed
      that Jasper killed Drood and was detected and exposed
      by Datchery, who turns out to be Helena Landless in
      disguise. Outlines the process by which this might
      happen in some detail.

941. Walters, J. Cuming. *The Complete Mystery of Edwin Drood:
      The History, Continuations, and Solutions 1870-1912.*
      London: Chapman and Hall, 1912.

      Compiles thirty-two different conclusions that various
      critics had formulated for *Drood* during the forty-two
      years after its publication.

942. Werner, Craig. "Fugal Structure in *The Mystery of Edwin
      Drood.*" *Dickens Studies Newsletter* 9 (1978): 77-80.

      Defends Sylvère Monod's thesis that the structure of
      Drood is fugal. (See item 920.) Dickens's approach to
      his material in *Drood* resembles the polyphonic approach
      to musical composition.

943. White, Allen H. "Language and Location in Charles Dickens'
      Bleak House." *Critical Quarterly* 20 (1978): 73-89.

      Contends that the repetition in *Bleak House*, including
      Inspector Bucket's duplication of Tulkinghorn's investi-
      gation, is deliberate. "The whole novel is constructed
      on a doubling-up of figures, moments and events which
      creates a reinforced connectedness."

944. Wilson, Edmund. "Dickens: The Two Scrooges." *The Wound
      and the Bow*. Boston: Houghton Mifflin, 1941, pp. 83-
      104.

      Observes that Jasper has two identities. One is the
      choirmaster, the other--brought on by opium--is that of
      a murderous Thuggee. Contends that Helena Landless would
      have been forced to hypnotize Jasper so that he could
      return to a mental state in which he could recall his
      crime.

945. Wilson, J.W. "Last Words on the *Drood* Mystery." *Dickensian*
      4 (1908): 103-104.

      Argues that the evidence in the novel points to the
      conclusion that John Jasper was a mesmerist.

946. Wing, George. "*Edwin Drood* and *Desperate Remedies*:
      Prototypes of Detective Fiction in 1870." *Studies in
      English Literature, 1500-1900* 13 (1973): 677-687.

      Examines *Drood* and Hardy's *Desperate Remedies* as
      early examples of the detective story. Contends that
      both are "immeasurably much more than detective fiction."

947. Winner, Anthony. "Character and Knowledge in Dickens:
      The Enigma of Jaggers." *Dickens Studies Annual* 3
      (1974): 100-121.

      Contends that Inspector Bucket, "tainted by profes-
      sional opacity, secrecy, and disguises," is an example
      of one of Dickens's most complex characters--the benign
      man who is sometimes forced to act in a manner contrary
      to his basic instincts. As such, Bucket prefigures the
      character Jaggers in *Great Expectations*.

948. Worth, George J. *Dickensian Melodrama: A Reading of
      the Novels*. Lawrence: University of Kansas, 1978,
      pp. 111-127.

      Argues that *Bleak House* is a novel in which order,
      design, and connection have been obscured. Inspector

Bucket is the only character able to make connections.
He serves as Dickens's agent in orchestrating a highly
successful melodrama of mystery.

DICKINSON, PETER (1927-   )

949.   Dickinson, Peter. "Superintendent Pibble." *The Great
       Detectives* (item 60), pp. 175-182.

       Dickinson states that he created Pibble because he
       wanted a life-like character who would be completely
       unlike James Bond--easily intimidated, "intelligent,
       fallible," and not sexually attractive.

DICKSON, CARR. See JOHN DICKSON CARR

DICKSON, CARTER. See JOHN DICKSON CARR

DIETRICH, ROBERT. See E.HOWARD HUNT

DISNEY, DORIS MILES (1907-1976)

950.   Mercier, J.F. "Doris Miles Disney: An Interview."
       Publishers Weekly 204 (13 August 1973): 24-25.

       States that believable characters are the strong point
       in Disney's novels and traces how many of her murder
       plots are created from personal events.

DOMINIC, R.B. See EMMA LATHEN

DOYLE, ARTHUR CONAN (1859-1930)

       *Sherlock Holmes, Sir Arthur Conan Doyle's legendary
       detective, is without a doubt the most famous figure
       in the literature of mystery and detection. Doyle's
       works have inspired well over 3,000 books and articles
       on the exploits of the great sleuth. Some of this out-
       put is genuine literary criticism; most of it is not.
       Baker Street whimsey has become a thriving industry
       among Holmes fans. It began when Ronald Knox satiri-
       cally applied the techniques of the higher criticism*

to Conan Doyle's works. This treatment caught on, and
many "critics" began to write about Holmes and Watson
as though they were real people; if Conan Doyle was
mentioned at all, he was referred to as Watson's
"literary agent." To give the user some idea of this
side of Conan Doyle commentary we have included a few
of the best-known examples of the whimsical or higher
criticism (so indicated in the annotations), but
nearly all of the section on Conan Doyle consists of
items that are genuine literary criticism.

BOOKS

951. Baring-Gould, William S., ed. *The Annotated Sherlock
Holmes*. New York: Clarkson N. Potter, 1967. 2 volumes,
688; 824pp.

All four novels and fifty-six short stories in which
Sherlock Holmes appears are included, with an introduc-
tion, copious notes, and a bibliography by Baring-Gould.
Often called the definitive study for the Holmes devotee.

952. Carr, John Dickson. *The Life of Sir Arthur Conan Doyle*.
New York: Harper and Brothers, 1949. 304pp.

A completely documented biography of Conan Doyle, only
a small part of which concerns his writing of the
Sherlock Holmes stories. Carr does draw several parallels
between the "mental processes" of Conan Doyle and Sherlock Holmes and in three pages describes the germination
of the idea of the "most famous character in the English
language."

953. Dakin, D. Martin. *A Sherlock Holmes Commentary*. New York:
Drake Publishers, 1972. 320pp.

Extensive notes on each of the Sherlock Holmes tales,
regarded by some as a supplement to Baring-Gould (item
951) for the Holmes devotee.

* Depken, Friedrich. *Sherlock Holmes, Raffles, and Their
Prototypes* (item 28).

Focuses on the influence of Poe and Gaboriau on Conan
Doyle's work.

954. De Waal, Ronald Burt. *The World Bibliography of Sherlock
Holmes and Dr. Watson: A Classified and Annotated List
of Materials Relating to Their Lives and Adventures*.
Boston: New York Graphic Society, 1974. 526pp.

Lists appearances (in all sources, including periodicals, individual books, collections, and foreign-language
editions) of the sixty Sherlock Holmes tales as well as
over 2,500 "Writings About the Writings" (most of which
are annotated) and other items such as Sherlock Holmes
in plays and films. Over 6,200 items are included. A
supplement to this work is scheduled for 1980.

955. Hall, Trevor H. *Sherlock Holmes and His Creator*. London:
     Duckworth, 1978. 155pp.

     Hall offers several essays on Sherlockiana, mostly
     tongue in cheek. The chapters on Doyle and T.S. Eliot,
     Doyle and Arsène Lupin, the origin of Sherlock Holmes,
     and Doyle and spiritualism are, however, genuine exer-
     cises in literary criticism.

956. Hardwick, Michael, and Molly Hardwick. *The Sherlock
     Holmes Companion*. Garden City, N.Y.: Doubleday, 1963.
     232pp.

     Contains a "who's who" of characters in the stories,
     synopses of the plots (without the solutions), many
     quotations, articles on Holmes, Watson, and Conan Doyle
     and the Sidney Paget illustrations.

957. Higham, Charles. *The Adventures of Conan Doyle: The
     Life of the Creator of Sherlock Holmes*. New York:
     W.W. Norton, 1976. 368pp.

     In the chapters on the Sherlock Holmes stories Higham
     maintains that, although they probably had real life
     prototypes, Holmes and Watson represent different aspects
     of Conan Doyle himself, each reflecting opposite sides
     of his personality.

958. Keating, H.R.F. *Sherlock Holmes: The Man and His World*.
     New York: Scribners, 1979. 160pp.

     Treats Sherlock Holmes as a real person but does not
     indulge in any speculation. The emphasis of the work is
     on the historical and cultural events of Holmes's time.
     Over half of the book consists of contemporary illus-
     trations of Holmes and illustrations and photographs of
     his world.

959. Liljegren, S.B. *The Irish Element in The Valley of Fear*.
     Uppsala: A.B. Lundequistska Bokhandeln, 1964. 47pp.

Liljegren argues that Conan Doyle's novel was inspired
by a talk with William J. Barnes, an American detective,
who told him about the Pinkertons and the Mollie Maguires.
He contends that, although Conan Doyle disguised the
Irish aspect of the story by anglicizing some of the
names of the characters, the Irish element is nonetheless distinct in the story; and indeed, "forms the
fundamental element of the novel."

960. McQueen, Ian. *Sherlock Holmes Detected: The Problems
of the Long Stories.* New York: Drake, 1974. 227pp.

Based on the concept that Holmes and Watson "were only
pretending to be characters of fiction and had employed
Conan Doyle to edit their scripts," McQueen examines
five major Holmes stories for clues to the lives of
Doyle's heroes outside of the stories.

961. Nordon, Pierre. *Conan Doyle: A Biography.* New York:
Holt, 1967. 370pp.

Nordon argues that there is a close association between
the character of Conan Doyle and that of his protagonist,
Sherlock Holmes. He contends that Holmes "is one of the
last incarnations of chivalry in the literature of the
English language."

962. Pearsall, Ronald. *Conan Doyle: A Biographical Solution.*
New York: St. Martin's Press, 1977. 208pp.

In the context of a biography of Conan Doyle, Pearsall
notes Doyle's debts to various mystery writers, from
Poe to Doyle's contemporaries. He cites various Victorian
treatises on criminology, which he contends were the
inspiration for much of Sherlock Holmes's vaunted deductive powers.

963. Pearson, Hesketh. *Conan Doyle.* New York: Walker and
Company, 1961. 256pp.

Originally published in England in 1943, this general
biography devotes a chapter to Sherlock Holmes, pointing
out Doyle's debt to Poe in both his conception of the
character of Holmes and in the construction of his
stories. Credits Conan Doyle with being "the first writer
to give vitality and personality to a detective."

964. Rosenberg, Samuel. *Naked Is the Best Disguise: The Death
and Resurrection of Sherlock Holmes.* Indianapolis:
Bobbs-Merrill, 1974. 203pp.

Argues that Conan Doyle was a very brilliant and subtle
writer who is underestimated when he is viewed as merely
a popular writer with some story-telling ability. Contends that "Moriarty is clearly based on Conan Doyle's
distinctly unfriendly attitudes" toward Nietzsche and
draws parallels between Holmes and Dionysus and Holmes
and Christ. States that Conan Doyle was an "omnivorous"
reader with a "phenomenal" memory, quite capable of
consciously using a wide range of literary, historical,
and philosophical references and symbols in his work.

965.   Sayers, Dorothy L. *Unpopular Opinions: Twenty-one Essays*.
       New York: Harcourt, Brace, 1947. 236pp.

       Contains four essays written between 1935 and 1945
       ("Holmes' College Career," "Dr. Watson's Christian
       Name," "Dr. Watson, Widower," "The Dates in *The Red-
       Headed League*") in which Sayers indulges in some humorous
       pseudo-scholarship on topics related to the Sherlock
       Holmes stories.

966.   Starrett, Vincent. *The Private Life of Sherlock Holmes*.
       New York: Macmillan, 1933. 214pp. London: Ivor Nichol-
       son and Watson, 1934. 199pp. New York: Haskell House
       Publishers, 1971. 199pp.

       One of the earlier and more famous books which essen-
       tially treats Sherlock Holmes as a real person, detail-
       ing his habits, methods, and personality. This book
       was revised and reprinted in 1960 (see item 967 below),
       but because many critics prefer this version, all three
       editions of it are listed.

967.   Starrett, Vincent. *The Private Life of Sherlock Holmes*.
       Chicago: University of Chicago Press, 1960. 155pp.
       London: George Allen and Unwin, 1961. 155pp.

       This is a revised and enlarged version of item 966
       above. Since many critics prefer the original, both
       editions of this version are listed.

968.   Weil-Nordon, P., ed. *Sir Arthur Conan Doyle: Centenary,
       1859-1959*. London: John Murray, 1959. 135pp.

       A profusely illustrated overview of Conan Doyle's life
       and literary career, with an admiring introduction by
       Weil-Nordon.

ARTICLES AND PORTIONS OF BOOKS

969. Adcock, A. St. John. "Sir Arthur Conan Doyle." *Bookman* (London) 43 (November 1912): 95-110. Reprinted *Living Age* 275 (28 December 1912): 778-787. Condensed in *Gods of Modern Grub Street: Impressions of Contemporary Authors*. New York: Frederick A. Stokes, 1923, pp. 83-89.

In a comprehensive biographical sketch of Doyle, Adcock argues that Doyle's works reflect the qualities of Doyle himself. They are "masculine, courageous, healthful," accentuating the positive, though not unmindful of "the darker facts of existence."

970. Barzun, Jacques, and Wendell Hertig Taylor. Preface to *The Hound of the Baskervilles*, by Arthur Conan Doyle. New York: Garland Publishing, 1976. Also printed in *A Book of Prefaces* (item 22), pp. 41-42.

Points out that this is Conan Doyle's only story in which there is "any serious consideration of the supernatural as an agent of death and revenge." There is a masterly blending of this supernatural element with significant details and a "truly Dickensian humor."

971. Bell, Joseph. "The Adventures of Sherlock Holmes." *Bookman* (London) 3 (December 1892): 79-81. Reprinted as "Mr. Sherlock Holmes." *A Study in Scarlet*, by Arthur Conan Doyle. London: Ward, Lock and Bowden, 1893, pp. xiii-xx. Also reprinted *Baker Street Journal* 2 (January 1947): 45-49.

In this article the man often called the prototype of Holmes observes that the technique of Holmes is essentially that of successful medical diagnosis. In addition, he contends that Conan Doyle is a born storyteller and "his stories are absolutely free from padding."

972. Brooks, Colin. "The Right Wrong Thing: Conan Doyle and the Spirit of the Nineties." *Bookman* (London) 79 (December 1930): 174-175.

Brooks argues that the 1890s reading public appreciated the Sherlock Holmes stories for the wrong reasons, i.e., Doyle's craftsmanship in creating memorable characters. Brooks asserts that a proper literary comparison is not between Doyle and Poe, but between Doyle and Jane Austen. The Holmes stories will someday be cherished as valuable costume pieces that accurately reflect English life in the 1890s.

*   Chandler, Frank Wadleigh. "The Literature of Crime-
         Detection." *The Literature of Roguery* (item 154),
         pp. 537-547.

         Contends that the success of the Sherlock Holmes
         character is partly due to Conan Doyle's combining Poe's
         analytical elements, Gaboriau's sensational ones, Dupin's
         reason, and LeCoq's energy in his portrayal and to his
         use of Poe's succinct presentation and Gaboriau's device
         of inserting the history of the criminal into the main
         narrative in order to explain his motive.

973.   Chesterton, G.K. "Sherlock Holmes." *A Handful of Authors:
         Essays on Books and Writers*. Edited by Dorothy Collins.
         New York: Sheed and Ward, 1953, pp. 168-174.

         Originally written for the *London Daily News* in 1901
         and 1907, the theme of these two short essays is that
         the detective story is a neglected popular art form
         that Conan Doyle has raised to its proper level by his
         "artistic seriousness." Maintains that Sherlock Holmes
         "is probably the only literary creation since the cre-
         ations of Dickens which has really passed into the life
         and language of the people."

974.   Christ, Jay Finley. "Sherlock and the Canons." *Baker
         Street Journal* 3 (January 1953): 5-12.

         Points out that *A Study in Scarlet* violates widely
         accepted conventions or "canons" of the detective story,
         such as "all 'proof' must be strictly logical" and that
         "the data must all be given fairly with the problem."
         Conlcudes that in spite of this the story is still
         "amusing and absorbing."

975.   Christensen, Peter. "The Nature of Evil in *The Hound
         of the Baskervilles*." *Baker Street Journal* 29 (Decem-
         ber 1979): 209-211, 213.

         Maintains that Conan Doyle suggests all evil is a
         sort of "reversion or throwback." He "emphasizes his
         theme by juxtaposing the forces of civilization and
         those of evil and chaos."

976.   Coleman, Arthur. "The Game's Afoot: Animal Imagery in
         the Sacred Writings." *Baker Street Journal* 22 (Decem-
         ber 1972): 222-225.

         Points out that "animal imagery is the most frequently
         utilized of all linguistic devices and appears with

remarkable consistency throughout the tales" and serves
as a means of indicating the "Victorian point of view
toward the nature of the world and the people in it."
Gives many examples from the stories.

977. Conroy, Peter V. "The Importance of Being Watson." *Texas
      Quarterly* 21 (Spring 1978): 84-103.

      Contends that Watson's function as narrator of the
      Sherlock Holmes stories is quite important to their
      involving the reader in their "very special suspense."

978. Deighton, Len. Introduction to *The Valley of Fear* by
      Arthur Conan Doyle. Garden City, N.Y.: Doubleday, 1977,
      pp. 7-13.

      Maintains that Conan Doyle was not only a link between
      the older school of detective fiction (Poe and Collins)
      and the new school (Sayers and Chandler), but also a
      recorder and "sometimes the prophet, of the remarkable
      new world of criminology." Also details Conan Doyle's
      medical and scientific background that formed his approach
      to detection.

*   Eames, Hugh. "Sherlock Holmes--Arthur Conan Doyle."
      Sleuths, Inc. (item 30), pp. 9-47.

      Contends that Holmes as a problem solver did not attempt
      to find out the truth about large, abstract questions
      but preferred intricate criminal puzzles that called for
      the examination of minute, seemingly unimportant facts.

979. Egan, Joseph J. "Conan Doyle's *The Adventure of the
      Creeping Man* as Stevensonian Analogue." *Studies in
      Scottish Literature* 7 (January 1970): 180-183.

      Details the parallels between *The Adventure of the
      Creeping Man* and Stevenson's *The Strange Case of Dr.
      Jekyll and Mr. Hyde*, the most compelling connection being
      their similar moral commentaries.

980. Fowles, John. Foreward and Afterword to *The Hound of the
      Baskervilles*, by Arthur Conan Doyle. Garden City, N.Y.:
      Doubleday, 1977, pp. 7-11, 186-196.

      Maintains that *The Hound of the Baskervilles* exhibits
      Conan Doyle's "unsurpassed narrative technique" and
      "superb caricatures" but fails in "ingenuity," "con-
      centrated wisdom (or love of reason)," and "circumstan-
      tiality," three qualities singled out by Jacques Barzun
      (item 117), as the prime requisite for a good tale.

981.   Fowles, John. "A Study in Scarlet." *New Statesman* 92
        (26 November 1976): 751-752.

        In the context of a review of *The Adventures of Conan
        Doyle*, by Charles Higham, argues that one element in
        the success of the Sherlock Holmes stories is based on
        a faulty premise: that everything can be solved by logic
        and analysis. Observes that "despite the sharp observa-
        tion of social appearances" in the stories, the "almost
        total lack of any social content" in them reduces "life
        to a picturesque and entertaining myth."

*   Gerber, Richard. "Name as Symbol: On Sherlock Holmes
        and the Nature of the Detective Story" (item 241).

        Gerber justifies this exhaustive semantic and psycho-
        logical analysis of the name "Sherlock Holmes" by stating
        that the name is a "signaling" name, one that is expressive
        in a concealed or subliminal manner and that analyzing
        the name is a way to obtain "insight into otherwise con-
        cealed depths." Since Holmes "also represents *the* hero
        of the detective novel," insight into his character also
        means obtaining insight into "the basic psychic structure
        of the detective novel."

982.   Greene, Graham. Introduction to *The Sign of Four*, by
        Arthur Conan Doyle. Garden City, N.Y.: Doubleday, 1977,
        pp. 7-10.

        Observes that "perhaps the reason why *The Sign of Four*
        has stayed indelibly in the memory is that in this book
        the great detective for the first time comes completely
        to life in all his complexity."

*   Haines, Helen E. "The Lure of Crime" (item 265), pp. 226-
        228.

        Maintains that Conan Doyle "brought humor, common sense
        and simple realism into the working-out of intricate
        crime problems." Concludes that "the Sherlock Holmes
        volumes are classics in their originality, skill of work-
        manship, their sustained interest and plausibility."

*   Haycraft, Howard. "Profile by Gaslight." *Murder for
        Pleasure* (item 36), pp. 45-61.

        Credits Doyle's creation of Sherlock Holmes with re-
        viving the Poe and Gaboriau formula but points out that
        the stories are, by today's standards, often "better
        fiction than detection." Doyles's only real originality
        lay in his creation of Holmes and Watson.

983. Haycraft, Howard. "The Time, the Place, and the Man."
      Sherlock Holmes' Greatest Cases, by Arthur Conan Doyle.
      New York: Franklin Watts, 1967, pp. 1-16.

      In this introduction, Haycraft states that a myth has
      grown up around Sherlock Holmes in which he is regarded
      as a real person and not a fictional character. Aimed
      at the person who is not familiar with Sherlock Holmes
      or Conan Doyle, the article gives a biographic sketch
      of Conan Doyle and "suggests" three reasons the stories
      have been so popular: the story-telling ability of Conan
      Doyle, their "flavor" of Victorian England, and "the
      character of Holmes himself."

984. Hill, Edwin C. "221-B, Baker Street." *Scribner's Magazine*
      100 (November 1936): 68.

      Observes that Conan Doyle based Sherlock Holmes on Dr.
      Joseph Bell, one of his professors, and that Sherlock
      Holmes has achieved a life of his own, just as D'Artagnan
      and Cyrano have.

985. Hoerr, Willmer A. "The Case of the Sundry Sources." *Baker
      Street Journal* 22 (December 1972): 215-218.

      Maintains that the successful combination of "the
      romantic and the realistic" in *The Hound of the Basker-
      villes* can be traced to several sources, particularly
      Dickens, "the Gothic school" of Ann Radcliffe and Monk
      Lewis, and Wilkie Collins.

986. Hollyer, Cameron. "Arthur Conan Doyle: A Case of Identity."
      *Pacific Quarterly: An International Review of Arts
      and Ideas* 3 (January 1978): 50-61.

      Argues that the vast amount of "paracriticism" (in
      which Holmes and Watson are treated as real people)
      written on the Sherlock Holmes stories makes serious
      criticism of them difficult. Examines at length two
      serious works of criticism on Conan Doyle, by John Fowles
      (item 980) and Samuel Rosenberg (item 964) and finds
      that "the lack of deeper meanings in the tales" disturbs
      Fowles; "their abundance delights Rosenberg." Concludes
      that the tales "will inevitably compel more serious
      critical attention."

987. Horwill, Herbert W. "Literature: Recent Fiction."
      Forum 37 (July 1905): 106-109.

In the context of a review of *The Return of Sherlock Holmes*, observes that Conan Doyle's ingenuity seems to be failing and concludes that the "impression of originality" and freshness created by the earlier stories is lacking.

988.   Iseminger, Gordon L. "Sherlock Holmes: Victorian Archetype." *Baker Street Journal* 29 (September 1979): 156-166.

Points out the various ways in which the character of Sherlock Holmes and his adventures provide insights into Victorian society, such as Holmes's attitude toward sex (discreet and prudent).

989.   Knox, Ronald. "Studies in the Literature of Sherlock Holmes." *Essays in Satire*. New York: E.P. Dutton, 1930, pp. 145-175. Reprinted *Seventeen Steps to 221B: A Collection of Sherlockian Pieces by English Writers.* Edited by James Edward Holroyd. London: George Allen and Unwin, 1967, pp. 30-45.

This article (first read at an Oxford debating society in 1911) was meant as a satire on the Higher Criticism, which Knox thought was damaging the foundations of Christianity by applying historical methodology to the study of the Bible. In the article Knox describes the theories of various fictional scholars (who have such names as Sauwosch and Piff-Pouff) about the Holmes stories. For example, one draws parallels between Watson and the chorus in *Agamemnon*, and another asserts that some of the tales are true and others are merely inventions of Watson.

990.   Labianca, Dominick A., and William J. Reeves. "Drug Synergism and the Case of 'The Disappearance of Lady Frances Carfax.'" *American Notes and Queries* 16 (January 1978): 68-70.

Points out that Lady Carfax could not have been revived from a chloroform-induced unconsciousness by an injection of ether, but states that Conan Doyle can be given the benefit of the doubt because the scientific community of the time may not have fully understood the properties of ether.

*   Lambert, Gavin. "Final Problems: Sir Arthur Conan Doyle." *The Dangerous Edge* (item 42), pp. 31-63.

In a survey of the Sherlock Holmes stories observes that Conan Doyle "had a poetic imagination which the skill of the stories and the examples of Holmes's intellect at work tend to obscure." Relates passages from the stories to forces and incidents in Conan Doyle's personal life. Also maintains that in the stories "the most powerful reiterated motive is greed."

991. Lauterbach, Edward. "Annotating the Holmes Saga." *Armchair Detective* 7 (February 1974): 119, 124.

A listing of annotated editions of Sherlock Holmes stories.

992. La Vallo, Frank. "The Case of the Deathless Detective." *Texas Quarterly* 11 (Summer 1968): 180-199.

Although Conan Doyle's historical novels and other aspects of his personal and professional life are mentioned, the article focuses mainly on the Sherlock Holmes stories, particularly on the Holmes-Watson relationship and Holmes's methods of detection.

993. LeBlanc, Maurice. "A Propos de Conan Doyle." *Les Annales Politiques et Littéraires* 95 (1 August 1930): 111. English translation printed *Baker Street Journal* 21 (June 1971): 100-102.

A tribute to Conan Doyle in which LeBlanc points out that Conan Doyle's popularity is due to "his great talent as a storyteller"--his ability "to choose, compose, arrange, and present the work in just the right way."

994. McCleary, G.F. "The Original of Sherlock Holmes." *On Detective Fiction and Other Things.* London: Hollis and Carter, 1960, pp. 34-51.

Argues that the real person upon whom Sherlock Holmes was based was Conan Doyle himself, although Dr. Joseph Bell was to some degree also an inspiration for the character.

995. Mackenzie, J.B. "Sherlock Holmes' Plots and Strategy." *Green Bag* 14 (September 1902): 407-411. Reprinted *Baker Street Journal Christmas Annual* 1 (1956): 56-61.

Criticizes Holmes's methods of deduction, arguing that "from unstable premises, he builds faulty conclusions." Also observes that "one of the least defensible of Holmes's practices ... is the making responsible officials

of Scotland Yard parties to compromises" that would cost
them their jobs in real life. Gives several examples from
the stories to illustrate his point.

996.   McLuhan, Marshall. "Sherlock Holmes vs. the Bureaucrat."
       Explorations 8 (October 1957): 10-12.

       Argues that Holmes is a hero for the ordinary man
       because he is an intuitive genius triumphing over the
       bureaucratic Scotland Yard.

997.   Marshall, Margaret. "Alkali Dust in Your Eyes." *American
       Scholar* 37 (Autumn 1968): 650-654.

       Points out that when Conan Doyle set part of *A Study
       in Scarlet* in Utah he put a range of mountains where
       there is actually only desert.

998.   Maurice, Arthur Bartlett. "Forty Years of Sherlock."
       Bookman 66 (October 1927): 160-162.

       Maintains that in the matter of popularity there has
       never been a fictional character comparable to Sherlock
       Holmes and that many people regard Holmes as a real
       person.

999.   Maurice, Arthur Bartlett. "Sherlock Holmes and His
       Creator." *Collier's* 41 (15 August 1908): 11-14.

       In addition to biographical details about Conan Doyle,
       Maurice observes that Sherlock Holmes is derived from
       both the detective stories of Poe and the appearance and
       personality of Dr. Joseph Bell, a professor of medicine
       under whom Conan Doyle studied. Also points out that
       the character of Holmes was in "a constant state of evo-
       lution" during the first four stories.

1000. Moore, John Robert. "Sherlock Holmes Borrows a Plot."
       Modern Language Quarterly 8 (March 1947): 85-90.

       Argues that Conan Doyle took the idea for "The Man
       with the Twisted Lip" from Thackeray's "Miss Shum's
       Husband" in *Yellowplush Papers*.

1001. Moorman, Charles. "The Appeal of Sherlock Holmes."
       Southern Quarterly 14 (January 1976): 71-82.

       Argues that the appeal of Sherlock Holmes lies not
       in the characterization, plotting, or writing style of
       the stories but in their abundance of detail, which
       creates a world.

1002. Morley, Christopher. "An American Gentleman." *Saturday Review* 30 (20 September 1947): 16-17.

Argues that Conan Doyle was influenced by *The Dynamiter* by Robert Louis and Fanny Stevenson.

1003. Morley, Christopher. "In Memoriam: Sherlock Holmes." *Saturday Review* 7 (2 August 1930): 21. Reprinted *The Complete Sherlock Holmes*, Volume 1. Garden City, N.Y.: Doubleday, Doran, 1930, pp. vii-xiv. Reprinted *Internal Revenue*. Garden City, N.Y.: Doubleday, Doran, 1933, pp. 70-80. Reprinted *Prefaces Without Books: Prefaces and Introductions to Thirty Books*. Austin: University of Texas Humanities Research Center, 1970, pp. 22-27.

Maintains that the "Sherlock Holmes saga is a triumphant illustration of art's supremacy over life." It is the characters and relationship of Holmes and Watson that Sherlockians like to discuss and argue about, and for this reason the stories can be read many times.

1004. Morley, Christopher. Introduction and Annotations in *Sherlock Holmes and Dr. Watson: A Textbook of Friendship*. Edited by Christopher Morley. New York: Harcourt, Brace, 1944. 366pp.

Morley's introduction points out that Conan Doyle was influenced by Robert Louis Stevenson and Edgar Allan Poe and that "few writers have made more efficient use in fiction of their own experiences." Also, the stories are annotated to explain references that might not be clear to the reader who is unfamiliar with Victorian England. The stories included are *A Study in Scarlet*, *The Sign of Four*, *The Final Problem*, *The Adventure of the Empty House*, and *The Adventure of the Bruce-Partington Plans*.

1005. Morley, Christopher. Introduction to *The Adventure of the Blue Carbuncle*, by Arthur Conan Doyle. New York: Baker Street Irregulars, 1948, pp. 9-16. Reprinted as "A Christmas Story Without Slush." *The Ironing Board*. Garden City, N.Y.: Doubleday, 1949, pp. 95-101.

Argues that *The Blue Carbuncle*, also a Christmas season story, is "a far better work of art" than *A Christmas Carol* by Charles Dickens. It has exactly the right number of words and "nowhere breaks its chosen mood."

*   Murch, A.E. "Sherlock Holmes." *The Development of the
       Detective Novel* (item 51), pp. 167-191.

       Argues that Holmes was immensely popular because he
       was like earlier fictional detectives but also was more
       brilliant, had a "good social and cultural background,"
       was a scientist, and was English rather than French.
       Notes Conan Doyle's debt to Poe as well as the greater
       humanity, excitement, and importance of setting in the
       Holmes stories. Also observes that Conan Doyle combined
       the intellectual and the sensational types of detective
       stories.

1006. "The Novels of Sir Arthur Conan Doyle." *Quarterly Review*
       200 (July 1904): 158-179. Reprinted *Living Age* 242
       (10 September 1904): 641-654.

       In the context of a review of a collected edition of
       Conan Doyle's novels (1903), the reviewer admits to a
       preference for the Sherlock Holmes stories over Conan
       Doyle's other works but observes that they "do not lend
       themselves as inspiring topics to criticism," partly
       because they are too short to allow study of character
       and partly because they follow a formula.

1007. O'Faolain, Sean. "Good Night, Sweet Sherlock." *Playboy*
       22 (January 1975): 109.

       Contends that Sherlock Holmes is irrelevant to the
       modern world, which has lost faith in the powers of the
       intellect. Conan Doyle's stories now have value only
       as nostalgia.

1008. O'Toole, L.M. "Analytic and Synthetic Approaches to
       Narrative Structure: Sherlock Holmes and 'The Sussex
       Vampire.'" *Style and Structure in Literature: Essays
       in the New Stylistics.* Edited by Roger Fowler. Oxford:
       Basil Blackwell, 1975, pp. 143-176.

       This is an application of the structural-semiotic
       approach of generative poetics to a Sherlock Holmes
       story. The focus is on the methodology as much as the
       story itself, and many complex diagrams and symbols are
       used. O'Toole begins with the observation that the
       theme of the Holmes stories is "the triumph of reason
       over the irrational" and also remarks that "The Sussex
       Vampire" is "so neat in its structure, and so mannered
       in its style" that one might suspect it is self-parody
       by Conan Doyle.

*   Ousby, Ian. "Arthur Conan Doyle." *Bloodhounds of Heaven*
       (item 55), pp. 139-175.

       Contends that Conan Doyle's Sherlock Holmes stories
       do not try to "engage the reader's sensibilities" nor
       do they "insult his intelligence." Argues also that the
       portrayal of Holmes "carries the Mid-Victorian respect
       for the detective to new heights of hero-worship."

1009. Peck, Harry Thurston. "A Chat About Sherlock Holmes."
       Independent 53 (21 November 1901): 2757-2760.

       Contends that in the best Sherlock Holmes stories
       Conan Doyle is "as ingenious as Gaboriau, as imaginative
       as Poe," and adds "the human element."

*   Peck, Harry Thurston. "The Detective Story" (item 398).

       Contends that Conan Doyle "is the supreme writer of
       detective stories" because of the simplicity and candor
       of his plots and because his characters "are living,
       breathing human beings." Argues that the "Sherlock
       Holmes stories are not only immensely superior to ...
       Gaboriau's, but in some respects the best of them are
       better" than Poe's detective stories. Singles out *The
       Speckled Band* as the best of the stories.

1010. Poston, Lawrence, III. "The D'Urbervilles and the
       Baskervilles: Two Sets of Noble Kinsmen?" *Baker Street
       Journal* 22 (December 1972): 212-214.

       Points out parallels between *The Hound of the Basker-
       villes* and Thomas Hardy's *Tess of the D'Urbervilles*,
       such as "both novels hint at a fate beyond the control
       of the characters." Singles out Chapter 13 of *The Hound
       of the Baskervilles* as having a "possible source" in
       Chapter 24 of *Tess*.

1011. Pratt, Fletcher. Introduction to *The Later Adventures
       of Sherlock Holmes*, by Arthur Conan Doyle. New York:
       Limited Editions Club, 1952. Reprinted *Introducing
       Mr. Sherlock Holmes*. Edited by Edgar W. Smith. Morris-
       town, N.J.: Baker Street Irregulars, 1959.

       After pointing out that the detective novel usually
       has some padding to make it long enough, Pratt argues
       that *The Hound of the Baskervilles* is not only the
       single case in which Conan Doyle "produced an absolutely
       pure detective story in the long form, but one of the
       few in which any one ever did," and observes that the
       work has realism of both architecture and detail.

1012.   Ratcliffe, S.K. "Arthur Conan Doyle." *New Statesman* 35
        (12 July 1930): 442.

        Contends that in Sherlock Holmes Conan Doyle created
        a character whom everyone knows. Observes that "for all
        his clumsiness of style," Conan Doyle was a good story-
        teller and agrees with Desmond MacCarthy in character-
        izing him "as a writer of 'good bosh.'"

1013.   Rauber, D.F. "Sherlock Holmes and Nero Wolfe: The Role
        of the 'Great Detective' in Intellectual History."
        Journal of Popular Culture 6 (Spring 1973): 483-495.
        Reprinted *Dimensions of Detective Fiction* (item 43),
        pp. 89-96.

        Just as Sherlock Holmes reflects the assumptions of
        classical physics, Nero Wolfe reflects the changes in
        that science produced by the emergence of sub-atomic
        phenomena. The difference is chiefly that Wolfe does not
        use straight clear logic based on physical objects as
        does Holmes.

1014.   Rexroth, Kenneth. "Sherlock Holmes." *Saturday Review*
        51 (27 April 1968): 53, 58.

        Contends that "the adventures of Sherlock Holmes form
        a great comic epic of Victorianism." Conan Doyle "catches
        and transmits the intense individualism and the universal
        consent, and instinctively emphasizes the source, of
        this vast, unstable, dynamic balance-empire."

1015.   Ritunnano, Jeanne. "Mark Twain vs. Arthur Conan Doyle
        on Detective Fiction." *Mark Twain Journal* 16 (Winter
        1971-1972): 10-14.

        Points out that Mark Twain's "A Double-Barrelled
        Detective Story" is a parody of Conan Doyle's Sherlock
        Holmes story, *A Study in Scarlet*. Bases her conclusion
        on a comparison of the two plots and maintains that the
        Conan Doyle story "depicts man as a free agent who acts
        with noble and unselfish motives" and that "man's in-
        tellect is a valuable tool in overcoming difficulties."
        Twain's parody, however, demonstrates that man is mean,
        selfish, vindictive, and not a free agent.

1016.   Roberts, Daisy Mae. "'The Red-Headed League' and 'The
        Rue Morgue.'" *Senior Scholastic* 32 (26 February 1938):
        19E-20E.

Points out that both stories have a first-person narrator, "character drawing of heroes, lucidity, orderliness, and cleverness of plot construction, use of various devices to establish reality and power of minute analysis."

1017. Roberts, S.C. "Baker Street Cult." *Time and Tide* 40 (30 May 1959): 628-629.

In a survey of Conan Doyle's literary career points out that the fact that most people think of him "in terms of Sherlock Holmes should not be allowed to obscure the vigour and variety of his works as a whole." Singles out *The Hound of the Baskervilles* as a "supreme example of the art of story-telling."

1018. Rose, Phyllis. "Huxley, Holmes and the Scientist as Aesthete." *Victorian Newsletter* 38 (Fall 1970): 22-24.

Contends that the Sherlock Holmes stories may be viewed as a "corrective commentary" on, or a parody of, T.H. Huxley's popularization of science. "In transferring the figure of the scientist to fiction, Doyle also converts the scientific method into art."

1019. Rosenberg, Samuel. "Introduction: The Case of the Missing Detective." *The Hound of the Baskervilles*, by Arthur Conan Doyle. New York: Schocken Books, 1975, pp. vii-xi.

Speculates that "Sherlock Holmes's absence from fifty pages of *The Hound of the Baskervilles* might ... be a continuation of Conan Doyle's undying antipathy" for Holmes, pointing out that Conan Doyle borrowed many of Poe's ideas, characters, and plot devices. To assuage his guilty feelings he killed Sherlock Holmes in order to write other types of literature.

*   Routley, Erik. "The Master." *The Puritan Pleasures of the Detective Story* (item 64), pp. 27-59.

Observes that the Sherlock Holmes stories are a "distillation of romantic literature" brought to a peak by the contrast between the two sides of Holmes's character: the "cold logical reasoner and the romantic remoteness." Concludes that Conan Doyle's contribution to the detective story was to transform detection from an "incident or an eccentricity" to a "literary form."

1020.   "Some Inconsistencies of Sherlock Holmes." *Bookman* 14
        (January 1902): 446-447.

        Points out that in *A Study in Scarlet* Holmes is por-
        trayed as knowing almost nothing about literature or
        philosophy but in the next story, Holmes cites "French
        aphorisms," quotes "Goethe in the original German," and
        demonstrates a familiarity with various authors.

1021.   Starrett, Vincent. "Enter Mr. Sherlock Holmes." *Atlantic
        Monthly* 150 (July 1932): 81-87. Reprinted *The Private
        Life of Sherlock Holmes* (item 966).

        Points out the conditions that made the birth of
        Sherlock Holmes possible: Conan Doyle's need for addi-
        tional income, his knowledge of detective fiction, and
        his acquaintance with Dr. Joseph Bell (upon whom Sher-
        lock Holmes is partly modeled).

1022.   Starrett, Vincent. "Oliver Wendell Holmes and Conan
        Doyle." *American Notes and Queries* 1 (1941): 42-43.

        Starrett contends that there is "no direct evidence"
        that Conan Doyle named his protagonist after Oliver
        Wendell Holmes.

1023.   Stewart-Gordon, James. "The Real Sherlock Holmes."
        Ottawa Journal 80 (16 January 1965): 35+. Condensed
        and printed as "The Case of the Durable Detective."
        Reader's Digest 86 (February 1965): 207-210.

        Reviews Conan Doyle's life and literary career. Ob-
        serves that some of the scientific detective methods
        used by Holmes, such as plaster casts to preserve and
        protect evidence, are still used today.

1024.   Stix, Thomas L. "Casual Comments on *The Crooked Man*."
        Baker Street Journal 12 (June 1962): 99-100.

        Points out weaknesses and inconsistencies in *The
        Crooked Man* but concludes that it should not be dis-
        missed lightly because in it Holmes states the "theory
        on which the detective story is based."

1025.   Stout, Rex. "Watson Was a Woman." *Saturday Review* 23
        (1 March 1941): 3-4, 16. Reprinted *The Art of the
        Mystery Story* (item 35). Also reprinted *The Saturday
        Review Gallery*. Edited by Jerome Beatty, Jr. New
        York: Simon and Schuster, 1959, pp. 114-120.

In this famous parody of Baker Street whimsey, Stout gives numerous examples to "prove" that Dr. Watson was really Mrs. Sherlock Holmes.

* Symons, Julian. "The Case of Sherlock Holmes." *Mortal Consequences* (item 74), pp. 63-75.

Contends that Conan Doyle's lack of "mechanical technical perfection" is more than compensated by his skill in storytelling. States that Holmes was "the Superman who was also the Great Outsider" and maintains that the "freshness of detail" and period atmosphere of the stories give "continual pleasure." Argues that Conan Doyle wrote "at least half a dozen" of the best twenty detective short stories.

* Thomson, H. Douglas. "Sherlock Holmes." *Masters of Mystery* (item 77), pp. 122-143.

Observes that Conan Doyle's characterization of Sherlock Holmes is a compromise between "intellectualism and humanism" and that Holmes's eccentricities mask the lack of depth in his character.

* Watson, Colin. *Snobbery with Violence* (item 78), pp. 180-184.

Contends that Conan Doyle's "final touch of genius in the creation of the ideal detective hero" was to place him safely in the past where his adventures could be viewed as either history or nostalgia.

1026. Watt, Donald J. "The Literary Craft of *The Hound of the Baskervilles*." *Baker Street Journal* 22 (December 1972): 207-211.

Maintains that *The Hound of the Baskervilles* is a very good "example of careful literary craftsmanship in a popular story." Conan Doyle shrewdly manipulates "structure, mood, and metaphor" to achieve a unified, completely realized narrative.

* Waugh, Arthur. "Wilkie Collins and His Mantle" (item 810).

Maintains that although Conan Doyle is the best of Wilkie Collins's successors, Collins is still preeminent. Cites specific scenes to explain his preference for *The Moonstone* over *The Hound of the Baskervilles*.

1027.   Wilson, Edmund. "Mr. Holmes, They Were the Footprints
        of a Gigantic Hound." *New Yorker* 21 (17 February 1945):
        66-70. Reprinted *A Literary Chronicle: 1920-1950*.
        Garden City, N.Y.: Doubleday, 1956, pp. 346-353.

        Contends that Conan Doyle's Sherlock Holmes stories
        are literature because they have imagination and style
        that most modern mystery stories lack. Cites several
        examples from the stories to illustrate his contention.

1028.   Wilson, Gary. "The Anomaly of *The Musgrave Ritual*."
        Baker Street Journal 25 (September 1975): 148-153.

        Maintains that Conan Doyle builds into the story's
        structure "unresolved problems" and "incomplete scenes"
        because "Doyle wants the reader to observe, as Holmes
        wants Watson to observe, a story in which loose ends
        are never tied, scenes become fragments of an incomplete
        whole, the supersleuth does not get his man."

DRESSER, DAVIS. See BRETT HALLIDAY

DU BOISGOBEY, FORTUNE (1821-1891)

*   Haycraft, Howard. *Murder for Pleasure* (item 36), pp.
        103-104.

        Observes that Du Boisgobey was a disciple of Gaboriau
        but his style was of a lesser quality.

*   Thomson, H. Douglas. *Masters of Mystery* (item 77), pp.
        109-114.

        States that though Du Boisgobey "relies on the same
        effects as Gaboriau, he is distressingly prolix." His
        one advantage is that he can control his numerous story
        plots more logically than Gaboriau.

DUERRENMATT, FRIEDRICH. See FRIEDRICH DÜRRENMATT

DUKE, WINIFRED (d. 1962)

1029.   Donaldson, Norman. "Winifred Duke: A Preliminary Survey."
        Armchair Detective 2 (January 1969): 94-96.

States that Duke's mysteries usually were based on
real-life murder cases and lists and discusses some of
the more important.

du MAURIER, DAPHNE (1907-   )

1030.   Bryden, Ronald. "Queen of the Wild Mullions." *Spectator*
        208 (20 April 1962): 514-515.

        Contends that du Maurier is beginning to receive
        much deserved critical praise for her cultured suspense
        novels.

1031.   Stockwell, LaTourette. "Best Sellers and the Critics:
        A Case History." *College English* 15 (January 1955):
        214-221.

        States that though du Maurier is widely read, rarely
        have her novels "been responsibly considered by serious
        critics. *Rebecca* is compared to Charlotte Brontë's *Jane
        Eyre*.

DUNCAN, ROBERT L. (1927-   ). Pseudonym: James Hall Roberts

1032.   Winks, Robin W. "Murder by Holocaust." *New Republic* 179
        (22 July 1978): 31-33.

        Contends that Duncan is one of the leading practitioners
        of a subgenre of thriller fiction: "international busi-
        ness intrigue in a foreign setting." Points out that
        "Duncan is interested in the clash of cultures" (six of
        his books "take place in or relate closely to Japan")
        and that his work shows "a strong sense of place, an
        awareness of how landscape, social environment, climate
        influence structure."

DUNCAN, W. MURDOCH (1909-1975). Pseudonyms: John Cassells,
    John Dallas, Neill Graham, Martin Locke, Peter Malloch,
    Lovat Marshall

1033.   Ireland, Donald. "W. Murdoch Duncan--Master of Mystery."
        Armchair Detective 9 (February 1976): 116-118.

        Maintains that Duncan emphasized characters as well
        as plots, and "was able to create atmosphere and pace
        in his stories, as well as providing the reader with a

real problem in detection." Also observes that he used
different styles for different pseudonyms.

DURAS, MARGUERITE (1914-)

1034. Eisenger, Erica M. "Crime and Detection in the Novels
       of Marguerite Duras." *Contemporary Literature* 15
       (Autumn 1974): 503-520.

       In her use of the themes and techniques of the detec-
       tive story Duras "emphasizes the human drama of moral
       involvement in the mystery of another's criminal act"
       rather than the puzzle element.

DURBRIDGE, FRANCIS (1912-). Joint pseudonym with James Douglas
   Rutherford McConnell (1915-): Paul Temple. Series character
   also named Paul Temple

1035. Adley, Derek. "The Paul Temple Saga." *Armchair Detective*
       9 (October 1976): 267-269.

       States that Durbridge based his character, Paul Temple,
       on a brief encounter with a man on a commuter train.
       Continues with a brief description of how the character
       has changed since the 1930s.

DÜRRENMATT, FRIEDRICH (1921-)

1036. Arnold, Armin. "Friedrich Dürrenmatt and Edgar Wallace."
       International Fiction Review 3 (1976): 142-144.

       Contends that Dürrenmatt's *Die Panne* is influenced by
       some works by Edgar Wallace, chiefly *The Four Just Men*.

1037. Holtan, Orley I. "Friedrich Dürrenmatt: The Detective
       Story as Moral Parable." *Armchair Detective* 5 (April
       1972): 133-136, 144.

       Contends that Dürrenmatt has made of the detective
       story "a moral or a metaphysical parable," missing the
       question of whether an absolute principle of justice
       exists.

1038. Leah, Gordon N. "Dürrenmatt's Detective Stories."
       Modern Languages 48 (June 1967): 65-69.

Argues that Dürrenmatt intends his three novels as parodies of the conventional detective story.

1039. Ramsey, Roger. "Parody and Mystery in Dürrenmatt's *The Pledge.*" *Modern Fiction Studies* 17 (Winter 1971-1972): 525-532.

Contends that Dürrenmatt parodies puzzle-solving but not "faith in mystery" in *The Pledge.*

1040. Wagner, Geoffrey. "Dürrenmatt and the *Kriminalroman.*" *Commonweal* 76 (22 June 1962): 324-326.

Argues that Dürrenmatt's works are virtual parodies of the detective story, especially in their use of chance.

1041. Wieckenberg, Ernst-Peter. "Dürrenmatts Detektivromane." *Text + Kritik* 56 (October 1977): 8-19.

By using an unsuccessful detective and an ambiguous case Dürrenmatt changed the detective story to reflect the complexities of life.

EGAN, LESLEY. See ELIZABETH LININGTON

ELLIN, STANLEY (1916-)

1042. Geller, Evelyn. "Stanley Ellin." *Wilson Library Bulletin* 35 (June 1961): 796.

States that Ellin is a modern master of the mystery/suspense story. Also traces the literary reaction to his short stories and three novels.

EUSTIS, HELEN (1916-)

1043. Barzun, Jacques, and Wendell Hertig Taylor. Preface to *The Horizontal Man*, by Helen Eustis. New York: Garland Publishing, 1976. Also printed in *A Book of Prefaces* (item 22), pp. 43-44.

Contends that in no other mystery novel have psychological clues "been used so extensively and confidently" as in this book.

EVANS, JOHN. See HOWARD BROWNE

EXBRAYAT, CHARLES HUBERT (1906-   )

1044.   Evernden, Margery. "America, où est-vous?: Speculations
        on Exbrayat." *Armchair Detective* 11 (July 1978):
        254-256.

        Although he has written a large number of "roman
        policiers" Exbrayat is unknown in America, possibly
        because of his choice of settings (southern Europe),
        his failure to create a "charismatic" detective featured
        in a series of novels, his esoteric sense of humor, and
        his interest in social classes.

FAIR, A.A. See ERLE STANLEY GARDNER

FAIRBAIRN, ROGER. See JOHN DICKSON CARR

FARJEON, B.L. (1838-1903)

1045.   Faderman, Lillian. "B.L. Farjeon: Victorian Novelist."
        Ph.D. dissertation, University of California at Los
        Angeles, 1967.

        States that Farjeon was popular with Victorian readers
        because his writing style and subject matter were based
        on what most pleased these readers.

1046.   "The Late B.L. Farjeon." *Bookman* 18 (September 1903): 1.

        Points out that although Farjeon had a very successful
        literary career, his popularity did not last.

FAULKNER, WILLIAM (1897-1962)

1047.   Brooks, Cleanth. "History, Tragedy and the Imagination
        in *Absalom, Absalom!*" *Yale Review* 52 (March 1963):
        340-351. Reprinted *William Faulkner: The Yoknapatawpha
        Country.* New Haven, Conn.: Yale University Press,
        1963, pp. 295-324.

        Absalom, Absalom! is from one point of view "a wonder-
        ful detective story, by far the best of Faulkner's
        several flirtations with the particular genre."

1048. Fiedler, Leslie. "William Faulkner: An American Dickens." *Commentary* 10 (October 1950): 384-387. Reprinted as "William Faulkner: Highbrow's Lowbrow." *No! In Thunder: Essays on Myth and Literature.* Boston: Beacon Press, 1960, pp. 111-118.

"The detective story is the inevitable crown of Faulkner's work" because, like most of the reading public, Faulkner is fond of the "switcheroo" and the surprise ending. Mentions but does not examine *Knight's Gambit* and *Intruder in the Dust.*

1049. French, Warren. "William Faulkner and the Art of the Detective Story." *The Thirties: Fiction, Poetry, Drama.* Edited by Warren French. Deland, Fla.: Everett Edwards, 1967, pp. 55-62.

The genre of the detective story seems "trivial and sub-literary" only because it usually attracts poor writers. In *Absalom, Absalom!* Faulkner showed that a detective story can be a work of art that deals "with man's tragic relationship to his social situation."

1050. Gidley, Mark (Mick). "Elements of the Detective Story in William Faulkner's Fiction." *Journal of Popular Culture* 7 (Summer 1973): 97-123. Reprinted *Dimensions of Detective Fiction* (item 43), pp. 228-246.

Argues that Faulkner liked detective fiction because of its "sense of surprise." Common to Faulkner's work as a whole and to detective writing is "the ability to conceal meaning." But none of Faulkner's works is satisfactory as a pure detective story because he--to his credit--does not make everything fall into place at the end.

1051. Holman, C. Hugh. "*Absalom, Absalom!*: The Historian as Detective." *Sewanee Review* 79 (Autumn 1971): 542-553.

That Faulkner read and wrote detective stories is reflected in *Absalom, Absalom!*, the construction of which is close to that of a standard detective story. The connection between the detective story and much of Faulkner's work is that "the detective story is ... concerned with understanding the past through interpretation."

1052. Howe, Irving. "Minor Faulkner." *Nation* 169 (12 November
       1949): 473-474.

       The stories in *Knight's Gambit* are detective stories,
       but they "fail to satisfy the needs of that form" even
       though the "detective apparatus" gets in the way of
       one's appreciation of the stories on any other level.

1053. Malraux, André. "A Preface for Faulkner's *Sanctuary*."
       Yale French Studies 10 (Fall 1952): 92-94.

       The importance of the detective story plot in *Sanc-
       tuary* is not in itself but that it "engenders ... an
       ill-assorted, powerful, and savagely personal world."

1054. Millgate, Michael. *The Achievement of William Faulkner*.
       Lincoln: University of Nebraska Press, 1978, pp.
       265-270.

       Knight's Gambit is a collection of short stories, each
       of which has the basic structure of the detective story,
       but the first, "Smoke," is little more than a poor
       example of the form, and the value of the rest is the
       development of the detective, Gavin Stevens, into "a
       staunch upholder of humanistic values."

1055. O'Connor, William Van. *The Tangled Fire of William
       Faulkner*. New York: Gordian Press, 1968, pp. 142-145.

       The genre of the detective story is not suited to
       Faulkner's language, themes, or subject matter. As a
       result, in Faulkner's detective stories the deduction
       is inclined to be "tricky and insignificant" while the
       characterization and themes are "out of keeping with
       the occasion."

1056. Rubin, Louis D., Jr. "Five Southerners." *Hopkins Review*
       3 (Spring 1950): 42-45.

       A mystery story can be literature only if the plot
       does not overshadow the characters and if one is tempted
       to re-read the story after one knows the solution to
       the mystery. *Intruder in the Dust* passes these "tests,"
       but *Knight's Gambit*, one of Faulkner's least important
       works, does not.

1057. Tallack, Douglas G. "William Faulkner and the Tradition
       of Tough-Guy Fiction." *Dimensions of Detective Fiction*
       (item 43), pp. 247-264.

Detective fiction written before the tough-guy period
"evokes crime and then purges it and is thus a completely
safe form." In tough-guy fiction, however, "respectable
society is honeycombed with corruption and hypocrisy."
This is the form which influenced Faulkner's *Sanctuary*.

FAUST, FREDERICK (1892-1944). Pseudonyms: Max Brand, Frederick
Frost, Walter C. Butler

1058.   Clark, Bill. "Max Brand and the Mystery Story." *Armchair
        Detective* 2 (July 1969): 255.

        Though known as a writer of Westerns, Brand (Frederick
        Faust) wrote several mystery and spy stories under three
        pseudonyms: Max Brand, Walter C. Butler, and Frederick
        Frost.

1059.   Easton, Robert. *Max Brand: The Big "Westerner."* Norman:
        University of Oklahoma Press, 1970. 330pp.

        This account of the life and writings (most of which
        were Westerns) of the prolific Brand contains scattered
        references to his mystery stories. Easton suggests that
        the mystery fiction was written solely for money and
        that Brand had little enthusiasm for it.

FEARING, KENNETH (1902-1961)

1060.   Barzun, Jacques, and Wendell Hertig Taylor. Preface to
        The Big Clock, by Kenneth Fearing. New York: Garland
        Publishing, 1976. Also printed in *A Book of Prefaces*
        (item 22), pp. 45-46.

        Points out that this mystery novel is "a mystery
        without a mystery" that remains gripping throughout,
        partly because of the narrative skill of Fearing.

FISH, ROBERT L. (1912-   ). Pseudonym: Robert L. Pike

1061.   Fish, Robert L. "Captain José da Silva." *The Great
        Detectives* (item 60), pp. 67-77.

        Fish points out several ways in which his detective
        differs from "most fictional policemen, or private-eye
        detectives": he is not stupid, can be injured, complains
        when hurt, exhibits normal emotional reactions, and has
        a bad temper.

FLEMING, IAN (1908-1964). Series character: James Bond

1062.   Amis, Kingsley. *The James Bond Dossier.* New York: New
        American Library, 1965. 142pp.

        Argues that Fleming's novels are reflections of
        society's aggressions, insecurities, and fantasies; ex-
        amines reasons for the enormous popularity of James
        Bond.

1063.   Amis, Kingsley. "M for Murder." *New Statesman* 69 (2
        April 1965): 540-541.

        States that Fleming rewrote the manuscript for *You
        Only Live Twice* due to criticism of the amount of
        violence and sadism. Amis states that the final version
        is weak and uninteresting, noting that "nobody can write
        at his best with part of his attention on puritanical
        readers over his shoulder."

*   Barzun, Jacques. "Meditations on the Literature of
        Spying." (item 115).

        Contends that the Bond novels were popular because
        they satisfied the reader's desire for action and
        adventure.

1064.   Bergonzi, Bernard. "The Case of Mr. Fleming." *Twentieth
        Century* 163 (March 1958): 220-228.

        States that Fleming's novels have no "ethical frame
        of reference"; rather, the novels are based on lurid
        sensation which is the "characteristic mode of fantasy
        of a dirty-minded schoolboy."

1065.   Bocca, Geoffrey. "The Spectacular Cult of Ian Fleming."
        Saturday Evening Post 236 (22 June 1963): 66-68.

        Observes that although Fleming designed Bond's back-
        ground to be similar to his own, Fleming's character is
        opposite; he abhors violence.

1066.   Boyd, Ann S. *The Devil with James Bond!* Richmond, Va.:
        John Knox Press, 1967. 123pp.

        Argues that throughout the Bond novels there is a
        basic underlying theme: the "destruction of today's
        seven deadlier sins, particularly apathy." States that
        Bond is a modern St. George who seeks out these sins
        and destroys them for the benefit of modern society.

1067. Boyd, Ann S. "James Bond: Modern Day Dragonslayer."
      Christian Century 82 (19 May 1965): 644-647.

      States that the Bond novels represent a layman's
      analysis of the relationship between the "demonic and
      individual responsibility" and maintains that Bond
      would sacrifice all to defend justice and humanity.

1068. Buono, Oreste del, and Umberto Eco, eds. *The Bond
      Affair*. London: Macdonald, 1966. 173pp.

      Unavailable for annotation. Contains eight essays.

1069. Carpenter, Richard C. "007 and the Myth of the Hero."
      Journal of Popular Culture 1 (Fall 1967): 80-89.

      Contends that Bond, more than any other modern literary
      hero, is a reproduction of the legendary heroes of the
      past; parallels drawn include embarking on a dangerous
      journey, encountering difficult obstacles, and suffering
      greatly in order to accomplish the mission.

*   Cawelti, John G. *Adventure, Mystery, and Romance* (item
      150), pp. 39-40.

      States that the Bond stories are a form of fantasy
      involving a superhero who has extraordinary abilities
      that help him defeat insuperable obstacles without harm
      to himself, either morally or physically.

1070. Clements, Robert J. "The European Literary Scene."
      Saturday Review 48 (7 August 1965): 22.

      Maintains that popularity can transform an ordinary
      novel into one of critical importance. Observes that
      if Fleming had remained just a writer of thrillers,
      critics would have ignored him. His phenomenal "over-
      night" success, however, meant that the Bond novels
      would be critically analyzed by sociologists and
      psychologists as well as literary critics.

1071. Cook, Bruce. "007: The Gentleman in Decline." *Catholic
      World* 203 (June 1966): 169-174.

      States that earlier mysteries had "gentleman-heroes"
      (such as Bulldog Drummond, Richard Hannay, and Sandy
      Arbuthnot) who reflected the authors' perceptions of
      their age: Bond cannot be included in this category
      since he reflects an "idea of a gentleman so modern
      and loose as to be totally meaningless."

1072.   Gallico, Paul. Introduction to *Gilt-Edged Bonds:*
        Casino Royale, From Russia, with Love, Doctor No, by
        Ian Fleming. New York: Macmillan, 1961, pp. v-xvi.

        Contends that James Bond and the novels in which he
        appears are immensely popular because they reflect the
        mores of the times. Bond is thus regarded as a hero
        by the public despite the fact that Fleming "never
        intended him to be one."

1073.   Grella, George. "James Bond: Culture Hero." *New Republic*
        150 (30 May 1964): 17-20. Reprinted *The Critic as*
        Artist: Essays on Books, 1920-1970. Edited by Gilbert
        A. Harrison. New York: Liveright, 1972, pp. 138-144.

        Maintains that Bond is accepted as a modern-day hero
        "savior of our culture," and states that "no secret
        agent could behave with such incompetence and still
        achieve such high renown." Also argues that most of
        Fleming's thrillers are based on myth and legends.

1074.   Hedman, Iwan. "Ian Fleming." *Armchair Detective* 5 (July
        1972): 216-219, 222.

        Hedman gives a biographical sketch of Fleming and
        points out that his newspaper experience and adventurous
        life are reflected in the Bond books. A checklist of
        items by and about Fleming is included.

1075.   Holbrook, David. *The Masks of Hate: The Problem of*
        False Solutions in the Culture of an Acquisitive
        Society. Oxford: Pergamon Press, 1972, pp. 67-144.

        An extended analysis of Fleming's *Goldfinger* is used
        to develop Holbrook's thesis that the false trends in
        our culture are based upon the mistaken belief "that
        man's primary drive is to pleasure, power, or self-
        assertion."

1076.   Hydak, Michael G. "Don Juan Bond." *Language Quarterly*
        14 (Spring-Summer 1976): 29-30, 33.

        Observes that Ian Fleming's James Bond was influenced
        by Tirso de Molina's Don Juan. Points out the similar-
        ities of the characters' moral ideals as well as their
        similar relationships with women. In French.

1077.   Johnson, Paul. "Sex, Snobbery and Sadism." *New States-*
        man 55 (5 April 1958): 430-432.

States that *Dr. No* has three basic elements which are "all unhealthy, all thoroughly English": sadism, sexual longing, and snobbish cravings. Johnson observes that the combination of these elements has created a "social phenomenon of some importance."

1078. Kirk, Russell. "Education of Presidents." *National Review* 15 (8 October 1963): 308.

Observes that detective stories were popular with several American Presidents, such as Franklin Roosevelt, Eisenhower, and Kennedy. Points out Kennedy's appreciation of Ian Fleming and the Bond novels.

1079. Lejeune, Anthony. "To Valhalla with Twin Exhausts." *National Review* 17 (7 September 1965): 776-777.

Maintains that Fleming viewed the detective novel as a fairy tale for adults and that he deliberately made them as glossy and sexually appealing as he could.

1080. "Man with the Golden Bond." *Time* 84 (21 August 1964): 22-23.

States that the best detective-heroes were always "superbly attuned to their own age" and that Bond has the perfect mixture of amorality and public responsibility for the sixties, an age "dedicated to affluence and to being with it."

1081. Marshment, Margaret. "Racist Ideology and Popular Fiction." *Race and Class* 19 (Spring 1978): 331-344.

Maintains that James Bond represents the England of the white, upper-class male.

1082. Martin, Bernard. "James Bond: A Phenomenon of Some Importance." *Cunning Exiles: Studies of Modern Prose Writers*. Edited by Don Anderson and Stephen Knight. London: Angus and Robertson, 1974, pp. 218-238.

Argues that the two most important reasons for the success of Fleming's novels were his use of fantasy in the plots and the anchoring of that fantasy to realistic and convincing detail. Thus he provided the reader with escape that always remained familiar.

1083. Muggeridge, Malcolm. "Books." *Esquire* 62 (December 1964): 36-38.

Observes that Fleming had devised a definite formula
that he felt would make the Bond novels popular: money,
sex, snobbishness, and violence.

1084. Newquist, Roy. "Ian Fleming's Last Interview." *Show* 4
       (November 1964): 62-63, 91.

       In this wide-ranging interview Fleming covers such
       topics as James Bond's development from a "straight-
       forward man who didn't really possess a total personal-
       ity" to a more rounded character "encrusted with manner-
       isms and belongings and individual characteristics" and
       the fact that Hammett, Chandler, E. Phillips Oppenheim,
       and Sax Rohmer influenced him.

1085. "Of Human Bondage." *Time* 79 (13 April 1962): 102-104.

       Contends that the most important reason for the popu-
       larity of James Bond is his "man-of-the-worldmanship"
       and his apparently universal expertise that feeds the
       reader's fantasies.

1086. "007 v. SMERSH." *Time* 79 (29 June 1962): 16.

       States that the Russian newspaper *Izvestia* considers
       the Bond novels to be a part of American propaganda
       against the Soviet Union; the Russians charge that
       Allen Dulles (former head of the CIA) recommended pro-
       paganda methods to Fleming who used them in *From Russia,
       with Love* and *Dr. No.*

1087. **Ormerod, David, and David Ward. "The Bond Game."** *London
       Magazine* 5 (May 1965): 41-55.

       Observes that many of the Bond novels are based upon
       ancient myths and psychological motifs that were used
       to exploit the reader's obsessions.

*   Palmer, Jerry. *Thrillers* (item 56).

       Devotes many pages to Fleming throughout and argues
       that Fleming's novels did not establish any new ideas
       for the spy novel but were simply modern examples of
       established formulas.

1088. Pearson, John. *James Bond: The Authorized Biography of
       007.* New York: William Morrow, 1973. 317pp.

       Pearson, the author of a biography of Fleming (item
       1089), in this book writes about James Bond as if he
       were a real person.

1089. Pearson, John. *The Life of Ian Fleming.* New York: McGraw, 1966. 352pp.

Observes that Fleming's early adventurous life was a model for that of James Bond and states that Fleming "succeeded in tapping his own unconscious" when writing the novels.

1090. "Playboy Interview: Ian Fleming." *Playboy* 11 (December 1964): 97-106.

In this interview, Fleming states that James Bond is a "creature of his era," reflecting the values and interests of modern society.

1091. Plomer, William. "Ian Fleming Remembered." *Encounter* 24 (January 1965): 64-66.

States that Fleming's novels express his straight-forward approach to his writing while incorporating his zest for living.

1092. Price, James. "Our Man in the Torture Chamber: The Novels of Ian Fleming." *London Magazine* 2 (July 1962): 67-70.

Observes Fleming's tongue-in-cheek attitude and growing ambivalence toward the Bond novels. Points out that the plots became progressively more far-fetched and that the "fantasies have grown more and more grandiose as volume succeeeded volume."

1093. Richler, Mordecai. "James Bond Unmasked." *Commentary* 46 (July 1968): 74-81. Reprinted *Mass Culture Revisited.* Edited by Bernard Rosenberg and David Manning White. New York: Van Nostrand, 1971, pp. 341-355. Also reprinted *Notes on an Endangered Species and Others.* New York: Alfred A. Knopf, 1974, pp. 3-35.

Richler finds Fleming's books "morally repugnant" and contends that Fleming "sniffed plotters, either colored or with Jewish blood, perpetually scheming at the undoing of the England he cherished. This, largely, is what James Bond is about." Includes many examples from the novels in support of this thesis.

1094. Snelling, O.F. *007, James Bond: A Report.* New York: New American Library, 1964. 127pp.

Contends that James Bond is the "livingest" character since Sherlock Holmes, that he is real in a way that The Saint, Philip Marlowe, and Inspector Maigret never are. In this respect his predecessors are the pre-World War II characters Richard Hannay, Bulldog Drummond, and Jonah Mansel, even though Bond does not follow their code of honor or morality. Analyzes Bond's image, women, adversaries, and future.

1095. "Sorry to Have Troubled You." *Newsweek* 64 (24 August 1964): 37.

Argues that in spite of all the violence, the Bond novels are a "series of civilized acts." In an age of anti-heroes Bond is a popular hero who has the freedom to destroy modern oppressors and demolish fears.

1096. Starkey, Lycurgus M., Jr. *James Bond's World of Values.* Nashville: Abingdon Press, 1966. 96pp.

States that Bond is popular because he represents the values of a modern, affluent culture and maintains that Bond's world challenges the Christian ethic in five areas: sex, sadism, status, leisure time, and nationalism.

*   Symons, Julian. "An End to Spying: Or, From Pipe Dream to Farce." (item 488).

Briefly surveys comments by critics on the Bond novels and argues that "the modern spy story starts with Bond, which is to say that it starts with a pipe dream." Also contends that Bond was popular partly because he "exemplified the effectiveness of individual violence" at a time when many readers felt they were only powerless parts of an organization. Also maintains that "an element of self-mockery" in the books allowed the reader to enjoy them without taking them too seriously.

1097. "Upper-Crust Low Life." *Time* 71 (5 May 1958): 84.

Observes that many critics consider the Bond novels to be a mixture of sophisticated taste and bad writing and that Fleming is often considered a dilettante who constructs unlikely thrills; he has been called a "kind of Mickey Spillane in gentleman's clothing."

*   Watson, Colin. *Snobbery with Violence* (item 78), pp. 233-251.

Argues that the James Bond novels did not represent a new type of thriller; they actually "repeated every prescription in the pharmacopoeia of crime and spy fiction."

1098.   Webb, Bernice Larson. "James Bond as Literary Descendant
        of Beowulf." *South Atlantic Quarterly* 67 (Winter
        1968): 1-12.

        States that *Beowulf* and the Bond novels are both tradi-
        tional hero-romances and have such common elements as
        improbable adventures, a heroic leader, and an absence
        of romantic love.

1099.   Zeiger, Henry A. *Ian Fleming: The Spy Who Came in with
        the Gold*. New York: Duell, 1965. 150pp.

        Argues that Fleming needed a hero figure and created
        one in the character of James Bond, who was modeled
        after several friends of Fleming.

FOOTNER, WILLIAM HULBERT (1879-1944)

1100.   Morley, Christopher D. "In Memoriam." *The Ironing Board*.
        New York: Doubleday, 1949, pp. 167-172.

        Points out how Footner's personal life influenced his
        writing and very briefly surveys several of his charac-
        ters and mystery titles.

1101.   Overton, Grant M. "Where the Plot Thickens." *When Winter
        Comes to Main Street*. New York: George H. Doran. 1922,
        pp. 74-75.

        Observes that Footner "has a special gift for the
        picturesque character."

FORD, LESLIE. Pseudonym of Zenith Jones Brown (1898-   ). Other
        pseudonym: David Frome

1102.   Dueren, Fred. "Evan Pinkerton." *Armchair Detective* 7
        (May 1974): 193-194.

        A description of Frome's character, Evan Pinkerton,
        in which Dueren observes that Pinkerton's interest in
        detective work was due to his friendship with Inspector
        John Bull of Scotland Yard, whose work he romanticized.
        Timid and unassertive himself, Pinkerton used "his
        almost feminine intuition and common sense" to help
        Bull solve his cases.

1103.   Ford, Leslie. "Why Murder Fascinates Me." *Good House-
        keeping* 110 (May 1940): 37.

States that what interests her most in writing a
mystery novel is the "psychological or emotional state"
of a person who sees murder as the only solution to a
problem.

*   Haycraft, Howard. *Murder for Pleasure* (item 36), pp.
        209-210.

Points out that the *Pinkerton Tales* published under
Brown's pseudonym, David Frome, are not as stylized as
would be expected in a straightforward crime narrative.

1104.   Shore, Jane. "Profile of a Mystery Writer." *Saturday
        Review* 20 (9 September 1939): 10-11.

States that Ford's mysteries are notable for their
intelligence, witty dialogue and for well-bred sophisticated characters. She "is at her best in writing
backgrounds and minor characters."

FORSYTH, FREDERICK (1938-   )

1105.   Wolfe, Peter. "Stalking Forsyth's Jackal." *Armchair
        Detective* 7 (May 1974): 165-174.

In a detailed plot analysis of *The Day of the Jackal*
(1971), points out elements of the smoothly-knit plot
that contribute to the book's "relentless buildup."
Observes that "the characters reveal themselves in
action, mostly physical, rather than in thought or
moral decision."

FOWLES, JOHN (1926-   )

1106.   Brownell, David. "John Fowles' Experiments with the
        Form of the Mystery Story." *Armchair Detective* 10
        (April 1977): 184-186.

Contends that Fowles's short story "The Enigma"
(published in *The Ebony Tower*) successfully accomplishes
the "technical experiment" of writing a mystery story
that does not solve the mystery.

FOX, SEBASTIAN. See GERALD BULLETT

FRANCIS, DICK (1920-)

1107. Bauska, Barry. "Endure and Prevail: The Novels of Dick Francis." *Armchair Detective* 11 (July 1978): 238-244.

Argues that while Francis's heroes are not James Bond types but rather dull, ordinary people who have suffered either physical or psychological problems, they are really romantic heroes.

1108. Cantwell, R. "Mystery Makes a Writer." *Sports Illustrated* 28 (25 March 1968): 76-88.

Points out that Francis uses his considerable racing and horse raising knowledge as background for his mysteries.

1109. Durrant, Digby. "Born Winner." *London Magazine* 14 (June/July 1974): 90-93.

Observes that Francis's success can be attributed to his fast-paced action and ingenious and thoroughly researched plotting.

FRAZER, ROBERT CAINE. See JOHN CREASEY

FREEDGOOD, MORTON. See JOHN GODEY

FREELING, NICOLAS (1927-). Series character: Inspector Van der Valk

1110. "Authors and Editors--Nicolas Freeling." *Publishers Weekly* 191 (29 May 1967): 25.

States that Freeling's character, Inspector Van der Valk, is popular because he sometimes finds a "most unpolice-like" solution to a crime.

1111. Freeling, Nicolas. "Inspector Van der Valk." *The Great Detectives* (item 60), pp. 247-257.

Freeling states that he created Van der Valk because he wanted a detective "who would be a recognizable human being."

FREEMAN, R. AUSTIN (1862-1943). Series character: Dr. Thorndyke

1112. Adams, John. "Mr. R. Austin Freeman." *Bookman* (London)
       44 (April 1913): 6-7.

       Argues that Freeman's mystery novels are above average
       because of Freeman's acknowledged "authority on the
       subjects he is dealing with."

1113. Barzun, Jacques, and Wendell Hertig Taylor. Preface to
       The Singing Bone, by R. Austin Freeman. New York:
       Garland Publishing, 1976. Also printed in *A Book of
       Prefaces* (item 22), pp. 47-48.

       Points out that this novel uses two of Freeman's
       innovations--the "inverted" detective story and his
       skillful "use of fingerprints." The inverted detective
       novel tells the story twice, once "as the facts of the
       crime occur, and again as the detective goes to work
       on the clues."

1114. Bleiler, E.F. Introduction to *The Best Dr. Thorndyke
       Detective Stories*, by R. Austin Freeman. New York:
       Dover, 1973, pp. v-ix.

       Contends that Freeman was a leading exponent of the
       "scientific detective story" and "the philosopher turned
       detective." He developed several techniques that his
       detective, Dr. Thorndyke, used to solve crimes, such
       as blood examination and footprint preservation.

1115. Donaldson, Norman. "A Freeman Postscript." *The Mystery
       and Detection Annual 1972* (item 16), pp. 86-92.

       Observes that the strongest point of Freeman's
       Thorndyke stories is their scientific foundation. Ana-
       lyzes "The Blue Diamond Mystery."

1116. Donaldson, Norman. *In Search of Dr. Thorndyke: The Story
       of R. Austin Freeman's Great Scientific Investigator
       and His Creator*. Bowling Green, Ohio: Bowling Green
       University Popular Press, 1971. 288pp.

       Donaldson argues that most of Freeman's life and
       personality is in the Dr. Thorndyke books, particularly
       his attention to detail and his scientific interest
       and training. Also stresses Freeman's invention of the
       "inverted" detective story, in which the crime is de-
       scribed in the first part and the detection in the
       second part (often the reader knows who committed the
       crime).

1117. Donaldson, Norman. "The Penrose Mystery." *Armchair Detective* 2 (January 1969): 108-111.

States that conversations with Ronald Jessup, an amateur archaeologist, gave Freeman the idea for a hiding place for a body in *The Penrose Mystery* and that the book then inspired an excavation of the site described. Includes an excerpt from a letter from Jessup.

1118. Donaldson, Norman. "R. Austin Freeman." *Armchair Detective* 1 (January 1968): 32-36.

Argues that Freeman had wide knowledge that he used in his novels, but only as an essential part of the story. His books provide intellectual rather than visceral pleasures. Includes a checklist.

1119. Freeman, R. Austin. "Meet Dr. Thorndyke." *Meet the Detective* (item 45), pp. 129-138. Reprinted *Dr. Thorndyke's Crime File*, by R. Austin Freeman. Edited by P.M. Stone. New York: Dodd, Mead, 1941, pp. ix-xv.

Freeman states that as a medical student he became interested in medical jurisprudence and saw the value of physical facts that would be apparent only to a trained medical practitioner. He later had Thorndyke adopt this method of investigation.

* Haycraft, Howard. *Murder for Pleasure* (item 36), pp. 67-71.

Contends that Freeman "was the true and undoubted 'parent' of the scientific detective story."

1120. Heenan, Michael G. "A Note on the Chronology of the Dr. Thorndyke Novels." *Armchair Detective* 9 (November 1975): 52-54.

Annotated list of the twenty-one Dr. Thorndyke novels and forty short stories.

1121. Lofts, W.O.G., and D.J. Adley. "Was 'Jack Wylde' Really R. Austin Freeman?" *Armchair Detective* 7 (August 1974): 247-250.

Maintains there is a possibility that Freeman wrote juvenile detective stories under the pseudonym Jack Wylde.

1122.   "R. Austin Freeman." *Wilson Library Bulletin* 3 (November
        1928): 322.

        Contends that Freeman has gained a deserved reputation
        as one of the best writers of scientific detective
        stories. His particular care with the accuracy of the
        experiments performed by his main character, Dr. Thorn-
        dyke, has greatly contributed to the plausibility of
        his detective stories.

*   Routley, Erik. *The Puritan Pleasures of the Detective
        Story* (item 64), pp. 63-72.

        Contends that Freeman's lack of literary style makes
        reading his Dr. Thorndyke stories pleasureless. They
        do retain some interest, however, "because of their
        author's single-minded devotion to the task of showing
        'science' as relevant to that everyday life which de-
        tective stories deal with."

*   Thomson, H. Douglas. *Masters of Mystery* (item 77), pp.
        168-176.

        Argues that Freeman's emphasis on the scientific
        "constituted an admirable reaction to the wild guess-
        work of some of Thorndyke's contemporaries."

FROME, DAVID. See LESLIE FORD

FROST, FREDERICK. See FREDERICK FAUST

FUTRELLE, JACQUES (1875-1912)

1123.   Freedman, Benedict. "The Thinking Machine." *The Mystery
        and Detection Annual 1972* (item 16), pp. 79-85.

        Argues that what makes Futrelle's stories "permanently
        readable" is that he "has introduced elements of doubt,
        even mockery, into his portrait of the perfect deduc-
        tive thinker."

1124.   Gilbert, Elliot L. "Murder Without Air: Jacques Futrelle."
        New Republic 177 (30 July 1977): 33-34.

        States that the popular appeal of Futrelle's tale
        The Problem of Cell 13 is due to its being "nothing
        less than an ingenious rewriting of the Easter myth for
        the modern sensibility."

* Haycraft, Howard. *Murder for Pleasure* (item 36), pp. 85-87.

 Contends that Futrelle brought a freshness to the detective novel with his style, which is straightforward and free of pomposity.

GABORIAU, ÉMILE (1832-1873)

1125. Bleiler, E.F. Introduction to *Monsieur LeCoq*, by Émile Gaboriau. New York: Dover Publications, 1975, pp. v-xxviii.

 Bleiler points out that a "scandal of the sexual sort" provided the common theme in Gaboriau's novels and also analyzes LeCoq, the detective in five of Gaboriau's works.

1126. Bonniot, Roger. "A la Recherche d'Émile Gaboriau." *Europe* no. 571-572 (November-December 1976): 55-60.

 Points out that the centenary of Gaboriau's birth passed almost unnoticed in France and that there is insufficient documentation for the researcher interested in studying his life and literary career. Contends that a study of what is known about Gaboriau's life leads one to the conclusion that some parts of his books are autobiographical.

1127. **Cambiaire, Célestin Pierre.** "Poe and Émile Gaboriau." *The Influence of Edgar Allan Poe in France.* New York: G.E. Steckert, 1927, pp. 264-280.

 Points out examples of Poe's influence on Gaboriau, particularly in the methods his detective hero used, such as close observation. Concludes that "Gaboriau writes novels, while Poe writes short stories."

1128. **Curry, Nancy E.** "The Life and Work of Émile Gaboriau." Ph.D. dissertation, University of Kentucky, 1971.

 Argues that Gaboriau's novels display great originality in presenting the detectives and their methods of extremely rational deduction. Also contends that Gaboriau brings his characters to life in the manner of Balzac.

* Haycraft, Howard. *Murder for Pleasure* (item 36), pp. 30-36.

States that Gaboriau wrote novels which "made use of
detection as one of several themes." His weakness,
according to modern detective fiction standards, is in
the implausibility of his plots.

*   Murch, A.E. "The Rise of the Roman-Policier." *The Development of the Detective Novel* (item 51), pp. 121-
128.

Credits Gaboriau with originating the "roman-policier"
in which "the reader's attention is focussed on the
detection, not the commission, of crime" and with en-
riching detective fiction "by his perception of the
suspense-value of the 'red herring.'"

*   Peck, Harry Thurston. "The Detective Story." (item 398).

Maintains that Gaboriau "is a link between Edgar Allan
Poe and Conan Doyle." He combined an "understanding of
human nature" with the mathematical reasoning of Poe
and in his best detective novel, *Monsieur LeCoq*, "introduced a new type of deductive reasoner which suggested
to Conan Doyle the interesting Mycroft Holmes, brother
of Sherlock Holmes."

1129.   [Sayers, Dorothy L.] "Émile Gaboriau, 1835-1873: The
Detective Novelist's Dilemma." *Times Literary Supplement* 2 November 1935, pp. 677-678.

Argues that Gaboriau was a novelist who believed the
"detective problem could never stand as a book by itself."
He thought that "the character interest was as necessary
as the plot interest."

*   Symons, Julian. *Mortal Consequences* (item 74), pp. 49-53.

Observes that Gaboriau was the first mystery writer
to use such detective techniques as plaster casts of
footprints and setting the time of death. Concludes that,
along with Collins and Poe, Gaboriau created the mold
for the detective.

*   Thomson, H. Douglas. "The French Detective Story."
Masters of Mystery (item 77), pp. 93-108.

Contends that though Gaboriau had definite opinions
on what the detective story ought to be, he could not
"make up his mind as to what constituted the ideal construction" of plot. *L'Affaire Lerouge* and *Le Crime
d'Orcival* are analyzed in detail.

1130.   Williams, Valentine. "Gaboriau: Father of the Detective
        Novel." *National Review* 82 (December 1923): 611-622.

        Contends that Gaboriau is the "indisputable" father
        of the detective novel because he took Poe's basic form
        and added to it not only an intricate puzzle but also
        living characters, "brisk dialogue and a keen percep-
        tion of 'situations.'"

1131.   "The Works of Gaboriau." *Bookman* 12 (October 1900):
        106-107.

        Argues that Gaboriau was undeservingly passed over
        by critics as a mere creator of detective stories.

GARDNER, ERLE STANLEY (1889-1970). Pseudonyms: A.A. Fair,
   Carleton Kendrake, Charles J. Kenny. Series character: Perry
   Mason

1132.   Barzun, Jacques, and Wendell Hertig Taylor. Preface to
        The Case of the Crooked Candle, by Erle Stanley
        Gardner. New York: Garland Publishing, 1976. Also
        printed in *A Book of Prefaces* (item 22), pp. 49-50.

        Contends that this novel shows Gardner's inventive
        powers and gift for exposition and dialogue at their
        best as well as demonstrating Gardner's solid knowledge
        of the law and medical jurisprudence.

1133.   "The Case of the Indefatigable Gardner." *Saturday
        Evening Post* 214 (30 May 1942): 4.

        Quotes Gardner saying that he writes detective fiction
        "that moves right along," but that it does not have to
        have "action" in order to have "motion."

1134.   Hanscom, Leslie. "Man of Mystery." *Newsweek* 55 (18 Janu-
        ary 1960): 53-56.

        States that Gardner's rule in writing a mystery novel
        is never to tell the reader everything. Gardner purposely
        does not fully describe Perry Mason so the reader can
        make him conform to his own physical ideal.

1135.   "Heroes Who Shoot Straight." *Time* 53 (9 May 1949):
        108, 110.

        Gardner was a "rough and tumble" lawyer in Southern
        California when he began his career as a writer, even-

tually becoming the best-selling author alive because
of his "stream of action technique," "ingenious but
credible solutions," and "direct, undecorated prose"
plus an ability to write four books a year. The detective story, Gardner says, "reassures the reader about
life, makes him believe that justice always triumphs."

1136. Hibbs, Ben. "The Writing Lawyer of Rancho del Paisano."
       Reader's Digest 83 (August 1963): 160-168.

       Says that Gardner believes that the three main benefits
       the reader gets from a mystery story are the satisfac-
       tion of seeing good triumph, stimulating mental exercise,
       and "sheer fun."

1137. Hughes, Dorothy B. *Erle Stanley Gardner: The Case of
       the Real Perry Mason*. New York: William Morrow, 1978.
       350pp.

       Argues that "Mason was Gardner," dramatized and glam-
       orized a bit. Gardner's interest was in the "fighting
       ability" and the "loyalty" of his hero. Hughes points
       out several minor motifs in Gardner's work and the fact
       that he used no "Watson" character to act as a sounding
       board for his hero.

1138. Jackson, Joseph Henry. "The Case of the Mystery Writer."
       Saturday Review 18 (16 July 1938): 10-12.

       Contends that Gardner is successful partly because he
       created a new kind of hero, the lawyer-detective, and
       partly because he received good training in his early
       writings in constructing plots.

1139. Johnston, Alva. "The Case of Erle Stanley Gardner."
       Saturday Evening Post 219 (5 October 1946): 9+;
       219 (12 October 1946): 26+; 219 (19 October 1946):
       24+. Reprinted as a book: *The Case of Erle Stanley
       Gardner*. New York: William Morrow, 1947. 87pp. Also
       condensed in *Reader's Digest* 50 (January 1947): 11-15.

       States that Gardner's formula is a surprise solution
       produced by Perry Mason's courtroom cross-examination
       and observes that "one source of Gardner's popularity
       is undoubtedly the average American's fondness for
       legal problems."

1140. "A Matter of Loyalty." *Newsweek* 75 (23 March 1970):
       114.

This obituary notes Gardner's phenomenally successful
sales and his equally phenomenal energy and output. His
Perry Mason mysteries are described as carefully plotted
and "legally impeccable courtroom dramas."

1141. Morton, Charles W. "The World of Erle Stanley Gardner."
       Atlantic 219 (January 1967): 79-86, 91.

       Contends that Gardner's mystery novels are popular
       because of the "real-life quality of his characters
       and their problems" and the action, tension, and unex-
       pected endings of his plots.

1142. Mundell, E.H. *Erle Stanley Gardner: A Checklist.* Kent,
       Ohio: Kent State University Press, 1968. 91pp.

       Primary bibliography.

1143. Robbins, Frank E. "The Firm of Cool and Lam." *Michigan
       Alumnus Quarterly Review* 59 (Spring 1953): 222-228.
       Reprinted *The Mystery Writer's Art* (item 54), pp.
       136-148.

       Surveys Gardner's A.A. Fair novels about the exploits
       of Bertha Cool and Donald Lam, extracting biographical
       information about the protagonists.

GARVE, ANDREW. Pseudonym of Paul Winterton (1908-)

1144. Barzun, Jacques, and Wendell Hertig Taylor. Preface to
       No Tears for Hilda by Andrew Garve. New York: Garland
       Publishing, 1976. Also printed in *A Book of Prefaces*
       (item 22), pp. 51-52.

       Contends that the hallmark of Garve's work is his
       ability to present successfully both aspects of the
       detective story--the detective and his quarry--in terse,
       vivid descriptive prose which is expertly demonstrated
       in this novel.

GIBSON, WALTER B. (1897-). Pseudonym: Maxwell Grant. Series
   character: Lamont Cranston (The Shadow)

1145. Cox, J. Randolph. "That Mysterious Aide to the Forces
       of Law and Order." *Armchair Detective* 4 (July 1971):
       221-229.

Surveys the masked avenger in pulp fiction but concentrates on The Shadow. Contends that compared to the
other pulp stories, the exposition was less obvious
in The Shadow series and there was more character development.

1146.   Goulart, Ron. "A.K.A. The Shadow." *Cheap Thrills: An
        Informal History of the Pulp Magazine.* New Rochelle,
        N.Y.: Arlington House, 1972, pp. 43-58.

        Gibson began writing The Shadow stories as an assign-
        ment from the publisher and was much influenced by
        LeBlanc.

1147.   Grant, Maxwell. "The Shadow." *The Great Detectives*
        (item 60), pp. 207-216.

        The Shadow created himself, states Grant. The secret
        of his popularity and success was that "his escapes
        were worked out beforehand, so that they never exceed the
        bounds of plausibility when detailed in narrative form."

1148.   Lauterbach, Edward. "Gibson's Non-Shadow Detective."
        Armchair Detective 6 (October 1972): 33-34.

        A Blonde for Murder is an above average pulp novel,
        but it is not remarkably different from his stories
        about The Shadow.

1149.   "The Man Who Cast the Shadow." *Newsweek* 69 (16 January
        1967): 10.

        Contends that The Shadow began the trend toward the
        superhero upon his appearance in 1931 in *The Shadow
        Magazine*. Gibson states that The Shadow stories were
        "formula writing" but that the secret of writing them
        or anything else is a "fresh point of view."

GILBERT, MICHAEL (1912-   )

1150.   Barzun, Jacques, and Wendell Hertig Taylor. Preface to
        Smallbone Deceased, by Michael Gilbert. New York:
        Garland Publishing, 1976. Also printed in *A Book of
        Prefaces* (item 22), pp. 53-54.

        Contends that Gilbert's adeptness at writing satire,
        his "wide knowledge of human perversity," and inventive
        plots that combine wit and ingenuity are excellently
        demonstrated in this novel.

1151. Gilbert, Michael. "Patrick Petrella." *The Great Detectives* (item 60), pp. 167-174.

Gilbert conceived the idea for his fictional detective in church after reading Christina Rossetti's "Who has seen the wind?" Almost all of Petrella's later development is traceable to that first conception of his character.

GODEY, JOHN. Pseudonym of Morton Freedgood (1912-)

1152. Cooper, Arthur. "Subway Connection." *Newsweek* 81 (5 March 1973): 82-84.

In this review of *The Taking of Pelham One Two Three* Cooper contends that Godey's plot is taut and suspenseful and that the book contains sharp observations on city politics, revolutionaries, and the sub-culture of over-achievers. Godey creates striking verisimilitude by providing minute details about subways.

GODWIN, WILLIAM (1756-1836)

1153. McCracken, David. Introduction to *Caleb Williams*, by William Godwin. New York: Oxford University Press, 1970, pp. vii-xxvi.

Contends that Godwin, through deft use of a narrative technique, builds and maintains interest and suspense and concludes that the novel has withstood the test of time as a "novel of adventure, psychology, and politics."

1154. Ousby, Ian. "'My Servant Caleb': Godwin's *Caleb Williams* and the Political Trials of the 1790's." *University of Toronto Quarterly* 44 (Fall 1974): 47-55. Revised and printed as "Thief-Taking and Thief-Making: *Caleb Williams.*" *Bloodhounds of Heaven* (item 55), pp. 19-42.

Argues that *Caleb Williams* is notable for its portrayal of a "typical thief-taker" based on contemporary attitudes and because it is the first English novel to show a "sustained interest in the theme of detection."

1155. Saintsbury, George. *The English Novel*. New York: E.P. Dutton, 1924, pp. 168-169.

Saintsbury mentions *Caleb Williams* because it is "in a sense" the first example of the popular genre, the detective novel, but he states that "it is impossible to sympathize with a hero who is actuated by the very lowest of human motives, sheer inquisitiveness."

*   Symons, Julian. *Mortal Consequences* (item 74), pp. 19-22.

Argues that Godwin's *Caleb Williams* (1794) is the forerunner of contemporary detective fiction, its primary importance lying in its reversal of the assumptions usually made in detective fiction: law and the establishment are portrayed as wholly corrupt and evil and the criminal's heroic nature is glorified.

1156.   Woodcock, George. "Things as They Might Be: Things as They Are: Notes on the Novels of William Godwin." *Dalhousie Review* 54 (Winter 1974-75): 685-697.

Contends that *Caleb Williams* foreshadows the modern "metaphysical thriller" and the classic detective story because of its combination of moral and psychological complexity with suspense and pursuit.

GODWIN, WILLIAM, JR. (d. 1832)

1157.   Adams, Donald K. "Recalled and Awakened: The Romantic Fiction of William Godwin, Jr." *The Mystery and Detection Annual 1973* (item 17), pp. 142-166.

Detailed analysis of *Transfusion, or the Orphans of Unwalden*, a forgotten Godwin novel. Argues that, though Godwin had weaknesses as a writer, he was adept at creating suspense.

GOEDSCHE, HERMANN O.F. See JOHN RETCLIFFE

GOODRUM, CHARLES A. (1923-   )

1158.   Goodrum, Charles A. "Writing the Library Whodunit." *American Libraries* 8 (April 1977): 194-196.

Goodrum, a librarian, states that he wrote *Dewey Decimated* because he likes pre-1955 mysteries in which the puzzle is more important than sex and violence and he thought the genre should have a librarian-detective.

GORDONS, THE. Byline of GORDON GORDON (1912-   ) and MILDRED
GORDON (1912-   )

1159.   Gordon, Mildred, and Gordon Gordon. "A Story that Goes
Some Place." *Writer* 79 (November 1966): 11-14.

The Gordons state that plot, "a story that goes some
place," is the basis of their writing. "Nothing helps
a plot as much as research," they say, but details
must not get in the way of the story.

GOULART, RON (1933-   ). Pseudonym: Kenneth Robeson, which was
also used by Lester Dent

1160.   Banks, R. Jeff. "Goulart's Version of the Avenger: New
Wine, Old Bottles and Something Extra." *Armchair
Detective* 9 (February 1976): 122-124.

Points out such differences between the Avenger series
of pulp novels written by Ron Goulart and the earlier
ones as the absence of the "trap-escape-trap" formula
and the addition of "easily identifiable pulp, mystery
and movie stars as characters."

GOULD, CHESTER (1900-   ). Series character: Dick Tracy

1161. Bainbridge, John. "Chester Gould: The Harrowing Adventures
of His Cartoon Hero, Dick Tracy, Give Vicarious Thrills
to Millions." *Life* 17 (14 August 1944): 43-46, 51-53.

Gould contends that the only aim of his Dick Tracy
comic strip is to entertain and that he tries to avoid
political or ideological overtones. Gould says that he
incorporates three basic elements into every Tracy
episode: the crime, the chase, and the capture, and
spends about sixty percent of his time writing the
dialog, the other forty percent drawing the strip.

1162.   Berchtold, William E. "Men of Comics." *New Outlook* 165
(May 1935): 43-47, 64.

Argues that the trend in comic strips is towards the
tragic (as opposed to the funny) and singles out Gould
as a leading practitioner of the tragic strip. Also
argues that Gould is second only to the creator of
Little Orphan Annie in his ability to build and sustain
reader interest.

1163. Bester, Alfred. "King of the Comics." *Holiday* 23 (June 1958): 135+.

Contends that Gould's Dick Tracy comic strip is a "morality play" in which the good and bad are clearly discernible.

1164. Gould, Chester. "Dick Tracy." *The Great Detectives* (item 60), pp. 237–245.

Gould says he created Tracy as a detective who could catch criminals and restore respect for law which was at a low ebb at the time (1931) and contends that Tracy is both a "cerebral and physical detective, depending upon what each situation calls for."

1165. Phelps, Donald. "Rogues Gallery/Freak Show." *Prose* 4 (Spring 1972): 133–149.

Though deficient in suspense and characterization, Gould's *Dick Tracy* exhibits a "reckless, feckless, hyperbolic imagination."

1166. "Top Cop." *Newsweek* 58 (16 October 1961): 102, 105–106.

In this story on the occasion of the thirtieth birthday of the Dick Tracy comic strip, *Newsweek* quotes Gould as saying the ideas for his villains come from observation, imagination, and topical interests and that he deliberately makes them so ugly that the reader will immediately recognize that they are villains.

GRAFTON, C.W. (1909–   )

1167. Barzun, Jacques, and Wendell Hertig Taylor. Preface to *Beyond a Reasonable Doubt*, by C.W. Grafton. New York: Garland Publishing, 1976. Also printed in *A Book of Prefaces* (item 22), pp. 55–56.

Contends that the originality of the novel lies in "the superbly maintained suspense of the first-person narrative and even more to the extraordinary ingenuity with which the details of the true and of the falsified sequence of events are dovetailed with one another."

GRAHAM, NEILL. See W. MURDOCK DUNCAN

GRAINGER, FRANCIS EDWARD. See HEADON HILL

GRANT, MAXWELL. See WALTER B. GIBSON

GRAYSON, RUPERT

1168. Grayson, Rupert. "Meet Gun Cotton." *Meet the Detective* (item 45), pp. 42-50.

States that he identifies closely with his protagonist, Gun Cotton, but does not fully understand him because he has "many facets to his character."

GREEN, ANNA KATHARINE (1846-1935)

1169. Barzun, Jacques, and Wendell Hertig Taylor. Preface to *The Circular Study*, by Anna Katharine Green. New York: Garland Publishing, 1976. Also printed in *A Book of Prefaces* (item 22), pp. 57-58.

Argues that Green may deserve credit for inventing the first series character in detective fiction with the creation of Ebenezer Gryce (1878) and that she was ahead of her contemporaries in her handling of clues.

1170. Collins, Wilkie. "Wilkie Collins on *The Leavenworth Case*." *Critic* 22 (28 January 1893): 52.

The Critic printed this letter Wilkie Collins had written to one of its readers in 1883. In the letter Collins praises Green's powers of invention, imagination, and belief in what she writes.

1171. Cornillon, John. "A Case for Violet Strange." *Images of Women in Fiction: Feminist Perspectives*. Edited by Susan K. Cornillon. Bowling Green, Ohio: Bowling Green University Popular Press, 1972, pp. 206-215.

In Violet Strange, Green created a character with a dual character: she plays the "airy little being" as well as being a detective, sometimes using the first persona to gather information for the second. She uses her detective work to aid women and when she marries, she chooses a man of "egalitarian temperament."

1172.   "Godmother of Mystery Stories." *Publishers Weekly* 127
        (27 April 1935): 1679.

        Brief obituary which argues that her *The Leavenworth
        Case* (1878) might be the beginning of the great popu-
        larity of the mystery story. Quotes Green that good
        mystery should have a clear and concise plot with a
        "queer turn that has never before been attempted."

1173.   Harkins, Edwin F. "Anna Katharine Green." *Famous Authors
        (Women)*. Boston: L.C. Page, 1901, pp. 91-106.

        States that Green's upbringing as the daughter of a
        well-known lawyer may have stimulated her imagination
        and strengthened her ability to deal with complex
        psychological problems. Green shows great skill in con-
        structing her stories as well as having the imagination
        and perception required for writing "police-court
        literature." Harkins concludes that "even if one does
        not approve of this sort of literature, she writes
        artistically" and predicts that her detective novels
        will be read by future generations.

*   Haycraft, Howard. *Murder for Pleasure* (item 36), pp.
        83-85.

        Maintains that Anna Katharine Green is important in
        the development of American detective fiction largely
        because of her carefully constructed plots, her early
        appearance in the genre, and her great popularity. Her
        novel *The Leavenworth Case* (1878) is a truly significant
        milestone of the genre.

*   Murch, A.E. *The Development of the Detective Novel*
        (item 51), pp. 158-164.

        Argues that in Green's novels the main interest is
        in the detection theme and that in her work can be
        first discerned, "in its entirety, the pattern that
        became characteristic of most English detective novels
        written during the following fifty years": a puzzle
        followed by enigmatic or false clues that temporarily
        delay the investigation and finally the triumphant
        unmasking of the criminal, usually someone not suspected
        until the climax.

1174.   Overton, Grant Martin. "Anna Katharine Green." *Women
        Who Make Our Novels*. New York: Moffat, Yard, 1922,
        pp. 204-214.

Contends that every one of Green's novels is "wretchedly" written, but her plots are carefully constructed, and she makes their surprising endings plausible.

1175. Woodward, Kathleen. "Anna Katharine Green." *Bookman* 70 (October 1929): 168-170.

In a wide-ranging interview, Green states that her writing is heavily influenced by Gaboriau and that the mystery writer has a responsibility not to mislead the reader by false clues but rather to outwit him.

GREENE, GRAHAM (1904-)

1176. Adamson, Judy, and Philip Stratford. "Looking for the Third Man: On the Trail in Texas, New York, Hollywood." *Encounter* 50 (June 1978): 39-46.

A study of the writing and publication of *The Third Man*, and of the textual changes in its American and cinematic versions. Finds that Lime's character is softened to make him acceptable to American audiences.

1177. Alley, Kenneth D. "*A Gun for Sale*: Graham Greene's Reflection of Moral Chaos." *Essays in Literature* 5 (1978): 175-185.

Argues that *A Gun for Sale* (American title: *This Gun for Hire*) is more than a mere entertainment. It represents Greene's "full scale attack upon the idealistically simplistic and illusory social attitudes implicit in the traditional mystery or detective story." It is his vision of "a world gone morally awry."

1178. Alloway, Lawrence. "Symbolism in 'The Third Man.'" *World Review* 13 (March 1950): 57-60.

Notes a biblical echo in the story's title--a reference to the journey to Emmaus; the third man is the resurrected Christ. In addition, the names Harry Lime and Holly Martin refer to trees. Holly killing Lime recalls the rituals described in *The Golden Bough*. Greene ties the theme of renewal to that of despair in his thriller.

1179. Atkins, John Alfred. *Graham Greene*. London: Calder and Boyars, 1966. 257pp.

Surveys Greene's career and finds him to be "a tough-
minded writer who is greatly impressed by the power of
accident and misinterpretation." Contends that too many
critics fix upon Greene's religious themes, ignoring
the life behind them.

1180.   Auden, W.H. "The Heresy of Our Time." *Renascence* 1
        (Spring 1949): 23-24. Reprinted *Graham Greene: A
        Collection of Critical Essays*. Edited by Samuel
        Hynes. Englewood Cliffs, N.J.: Prentice-Hall, 1973,
        pp. 93-94.

        The thriller resembles the epic except that its war
        is secret and there is no compassion for the other
        side. Greene, Auden contends, avoids "this crudity
        without sacrificing the drama, by relating the thriller
        to another literary form, the allegory."

1181.   Bedard, Bernard J. "The Thriller Pattern in the Major
        Novels of Graham Greene." Ph.D. dissertation, Uni-
        versity of Michigan, 1959.

        Argues that the same "thriller pattern"--an outcast
        "is pursued through a corrupt and violent world by
        grotesques" until "his sense of justice causes him to
        rebel; the pursuit is reversed"--exists in *Brighton
        Rock*, *The Power and the Glory*, *The Heart of the Matter*,
        and *The End of the Affair* as in Greene's outright
        thrillers. Greene adapted these thriller patterns in
        his serious novels to present a "meaningful religious
        experience" to his readers.

1182.   Boardman, Gwenn R. *Graham Greene: The Aesthetics of
        Exploration*. Gainesville: University of Florida Press,
        1971, pp. 34-42.

        Points out that the detective story is, according to
        Greene's own statement, "the pursuit of exact truth"
        and that in his detective stories Greene "never loses
        sight of either the Divine Judge or the dramatic irony
        of 'poetic justice.'" Singles out *This Gun for Hire* to
        illustrate this point because it "meets all the criteria
        for Greene's special variety of 'fairy story.'"

1183.   De Vitis, A.A. "Allegory in *Brighton Rock*." *Modern
        Fiction Studies* 3 (Autumn 1957): 216-224.

        Contends that *Brighton Rock* "is in the tradition of
        the detective story." Cites parallels between this,
        Greene's first explicitly religious novel, and his

earlier thrillers. The story is an allegory of good
and evil.

1184. De Vitis, A.A. *Graham Greene*. New York: Twayne, 1964.
175pp.

Distinguishes Greene's thrillers from his more serious
novels by the absence of overt preoccupation with religious and ethical problems in the thrillers. Notes
that *Brighton Rock* combined Catholicism and the detective tradition.

1185. De Vitis, A.A. "Religious Aspects in the Novels of
Graham Greene." *The Shapeless God: Essays on Modern
Fiction*. Edited by Harry J. Mooney, Jr., and Thomas
F. Staley. Pittsburgh: University of Pittsburgh Press,
1968, pp. 41-65.

Analyzes Greene's serious novels and contends that
Brighton Rock combines thriller conventions with religious theories in an attempt to explain the nature of
right and wrong and good and evil.

1186. King, James. "In the Lost Boyhood of Judas: Graham
Greene's Early Novels of Hell." *Dalhousie Review* 49
(1969): 229-236.

Contends that Raven in *A Gun for Sale* (American title:
This Gun for Hire) is the prototype for Pinkie of
Brighton Rock. Both characters "are young criminals
who should have been inmates of seminaries rather than
murderers."

1187. Kunkel, Francis L. "A Critical Study of Graham Greene."
Ph.D. dissertation, Columbia University, 1959.

Contends that although Greene's thrillers may be distinguished from his more serious works by their greater
use of melodrama, their relative lack of character
development, and concession to a happy ending, they
nonetheless "dramatize moral problems of far-reaching
significance."

1188. Kunkel, Francis L. *The Labyrinthine Ways of Graham
Greene*. New York: Sheed and Ward, 1959. 181pp.

Distinguishes between Greene's serious novels and his
entertainments, which include most of his detective/
thriller fiction. The entertainments are distinguished
by a tendency to melodrama, a relative lack of character
development, and a happy ending.

*   Lambert, Gavin. *The Dangerous Edge* (item 42), pp. 132-
      170.

      In an extensive survey of Greene's career, interprets
      the persistent themes in Greene's work in light of his
      psychological development. Contends that Greene's early
      discovery that "belief needs betrayal to prove its
      strength" is the key to understanding his work.

1189. Lodge, David. *Graham Greene*. New York: Columbia Univer-
      sity Press, 1966. 48pp.

      In brief analyses of each of Greene's novels, Lodge
      finds connections between the thrillers and the religi-
      ous novels. Observes that much of the critical hostility
      to Greene is directed at his Catholicism.

1190. Lodge, David. "Graham Greene." *Six Comtemporary British
      Novelists*. Edited by George Stade. New York: Columbia
      University Press, 1976, pp. 1-56.

      Surveys Greene's literary career. Contends that
      Stamboul Train, Greene's first entertainment, was the
      novel that opened up his career. Greene's thrillers
      stress the themes of treachery and betrayal.

1191. McCall, Dan. "*Brighton Rock*: The Price of Order."
      English Language Notes 3 (1966): 290-294.

      Contends that *Brighton Rock* is a detective story, but
      one with philosophical underpinnings. It "embodies a
      movement from disorder to order." Evil "consists in
      sin against order; the evil is judged and the order is
      maintained" by traditional Catholicism.

1192. McDonald, James L. "Graham Greene: A Reconsideration."
      Arizona Quarterly 27 (1971): 197-210.

      Argues that Greene is more than a doctrinal Catholic
      writer. In both his thrillers and his religious works
      "he confronted the political and social climate of his
      time ... and honestly defined their moral dimensions."

1193. Manly, Jane. "Graham Greene: The Insanity of Innocence."
      Ph.D. dissertation, University of Connecticut, 1969.

      Observes that for Greene, innocence is a form of
      insanity. Divides Greene's works into those dealing
      with the innocents who destroy both themselves and
      others and those with more mature protagonists who have
      put aside disastrously romantic attachments to abstrac-
      tions.

1194. O'Donnell, Donat. "Graham Greene." *Chimera* 5 (Summer
       1947): 18-30.

       Argues that almost all of Greene's works are thrillers
       because "one senses in them the very motives which make
       people read thrillers; hatred of organized society,
       longing for destruction."

1195. O'Grady, Walter A. "Political Contexts in the Novels
       of Graham Greene and Joyce Cary." Ph.D. dissertation,
       University of Toronto, 1971.

       Observes that some of Greene's thrillers deal with
       the "inadequacy of human law as a basis for social
       order." Others demonstrate the chaos that results from
       an attempt to build a Utopia.

1196. Pryce-Jones, David. *Graham Greene.* Edinburgh: Oliver
       and Boyd, 1973. 126pp.

       Observes that Greene's thrillers lack the central
       religious issue of his serious novels. Their themes
       are "pursuit and betrayal, the corruption of innocence,
       and the impossibility of rejecting past unhappiness."

1197. Scott, Carolyn D. "The Urban Romance: A Study of Graham
       Greene's Thrillers." *Graham Greene.* Edited by Harry
       J. Cargas. St. Louis, Mo.: B. Herder, [1969], pp.
       1-28.

       Argues that "Greene's thrillers ... catch the aesthet-
       ic of our age," that he uses a popular art form to
       make a statement about man.

1198. Slate, Audrey. "Technique and Form in the Novels of
       Graham Greene." Ph.D. dissertation, University of
       Wisconsin, 1960.

       Contends that Greene's novels after *Brighton Rock*
       are "religious thrillers." They combine suspense with
       a serious subject matter.

1199. Spier, Ursula. "Melodrama in Graham Greene's *The End
       of the Affair.*" *Modern Fiction Studies* 3 (1957):
       235-240.

       Maintains that, although Greene deliberately tried
       to eliminate the melodramatic, or thriller, elements
       from *The End of the Affair,* the novel nonetheless
       contains many plot devices--the pursuit, the detective--
       that are present in his thrillers. They are, however,
       used to good effect.

1200.   Stenberg, Carl E. "The Quest for Justice in the Fiction
         of Graham Greene." Ph.D. dissertation, University of
         Connecticut, 1969.

         Contends that the quest for justice is a characteristic
         feature of Greene's thrillers as well as of his more
         serious novels.

1201.   Stratford, Philip. *Faith and Fiction: Creative Process
         in Greene and Mauriac.* Notre Dame, Ind.: University
         of Notre Dame Press, 1964, pp. 111-139.

         Contends that Greene's thrillers had a seriousness
         of artistic purpose that remained consistently high.
         Stamboul Train was the first novel in which Greene
         properly attended to the mechanics of his craft.

1202.   Stratford, Philip. "Graham Greene: Master of Melodrama."
         Tamarack Review 19 (Spring 1961): 67-86.

         Notes similarities--particularly in the theme of
         pursuit--between Greene's thrillers and his religious
         work. Argues that, although many of Greene's novels
         are undeniably melodramatic, the melodrama is under
         control. Greene uses it to serve his own ends rather
         than gratuitously.

1203.   Wolfe, Peter. *Graham Greene: The Entertainer.* Carbon-
         dale: Southern Illinois University Press, 1972. 181pp.

         A detailed study of Greene's thrillers. Contends that
         Greene's skill lies in his ability to control his
         readers' responses. The thrillers, with their emphasis
         on violence, reflect Greene's belief in "the nearly
         boundless potential for evil in human nature."

1204.   Wyndham, Francis. *Graham Greene.* London: Longmans,
         Green, 1962. 32pp.

         Contends that the literal element of pursuit in
         Greene's novels--pursuit of a criminal, of a traitor,
         of a victim--symbolizes the pursuit of man's soul by
         God.

1205.   Zabel, Morton Dauwen. "The Best and the Worst." *Craft
         and Character.* New York: Viking Press, 1957, pp.
         76-96. Reprinted *Graham Greene: A Collection of
         Critical Essays.* Edited by Samuel Hynes. Englewood
         Cliffs, N.J.: Prentice-Hall, 1973, pp. 30-48.

Argues that because of the corrupt values of contemporary society the thriller "must become moral."
This is the challenge Greene has met.

GRIERSON, FRANCIS D. (1888-)

1206. Grierson, Francis D. "Meet Professor Wells." *Meet the
       Detective* (item 45), pp. 71-79.

       States that he regards Wells as a friend, not merely
       a character in a book and that he is based on an eminent
       scientist.

GRILE, DOD. See AMBROSE BIERCE

HAGGARD, WILLIAM. Pseudonym of Richard Henry Michael Clayton
(1907-)

1207. Winks, Robin W. "Murder Without Blood." *New Republic*
       177 (30 July 1977): 30-33.

       "Professionalism, style, nuance, the difference be-
       tween what appears to happen and what does happen" are
       what Haggard's books are about. His books have no un-
       necessary bloodletting, and Haggard has "sympathy and
       insight" into all his characters as well as a fine
       subtle style.

HALL, ADAM. Pseudonym of Elleston Trevor (1920-)

1208. Hall, Adam. "Quiller." *The Great Detectives* (item 60),
       pp. 185-192.

       Quiller is often described as the "quintessential
       corporate operator," very professional, very efficient,
       and very cold.

HALLIDAY, BRETT. Pseudonym of Davis Dresser (1904-1977). Other
pseudonym: Asa Baker. Joint pseudonym with Kathleen Rollins:
Hal Debrett. Joint pseudonym with (Walter) Ryerson Johnson
(1901-): Matthew Blood

1209. Halliday, Brett. "Michael Shayne." *The Great Detectives*
       (item 60), pp. 219-225.

Halliday states that his fictional detective hero
has "no special or esoteric knowledges to help him
solve his cases." This enables the reader to identify
more readily with Shayne.

*   Ruehlmann, William. *Saint with a Gun* (item 65), pp.
        114-117.

        Contends that Halliday's detective, Mike Shayne, is
        a heroic figure because he is sensitive and sentimental
        with idealistic motives. Also argues that in his crea-
        tion of Shayne, Halliday has been greatly influenced
        by Dashiell Hammett's Sam Spade.

HALLIDAY, MICHAEL. See JOHN CREASEY

HAMILTON, DONALD (1916-   ). Series character: Matt Helm

1210.   Erisman, Fred. "Western Motifs in the Thrillers of
        Donald Hamilton." *Western American Literature* 10
        (February 1976): 283-292.

        Hamilton's thrillers resemble Westerns in their setting
        (Matt Helm is a resident of New Mexico) and the hero's
        use of direct action, but the hero does not have the
        sense of absolute right and wrong of the conventional
        Western.

1211.   Hamilton, Donald. "Matt Helm." *The Great Detectives*
        (item 60), pp. 121-126.

        Hamilton states that he created the tough, professional
        Helm as an antidote to weak, sentimental amateurs and
        that the character "put himself together."

1212.   Winks, Robin W. "The Sordid Truth: Donald Hamilton."
        New Republic 173 (26 July 1975): 21-24.

        Hamilton is a direct descendant of John Buchan (author
        of *The Thirty-Nine Steps*) though there is a moral am-
        bivalence in Hamilton's hero's actions that makes his
        portrayal of espionage more realistic than that of
        Buchan. Hamilton has a good "eye and ear for landscape."

HAMMETT, DASHIELL (1894-1961)

1213. Adams, Donald K. "The First Thin Man." *The Mystery and Detection Annual 1972* (item 16), pp. 160-177.

Describes an unfinished sixty-five-page manuscript by Dashiell Hammett called "The Thin Man" that he abandoned some time before writing the novel called *The Thin Man*. The two are different but have a "similarity in mood, setting, and general character outline."

1214. Alvarez, A. "The Thin Man." *Spectator* 216 (11 February 1966): 169-170. Reprinted as "Dashiell Hammett." *Beyond All This Fiddle: Essays 1955-1967*. New York: Random House, 1969, pp. 208-212.

Alvarez states that he finds "most detective stories unreadable" but that Hammett's books "with their elegant plots and stripped, clean writing" are an exception. Also argues that Hammett "has a genius, and part of it lies in his ability to make corruption seem normal without ever quite endorsing it."

1215. Asbury, Herbert. "*Red Harvest*." *Bookman* 69 (March 1929): 92.

Argues that "it is doubtful if even Ernest Hemingway has ever written more effective dialogue" than Hammett. The writing style of Hammett, Asbury notes, is devoid of literary frills and has "an amazing clarity and compactness."

1216. Bazelon, David T. "Dashiell Hammett's Private Eye: No Loyalty Beyond the Job." *Commentary* 7 (May 1949): 467-472. Reprinted *The Scene Before You: A New Approach to American Culture*. Edited by Chandler Brossard. New York: Rinehart, 1955, pp. 180-190.

Contends that "the core of Hammett's art is his version of the masculine figure in American society." In Hammett's world "to an extent, *competence* replaces moral stature as the criterion of an individual's worth."

1217. Blair, Walter. "Dashiell Hammett: Themes and Techniques." *Essays on American Literature in Honor of Jay B. Hubbell*. Edited by Clarence Gohdes. Durham, N.C.: Duke University Press, 1967, pp. 295-306.

Points out that critics frequently compare Hammett to Hemingway, largely because they both wrote about

similar themes—disillusionment, cynicism, courage, and
honor. Cites as two of Hammett's virtues his handling
of point of view and his technique of giving his characters "outward aspects incongruous with their actual
natures."

*   Cawelti, John G. "Hammett, Chandler, and Spillane."
      Adventure, Mystery, and Romance (item 150), pp.
      162-191.

      Argues that "Hammett's power as a writer does not
      lie in his greater fidelity to the realistic details
      of crime and punishment but in his capacity to embody
      a powerful vision of life in the hard-boiled detective
      formula."

*   Chandler, Raymond. "The Simple Art of Murder." (item
      156).

      Argues that Hammett was part of "a rather revolutionary
      debunking of both the language and material of fiction,"
      and that he "gave murder back to the kind of people
      that commit it for reasons, not just to provide a corpse"
      for a literary detective.

*   Crider, Allen B. "The Private Eye Hero: A Study of the
      Novels of Dashiell Hammett, Raymond Chandler, and
      Ross Macdonald." Ph.D. dissertation, University of
      Texas at Austin, 1972 (item 666).

      Observes that Hammett was the first "hard-boiled"
      detective writer to attract serious attention. Crider
      argues that Hammett's characters "live in a society
      which is in a state of dissolution, and they adapt
      themselves to it by accepting the fact that an indivi-
      dual is ultimately alone."

*   Eames, Hugh. "Sam Spade—Dashiell Hammett." *Sleuths,*
      Inc. (item 30), pp. 98-140.

      Outlines Hammett's background as a Pinkerton man and
      points out that he was "an alternative to the genteel
      tradition in detective fiction." Contends that the
      women in Hammett's stories have been overlooked and
      that the comment of the Continental Op to one is an
      apt description of most of them: "You're a cold blooded
      hussy."

1218. Edenbaum, Robert I. "The Poetics of the Private Eye:
The Novels of Dashiell Hammett." *Tough Guy Writers
of the Thirties* (item 46), pp. 80-103. Reprinted *The
Mystery Writer's Art* (item 54), pp. 98-108.

Characterizes Hammett's tough-guy hero as "free of
sentiment, of the fear of death, of the temptations of
money and sex."

* Finch, G.A. "From Spade to Marlowe to Archer: An Essay"
(item 674).

Contends that Hammett created in *The Maltese Falcon*
such a powerful, sustained portrait of a private detective that he provided an outstanding model for Chandler
and Ross Macdonald to emulate. Also argues that *The
Maltese Falcon* is the first detective novel to "join
a refined and careful style with a wholly persuasive
character." Concludes that without Hammett we might
not have had the work of Chandler and Macdonald.

1219. Gardner, Erle Stanley. "Getting Away with Murder."
Atlantic Monthly 215 (January 1965): 72-75.

States that Hammett dazzled his editors at *Black
Mask* with his knowledge of underworld language and that
its use in his stories influenced other mystery writers
to copy this writing style.

1220. Grella, George. "The Wings of the Falcon and the Maltese
Dove." *A Question of Quality: Popularity and Value
in Modern Creative Writing.* Edited by Louis Filler.
Bowling Green, Ohio: Bowling Green University Popular
Press, 1976, pp. 108-114.

Points out similarities in technique, subject matter,
and moral vision between Henry James and Dashiell
Hammett, using James's novel *The Wings of the Dove* and
Hammett's *The Maltese Falcon* as a basis for comparison.
Contends that both authors had a sense of the corrupting
power of money and "of the evil possibilities in the
world they portray." Concludes that Hammett "is possibly
the most Jamesian of all detective novelists."

1221. Handlin, Oscar. "Reader's Choice: Dashiell Hammett."
Atlantic Monthly 218 (July 1966): 136-139.

States that Hammett transformed the detective character from a guardian of good against evil, a knightly
figure, to a realistic individual who had faults in

addition to virtues but whose self value was more
important than the case.

*   Haycraft, Howard. *Murder for Pleasure* (item 36), pp.
       168-173.

       Points out that the action in Hammett's novels is
       "machine-gun paced and so violent that in the first
       two books particularly, it occasionally defeats the
       purpose by exhausting the reader's receptive and reac-
       tive capacities."

1222. Hulley, Kathleen. "From the Crystal Sphere to Edge
       City: Ideology in the Novels of Dashiell Hammett."
       Myth and Ideology in American Culture. Edited by
       Regis Durand. Lille: University de Lille, 1976, pp.
       111-127.

       Analyzes the narrative shift from early traditional
       detective fiction (with its sense of order and reason)
       to the hard-boiled school, which incorporates violence
       and chaos. Shows that the latter characteristics are
       exemplified in *Red Harvest* (1929) and *The Glass Key*
       (1931).

1223. Kenney, William P. "The Dashiell Hammett Tradition
       and the Modern Detective Novel." Ph.D. dissertation,
       University of Michigan, 1964.

       Argues that the works of Dashiell Hammett "not only
       reject the older form" of the detective novel "but
       challenge the moral and metaphysical assumptions on
       which that form was based." Also contends that Hammett
       has been unable to resolve "the conflict between the
       restraints imposed by the detective framework and the
       freedom the novelist seeks to exercise in the other
       elements of his fiction," and it "seems likely that no
       satisfactory solution is possible."

1224. Layman, Richard. *Dashiell Hammett: A Descriptive
       Bibliography.* Pittsburgh: University of Pittsburgh
       Press, 1979. 185pp.

       A primary bibliography that includes such details
       as pagination, contents, typography, and date of publi-
       cation for Hammett's works.

1225. Leverence, John. *"The Continental Op." Journal of
       Popular Culture* 9 (Winter 1975): 741-743.

Contends that the *Continental Op* stories as examples of Hammett's art are inconsequential and unimaginative but were a framework for the development of the hard-boiled detective genre. His key writing method in these short stories is the use of juxtapositions.

1226. Malin, Irving. "Focus on *The Maltese Falcon*: The Metaphysical Falcon." *Tough Guy Writers of the Thirties* (item 46), pp. 104-109.

Contends that "in its many symbolic, odd descriptions and conversations *The Maltese Falcon* transcends the hard-boiled school of detective writing" and becomes not merely "physical" but "metaphysical." Cites many examples from the novel to illustrate his thesis.

1227. Marcus, Steven. Introduction to *The Continental Op*, by Dashiell Hammett. New York: Random House, 1974, pp. ix-xxix. Also printed as "Dashiell Hammett and the Continental Op." *Partisan Review* 41 (1974): 362-377. Reprinted *Representations: Essays on Literature and Society*. New York: Random House, 1975, pp. 311-321.

Maintains that Hammett transformed the detective story into literature. Quotes and analyzes an extended passage that he contends is the key to Hammett's work because it embodies his view of the "ethical irrationality of existence."

1228. Morris, Homer H. "Dashiell Hammett in the Wasteland." *Midwest Quarterly* 19 (Winter 1978): 196-202.

Contends that Hammett viewed the world as a "vast wasteland" in which wealth and power corrupt. Because Hammett chose to "set his crimes in a believable and recognizable environment" he deserves consideration as a serious novelist and short story writer.

1229. Moss, Leonard. "Hammett's Heroic Operative." *New Republic* 154 (8 January 1966): 32-34.

Contends that Hammett's finest novel is *Red Harvest*, which has a rapid and direct storyline without the pretentiousness of *The Maltese Falcon*. Hammett's best character, Moss adds, is not Sam Spade, but the detective in the *Continental Op* stories.

1230. Mundell, E.H. *A List of Original Appearances of Dashiell Hammett's Magazine Work*. Kent, Ohio: Kent State University Press, 1968. 52pp.

A primary bibliography which includes the first 25 to 30 words of each story for purposes of identification.

1231.   "The New School of Murder Mystery." *Literary Digest* 118 (1 September 1934): 25.

States that Dashiell Hammett may be ushering in a new era in detective fiction. His detectives ("rough, coarse, and brutal") are the first not to remind one of Sherlock Holmes.

1232.   Nolan, William F. *Dashiell Hammett: A Casebook.* Santa Barbara, Calif.: McNally and Loftin, 1969. 189pp.

Traces both Hammett's life and writing, stressing the importance to his writing of his experience as a Pinkerton man. Also argues that "his protagonists usually combined the cynic and the idealist" and that his style was simply the attempt "to reproduce, in dramatic terms, the lean speech of the man who says nothing more than he has to." Includes a checklist of Hammett's published works and writings about him.

1233.   Nolan, William F. "The Hammett Checklist Revisited." *Armchair Detective* 6 (August 1973): 249–254.

This is an updating of the primary and secondary checklist in Nolan's *Dashiell Hammett: A Casebook* (item 1232).

1234.   Nolan, William F. "Revisiting the Revisited Hammett Checklist." *Armchair Detective* 9 (October 1976): 292–295, 324–329.

A further updating of the checklist begun in Nolan's *Casebook* (item 1232) and continued in "The Hammett Checklist Revisited" (item 1233).

1235.   Nolan, William F. "Shadowing the Continental Op." *Armchair Detective* 8 (February 1975): 121–123.

A listing of all *Continental Op* titles published.

1236.   Occhiogrosso, Frank. "Murder in the Dark: Dashiell Hammett." *New Republic* 177 (30 July 1977): 28–30.

Points out that Hammett's major contribution to the mystery story was the creation of a detective who relied more on his ability to read people than on reasoning out clues.

1237. Parker, Dorothy. "Oh, Look--Two Good Books!" *New Yorker* 7 (25 April 1931): 83-84. Reprinted as "Oh, Look--A Good Book!" *Constant Reader*. New York: Viking Press, 1970, pp. 134-137.

Parker finds Hammett's plots "nuisances," but praises his creation of Sam Spade and contends that "he is a good, hell-bent, cold-hearted writer, with a clear eye for the ways of hard women and a fine ear for the words of hard men, and his books are exciting and powerful."

* Parker, Robert B. "The Violent Hero, Wilderness Heritage and Urban Reality: A Study of the Private Eye in the Novels of Dashiell Hammett, Raymond Chandler, and Ross Macdonald." Ph.D. dissertation, Boston University, 1971 (item 689).

Argues that "the violent hero of the modern hard-boiled detective story is Adam in the city"; he has frontier values but operates in an urban setting.

1238. Paterson, John. "A Cosmic View of the Private Eye." *Saturday Review* 36 (22 August 1953): 7-8, 31-33.

Points out that Hammett's detective characters are the first in the category of "the transcendant sleuth." Also notes the tragic implications of defeat and the atmosphere of futility in Hammett's works.

1239. Pattow, Donald J. "Order and Disorder in *The Maltese Falcon*." *Armchair Detective* 11 (April 1978): 171.

Contends that Hammett uses the structural device of pairing, such as lovers or business partners, to establish "the appearance of order. As the novel progresses, however, the order is revealed to be illusory, a facade masking a world in which no one can be trusted ... a world, in short, of disorder."

1240. Phelps, Donald. "Dashiell Hammett's Microcosmos." *National Review* 18 (20 September 1966): 941-942.

Contends that "Hammett fused the tempo, violence, and fantasy of pulp mystery writing with his own character, which ... had about it much of the nine-teenth century--graceful, autocratic, humanely rational."

*   Ruehlmann, William. *Saint with a Gun* (item 65), pp.
         73-75.

         Argues that *The Maltese Falcon* is an examination
         of the consequences of Sam Spade's code, not praise
         for it.

1241.   Sale, Roger. "The Hammett Case." *New York Review of
         Books* 22 (6 February 1975): 20-22.

         Argues that *The Glass Key* is Hammett's best work
         because in that novel he "tries to make the style of
         his hero matter."

1242.   Sanderson, Elizabeth. "Ex-Detective Hammett." *Bookman*
         74 (January-February 1932): 516-518.

         By creating "the flesh and blood figures of any good
         novel" and disregarding the old rules for detective
         stories, Hammett has written "four of the best detective
         stories ever published." He is also "a master of
         terse, abrupt prose."

*   Symons, Julian. *Mortal Consequences* (item 74), pp.
         137-144.

         Argues that Hammett's popularity was based on his
         rugged individualistic writing style, not (as Chandler
         has stated in item 156) because he "gave murder back to
         the kind of people that commit it for reasons, not
         just to provide a corpse." Briefly analyzes Hammett's
         five full-length novels.

1243.   Thompson, George J. "The Problem of Moral Vision in
         Dashiell Hammett's Detective Novels." Ph.D. disserta-
         tion, University of Connecticut, 1972. Reprinted
         Armchair Detective 6 (May 1973): 153-156; 6 (August
         1973): 213-225; 7 (1973): 33-40; 7 (May 1974): 178-
         192; 7 (August 1974): 270-280; 8 (November 1974):
         27-35; 8 (February 1975): 124-130.

         Argues that Hammett's novels are unlike traditional
         detective stories in that they have "an extremely
         ambiguous moral vision" and do not leave the reader
         with the sense that "the world is appreciably better
         off" because of what the protagonist has done. Thompson
         treats each of the novels at some length. In *Red Harvest*,
         he argues, the ending "is neither a condemnation of
         the Op and his methods or an unqualified approval."
         In *The Dain Curse* Hammett's detective "posits meaning

and value *in spite* of the absurdity he sees about him."
In *The Maltese Falcon* Sam Spade's rejection of Brigid
O'Shaughnessy at the end "is at once pragmatic and
moral." Thompson argues further that in *The Glass Key*
Hammett's moral vision is bleak because of the "implication that even moral action exacts a terrible price."
The last novel, *The Thin Man*, in one sense then, is
the darkest of all because it suggests the almost total
alienation of modern man."

1244.   Wolfe, Peter. *Beams Falling: The Art of Dashiell
        Hammett.* Bowling Green, Ohio: Bowling Green Univer-
        sity Popular Press, 1980. 168pp.

        Wolfe examines Hammett's works in detail, finding a
        "personal vision that expresses itself in movement and
        conflict," and he maintains that Hammett offers "a
        vision of America undergoing fast and widescale change."

1245.   Wolfe, Peter. "Sam Spade: Lover." *Armchair Detective*
        11 (October 1978): 366-371.

        Contends that the concentration on Spade's "toughness"
        has ignored the "tenderness and subtlety" of his char-
        acter and his "feminine sensitivity to atmosphere and
        textures." Illustrates these aspects in a detailed
        examination of Spade's relationship with Brigid
        O'Shaughnessy.

HANSEN, JOSEPH (1923-). Pseudonym: Rose Brock

1246.   Forrest, Alan. "Gay Eye." *Books and Bookmen* 18 (August
        1973): 6.

        A short interview with Hansen, who has created a
        private eye insurance investigator who is a homosexual.
        Hansen wants readers to see homosexuality as something
        other than "bizarre and alien."

HANSHEW, THOMAS W. (1857-1914). Series character: Hamilton
Cleek

1247.   Cox, J. Randolph. "Cleek and His Forty Faces: or, T.W.
        Hanshew, a Dime Novelist Who Made Good." *Dime Novel
        Roundup* 42 (15 March 1973): 30-34; 42 (15 April 1973):
        41-43.

        Traces Hanshew's character Cleek through several
        books and reports that little is known of Hanshew's life.

HARBAGE, ALFRED BENNET. See THOMAS KYD

HARE, CYRIL. Pseudonym of Alfred Alexander Gordon Clark (1900–1958)

1248.   Barzun, Jacques, and Wendell Hertig Taylor. Preface to
        When the Wind Blows, Cyril Hare. New York: Garland
        Publishing, 1976. Also printed in *A Book of Prefaces*
        (item 22), pp. 59–60.

        This novel is a classic, the authors argue, because
        of the well-paced plot, amusing characterization,
        credible combination of official amateur detection,
        and well-placed clues.

1249.   Shibuk, Charles. "Cyril Hare." *Armchair Detective* 3
        (October 1969): 28–30.

        Contends that Hare "remains one of the best British
        writers of detective stories." Includes checklist with
        commentary.

1250.   Strout, Cushing. "Murder with Manners." *New Republic*
        177 (30 July 1977): 34–36.

        Argues that an amateur is often the best writer of
        mystery stories. Hare was a judge in England, and his
        stories "are as low-keyed and well-ordered as an
        English court." When the culprit is finally revealed,
        "the effect is surprising and the method simple."

HARRINGTON, JOSEPH (1903–   )

1251.   Hays, R.W. "Joseph Harrington's First Three Books."
        Armchair Detective 4 (January 1970): 104–106.

        Contends that Harrington's three novels, *The Last
        Known Address* (1965), *Blind Spot* (1966), and *The Lost
        Doorbell* (1969), continue the tradition of the police
        procedure story, first introduced by Gaboriau in
        Monsieur LeCoq (1869), in which the "detective is
        presented with the problem of identification of a man
        who, upon being arrested, refuses to identify himself."
        One of Harrington's themes is criticism of the judicial
        system for letting too many criminals go free.

HAWTHORNE, JULIAN (1846-1934)

1252. Bassau, Maurice. *Hawthorne's Son: The Life and Literary Career of Julian Hawthorne*. Columbus: Ohio State University Press, 1970, pp. 180-211.

Bassau dismisses Hawthorne's detective stories with a few plot synopses and such comments as "glittering rubbish."

HEAD, MATTHEW. Pseudonym of John Edwin Canaday (1907-)

1253. Barzun, Jacques, and Wendell Hertig Taylor. Preface to *The Congo Venus*, by Matthew Head. New York: Garland Publishing, 1976. Also printed in *A Book of Prefaces* (item 22), pp. 61-62.

Contends that the novel is a classic because of the memorable characters (particularly the woman detective), the exotic setting, and the cultural variety.

1254. "Canaday Affair." *New Yorker* 39 (4 January 1964): 20-22.

Head's books are "well-written and psychologically interesting." Head is the pseudonym used by John Canaday, now art critic of the *New York Times*, who said in an interview that he tried to tell more about the murderer and the person murdered than does the usual mystery novel. He no longer writes mystery novels.

HENNISSART, MARTHA. See EMMA LATHEN

HEXT, HARRINGTON. See EDEN PHILLPOTTS

HEYER, GEORGETTE (1902-1974)

1255. Barzun, Jacques, and Wendell Hertig Taylor. Preface to *A Blunt Instrument*, by Georgette Heyer. New York: Garland Publishing, 1976. Also printed in *A Book of Prefaces* (item 22), pp. 63-64.

Argues that the novel is a classic because of Heyer's success in handling clues, plotting suspense, and employing "an ironic treatment of characters."

HIGHSMITH, PATRICIA (1921-   )

1256.   Brophy, Brigid. "Bartleby the Scriptwriter." *New Statesman*
        70 (29 October 1965): 664-665. Reprinted as "Highsmith."
        Don't Never Forget: Collected Views and Reviews. New
        York: Holt, Rinehart and Winston, 1967, pp. 149-155.

        In the context of a review of *A Suspension of Mercy*
        contends that not only is Highsmith an outstanding
        writer of crime fiction but also an excellent novelist
        who enlarges the genre of detective fiction with her
        "psychological naturalism."

1257.   Hamilton, Ian. "Patricia Highsmith, an Interview." *New
        Review* (London) 4 (August 1977): 31-36.

        Highsmith says that her interest in odd personalities
        possibly comes from reading *The Human Mind* by Karl
        Menninger when she was ten. Also states that she has no
        particular reason for writing crime stories instead of
        any other kind of fiction.

*   Symons, Julian. *Mortal Consequences* (item 74), pp. 182-
        185.

        Contends that Highsmith is the most important contem-
        porary practitioner of the crime novel because of her
        largely successful fusion of plot and characters.

1258.   Symons, Julian. "Patricia Highsmith: Criminals in Society."
        London Magazine 9 (June 1969): 37-43.

        Argues that Highsmith's books are "profound and subtle"
        studies of character, usually featuring the male charac-
        ters "locked together in a dislike and even hatred that
        often strangely contains love." She takes what may be
        a trivial or far-fetched idea and makes it "terrifyingly
        real."

1259.   "The Talented Miss Highsmith." *Times Literary Supplement*
        24 September 1971, pp. 1147-1148.

        Argues that Highsmith "has persistently used the crime
        story as a means of revealing and examining her own
        deepest interests and obsessions." A main obsession is
        "the threat of irrationality" in everyone. She has
        "gifts of insight" and "real powers of description,
        dialogue and dramatic timing." She should, the author
        contends, break away from the formulas of the crime
        story.

HILL, HEADON. Pseudonym of Francis Edward Grainger (1857-1927)

1260. Bengis, Nathan L. "Plots for Sale--Cheap; Apply: 221B."
       Armchair Detective 1 (July 1968): 116-117.

       Contends that many of the tales in *Zambra the Detec-*
       tive by Headon Hill are influenced by Conan Doyle stories.
       Lists and discusses each one.

HILTON, JAMES (1900-1954). His only mystery/detection work was
first published under the pseudonym of Glen Trevor and then
republished under his real name.

1261. Barzun, Jacques, and Wendell Hertig Taylor. Preface to
       Was It Murder?, by James Hilton. New York: Garland
       Publishing, 1976. Also printed in *A Book of Prefaces*
       (item 22), pp. 65-66.

       Observes that Hilton's only mystery novel has an en-
       gaging setting (an English boarding school), and a casual
       air and pace that add to its appeal, making it a highly
       successful effort in the genre.

1262. Shibuk, Charles. "Three British Experiments from the
       Mainstream." *Armchair Detective* 3 (October 1969): 80.

       Contends that Hilton's *Was It Murder?* is "more than
       competent, but far from inspired."

HIMES, CHESTER (1909-)

1263. Bakish, David. "Chester Himes." *Encyclopedia of World*
       Literature in the Twentieth Century, Volume IV. New
       York: Frederick Ungar, 1975, pp. 159-161.

       Argues that Himes's most recent detective novel, *Blind*
       Man with a Pistol (1969), has darker humor than the
       earlier ones as well as "skillful surrealism."

1264. Campenni, Frank J. "Black Cops and/or Robbers: The
       Detective Fiction of Chester Himes." *Armchair Detec-*
       tive 8 (May 1975): 206-209.

       Maintains that Himes "brilliantly captures the essence
       of Harlem and of representative black life in urban
       America through the metaphor of the detective story."
       Includes checklist.

1265.   Campenni, Frank J. "Chester Himes." *American Novelists Since World War II*. Edited by Jeffrey Halterman and Richard Layman. Detroit: Gale Research, 1978, pp. 240-244.

Argues that writing detective novels liberated Himes from "writing tendentious protest fiction." Uses examples to show the density of detail in the detective novels. That the detectives use illegal methods and many of the criminals disguise themselves as police illustrates the thesis behind all Himes's work: "blacks dwell in an absurdist world where white-designed categories do not apply."

1266.   Chelminski, Rudolph. "The Hard-Bitten Old Pro Who Wrote Cotton." *Life* 69 (28 August 1970): 60-61.

Himes first started writing in prison and in emulation of Dashiell Hammett, but it was twenty-five years before he wrote his detective stories. Quotes Himes saying that his books "are as authentic as *The Autobiography of Malcolm X*."

1267.   Feuser, Willfried. "Prophet of Violence: Chester Himes." *African Literature Today* 9 (1978): 58-76.

Himes's detective novels reveal the same preoccupation with white oppression of blacks that his other works have. The detective novels usually have a "treasure-hunt" plot with little or no emphasis on abstract logic. They evoke the atmosphere of Harlem.

1268.   Kane, Patricia, and Doris Y. Wilkinson. "Survival Strategies: Black Women in *Ollie Miss* and *Cotton Comes to Harlem*." *Critique* 16 (1974): 101-109.

Iris, a minor character in *Cotton Comes to Harlem*, is shown in several instances surviving the attempted dominance of "male authority figures."

1269.   Lee, A. Robert. "Hurts, Absurdities and Violence: The Contrary Dimensions of Chester Himes." *Journal of American Studies* 12 (1978): 99-114.

In an article chiefly concerned with Himes's non-detective work, Lee contends that the detective novels imaginatively use Himes's considerable insight into Harlem ghetto and underworld life.

1270. Lee, A. Robert. "Violence Real and Imagined: The World of Chester Himes' Novels." *Negro American Literature Forum* 10 (1976): 13-22.

Argues that the Harlem in Himes's detective novels "approaches inspired surrealism" and that "violence become a form" is the link between his detective and his other novels even though in his non-detective novels there is not the extreme overt violence seen in the detective ones.

1271. Lundquist, James. *Chester Himes*. New York: Ungar, 1976. 166pp.

In his one chapter on Himes's detective novels, Lundquist contends that Himes "developed a new form of the detective story" and "found a means of expressing his vision of a racially obsessed and decadent America that none of his earlier books quite afforded."

1272. Margolies, Edward. "The Thrillers of Chester Himes." *Studies in Black Literature* 1 (Summer 1970): 1-11.

Argues that the Harlem in Himes's detective novels is a comic intensification of the black experience in America and that Himes carries the pulp magazine formula to its "logical absurdity."

1273. Micha, René. "Les Paroissiens de Chester Himes." *Temps Modernes* 20 (1965): 1507-1523.

Argues that Himes's detective novels are more interesting than his "major" works because he is free from theses and a nineteenth-century idea of the form of the novel.

1274. Milliken, Stephen F. "The Continental Entertainer." *Chester Himes*. Columbia: University of Missouri Press, 1976, pp. 207-269.

Contends that "speed and surprise" are the main elements of Himes's detective novels.

1275. Mok, Michael. "PW Interviews: Chester Himes." *Publishers Weekly* 201 (3 April 1972): 20-21.

Himes states that the two policemen in his detective novels are based on two Los Angeles policemen of the 1940s, though he made them more humane. In these novels he created a Harlem of his own; it is not meant to be exactly realistic.

1276. Nelson, Raymond. "Domestic Harlem: The Detective Fiction
       of Chester Himes." *Virginia Quarterly Review* 48
       (Spring 1972): 260-276. Reprinted *Dimensions of
       Detective Fiction* (item 43), pp. 162-173.

       "What was new about Himes's series of detective novels
       was its variety of character types, its grotesque comedy
       of violence, and its sparse, descriptive style." The
       first, *For Love of Imabelle*, is more a naturalistic
       novel than a detective story. Himes uses the form of
       the detective story, which he says is very American,
       and uses the "bad niggers" of black folklore as his
       detectives. Includes some analyses of individual novels.

1277. Oakes, Philip. "The Man Who Goes Too Fast: A Profile of
       Chester Himes." *Sunday London Times Magazine* 9 Novem-
       ber 1969, pp. 69, 71.

       Contends that Himes is "a realist who deals in bloody
       nihilism."

1278. Reilly, John M. "Chester Himes' Harlem Tough Guys."
       Journal of Popular Culture 9 (Spring 1976): 935-947.

       Argues that "tough-guy fiction" is particularly con-
       genial to the black experience and that Himes's detective
       novels constitute a cycle which emphasize "the status
       of Harlem as an internal colony" and "social relations
       determined by exclusion and oppression."

HODGSON, WILLIAM HOPE (1877-1918)

1279. Christensen, Peter. "William Hope Hodgson: *Carnaki the
       Ghost-Finder*." *Armchair Detective* 12 (Spring 1979):
       122-124.

       Contends that the six stories of the first edition of
       Carnaki the Ghost-Finder "constitute a coherent and
       meaningful whole." In these stories is an interplay
       between the supernatural and the logical in which any-
       thing is possible.

HOLMES, GORDON. See M.P. SHIEL

HOLTON, LEONARD. Pseudonym of Leonard Patrick O'Connor Wibberley
(1915-   )

1280. Holton, Leonard. "Father Bredder." *The Great Detectives*
       (item 60), pp. 25-35.

       Holton does not like violence and says he has no
       talent for intricate plotting; therefore, he created
       Father Bredder, a "nonfussy and nonviolent" detective,
       who also gives the stories a spiritual quality.

HOPLEY, GEORGE. See CORNELL WOOLRICH

HORLER, SYDNEY (1888-1954)

1281. Horler, Sydney. "Meet Tiger Standish." *Meet the Detective*
       (item 45), pp. 61-70.

       Horler responds to accusations that he is a snob by
       arguing that the "public likes its heroes to be well
       born" and admits that Tiger Standish is his favorite
       among the fictional characters he has created.

*   Watson, Colin. "Excitable Sydney Horler." *Snobbery with
       Violence* (item 78), pp. 85-93.

       Contends that Horler's glorification of the qualities
       exemplified by his detective, Tiger Standish--courage,
       athleticism, and virility--was not designed cynically
       to appeal to the public but represented his own personal
       beliefs.

HORNUNG, ERNEST WILLIAM (1866-1921)

*   Butler, William Vivian. *The Durable Desperadoes* (item
       25), pp. 27-38.

       Maintains that Hornung's Raffles was the first really
       successful gentleman outlaw in English detective fiction.

*   Chandler, Frank Wadleigh. "Raffles and Company." *The
       Literature of Roguery* (item 154), pp. 515-521.

       Contends that the gentleman thief, Raffles, owes most
       of his characteristics to Conan Doyle's Sherlock Holmes.
       Raffles, however, is a rogue and adventurer whose moral
       and intellectual disadvantages must be offset by extremely
       difficult exploits that require qualities such as nerve,
       wit, cleverness, and breeding.

*   Murch, A.E. *The Development of the Detective Novel*
         (item 51), pp. 193-195.

         States that Hornung conceived his "rogue hero,"
         Raffles, as Sherlock Holmes turned inside out and even
         constructed his stories along the lines of Conan Doyle's
         Holmes stories.

*   Orwell, George. "Raffles and Miss Blandish" (item 709).

         Argues that Hornung's *Raffles* and James Hadley Chase's
         No Orchids for Miss Blandish can be compared sociologic-
         ally because both concentrate on the criminal rather
         than the detective and both are "morally equivocal."

*   Watson, Colin. "A Very Decent Sort of Burglar." *Snobbery
         with Violence* (item 78), pp. 45-52.

         Contends that the popularity of Hornung's novels
         featuring Raffles is largely due to the "flamboyant
         character and preposterous situation" which character-
         izes them, while the appeal of the Raffles character
         is partly due to his appearing to be above the law.

HOUSEHOLD, GEOFFREY (1900-   )

1282.   Barber, Michael. "Lives and Times of Geoffrey Household."
         Books and Bookmen 19 (January 1974): 40-42.

         Barber says that Household writes "thrillers designed
         to be read as literature" (a phrase coined by Ian
         Fleming). In the interview Household says he dislikes
         crime and violence; his ideal is to get his hero in
         trouble with everyone without actually being "what is
         commonly called a criminal."

HUGHES, DOROTHY B. (1904-   )

1283.   Bannon, Barbara A. "PW Interviews: Dorothy B. Hughes."
         Publishers Weekly 213 (13 March 1978): 6-7.

         The introduction to the interview argues that Hughes's
         books excel as suspense, as psychological studies, and
         as analyses of social problems. In the interview Hughes
         credits editor Marie Fried Rodell with teaching her to
         make her writing economical. She says that she used
         black characters in key roles beginning in the 1940s
         because she has a long-time friend who is black.

HUNT, E. HOWARD (1918-   ). Pseudonyms: Gordon Davis, Robert
Dietrich, John Q, David St. John

1284.   Davis, Earle. "Howard Hunt and the Peter Ward-CIA Spy
         Novels." *Kansas Quarterly* 10 (Fall 1978): 85-95.

         Summarizes Hunt's novels featuring Peter Ward, who
         is supposed to be an American James Bond and points out
         that they exhibit Hunt's extremely conservative political
         views. Davis also speculates on the connection between
         the novels and Hunt's work in the CIA at the time.

1285.   "E. Howard Hunt, Master Storyteller." *Time* 101 (11 June
         1973): 20-21.

         Describes Hunt's spy novels as "predictable concoctions
         of espionage and sex in exotic settings."

1286.   Lingeman, Richard R. "Hunt as Author: A Critic's Ap-
         praisal." *New York Times Magazine* 3 June 1973, pp.
         46-47.

         Hunt's writing, Lingeman contends, exhibits insider's
         details, a "brand-name dropping" pseudo-sophistication,
         a right-wing world view, and a flat style.

1287.   Vidal, Gore. "The Art and Arts of E. Howard Hunt." *New
         York Review of Books* 20 (13 December 1973): 6-19.
         Reprinted *Matters of Fact and of Fiction: Essays,
         1973-1976.* New York: Random House, 1977, pp. 207-235.

         Vidal states that the prime characteristics of Hunt's
         writing are anti-communism, daydreaming, and a vigilante
         sense of law and order.

HUNT, KYLE. See JOHN CREASEY

HUNTER, EVAN. See ED McBAIN

HUXLEY, ELSPETH (1907-   )

1288.   Barzun, Jacques, and Wendell Hertig Taylor. Preface to
         The African Poison Murders, by Elspeth Huxley. New
         York: Garland Publishing, 1976. Also printed in *A
         Book of Prefaces* (item 22), pp. 67-68.

In meeting the challenges of creating the atmosphere
and feeling of British East Africa before World War II,
in building suspense in her policeman's legal proceedings
in solving a double murder, and in integrating diverse
elements effortlessly into her plot, Huxley has, the
authors contend, created a tensely textured mystery.

INNES, MICHAEL. Pseudonym of J.I.M. Stewart (1906-   )

1289. Barzun, Jacques, and Wendell Hertig Taylor. Preface to
       The Daffodil Affair, by Michael Innes. New York:
       Garland Publishing, 1976. Also printed in *A Book of
       Prefaces* (item 22), pp. 69-70.

       Contends that the novel is not representative of
       Innes's work, but nonetheless is a classic because of
       Innes's successful handling of the bizarre motive and
       interplay of distrust, anxiety, espionage, and crime
       combined with a swiftly paced narrative and thoughtful
       style.

1290. Innes, Michael. "John Appleby." *The Great Detectives*
       (item 60), pp. 9-15.

       States that his detective, John Appleby, is intended
       to provide "civilized" entertainment as much as to
       pursue criminals. His favorite haunts—the great country
       house or ducal mansion—are really extensions "of the
       sealed room, defining the spatial, the territorial
       boundaries of a problem."

*   Routley, Erik. "Politeness and Protest: Michael Innes."
       The Puritan Pleasures of the Detective Story (item
       64), pp. 157-169.

       States that Innes "celebrates the academic in detective
       fiction," writing with precision and fastidiousness but
       without passion. He emphasizes narrative much more than
       plot and character, concentrating on the delight of the
       story rather than the delight of the pursuit.

IRISH, WILLIAM. See CORNELL WOOLRICH

JACOBS, W.W. (1863-1943)

1291. Harkey, Joseph H. "Foreshadowing in 'The Monkey's Paw.'"
       Studies in Short Fiction 6 (1969): 653-654.

Argues that four elements in the opening paragraphs
foreshadow the entire tale.

1292. Priestley, J.B. "In Praise of Mr. Jacobs." *London
        Mercury* 9 (November 1923): 26-36. Reprinted *Figures
        in Modern Literature.* London: Bodley Head, 1924, pp.
        103-123.

        Argues that Jacobs deserves a better critical reputa-
        tion than he has but bases this argument on his non-
        mystery stories. States that Jacobs does not have a
        sufficiently poetic mind to write a first-class horror
        story.

JAMES, P.D. (1920-   ). Series character: Adam Dalgliesh

1293. Bakerman, Jane S. "'From the Time I Could Read, I
        Always Wanted to Be a Writer': Interview with P.D.
        James." *Armchair Detective* 10 (January 1977): 55-57,
        92.

        In a wide-ranging interview James discusses her detec-
        tive Adam Dalgliesh whom she tries not to make senti-
        mental or infallible. James concludes the interview by
        stating that "as a writer, I would like to be remembered
        as an honest and original craftsman, who was able to
        give pleasure, and entertainment ... and to have troubled
        to try and do it well."

1294. Bannon, Barbara A. "PW Interviews: P.D. James." *Publishers
        Weekly* 209 (5 January 1976): 8-9.

        James's works are "psychologically subtle" and the
        detective in her novels is "quite possibly the most
        intellectual detective of our time." In the interview
        James reveals her distaste for the "English country
        house mystery" featuring an amateur detective.

1295. Dix, Winslow. "Murder with Character: People Populate
        P.D. James's Mysteries." *Books and Arts* 1 (14 Septem-
        ber 1979): 13.

        Argues that James's vivid characterizations are more
        outstanding than those of other contemporary mystery
        writers. Contends that she can be considered a serious
        novelist.

1296. Winks, Robin W. "Murder and Dying."*New Republic* 195
        (31 July 1976): 31-32.

James shows a greater awareness of the complexity of
human beings than did Dorothy Sayers. All James's books
are "realistic portrayals of life and death among the
ill and dying." Her style is one of nuance and indirec-
tion. *Shroud for a Nightingale* is her best book, with
"mood, pace, style and atmosphere ... in perfect
balance."

1297. Wyndham, Francis. "The Civilized Art of Murder." *Times
       Literary Supplement* 13 December 1974, p. 1419.

       Argues that James has revitalized the classical detec-
       tive story. She has a literate style and her conclusions
       "come as a surprise without straining credibility."
       The generally old-fashioned air of her works is often
       contradicted by a "modern melancholy" and by her accurate
       social and psychological observations.

JESSE, F. TENNYSON (1889?-1958). Pseudonym: Beamish Tinker

1298. Jesse, F. Tennyson. Foreword to *Solange Stories*. New
       York: Macmillan, 1931, pp. ix-xvi.

       Argues that "the fun of anything consists in its
       limitations" and with fewer restrictions in other forms
       of literature it is only in detective fiction that one
       can write within definite limitations. States that in
       her stories she tries to keep strictly within the rules
       but occasionally strays.

JOHNSON, WALTER RYERSON. See BRETT HALLIDAY

KAMINSKY, STUART (1936-)

1299. Lachtman, Howard. "California Dreamin': Shamus in
       Golden Age of Hollywood." *Los Angeles Times Book
       Review* 2 December 1979, p. 3.

       Maintains that although Kaminsky's detective, Toby
       Peters, begins as a derivative of such classic detec-
       tives as Sam Spade and Philip Marlowe, he becomes "an
       authentic character in his own right." Kaminsky includes
       in his detective novels such real people as the Marx
       Brothers and Raymond Chandler, and states that he
       chooses "actors and writers I admire ... historical
       characters who represent some kind of enigma I want to

explore," and blends them with swift-paced, succinct action to mix murder with nostalgia.

KEATING, H.R.F. (1926-)

1300. Keating, H.R.F. "Inspector Ghote." *The Great Detectives* (item 60), pp. 111-117.

Described by his creator as persistent, shrewd, and knowledgeable about police procedures, Inspector Ghote appears in novels that are based upon such abstract themes as perfectionism.

1301. Pettersson, Sven-Ingmar. "H.R.F. Keating." *Armchair Detective* 8 (August 1975): 277-279, 270 [*sic*].

In Keating's books, the crime is less important than either the theme, the "message," or the characters. Includes checklist and commentaries on individual works.

KEELER, HARRY STEPHEN (1890-1967)

1302. Beauchesne, Bernard. "Harry Stephen Keeler: Mystery Writer Extraordinary." *Armchair Detective* 1 (July 1968): 143-149.

Gives a brief biography of Keeler and describes his method of plotting a "web work" mystery by assembling randomly selected newspaper crime clippings. Includes a checklist of his writings.

1303. Nevins, Francis M., Jr. "Harry Stephen Keeler's Screwball Circus." *Armchair Detective* 5 (July 1972): 209-213.

The longest Keeler series with a human continuing character is the *Circus Sextology*. It shows that Keeler had an "unfettered delight in creation" and the "craftsmanship of a computer." Includes summaries of the novels and two maps of the territory covered in the first book in the series.

1304. Nevins, Francis M., Jr. "Hick Dick from the Sticks: Harry Stephen Keeler's Quiribus Brown." *Armchair Detective* 7 (August 1974): 251-252.

Details long and curious process which led Keeler to invent the character Quiribus Brown and write the book which features him, *The Murdered Mathematician*.

1305. Nevins, Francis M., Jr. "Murder like Crazy." *New Republic*
       177 (30 July 1977): 25-28.

       Argues that Keeler's novels "form a self-contained
       world of monstrously complicated intrigues, half farce ...
       half radical social criticism." States that Keeler in-
       vented the "webwork novel" in which hundreds of events
       turn out to be mathematically connected.

1306. Nevins, Francis M., Jr. "The Wild and Woolly World of
       Harry Stephen Keeler." *Journal of Popular Culture* 3
       (Spring 1970): 635-643; 4 (Fall 1970): 410-418; 5
       (Winter 1971): 521-529; 7 (Summer 1973): 159-171.

       Argues that Keeler was a committed radical humanist
       who wrote zany masterpieces, "a man so far ahead of
       his time we have still not caught up to him." His most
       characteristic device is a system of interlocked coin-
       cidences. Uses discussions of Keeler's important novels
       to support his contentions.

1307. Nevins, Francis M., Jr. "The Wild and Woolly World of
       Harry Stephen Keeler: Scenes from the Last Act."
       Armchair Detective 3 (January 1970): 71-76. Also
       printed in *Challenges in American Culture*. Edited by
       Ray B. Browne, Larry Landrum, and William K. Bottoroff.
       Bowling Green, Ohio: Bowling Green University Popular
       Press, 1970, pp. 251-257.

       States that Keeler is "the sublime nutty genius of
       crime fiction," but that his popularity declined so
       much that his books written during the 1950s and 1960s
       were either not published or published only in Spain
       or Portugal. Nevins describes a few of these novels.

1308. Nevins, Francis M., Jr. "The Worst Legal Mystery in
       the World." *Armchair Detective* 1 (April 1968): 82-85.

       Contends that Keeler's novel, *The Amazing Web* (1930),
       is a classic of the genre and gives a detailed plot
       summary of the novel to support his contention.

KEENE, CAROLYN. Pseudonym used for all the Nancy Drew stories.
    The first three were written by Edward L. Stratemeyer (1862-
    1930). All the rest were written by his daughter, Harriet
    L. Adams.

1309. Jones, James P. "Nancy Drew: WASP Super Girl of the
      1930's." *Journal of Popular Culture* 6 (Spring 1973):
      707-717.

      Concentrating on the first eighteen volumes of the
      series (published between 1930 and World War II), con-
      tends that the Nancy Drew books are stereotypical "for-
      mula fiction" that represent upper middle-class
      America's mores and values.

1310. Kagan, Julia. "Nancy Drew--18 Going on 50." *McCall's*
      100 (July 1973): 27.

      Notes the continuing success of the Nancy Drew books.
      Quotes Keene as saying Nancy is interesting because of
      her thinking processes and quotes a sociologist as
      saying Nancy can compete with a boy without upsetting
      sexual role definitions. Concludes that essentially
      Nancy Drew is a fantasy figure.

1311. Keene, Carolyn. "Nancy Drew." *The Great Detectives*
      (item 60), pp. 81-86.

      Contends that the impact of the Nancy Drew series is
      so large because teenagers basically want a fictional
      hero or heroine they can admire.

1312. Koff, Rochelle. "Harriet Adams." *Fort Lauderdale News*
      23 April 1975. Reprinted *Authors in the News*, Volume
      2. Edited by Barbara Nykoruk. Detroit: Gale Research,
      1976, p. 1.

      After surveying the history of the Nancy Drew series
      and Adams's background, points out that Adams has re-
      written the first three books in the series "to make
      them more appealing to a modern audience." Adams
      maintains that the books are still popular partly be-
      cause they are fast-paced and full of action.

1313. Mason, Bobbie Ann. "Nancy Drew: The Once and Future
      Prom Queen." *The Girl Sleuth* (item 48), pp. 48-75.

      Argues that the Nancy Drew series draws a picture of
      "a fading aristocracy, threatened by the restless lower
      classes." It is Nancy's task to define class lines,
      property, and order. As a girl detective she has the
      best of both the child's and adult's worlds--protected
      and free to have adventures.

1314.   Nye, Russel. *The Unembarrassed Muse: The Popular Arts
        in America.* New York: Dial Press, 1970, pp. 85-87.

        Outlines the conventional plot of a Nancy Drew book
        and states that Nancy appeals to the eleven to fifteen
        age group, who see her as what they wish to be--"poised,
        capable, self-sufficient."

1315.   Prager, Arthur. "The Secret of Nancy Drew." *Rascals at
        Large, or, The Clue in the Old Nostalgia.* Garden City,
        N.Y.: Doubleday, 1971, pp. 71-95. [Chapter is expanded
        from article originally published in *Saturday Review*
        52 (25 January 1969): 18-19, 34-35.]

        Argues that the immense and continuing appeal of Nancy
        Drew is that she is a fantasy figure but close enough
        to real life that a pre-teen girl can identify with
        her. Details the simple, unvarying patterns of the plots
        and the secure, conservative world in which they take
        place.

1316.   Zacharias, Lee. "Nancy Drew: Ballbuster." *Journal of
        Popular Culture* 9 (Spring 1976): pp. 1027-1038.

        Nancy Drew is not a realistic character; she is "the
        epitome of superiority, confidence, and control." She
        solves the mysteries of life, and "the solution is the
        American Dream, prosperity for the good guys, justice
        within the law." The title of the article refers to
        Nancy's desire to "reduce her villains to broken old
        men."

KEMELMAN, HARRY (1908-)

*   Lachman, Marvin. "Religion and Detection: Sunday the
        Rabbi Met Father Brown" (item 721).

        Using the format of a fictional conversation between
        Rabbi Small and Chesterton's Father Brown, Lachman
        points out that Rabbi Small's method of detection
        derives from his religious training in making fine
        distinctions and in considering all possibilities.

1317.   Maryles, Daisy. "PW Interviews: Harry Kemelman." *Publishers
        Weekly* 207 (28 April 1975): 8-9.

        Kemelman's novels featuring Rabbi David Small as a
        detective hero have the usual ingredients of the detec-
        tive story as well as "intellectual dialogues on reli-

gion and a careful portrayal of Jewish life in suburbia."
In the interview he states that his original purpose
in writing was to explain the Jewish religion in fiction.

1318. Phipps, Jennie. "His 'Sherlock' a Rabbi." *Fort Lauder-
       dale Sun-Sentinel* 20 January 1975. Reprinted *Authors
       in the News*, Volume 1. Edited by Barbara Nykoruk.
       Detroit: Gale Research, 1976, p. 265.

       Kemelman observes that his detective, Rabbi Small, is
       a "constructed" character "and not copied from similar
       people he has known." He is also quoted as saying that
       "a person like Rabbi Small wouldn't be tolerated in
       any synagogue. He's the sort of person every Rabbi
       would like to be, but if he behaved like that, he would
       lose his job."

KENDRAKE, CARLETON. See ERLE STANLEY GARDNER

KENDRICK, BAYNARD H. (1894-1977)

1319. Kendrick, Baynard H. "Duncan Maclain." *The Great
       Detectives* (item 60), pp. 129-140.

       Kendrick states that he was inspired to create his
       blind detective by the plight of a blind friend and the
       urging of Anne Mansfield Sullivan, Helen Keller's
       teacher. She challenged him to create a detective "who
       would never perform any feat in his detection or deduc-
       tion that couldn't be duplicated by someone totally
       blind."

KENNY, CHARLES J. See ERLE STANLEY GARDNER

KERSH, GERALD (1909-1968)

1320. Lauterbach, Edward S. "Smorgasbord Thriller." *Armchair
       Detective* 4 (April 1971): 165-167.

       Argues that Kersh's novel, *The Secret Masters*, is
       like a smorgasbord because it has elements of science
       fiction, the classical mystery story, and horror while
       basically it can be called a spy thriller.

KINDON, THOMAS

1321. Barzun, Jacques, and Wendell Hertig Taylor. Preface to
       Murder in the Moor, by Thomas Kindon. New York:
       Garland Publishing, 1976. Also printed in *A Book of
       Prefaces* (item 22), pp. 71-72.

       Observes that the book has a murder "committed for
       an original motive in a picturesque setting," a care-
       fully delineated villain, excellent deduction, a few
       eccentrics and a "sympathetic crook." All these elements
       are well integrated into the story and interest is
       prolonged "when everything looks finished."

KING, RUFUS (1893-1966)

1322. Purcell, J.M. "A Note on Rufus King's Series of Short
       Stories." *Armchair Detective* 12 (Fall 1979): 380.

       Contends that King's Colin Starr detective short
       stories series for *Redbook* (collected as *Diagnosis:
       Murder*, 1941) tried to reconcile the demands made by
       mystery fiction (everyone is under suspicion) and popu-
       lar magazine fiction (the reader wants to know who is
       good and who is bad). King's series of short stories
       featuring Stuff Driscoll are probably better known
       because of their more recent appearance and accessibil-
       ity.

KINGSLEY, SIDNEY (1906-)

1323. Porter, Thomas E. "Tragedy and the Private Eye: *Detec-
       tive Story.*" *Myth and Modern American Drama*. Detroit:
       Wayne State University Press, 1969, pp. 105-126.

       Explains the conventions of the detective story and
       the qualities associated with a tough detective hero
       and points out which ones are used in Sidney Kingsley's
       Broadway play *Detective Story* (1949).

KNOTT, FREDERICK (1918-)

1324. Kerr, Walter. "Me and Thee: My Malignant Mind." *Thirty
       Plays Hath November: Pains and Pleasure in the Con-
       temporary Theater*. New York: Simon and Schuster,
       1969, pp. 15-20.

States that the mystery form requires twists in the plot; it is a battle between the reader or viewer and the author. In his play *Wait Until Dark*, however, Knott is "simply fiddling around for two acts, *pretending* to be complicated."

KNOX, RONALD A. (1888-1957)

1325. Donaldson, Norman. "Ronald Arbuthnot Knox." *Armchair Detective* 7 (August 1974): 235-246.

Part I is a lengthy exploration of the "apostolic Knox." Part II, which covers his detective novels, particularly *The Viaduct Murder* and *Double-Cross Purposes*, concludes that Knox is "better with scenery than with characterizations, and better with minor characters than with major ones."

1326. Kingman, James. "In Defense of Ronald Knox." *Armchair Detective* 11 (July 1978): 299.

Argues that Knox is not read because too much is expected of his detective novels although if judged by normal standards they must be considered good. Concludes that Knox is therefore a victim of his own brilliance.

1327. Speight, Robert. *Ronald Knox the Writer*. London: Sheed and Ward, 1966, pp. 32-42.

Comments on each of the detective stories of Knox. States that he brought to the solution of *The Viaduct Murder* the "reasoning," "judgment," and "logic" he brought to his other work. Praises his use of atmosphere.

1328. Waugh, Evelyn. *The Life of the Right Reverend Ronald Knox*. London: Chapman and Hall, 1959. 358pp.

In the few references to Knox's detective fiction, Waugh argues that Knox regarded his detective stories purely as puzzles, as intellectual exercises, and had no concern for the psychology or morality of the crimes.

KURNITZ, HARRY. See MARCO PAGE

KYD, THOMAS. Pseudonym of Alfred Bennett Harbage (1901-1976)

1329. Barzun, Jacques, and Wendell Hertig Taylor. Preface to *Blood on the Bosom Divine*, by Thomas Kyd. New York:

Garland Publishing, 1976. Also printed in *A Book of Prefaces* (item 22), pp. 73-74.

Contends that Kyd avoids in this, his best novel, many of the architectural and psychological problems "associated with fictional murder on or near the stage." Besides an excellent handling of the mise-en-scène and personal relationships, Kyd also provides several deft humorous touches in depicting his detective and other characters.

LAING, ALEXANDER (1903-1976)

1330.   Lauterbach, Edward. "Horror, Detection and Footnotes." *Armchair Detective* 3 (October 1969): 12-13.

The *Cadaver of Gideon Wyck*, by Alexander Laing, is a novel of both horror and detection and uses footnotes for artistic effect.

LATHAM, AARON (1943-)

1331.   Steinberg, Sybil. "PW Interviews: Aaron Latham." *Publishers Weekly* 211 (27 June 1977): 12, 14.

Latham says that *Orchids for Mother* began with the idea of writing a non-fiction work on the CIA, but when he realized the CIA is "one of the greatest fiction machines in the country," he decided to write a novel instead. The two main characters in *Orchids for Mother* are based on real CIA people.

LATHEN, EMMA. Joint pseudonym of Mary J. Latsis and Martha Hennissart. Other joint pseudonym: R.B. Dominic

1332.   Bakerman, Jane S. "Women and Wall Street: Portraits of Women in Novels by Emma Lathen." *Armchair Detective* 8 (1974): 36-41.

"In the Lathen novels, the women characters are often more fully drawn, more able, and generally more nearly real people than is customary in the detective form," yet they are portrayed realistically and not idealized.

1333.   Brownell, David. "Comic Construction in the Novels of Emma Lathen and R.B. Dominic." *Armchair Detective* 9 (February 1976): 91-92.

The authors have enough detachment from their characters to make their books comic rather than tragic.

1334. Callendar, Newgate. "Criminals at Large." *New York
Times Book Review* 26 March 1972, p. 42.

In this review of *The Longer the Thread*, Callendar
makes the overall assessment of Lathen's work that
her dialog is "bright, observant and just this side of
cutesy." Minor characters are usually more lifelike
than her banker-detective, and her graceful manner
disarms criticism of her sentimental theme that good
always triumphs.

1335. Cawelti, John G. "Emma Lathen: Murder and Sophistication." *New Republic* 175 (31 July 1976): 25-27.

Lathen "is surely the most consistently superior
writer of classical detective writing in America today."
She concentrates more on the character of her detective
and the social milieu in which the crime was committed
than on clues and suspects. In addition, she has a gift
for comic satire.

1336. "Masters of White-Collar Homicide." *Forbes* 120 (1
December 1977): 89.

States that Lathen is the only writer of detective
stories specializing in "white-collar homicide."

LATSIS, MARY J. See EMMA LATHEN

LeBLANC, MAURICE (1864-1941). Series character: Arsène Lupin

1337. Bordillon, Henri. "Arsène Lupin, Balthazar et Dorothée."
Europe no. 604-605 (August-September 1979): 78-84.

Contends that the central figures in two of LeBlanc's
novels, Dorothée in *Dorothée Danseuse de Corde* (1923)
and Balthazar in *La Vie Extravagante du Professeur
Balthazar* (1925) present two perverted images of Lupin:
a feminine alter ego and a hollow, vain anti-hero.

1338. Buissiere, François. "Arsène Lupin: Homme de Lettres."
Europe no. 571-572 (November-December 1976): 61-71.

Points out the three-part nature of the protagonist
of the novel *L'Ile aux Trente Cercueils*.

1339.   Colin, Jean-Paul. "Modernisme ou Modernité du Langage
        Lupinien?" *Europe* no. 604-605 (August-September
        1979): 56-60.

        States that different modes of speech are used by
        Lupin--romantic, classic, and modern. These different
        styles are necessary because Lupin is accustomed to
        speaking with different social classes and must change
        his language and style of speech accordingly.

1340.   Dinguirard, J.C. "Le Lecteur en Peau de Lupin." *Europe*
        no. 604-605 (August-September 1979): 67-78.

        A semantic study of the name "Arsène Lupin."

1341.   Edwards, Oliver. "Boy's Own Caper." *London Times* 4
        November 1965, p. 14.

        Argues that LeBlanc had "an inexhaustible gusto and
        a gift for suspense" and that the atmosphere of his
        stories was one in which the impossible could happen.

1342.   Gayot, Paul. "Lupin Premier." *Europe* no. 604-605
        (August-September 1979): 20-23.

        Argues that in his Arsène Lupin stories, LeBlanc
        made important contributions to the puzzle novel, demon-
        strating that he was a geometrician as well as a poet.
        Also contends that LeBlanc surpasses not only Alexander
        Dumas and Conan Doyle but also Agatha Christie and
        S.S. Van Dine.

1343.   Lacassin, Francis. "L'Art de Cambrioler ... L'Histoire
        de France." *Europe* no. 604-605 (August-September
        1979): 24-34.

        After tracing notorious thieves in the history of
        France in order to place the character of Lupin in its
        proper context, Lacassin points out that Lupin's
        nationalism mirrored that of the age in which he appeared.

1344.   Limat, Maurice. "Monsieur Maurice LeBlanc: Écrivain
        Français." *Europe* no. 604-605 (August-September 1979):
        61-67.

        Contends that LeBlanc was an important writer who
        exhibited in his work three attributes all great writers
        must have: poetry, psychology, and action.

1345.   Meltzer, Charles Henry. "Arsène Lupin at Home." *Cosmo-
        politan* 54 (May 1913): 770-773.

Meltzer states that Arsène Lupin is an attractive
rascal but in his interview with LeBlanc finds the
author does not think his books could be a bad influence on anyone.

*   Murch, A.E. *The Development of the Detective Novel*
(item 51), pp. 195-197.

Contends that in LeBlanc's stories featuring Arsène
Lupin "'scientific' methods of detection play little if
any part" and that Lupin is most convincing as a gentleman burglar rather than as a detective.

1346.   Olivier-Martin, Yves. "Le Bal des Voleurs." *Europe* no.
604-605 (August-September 1979): 5-8.

Speculates that Lupin's character was an immediate
success partly because of the turn of the century atmosphere of anarchism that prevailed when he was created.
As a gentleman thief able to deal with any danger, he
appealed to members of all classes.

1347.   Olivier-Martin, Yves. "Esthétique du Gentleman-Cambri-
oleur." *Europe* no. 604-605 (August-September 1979):
35-42.

In the context of a semantic and sociological study
of the gentleman thief as he appeared in French literature before Lupin, Olivier-Martin points out characteristics that also appear in the Lupin myth such as pro-
tecting the weak and fooling the police.

1348.   Raymond, François. "Arsène Lupin et le Démon de la
Répétition." *Europe* no. 604-605 (August-September
1979): 42-49.

Pointing out the protean-like, many-sided nature of
the fictional Lupin--gentleman, thief, man of letters--
Raymond concludes that the popularity and appeal of
Lupin's character is partly due to the skill with
which LeBlanc makes the reader believe that all these
different personalities can exist at the same time in
Lupin or, conversely, that he can be totally one thing
and not another.

*   Thomson, H. Douglas. "The French Detective Story."
Masters of Mystery (item 77), pp. 118-121.

States that LeBlanc's detective, Arsène Lupin, is the
most famous French detective and contends that he is
a "parody of the conventional detective."

1349.   Vareille, Jean-Claude. "Modernité et Tradition." *Europe* no. 604-605 (August-September 1979): 50-55.

Points out some of the distortions in LeBlanc's Lupin stories, most of which were a result of popular misconceptions of science at the time they were written.

Le CARRÉ, JOHN. Pseudonym of David John Moore Cornwell (1931-)

1350.   Barber, Michael. "John Le Carré: An Interrogation."
        New York Times Book Review 25 September 1977, pp. 9,
        44-45.

        Le Carré attributes the present popularity of spy
        fiction to public cynicism about government. He begins
        writing his two characters in conflict but without a
        definite plan of how that conflict will progress or
        climax. He thinks the "norms and forms" of English
        society are an ideal background for suspense.

1351.   Bonfante, Jordan. "The Spy-Master Unmasked." *Life* 56
        (28 February 1964): 39-40, 43.

        Le Carré ascribes his successful depictions of spies
        and espionage in *The Spy Who Came In from the Cold* to
        his government experience and to a close study of the
        existing literature on the subject.

1352.   Bragg, Melvyn. "The Things a Spy Can Do." *Listener* 95
        (22 January 1976): 90.

        In this interview Le Carré says he likes to use the
        spy story to talk about politics, and he sees ordinary
        life as similar to that of a spy in that every relation-
        ship is fraught with tension.

1353.   Cameron, James. "The Case of the Hot Writer." *New York
        Times Magazine* 8 September 1974, pp. 55+.

        Argues that Le Carré brought "style and character and
        compassion and a rather haunting kind of verisimilitude"
        to the spy novel. Quotes Le Carré as saying the "people
        have always been fascinated by the anatomy of betrayal."

1354.   Crutchley, Leigh. "The Fictional World of Espionage:
        John Le Carré Interviewed by Leigh Crutchley." *Listener*
        75 (14 April 1966): 548-549.

        Le Carré says he developed his style while drafting
        items in the Foreign Office and that he has tried to
        show a world in which we are fighting the enemy with
        his own weapons.

1355.   Dean, Michael. "John Le Carré: The Writer Who Came In
        from the Cold." *Listener* 92 (5 September 1974): 306-
        307.

In this interview with Dean, Le Carré says that *The
Spy Who Came In from the Cold* was not written as an
anti-James Bond work and that too many people overlooked
the fact that it is a romantic book.

1356.   Fenton, James. "Le Carré Goes East." *New Review* 4
        (October 1977): pp. 31-34.

        Fenton, who worked for a time in Southeast Asia,
        finds *The Honourable Schoolboy*, which is set there,
        "inaccurate and unconvincing." He gives examples of
        the inaccuracies and states that Le Carré has become
        a prisoner of his own fame and has "lost contact with
        his talent."

1357.   Gillespie, Robert. "The Recent Future: Secret Agents
        and the Cold War." *Salmagundi* no. 13 (Summer 1970):
        45-60.

        Le Carré is "the best of the espionage lot ... his
        conclusions are close to what other serious fiction has
        been telling us about the world we have to live in,
        that it is physically shabby ... and spiritually sterile."

1358.   Grella, George. "John Le Carré: Murder and Loyalty."
        New Republic 31 (31 July 1976): 23-25.

        Argues that Le Carré is "one of the best living
        English writers," whose novels are not merely spy
        stories but "thoughtful, compassionate meditations on
        deception, illusion and defeat."

1359.   Greenway, H.D.S. "Travels with Le Carré: Writing Spy
        Thriller: *The Honourable Schoolboy*." *Newsweek* 90
        (10 October 1977): 102.

        Washington Post reporter Greenway assisted Le Carré
        in his research for *The Honourable Schoolboy*. He argues
        that Le Carré wanted credibility rather than total
        accuracy but that he did a thorough job of researching
        the background for the novel. He also contends that Le
        Carré's protagonist, Jerry Westerby, is Conrad's Lord
        Jim updated and turned inside out: Jim tried to rectify
        his breach of faith by a rigid code of conduct; Westerby
        finally rejects a code of conduct which he eventually
        realizes is immoral and cruel.

1360.   Johnson, Douglas. "Three Cards of Identity." *New Society*
        42 (3 November 1977): 247-248.

Argues that Le Carré's books are about reality and
identity and that, like Richard Adams and John Fowles,
Le Carré is "rooted in an English tradition of education, career, outlook and taste."

1361. Kanfer, Stefan. "The Spy Who Came In for the Gold."
       Time 110 (3 October 1977): 58-60, 67-68, 72.

       Contends that Le Carré's George Smiley is the most
       outstanding spy of his time, just as Le Carré is the
       most outstanding contemporary spy novelist and argues
       that Le Carré's success is partly due to his subject
       matter--espionage--which he both illuminates and human-
       izes.

1362. Maddocks, Melvin. "Le Carré at His Best with an Ethical
       Spy." *Life* 65 (25 October 1968): 6.

       In reviewing *A Small Town in Germany* Maddocks argues
       that Le Carré's attempt to write spy novels which are
       also literature sometimes produces pretentiousness and
       that his theme is the inescapable conflict between the
       ideal and the necessary. Maddocks concludes that Le
       Carré lacks "some extra margin of extravagance" that
       could make him a great novelist.

1363. Rutherford, Andrew. "The Spy as Hero: Le Carré and the
       Cold War." *The Literature of War: Five Studies in
       Heroic Virtue.* New York: Barnes and Noble, 1978, pp.
       135-156.

       Le Carré gives us not only exciting fantasies but
       also "political, moral, and psychological complexities."

1364. Watson, Alan. "Violent Image." *Sunday London Times*
       30 March 1969, pp. 55, 57.

       In this interview with Alan Watson, Le Carré states
       that though he writes about violence he is afraid of it
       and that he despises "the short answer in the perfectly
       made world" of the James Bond books.

LEE, MANFRED BENNINGTON. See ELLERY QUEEN

Le FANU, JOSEPH SHERIDAN (1814-1873)

1365. Begnal, Michael H. *Joseph Sheridan LeFanu.* Lewisburg,
       Penn.: Bucknell University Press, 1971. 87pp.

Argues that *Wylder's Hand* is Le Fanu's best work because of its strong narrative, paramount mystery and suspense, and compelling psychological portraits.

1366. Benson, E.F. "Sheridan Le Fanu." *Spectator* 146 (21 February 1931): 263-264.

Contends that producing terror is a most difficult art and that Le Fanu does it better than Poe. His technique is a "quiet, cumulative method leading up to intolerable terror." Uses *Uncle Silas* as an example.

1367. Bowen, Elizabeth. "*Uncle Silas*." *Collected Impressions.* London: Longmans, Green, 1950, pp. 3-17.

Argues that *Uncle Silas* was ahead of its time, being among the first of the psychological thrillers. States that it "derives its power from an inner momentum."

1368. Brownell, David. "Wicked Dreams: The World of Sheridan Le Fanu." *Armchair Detective* 9 (June 1976): 191-197.

Argues that "Le Fanu's territory as a writer is the realm of the unpleasant" and that in both his ghost stories and his mysteries the innocent as well as the guilty suffer. Brownell examines several of Le Fanu's works including *Wylder's Hand*, which he regards as Le Fanu's best novel.

* Ellis, Stewart Marsh. "Joseph Sheridan Le Fanu." *Wilkie Collins, Le Fanu and Others* (item 779), pp. 140-191.

Traces Le Fanu's interest in mystery stories to Irish tales he heard as a youth. States that *Wylder's Hand* is his best work, both for the compelling mystery and the "raw, jagged power" with which it is told.

1369. Kenton, Edna. "A Forgotten Creator of Ghosts." *Bookman* 69 (July 1929): 528-534.

Kenton finds the fact that Le Fanu has been forgotten inexplicable and calls him "the real forerunner of the 'psychic horror school.'"

* Murch, A.E. *The Development of the Detective Novel* (item 51), pp. 133-136.

Argues that *Checkmate* (1870-1871) is a landmark novel in detective fiction and "must be included in that small group of English detective stories which were written in the third quarter of the nineteenth century and influenced later fiction of this kind."

1370. Shroyer, Frederick B. "A Critical Survey of Representa-
       tive Works by Joseph Sheridan LeFanu and of Comments
       upon His Work." Ph.D. dissertation, University of
       Southern California, 1955.

       Argues that one of Le Fanu's most effective techniques
       is conveying a sense of "terror and suspense" by a
       description of nature. Also contends that Le Fanu in-
       troduced the character of the "psychic-doctor-detective,"
       which Shroyer traces through *Dracula* to the Father
       Brown stories.

*   Symons, Julian. *Mortal Consequences* (item 74), pp.
       55-57.

       Contends that Le Fanu is one of the most important
       writers in the development of mystery fiction and that
       his novel *Uncle Silas* (1864) compares favorably to
       Wilkie Collins's *The Woman in White*.

LeQUEUX, WILLIAM (1864- 1927)

*   Watson, Colin. "De Rigueur at Monte." *Snobbery with
       Violence* (item 78), pp. 53-59.

       Contends that LeQueux's romantic, escapist mystery
       fiction was directed at the English housewife who could
       not afford to travel and did not want her illusion of
       the romantic, fantastic world of the Riviera destroyed.

LEVIN, IRA (1929-)

1371. Lima, Robert. "The Satanic Rape of Catholicism in
       Rosemary's Baby." *Studies in American Fiction* 2
       (1974): 211-222.

       Lima traces the origins of the Satanists in *Rosemary's
       Baby* to the pseudepigraphical *Book of Enoch* (ca. A.D.
       200). By tracing the Satanic heresy through the ages,
       he demonstrates that the anti-Catholic imagery in
       Levin's book can be best understood in the context of
       traditional Satanism.

LEWIS, CECIL DAY. See NICHOLAS BLAKE

LEWIS, LANGE. Pseudonym of Jane Lewis Beynon (1915-)

1372. Barzun, Jacques, and Wendell Hertig Taylor. Preface to
       The Birthday Murder, by Lange Lewis. New York: Garland
       Publishing, 1976. Also printed in *A Book of Prefaces*
       (item 22), pp. 75-76.

Observes that the book shows Lewis's gift for brevity, smooth, succinct prose, and characterization.

LEWIS, MARY CHRISTIANNA MILNE. See CHRISTIANNA BRAND

LININGTON, ELIZABETH (1921-). Pseudonyms: Dell Shannon, Lesley Egan

1373. Shannon, Dell. "Lieutenant Luis Mendoza." *The Great Detectives* (item 60), pp. 149-153.

Offers a biography of her protagonist. "The cynicism, egotism, and sardonic humor are camouflage on Mendoza's part for a large and sentimental heart."

LINKS, J.G. See DENNIS WHEATLEY

LOCKE, MARTIN. See W. MURDOCH DUNCAN

LOCKRIDGE, RICHARD (1898-). Wrote many of his books with Frances Lockridge (1896-1963)

1374. Banks, R. Jeff. "Mr. & Mrs. North." *Armchair Detective* 9 (June 1976): 182-183.

Contends that Lockridge was inspired to turn his series of short stories featuring the husband and wife team of Mr. and Mrs. North into a detective novel by Dashiell Hammett's *The Thin Man* (1933), which also featured a husband and wife team and upon which a series of successful films was based. The author also contends that the most memorable element of Lockridge's novels is their humor.

1375. Filstrup, Chris, and Jane Filstrup. "An Interview with Richard Lockridge." *Armchair Detective* 11 (October 1978): 382-393.

In an interview that covers many aspects of Lockridge's writing, Lockridge emphasizes his love for New York City, the background for many of his novels, and his interest in strong characterizations as opposed to detailed plotting.

1376. Filstrup, Jane. "Murder for Two." *New Republic* 179 (22 July 1978): 35-38.

Maintains that Lockridge "is an American master of the urbane thriller" who uses rapidly paced, skillfully constructed plots, and series detectives who show "in

successive books character transformation and the
resolution of mild inner conflicts" to complement "the
intellectual appeal of the puzzle."

1377. Lockridge, Richard. "Mr. & Mrs. North." *Pages: The World
        of Books, Writers, and Writing*, Volume 1. Edited by
        Matthew J. Bruccoli and C.E. Frazer Clark, Jr.
        Detroit: Gale, 1976, pp. 254-257.

        Lockridge examines the growth of his two protagonists--
        Mr. and Mrs. North--from their origins in the *New Yorker*.
        His account is anecdotal and ranges from a discussion
        of his wife's role in writing the stories to a physical
        description of his two fictional detectives.

1378. Lockridge, Richard. "Mr. and Mrs. North." *The Great
        Detectives* (item 60), pp. 159-163.

        Traces the development of the Norths as sleuths from
        their beginnings in the casual comedies of the *New
        Yorker*. Jerry North is logical, slightly plodding--a
        perfect foil for his wife Pam's intuitive approach.

LUTZ, JOHN (1939-)

1379. Grochowski, Mary Ann. "An Interview with John Lutz."
        Armchair Detective 12 (Summer 1979): 276-279.

        Observes that Lutz's stories have "plausible plots,
        real life situations, taut suspense, and imaginative
        wit." Included is a checklist of short stories by Lutz.

McBAIN, ED. Pseudonym of Evan Hunter (1926-)

1380. McBain, Ed. "The 87th Precinct." *The Great Detectives*
        (item 60), pp. 88-97.

        McBain notes that his intent in writing the 87th
        Precinct novels was to portray a whole squadroom of
        detectives as a "conglomerate hero," though Steve
        Carella has emerged as a dominant figure. Likens the
        men of the 87th Precinct to a family; the squadroom is
        their home. New York City is a character in the novels,
        as is McBain himself.

McCLURE, JAMES (1939-)

1381. Wall, Donald C. "Apartheid in the Novels of James
        McClure." *Armchair Detective* 10 (October 1977): 348-
        351.

        Argues that apartheid provided McClure "with a richly

complicated cultural matrix within which to write his
three first-rate novels."

1382. White, Jean M. "Wahlöö/Sjöwall and James McClure:
       Murder and Politics." *New Republic* 175 (31 July 1976):
       27-29.

       James McClure, author of four South African police
       procedurals, shows that apartheid strips dignity and
       human feelings from both white and black, yet he is
       not didactic.

McCONNELL, JAMES DOUGLAS RUTHERFORD. See FRANCIS DURBRIDGE

McCURTIN, PETER

1383. Banks, R. Jeff. "Carmody: Sagebrush Detective." *Armchair
       Detective* 8 (November 1974): 42-43.

       Singles out two of McCurtin's Western novels, *Tough
       Bullet* (1970) and *Screaming on the Wire* (1972), as
       having strong detective elements. They feature Carmody,
       an outlaw with a code of honor who "displays an impres-
       sive knowledge of primitive forensic ballistics, a
       detective's nose for important evidence, and powers
       of intuitive reasoning."

McDONALD, GREGORY (1937-   )

1384. Randisi, Robert. "An Interview with Gregory McDonald."
       Armchair Detective 12 (Spring 1979): 134-135.

       McDonald states that in his first two mystery novels,
       Fletch (1974) and *Confess* (1976), he was trying "to be
       fun and entertaining." McDonald drew on his own news-
       paper background in creating the character of Fletch.

MACDONALD, JOHN. See ROSS MACDONALD

MacDONALD, JOHN D. (1916-   ). Series character: Travis McGee

1385. Abrahams, Etta C. "Travis McGee: The Thinking Man's
       Robin Hood." *New Dimensions in Popular Culture*. Edited
       by Russel B. Nye. Bowling Green, Ohio: Bowling Green
       University Popular Press, 1972, pp. 236-246.

       Contends that Travis McGee, "Robin Hood-detective,"
       is popular because McGee is given beliefs which tend
       to support or reaffirm the reader's own as well as
       making the reader's realization of his sexual fantasies
       possible through McGee's adventures.

*   Abrahams, Etta C. "Visions and Values in the Action
       Detective Novel: A Study of the Works of Raymond
       Chandler, Kenneth Millar and John D. MacDonald."
       Ph.D. dissertation, Michigan State University, 1973
       (item 657).

       Abrahams's dissertation studies the "attitudes, values
       and codes" of three private eyes, including MacDonald's
       Travis McGee. McGee, she asserts, is an outcast of
       society, sitting on his houseboat in Ft. Lauderdale
       and viewing "the chaos of modern America." But because
       McGee is a voluntary outcast, he is able to critique
       society from a position of moral superiority--indeed,
       from a position that affirms the traditional values of
       society that have been corrupted in contemporary times.
       Thus MacDonald's fiction is social criticism that
       paradoxically reinforces society's values.

1386. Benjamin, David A. "Key Witness." *New Republic* 173
       (26 July 1975): 28-31.

       Maintains that the success of the Travis McGee novels
       is chiefly due to the characterization of McGee
       himself (he has elements of Sam Spade, Philip Marlowe,
       and Lew Archer), the basic simplicity of the plots, and
       MacDonald's ability to, create "believable characters
       with whom we can identify." Concludes that the novels
       are "morality plays."

1387. Campbell, Frank D., Jr. *John D. MacDonald and the
       Colorful World of Travis McGee.* San Bernardino, Calif.:
       Borgo, 1977.

       Campbell's brief monograph is a breezy summary of
       MacDonald's Travis McGee novels--the title refers to
       MacDonald's habit of signalling the presence of Travis
       McGee in his books by including a color in the title--
       through *The Dreadful Lemon Sky.* The book is heavy on
       plot summary, although Campbell does discuss the devel-
       opment of MacDonald's protagonist over the course of
       the series.

1388. Doulis, Thomas. "John D. MacDonald: The Liabilities
       of Professionalism." *Journal of Popular Culture* 10
       (1976): 38-53.

       Doulis's thesis is that MacDonald is a better writer
       than his books might seem to indicate. Scattered
       throughout his large body of work are passages that
       indicate that MacDonald has lost a "craftsman's
       distance ... and found himself inside" the story he
       is telling. Doulis undertakes an extensive analysis
       of the Travis McGee novels to prove his point, and

concludes that MacDonald "provides an interesting example of the formula as aesthetic aid ... that has turned into handicap."

1389. Hills, Rust. "The Awesome Beige Typewriter." *Esquire* 84 (August 1975): 68, 136-137.

Hills describes a personal interview with John D. MacDonald, in which MacDonald discusses his writing habits. MacDonald admits to preferring style over plot, which Hills contends results in an occasional mechanical story.

1390. Hoyt, Charles Alva. "*The Damned*: Good Intentions: The Tough Guy as Hero and Villain." *Tough Guy Writers of the Thirties* (item 46), pp. 224-230.

Though Hoyt has little use for MacDonald's novel—he calls it "the grossest imitation Hemingway"—he argues that it is useful in illustrating the principal characteristics of latter-day tough guy writing. Indeed, the novel is unusually apt in this respect, since it contains not one but two tough guys, one successful and the other unsuccessful. The two protagonists have in common the primary characteristics of the tough guy: they both have a rigid code of honor, but they also believe that the end justifies the means. Thus they operate more often than not outside the law.

1391. Kelly, R. Gordon. "The Precarious World of John D. MacDonald." *Dimensions of Detective Fiction* (item 43), pp. 149-161.

Argues that the popularity of MacDonald's fiction is due to vivid portrayal of the "precariousness and vulnerability underlying life in American society" and illustrates his argument by focusing on one novel, *The Executioners* (1957), that best embodies these qualities.

1392. Kennedy, Veronica M.S. "The Prophet Before the Fact: A Note on John D. MacDonald's *The End of the Night*." *Armchair Detective* 7 (1973): 41.

Contends that *The End of the Night* is a prophetic novel with a "serious presentation of certain elements in modern society," particularly in equating the novel's multiple murders with "general corruption in society."

1393. Petersen, Clarence. "A MacDonald Festival: Happy Number Sixty-three, John D!" *Chicago Tribune Book World* 15 July 1973, pp. 1-2.

An apologia for MacDonald on the occasion of the publication of *The Scarlet Ruse*. Petersen surveys

MacDonald's career, attempting to separate the dross
from the gold; but he is nonetheless an unabashed MacDonald
enthusiast. This article is a significant early attempt
to elevate MacDonald from the ghetto of genre fiction.

1394.   Tolley, Michael J. "Color Him Quixote: MacDonald's
        Strategy in the Early McGee Novels." *Armchair Detec-*
        tive 10 (January 1977): 6-13.

        Contends that MacDonald's McGee novels merit serious
        critical attention because of their complexity and the
        complexity of the central character, Travis McGee, who
        is a subtle and varied image of the popular concept
        of Don Quixote, and thus, "one of the few acceptable
        hero types for this cynical age."

1395.   Wall, Donald C. "Ecology and the Detective Novel: The
        Contribution of John D. MacDonald." *Proceedings of*
        the Fifth National Convention of the Popular Culture
        Association, Chicago, Illinois, April 22-24, 1976.
        Compiled by Michael T. Marsden. Bowling Green, Ohio:
        Bowling Green University Popular Press, 1976, pp.
        265-281.

        Wall argues that MacDonald "has contributed a great
        deal to public knowledge about the nature, extent, and
        causes of our present environmental predicament." He
        quotes extensively from the Travis McGee novels on the
        subjects of air and water pollution and also demonstrates
        that MacDonald is not reluctant to lay the blame for
        this pollution at the feet of private industry.

MACDONALD, JOHN ROSS. See ROSS MACDONALD

MACDONALD, ROSS. Pseudonym of Kenneth Millar (1915-   ). Other
    pseudonyms: John Macdonald, John Ross Macdonald. Series
    character: Lew Archer

*   Abrahams, Etta C. "Visions and Values in the Action
        Detective Novel: A Study of the Works of Raymond
        Chandler, Kenneth Millar, and John D. Macdonald."
        Ph.D. dissertation, Michigan State University, 1973
        (item 657).

        Abrahams's dissertation studies the "attitudes, values
        and codes" of three private eyes, including Ross Mac-
        donald's (Kenneth Millar's) Lew Archer. Abrahams argues
        that detective fiction is social criticism that para-

doxically reinforces society's values. Archer, for instance, is an ex-policeman who left the force because it did not live up to his ideals. He continues to uphold the principle of justice while attacking the institutions that have corrupted those ideals.

*   Abrahams, Etta C. "Where Have All the Values Gone? The Private Eye's Vision of America in the Novels of Raymond Chandler and Ross Macdonald" (item 658).

Argues that Lew Archer is concerned with "nature and man's indifference to it," as well as such other social issues as "misguided and misunderstood" youth.

1396.   Barnes, Daniel R. "'I'm the Eye': Archer as Narrator in the Novels of Ross Macdonald." *Mystery and Detection Annual 1972* (item 16), pp. 178-190.

Argues that Macdonald's achievement as a writer of American detective fiction can be best realized through his detective narrator, Lew Archer, who reveals his character and adds to the reader's understanding of him through his narration. A "peculiar" feature of Archer's narration is his obsession with eyes; Macdonald uses bizarre eye imagery to emphasize Archer's "conscious or unconscious belief that he is the object of scrutiny, the observed rather than the observer."

1397.   Barzun, Jacques, and Wendell Hertig Taylor. Preface to *The Drowning Pool*, by Ross Macdonald. New York: Garland Publishing, 1976. Also printed in *A Book of Prefaces* (item 22), pp. 77-78.

Contends that in *The Drowning Pool* Macdonald is the first to use explicit sexual elements in detective fiction. In this book and its successors Macdonald creates a private detective (Lew Archer) "whose concern with society no less than his integrity and investigative skill make him a figure to believe in and admire."

1398.   Bruccoli, Matthew J. *Kenneth Millar/Ross Macdonald: A Checklist*. Detroit: Gale Research, 1971.

Primary bibliography.

1399.   Carroll, Jon. "Ross Macdonald in Raw California: Geography as Motive." *Esquire* 77 (June 1972): 148-149, 188.

Contends that Macdonald's works are "intricate, almost
nineteenth-century novels of character and situation."
Quotes Macdonald as contending that the problem in
Southern California is maintaining values in a non-
traditional society.

1400.   Carter, Steven R. "Ross Macdonald: The Complexity of
        the Modern Quest for Justice." *Mystery and Detection
        Annual 1973* (item 17), pp. 59-82.

        In this long, closely reasoned study covering many
        of Macdonald's Archer novels, Carter argues that the
        quest for justice is complex in Macdonald's work be-
        cause his characters are complex, rounded human beings.
        Thus, Macdonald's well-known interest in psychology is
        reflected in his expert characterizations.

*   Crider, Allen B. "The Private-Eye Hero: A Study of the
        Novels of Dashiell Hammett, Raymond Chandler, and
        Ross Macdonald." Ph.D. dissertation, University of
        Texas at Austin, 1972 (item 666).

        In his dissertation, Crider compares and contrasts
        the work of Macdonald and his predecessors. Macdonald
        began his career as an imitator of Raymond Chandler,
        Crider argues, but soon developed distinctive interests
        of his own. It is Macdonald's "overt interest" in
        psychology that differentiates him from Hammett and
        Chandler.

1401.   Dorinson, Zahana X. "Ross Macdonald: The Personal
        Paradigm and Popular Fiction." *Armchair Detective* 10
        (January 1977): 43-45, 87.

        Argues that Macdonald is an excellent mystery novelist
        but not a "serious" novelist because his novels are
        variations on detective story conventions. His novels
        exhibit careful craftsmanship and an individual, dis-
        tinguished style, content, and form that Dorinson terms
        "the personal paradigm." But Macdonald has not allowed
        himself the freedom which would permit originality, an
        "essential aspect of serious fiction."

1402.   Finch, G.A. "The Case of *The Underground Man*: Evolution
        or Devolution?" *Armchair Detective* 6 (August 1973):
        210-212.

        Contends that *The Underground Man* is weak as a detec-
        tive story and as a novel despite the view among "seri-
        ous" critics that Macdonald is now a novelist rather
        than a mere writer of detective stories.

*   Finch, G.A. "From Spade to Marlowe to Archer: An Essay"
        (item 673).

        After outlining the Hammett hero and style, Finch
        contends that Archer lacks the intensity of a Hammett
        hero and that Macdonald's style owes much more to
        Chandler than to Hammett.

1403.   Geherin, David J. "Archer in Hollywood: The 'Barbarous
        Coast' of Ross Macdonald." *Armchair Detective* 9
        (November 1975): 55-58.

        Macdonald has been using the materials of Hollywood
        in his novels for over twenty years, and "all of his
        fiction is influenced by, and expresses variations on
        that aspect of the American dream known as the Hollywood
        myth."

1404.   Grella, George. "Evil Plots." *New Republic* 173 (26
        July 1975): 24-26.

        Some of the outstanding characteristics of Macdonald's
        Lew Archer novels are the details of Southern California
        society, "highly wrought metaphors, the saintly private
        eye hero, the intensely complicated plots." The ex-
        cellence of the plots (which take on mythic overtones)
        is the characteristic that distinguishes the novels
        "from all other detective fiction."

1405.   Grogg, Samuel L., Jr. "Between the Mountains and the
        Sea: Ross Macdonald's Lew Archer Novels." Ph.D. dis-
        sertation, Bowling Green State University, 1974.

        Grogg, in this doctoral dissertation, traces the de-
        velopment of the detective genre, defines Lew Archer
        in the context of his predecessors, and outlines the
        major themes of Macdonald's Archer novels. Grogg argues
        that the detective genre is "a singularly appropriate
        form in which to represent the 'sense' of mental and
        physical life" in present day America, which is one
        of the primary goals in Macdonald's fiction.

1406.   Grogg, Samuel L., Jr. "Interview with Ross Macdonald."
        Journal of Popular Culture 7 (Summer 1973): 213-222.
        Reprinted *Dimensions of Detective Fiction* (item 43),
        pp. 182-192.

        In this interview, Ross Macdonald asserts that "I'm
        really trying to write about contemporary life. I've
        found the detective form useful for this." In his view,

the Archer novels are a "bridge" between the hard-boiled
detective story and the more formal narratives in the
mystery/detection genre.

1407.   Hazard, Johnnine. "The Detective Fiction of Kenneth
        Millar/Ross Macdonald." Ph.D. dissertation, Univer-
        sity of Chicago, 1974.

        Abstract unavailable.

1408.   Holtan, Judith, and Orley I. Holtan. "The Time-Space
        Dimension in the Lew Archer Detective Novels." *North
        Dakota Quarterly* 40 (1972): 30-41.

        The Holtans examine the adventures of Macdonald's
        famous private eye, and observe that he does a great
        deal of traveling, both geographically and temporally.
        This, they state, accurately reflects the California
        milieu in which Archer operates.

1409.   Kiell, N. "Very Private Eye of Ross Macdonald." *Litera-
        ture and Psychology* 27 (1977): 21-34; 27 (1977):
        67-73.

        Kiell's lengthy survey of the Lew Archer novels argues
        that the emphasis on eyes, private and otherwise, in
        these works, reflects Macdonald's "unresolved oedipal
        conflict."

*   Leonard, John. "I Care Who Killed Roger Ackroyd" (item
        325).

        In the context of a larger defense of mystery and
        detection, Leonard relates his efforts to have Macdonald's
        novels *The Chill*, *The Goodbye Look*, and *The Underground
        Man* reviewed by "respectable" critics in the *New York
        Times Book Review*.

1410.   Leonard, John. "Ross Macdonald, His Lew Archer and
        Other Secret Selves." *New York Times Book Review* 1
        June 1969, pp. 2, 19.

        Contends that with *The Doomstars* "a writer of detec-
        tive stories turned into a major American novelist,"
        who explores such themes as guilt, justice, mercy, and
        exile.

1411.   Macdonald, Ross. "Lew Archer." *The Great Detectives*
        (item 60), pp. 19-24.

The title is a bit misleading; Archer is never mentioned in this essay, although important aspects about
his creator's attitude toward him may be inferred from
the article. Instead, Macdonald discusses his conception of "the private investigator," in both fiction
and real life. Self-knowledge, he argues, and a cor-
responding knowledge of the world, is what the serious
private eye strives for and uses in his work.

* Macdonald, Ross. "The Writer as Detective Hero" (item
338).

Commenting that he created his detective, Lew Archer,
"from the inside out," Macdonald emphasizes the close,
emotional relationship between a writer and his detective. He concludes, however, that in his later novels
Archer has become less of a "fantasy projection" of
himself.

* Macdonald, Ross. "Writing *The Galton Case*" (item 339).

Comments on the "connections between a writer and his
fiction" with specific reference to his mystery novel
The Galton Case, in which his "ego is dispersed through
several characters" and he is involved with them to the
extent of his "imaginative strength."

1412. Mulqueen, James E. "Three Heroes in American Fiction."
Illinois Quarterly 36 (1974): 44–50.

Mulqueen compares Macdonald's Lew Archer to Cooper's
Natty Bumppo and Owen Wister's Virginian. They have,
he argues, a great deal in common: they are all of
humble origin, they are all courageous, and they all
have their own individualistic moral code. Indeed, he
avers, it is their moral integrity that is their most
important common denominator.

* Parker, Robert Brown. "The Violent Hero, Wilderness
Heritage and Urban Reality: A Study of the Private
Eye in the Novels of Dashiell Hammett, Raymond
Chandler and Ross Macdonald." Ph.D. dissertation,
Boston University, 1971 (item 689).

This doctoral dissertation advances the argument that
the modern hard-boiled private eye is "Adam in the city,"
who must confront the twentieth-century city with a
system of values "rooted in the nineteenth century
frontier." Thus Macdonald's Lew Archer and the other

detectives Parker discusses use their virtues--strength,
courage, etc.--to support their own private system of
values, which are often at odds with the values of the
societies in which they live.

1413.   Pry, Elmer R., Jr. "Lew Archer's 'Moral Landscape.'"
        Armchair Detective 8 (February 1975): 104-107.
        Reprinted *Dimensions of Detective Fiction* (item 43),
        pp. 174-181.

        Contends that Macdonald's detective, Lew Archer, is
        "both observer/narrator and a representative citizen"
        of his California environment whose final summing up
        of the "moral landscape" is that California was a
        potential Garden of Eden where values have become per-
        verted and confused.

1414.   Pry, Elmer R., Jr. "Ross Macdonald's Violent California:
        Imagery Patterns in *The Underground Man.*" *Western
        American Literature* 9 (1974): 197-203.

        Pry argues that Macdonald's work merits serious
        literary study. He examines *The Underground Man's*
        imagery patterns and discovers two sustained symbols:
        fire and the search for a father. These patterns are
        consistent with both the plot of the novel and with
        Macdonald's vision as a writer, and this consistency
        "confirms the judgment that Ross Macdonald is a 'seri-
        ous' literary man."

*   Ruehlmann, William. *Saint with a Gun* (item 65), pp.
        105-114.

        Though Ruehlmann's primary thesis is that "private
        eye novels are vigilante literature," he notes that
        Macdonald's Lew Archer is an exception to this rule. He
        observes that Archer's sense of personal guilt--over
        his broken marriage, his failure to complete college,
        and other, even more subtle reasons--"makes him more
        prone to pity than punishment."

1415.   Sipper, Ralph B. "An Interview with Ross Macdonald."
        The Mystery and Detection Annual 1973 (item 17),
        pp. 53-58.

        In this interview, Macdonald discusses the philosophy
        behind his writing. He argues that detective novels
        should depict society as it changes, but admits that
        "the individual human being is what interests me most."

1416. Sokolov, Raymond A. "The Art of Murder." *Newsweek* 77
       (22 March 1971): 101+.

       This well-known *Newsweek* cover story, which for many
       marked the "serious" acceptance of Macdonald, identifies
       the trademarks of his work as "the broken family and
       the search for the lost father." Quotes Macdonald say-
       ing that his hero, Lew Archer, is "a transitional figure
       between a world that is breaking up and one coming into
       being in which relationships and people will be impor-
       tant."

1417. Speir, Jerry. *Ross Macdonald.* New York: Ungar, 1978.
       182pp.

       Speir observes that the theme of Macdonald's novels
       is "the struggle of the self for identity," and argues
       that the novels mirror not only what he terms the
       "cultural mythology" of the detective novel, but also
       Macdonald's personal effort to understand the world and
       his own place in it. Macdonald is concerned with show-
       ing how and why the world is as it is.

*   Symons, Julian. *Mortal Consequences* (item 74), pp.
       182-184.

       Symons advances the unusual argument that Macdonald's
       writing has suffered because of his use of Lew Archer
       as the recurring central figure of most of his novels.
       The "impression that Macdonald has not put enough of
       himself into his books, that he has been too easily
       content with the things he can do well, remains."

1418. Tutunjian, Jerry. "A Conversation with Ross Macdonald."
       Tamarack Review 42 (1974): 66-85.

       In this wide-ranging interview, Macdonald discusses
       his Canadian background and influences, his opinion
       of his own work and that of his colleagues, and the
       California dream versus the California nightmare.

1419. Wolfe, Peter. *Dreamers Who Live Their Dreams: The World
       of Ross Macdonald's Novels.* Bowling Green, Ohio:
       Bowling Green University Popular Press, 1976. 346pp.

       In an in-depth analysis of the Lew Archer novels,
       Wolfe argues that Macdonald views the city as a maze.
       Lew Archer's task is to solve its riddle.

McGERR, PATRICIA (1917-)

1420.   Barzun, Jacques, and Wendell Hertig Taylor. Preface to
        Pick Your Victim, by Pat McGerr. New York: Garland
        Publishing, 1976. Also printed in *A Book of Prefaces*
        (item 22), pp. 79-80.

        Points out that this book is unique because it re-
        verses both the standard problem and its form: the
        criminal, not the victim, is known to a distant group
        of inquirers, and the crime itself is not mysterious
        at the time and place it occurs.

McGUIRE, PAUL (1903-)

1421.   Barzun, Jacques, and Wendell Hertig Taylor. Preface to
        A Funeral in Eden, by Paul McGuire. New York: Garland
        Publishing, 1976. Also printed in *A Book of Prefaces*
        (item 22), pp. 81-82.

        Points out that the novel achieves a perfect balance
        between its exotic setting (a Pacific island) and its
        plot.

MACHEN, ARTHUR (1863-1947)

1422.   Cassazza, Alice Catherine. "Arthur Machen's Treatment
        of the Occult and a Consideration of Its Reception
        in England and America." Ph.D. dissertation, Univer-
        sity of Southern California, 1971.

        In this dissertation, Cassazza argues that Machen's
        fiction is best understood in light of his avowed
        interest in the occult. Cassazza uses *The Hill of
        Dreams* and "The Bowmen" as primary examples in making
        her point.

1423.   Gekle, William Francis. *Arthur Machen: Weaver of Fantasy.*
        Millbrook, N.Y.: Round Table Press, 1949.

        Gekle argues that Machen had one theme: "The sense
        of the eternal mysteries ... hidden beneath the crust
        of common and commonplace things." He notes the in-
        fluence of Poe on Machen's work, and asserts that
        Machen's early work was his best.

*   Letson, Russell Francis, Jr. "The Approaches to Mys-
       tery: The Fantasies of Arthur Machen and Algernon
       Blackwood." Ph.D. dissertation, Southern Illinois
       University, 1975 (item 594).

       In this dissertation, Letson investigates the fantasy
       genre via an analysis of Machen and Algernon Blackwood.
       Machen, he asserts, is a more pessimistic writer than
       Blackwood. He argues that Machen's two central themes
       are Faustian temptation and the lost felicity of Eden;
       and that in Machen's work, man's search for this lost
       Eden always ends in horror.

1424. Matteson, Robert S. "Arthur Machen: A Vision of an
       Enchanted Land." *Personalist* 46 (1965): 253-268.

       Matteson argues that, although Machen is a lesser
       writer, he is nonetheless deserving of study. Machen's
       first books, he asserts, were failures. *The Hill of
       Dreams* and *The White People* are the best examples of
       Machen's theme of the mystic vision leading only to
       horror.

1425. Nash, Berta. "Arthur Machen Among the Arthurians."
       Minor British Novelists. Edited by Charles A. Hoyt.
       Carbondale: Southern Illinois University Press,
       1967, pp. 109-120.

       In a survey of Machen's writings, Nash argues that
       Machen's theme is the dualistic nature of man. Most
       of his stories emphasize the dark side of man's nature,
       but in *The Great Return*, a retelling of the Arthurian
       Grail legend, he emphasizes the positive, joyful side.

1426. Petersen, Karl M. "Arthur Machen and the Celtic
       Renaissance in Wales." Ph.D. dissertation, Louisiana
       State University, 1973.

       In this dissertation, Petersen asserts that Machen
       is best understood as a part of the Celtic Renaissance
       of the 1890s. He argues that Machen uses traditional
       Welsh themes of the supernatural in his work.

1427. Reynolds, Aidan, and William Charlton. *Arthur Machen:
       A Short Account of His Life and Work*. London: John
       Baker, 1963, pp. 47-52.

       Points out that in *The Three Impostors* Machen was
       trying to emulate Robert Louis Stevenson's *New Arabian
       Nights* and concludes that Machen's book is imaginative
       and sophisticated if not "particularly profound."

1428. Sweetser, Wesley D. *Arthur Machen.* New York: Twayne,
       1964. 175pp.

       In a comprehensive survey of Machen's work, Sweetser
       argues that Machen's relative obscurity is due to his
       proficiency at several genres, including the novel and
       short story, and several styles. He asserts that
       Machen can best be understood as a mirror of the times
       in which he lived.

1429. Sweetser, Wesley D. "The Works of Arthur Machen: An
       Analysis and Bibliography." Ph.D. dissertation,
       University of Colorado, 1958.

       In this dissertation, Sweetser argues that Machen's
       "single transcendental theme" is that "the reality
       which lies hidden beneath the surface can never be
       found and never be revealed."

MacINNES, HELEN (1907-)

1430. Becker, Mary H. "Politics in the Spy Novels of Helen
       MacInnes and Dorothy Gilman." *Proceedings of the
       Fifth National Convention of the Popular Culture
       Association, Chicago, Illinois, April 22-24, 1976.*
       Compiled by Michael T. Marsden. Bowling Green, Ohio:
       Bowling Green University Popular Press, 1976, pp.
       748-754.

       Becker argues that in MacInnes's novels, power
       politics is always presented as evil, or at best
       resulting in evil. MacInnes's political intrigues are
       always portrayed as tawdry, unglamorous affairs. Thus
       it is no coincidence that MacInnes's totalitarian power
       brokers are defeated by individuals--usually amateur
       heroes such as scholars, writers, or artists.

MACKINTOSH, ELIZABETH. See JOSEPHINE TEY

MacNEIL, NEIL. See W.T. BALLARD

McNEILE, H.C. (1888-1937). Pseudonym: Sapper

1431. McNeile, H.C. "Meet Bull-Dog Drummond." *Meet the Detec-
       tive* (item 45), pp. 13-19.

McNeile states that he tried to make Drummond "a
typical Englishman, who lives clean, loves sports, and
fights hard."

* Usborne, Richard. "Sapper." *Clubland Heroes* (item 629),
pp. 143-202.

Maintains that Sapper is a gifted storyteller although
his plots and characters varied little in his later
books. For most of his heroes "sport is a perfectly
sufficient end in itself." Examines such Sapper heroes
as Bulldog Drummond, Ronald Standish, and Jim Maitland,
and one adversary, Carl Peterson.

* Watson, Colin. "The Bulldog Breed." *Snobbery with
Violence* (item 78), pp. 63-71.

Contends that Bulldog Drummond was a "fictional extension" of his creator, "Sapper" McNeile, and that
Drummond's great popularity in England was due to such
qualities as patriotism and loyalty to friends.

MAJOR, CLARENCE (1936-)

1432. McCaffery, Larry, and Sinda Gregory. "Major's *Reflex
and Bone Structure* and the Anti-Detective Tradition."
Black American Literature Forum 13 (Summer 1979):
39-45.

Contends that the traditional detective novel, based
on a nineteenth-century reverence for reason, is being
rejected and even parodied by contemporary writers. In
Clarence Major's *Reflex and Bone Structure*, although
there are the "elements of a fairly conventional murder
mystery," there is also a narrator who states that he
is constructing the story, and there is no conventional
explanation at the end.

MAKIN, WILLIAM J. (1894-)

1433. Lofts, W.O.G. "It's All in the Face." *Armchair Detective*
7 (February 1974): 109-110.

After commenting briefly on the theory that criminals
can be detected by their features (a theory propounded
by Lombroso in 1864), singles out William J. Makin's
detective, Jonathan Jow, as one "who solved crimes by

the expressions and features on a face." Gives examples
of this talent from Makin's stories.

MALLOCH, PETER. See W. MURDOCH DUNCAN

MARQUAND, JOHN P. (1893-1960)

1434. Holman, C. Hugh. *John P. Marquand.* Minneapolis:
       University of Minnesota Press, 1965, pp. 18-19.

       States that the Mr. Moto books are "spy thrillers
       of a very high order, but they lack the tight construc-
       tion of the detective story." Holman contends, however,
       that their chief importance may be that they financed
       Marquand's rebellion against the commercial writing
       he had been doing before.

1435. Rausch, George J. "John P. Marquand and Espionage
       Fiction." *Armchair Detective* 5 (July 1972): 194-198.

       Marquand wrote six espionage novels, each containing
       I.A. Moto, a Japanese agent; but the protagonists are
       usually "harmless Americans caught up in international
       intrigue." Marquand perceived the major themes of the
       genre, Rausch argues, and handled them well "when he
       chose to do so."

MARRIC, J.J. See JOHN CREASEY

MARSH, NGAIO (1899-)

1436. Bargainnier, Earl F. "Ngaio Marsh's 'Theatrical'
       Murders." *Armchair Detective* 10 (April 1977): 175-181.

       Points out that Marsh's "lifelong involvement with
       the theatre" forms the backdrop for eight of her detec-
       tive novels and that "the fusion of plot, setting and
       atmosphere" in each reflects her knowledge of the
       theater. Gives examples from each of the novels to
       illustrate his points.

1437. Barzun, Jacques, and Wendell Hertig Taylor. Preface to
       A Wreath for Rivera, by Ngaio Marsh. New York: Garland
       Publishing, 1976. Also printed in *A Book of Prefaces*
       (item 22), pp. 83-84.

Contends that Marsh reaches a "high point of inventiveness" with the creation of an eccentric, uninhibited lord in this novel.

1438. Marsh, Ngaio. "Roderick Alleyn." *The Great Detectives* (item 60), pp. 3-8.

Marsh created her protagonist fairly easily. "From the beginning I discovered that I knew quite a lot about him." The character seemed so natural that he would have entered his author's life in some fashion even if she hadn't taken up writing detective fiction.

* Panek, LeRoy. "Ngaio Marsh." *Watteau's Shepherds* (item 57), pp. 185-197.

Observes that Marsh does not allow principal evidence to play an important part in detection in her novels but instead focuses on a "series of interviews as the essence of routine."

* Routley, Erik. *The Puritan Pleasures of the Detective Story* (item 64), pp. 146-149.

Points out that Marsh has "a gift equal to that of Dorothy Sayers for communicating character" but that she is different from both Dorothy Sayers and Margery Allingham in that "she is never oppressed by any sense of the evil which righteousness is at war with."

1439. White, Jean M. "Murder Most Tidy: Ngaio Marsh." *New Republic* 177 (30 July 1977): 36-38.

Contends that Marsh is one of the best practitioners of "the stylishly-told traditional British mystery, with discreet murder among civilized enemies." Her work is characterized by clever plots, "impeccable" literary style, and "bizarre" murder weapons.

MARSHALL, LOVAT. See W. MURDOCH DUNCAN

MASON, A.E. (1865-1948)

1440. Mason, A.E. "Meet Hanaud." *Meet the Detective* (item 45), pp. 20-35.

States that he deliberately made his protagonist the opposite of the "superhuman passionless amateur" of the Sherlock Holmes mode.

MAUGHAM, W. SOMERSET (1874-1965)

1441.   "Cloak Without Dagger." *Times Literary Supplement* 8
        February 1963, p. 92.

        Points out that the Ashenden novels are loosely
        based on personal experiences of Maugham; thus the
        stories have a high level of style and characterization.

1442.   Cody, Richard. "Secret Service Fiction." *Graduate
        Student of English* 3 (Summer 1960): 6-12.

        States that *Ashenden* was one of the most influential
        thrillers of the 1920s since it anticipated the realistic
        and cynical style of Eric Ambler and Graham Greene.

1443.   Dottin, Paul. "Livres." *Revue Anglo-Americaine* 6
        (February 1929): 285.

        Argues that the hero in *Ashenden* represents a degraded
        autobiographical view of Maugham; also states that
        Ashenden is more intense, the realism more cruel, and
        the characterization more shrewd than in earlier novels.

1444.   Heywood, C. "Somerset Maugham's Debt to *Madame Bovary*
        and Miss Braddon's *The Doctor's Wife*." *Etudes Anglais*
        19 (1966): 64-69.

        States that Maugham had read *The Doctor's Wife* at
        the beginning of his writing career and was influenced
        by Braddon's use of "truth" in the treatment of psycho-
        logical motivations.

1445.   "New Novels." *Times Literary Supplement* 12 April 1928,
        p. 270.

        Maintains that *Ashenden* is not really a novel but a
        series of disconnected episodes strung together "with
        no very great enthusiasm."

1446.   Way, Oliver. "Modern Life in Books." *Graphic* 120 (7
        April 1928): 22.

        States that *Ashenden*, "the very triumph of realism,"
        strips away the romance from the Secret Service.

1447.   Whitehead, John. "'Whodunit' and Somerset Maugham."
        Notes and Queries 21 (October 1974): 370.

        Observes that the term "who done it" (or "whodunit")
        originated from Maugham's short story "The Creative
        Impulse," published in 1926.

MERCER, CECIL WILLIAM. See DORNFORD YATES

MILLAR, KENNETH. See ROSS MACDONALD

MILLER, BILL. See WADE MILLER

MILLER, WADE. Joint pseudonym of Robert Wade (1920-   ) and
Bill Miller (1920-1961)

1448. Lachman, Marvin. "The Man Who was Thursday." *Armchair
       Detective* 8 (May 1975): 179, 184.

       Contends that Wade and Miller "wrote six very
       readable, remarkably consistent novels--and then quit
       while they were ahead." Their chief creation was the
       detective Max Thursday.

MILNE, A.A. (1882-1956)

1449. Barzun, Jacques, and Wendell Hertig Taylor. Preface to
       The Red House Mystery, by A.A. Milne. New York:
       Garland Publishing, 1976. Also printed in *A Book of
       Prefaces* (item 22), pp. 85-86.

       States that *The Red House Mystery* was intended to be
       a fanciful, enjoyable novel closer in style to Milne's
       children's books than to the established "hard-boiled"
       school.

*   Chandler, Raymond. "The Simple Art of Murder" (item
       156).

       Chandler criticizes the classical mystery story,
       using Milne's *The Red House Mystery* as an example. He
       calls it "an agreeable book, light, amusing" but states
       that its premise (that a man could impersonate someone
       else without being discovered even after he is murdered)
       makes it impossible to accept the book as "a problem
       of logic and deduction," which is the only way it can
       be accepted. Explains seven fallacies in the book.

*   Panek, LeRoy. "A.A. Milne." *Watteau's Shepherds* (item
       57), pp. 64-71.

Although Milne wrote only one mystery novel, *The Red House Mystery* (1922), it set a pattern that succeeding detective fiction writers of the Golden Age would follow. It was Milne's novel that Raymond Chandler (item 156) singled out as representative of what was wrong with detective fiction between the wars: "comfortable, pretty, mild amusements which do not inspire sublime emotions or probe the basic mysteries of life."

1450. Swann, Thomas Burnett. *A.A. Milne*. New York: Twayne, 1971, pp. 98-99, 104-108, 111-112.

Observes that the success of Milne's *The Red House Mystery* lies in the meticulously individualized characters who are placed against realistic backgrounds.

MITCHELL, GLADYS (1901-). Pseudonym: Malcolm Torrie

1451. Pike, B.A. "In Praise of Gladys Mitchell." *Armchair Detective* 9 (October 1976): 250-260.

This item consists of an interview and separate biographical and critical sections by Pike. In the interview about her writing methods and her detective, Dame Beatrice, Mitchell states that she finds each novel "difficult to write" because she seldom follows a plan. The biographical and critical sections place her work in context and sum up her work as varied, colorful and inventive. "Repeatedly, the sheer verve of the narrative, the teasing intricacy and driving energy of the action carry the reader over obscurities of motive, and improbabilities of character and incident."

MONTGOMERY, ROBERT BRUCE. See EDMUND CRISPIN

MORRAH, DERMOT (1896-1974)

1452. Barzun, Jacques, and Wendell Hertig Taylor. Preface to *The Mummy Case*, by Dermot Morrah. New York: Garland Publishing, 1976. Also printed in *A Book of Prefaces* (item 22), pp. 87-88.

Observes that Morrah is both entertaining and witty about academic conventions, students, and dons at a college of Oxford University.

MORRISON, ARTHUR (1863-1945)

1453. Bell, Jocelyn. "A Study of Arthur Morrison." *The English Association: Essays and Studies.* Edited by Arundell Esdaile. London: John Murray, 1952, pp. 77-89.

Contends that although Morrison's writing style compares favorably with that of Conan Doyle's, his plots and characterizations are less imaginative.

1454. Pritchett, V.S. *The Living Novel and Later Appreciations.* New York: Vintage Books, 1967, pp. 206-212.

States that Morrison had the ability of "writing on different planes and varying perspectives" and that this ability gave his novels a human drama of their own. Analyzes *The Hole in the Wall*, a mystery set in the East End of London.

MORTON, ANTHONY. See JOHN CREASEY

MURPHY, WARREN B. (1933-)

1455. Lochte, Dick. "Created, the Destroyer: An Interview with Warren Murphy." *Armchair Detective* 11 (July 1978): 284-286.

In this interview Murphy describes how he writes the Destroyer series in partnership with Richard Sapir.

OLDEN, MARC

1456. Randisi, Robert J. "An Interview with Marc Olden." *Armchair Detective* 12 (Fall 1979): 324-327.

Olden states that he was inspired to write the first book in his *Black Samurai* series of martial arts novels by an item in a "gossip column" and that his favorite mystery writers are Poe and Dashiell Hammett.

OLIVER, GEORGE. See OLIVER ONIONS

ONIONS, OLIVER. Pseudonym of George Oliver (1873-1961)

1457. Barzun, Jacques, and Wendell Hertig Taylor. Preface to *In Accordance with the Evidence*, by Oliver Onions.

New York: Garland Publishing, 1976. Also printed in
A Book of Prefaces (item 22), pp. 89-90.

Points out that Onions's object--"to tell how and why
a murderer works himself up to his deliberate deed"--
is done without boring or irritating the reader.

1458.   Swinnerton, Frank. "The Younger Novelists." *The Georgian
        Literary Scene*. London: J.M. Dent, 1938, pp. 218-220.

Singles out *In Accordance with the Evidence* as a
"brief masterpiece of grimness" that is unsurpassed in
its own genre. States that Onions's excellent use of
the first-person narrative is a key element of the
atmosphere of the book.

OPPENHEIM, E. PHILLIPS (1866-1946). Pseudonym: Anthony Partridge

1459.   Adcock, A. St. John. *Gods of Modern Grub Street*.
        London: Sampson Law, 1923, pp. 263-270.

States that Oppenheim constructs baffling plots and
builds suspense from the first page, but his greatest
achievement is that he takes the readers outside their
own experiences, appealing to their imagination.

1460.   Gadney, Reg. "Switch Off the Wireless--It's an Oppen-
        heim." *London Magazine* 10 (June 1970): 19-27.

Points out that among modern readers Oppenheim's
novels are largely unknown; attributes this to the
underlying snobbery of the stories with values meant
for, and understood by, a pre-war society.

1461.   "100th." *Time* 28 (20 July 1936): 70.

States that Oppenheim viewed his novels only as a
form of entertainment; he preferred a romantic plot
to reality.

1462.   Overton, Grant. "A Great Impersonation by E. Phillips
        Oppenheim." *Cargoes for Crusoes*. New York: D. Apple-
        ton, 1924, pp. 126-142.

Contends that Oppenheim's work is distinguished by
his confidential, informal manner with the reader, his
leisureliness, and his spontaneity. Singles out *The
Way of These Women* as a good example of his technique.

* Watson, Colin. *Snobbery with Violence* (item 78), pp. 59-61.

Points out that crime was not the primary ingredient of Oppenheim's novels; his preoccupation was with the setting of the story, the luxury and elegance of high life.

ORCZY, BARONESS EMMUSKA (1865-1947)

* Murch, A.E. *The Development of the Detective Novel* (item 51), pp. 209-212.

Points out that the Baroness Orczy was determined to create a detective-hero who was in no way reminiscent of any other detective and thus created a nameless old man whose sympathies were always with the criminal.

OTTOLENGUI, RODRIGUES (1861?-1937)

1463. Taylor, Wendell Hertig. "Rodrigues Ottolengui (1861-1937): A Forgotten American Mystery Writer." *Armchair Detective* 9 (June 1976): 181.

Observes that Ottolengui's books deserve to be revived because of the pleasant writing, good psychology, and good characterization that are their hallmarks. Brief comments on several illustrate his contention.

1464. Wright, Richardson. "Forgotten Dentures: Molars and Murders in Old New York." *Saturday Review* 27 (1 January 1944): 8, 21.

Describes the literary career of Dr. Rodrigues Ottolengui, a New York dentist, who published his first mystery story, "An Artist in Crime," in 1921. In that story he introduced the two amateur detectives, Robert Leroy Mitchell and John Barnes, who would appear in several more of his stories.

PACKARD, FRANK L. (1877-1942)

1465. Guiterman, Arthur. "Frank L. Packard and His Miracle Men." *Bookman* 51 (June 1920): 466-470.

Maintains that Packard viewed his detective stories not as profound literature but as modern fairy tales intended solely to divert and thrill the reader.

*   Overton, Grant. "Frank L. Packard Unlocks a Book."
       Cargoes for Crusoes (item 1462), pp. 330-347.

       Contends that Packard does not write "with literary
       distinction" but that he is a "master of plot and of
       incident" in whose works can be found the interweaving
       of the "themes of sacrifice and regeneration."

PAGE, MARCO. Pseudonym of Harry Kurnitz (1907-1968)

1466. Barzun, Jacques, and Wendell Hertig Taylor. Preface to
       The Shadowy Third, by Marco Page. New York: Garland
       Publishing, 1976. Also printed in *A Book of Prefaces*
       (item 22), pp. 91-92.

       Points out the differences between humor and cynicism
       in English and American detective novels, observing
       that *The Shadowy Third* is a lighthearted, intelligent
       farce.

PARTRIDGE, ANTHONY. See E. PHILLIPS OPPENHEIM

PENTECOST, HUGH. Pseudonym of Judson Philips (1903-)

1467. Pentecost, Hugh. "Pierre Chambrun." *The Great Detectives*
       (item 60), pp. 47-55.

       Pentecost states that his character Pierre Chambrun,
       a hotel manager who also solves crimes, was conceived
       as the protagonist of only one book. He was, however,
       so popular that Pentecost wrote a series of books in
       which he is featured. In keeping with the practice
       established in the first book, Chambrun is always
       presented through the eyes of other characters in the
       novel.

PERDUE, VIRGINIA (1899-1945)

1468. Barzun, Jacques, and Wendell Hertig Taylor. Preface to
       Alarum and Excursion, by Virginia Perdue. New York:
       Garland Publishing, 1976. Also printed in *A Book of
       Prefaces* (item 22), pp. 93-94.

       Contends that one of the strengths of Perdue's plot
       is the new motive supplied after the mystery is sup-
       posedly solved that helps keep "things going beyond
       the end of the story."

PHILIPS, JUDSON. See HUGH PENTECOST

PHILLPOTTS, EDEN (1862-1960). Pseudonym: Harrington Hext

1469. Barzun, Jacques, and Wendell Hertig Taylor. Preface to
       Found Drowned, by Eden Phillpotts. New York: Garland
       Publishing, 1976. Also printed in *A Book of Prefaces*
       (item 22), pp. 95-96.

       States that the success of Phillpotts's mysteries
       is due to his skillful use of atmosphere supported by
       realistic characters and speech.

1470. Follett, Helen Thomas, and Wilson Follett. *Some Modern
       Novelists*. New York: Holt, 1919, pp. 179-205.

       Argues that Phillpotts was not a successful writer
       because he used so much creativity and imagination
       that he failed to have a concrete subject to write
       about. States that he confused the material with the
       subject.

1471. Howells, W.D. "The Fiction of Eden Phillpotts." *North
       American Review* 190 (1909): 15-22.

       Observes that although Phillpotts believed that a
       story could be constructed around an adventure, his
       writing often showed the strain and effort of trying
       to relate action to an improbable scene.

1472. Moult, Thomas. "Eden Phillpotts: A Critical Apprecia-
       tion." *Bookman* (London) 74 (September 1928): 290-292.

       Points out that compassion and humanity characterize
       Phillpotts's novels. Also observes that in *The Secret
       Woman* even the murderess "speaks as a saint ... and
       in her inspired utterance lies truth and wisdom."

1473. Rowland, John. "Phillpotts's Detective Fiction." *Eden
       Phillpotts: An Assessment and a Tribute*. Edited by
       Waveney Girvan. London: Hutchinson, 1953, pp. 135-
       151.

       Maintains that Phillpotts's detective fiction de-
       serves to be ranked with that of Wilkie Collins because
       of the "interplay of character and environment" that
       is "the fundamental basis of almost all the crime
       novels." Also contends that Phillpotts's work in the
       genre has helped to establish "the detective story
       as a 'respectable' form of literature."

1474.   White, Mary Ogden. "With Eden Phillpotts on Dartmoor."
        Outlook 91 (23 January 1909): 195-205.

        States that the narrative in Phillpotts's mysteries
        becomes elaborate to the point of being overwrought,
        thus adding "cheapness of tragedies" and emotions
        that never appear realistic. Observes that the reiter-
        ated motif is "overworked to a point of exasperation."

PIKE. ROBERT L. See ROBERT L. FISH

POE, EDGAR ALLAN (1809-1849). Series character: C. Auguste
        Dupin

1475.   Asarch, Joel Kenneth. "A Telling Tale: Poe's Revisions
        in 'The Murders in the Rue Morgue.'" *Library Chronicle*
        41 (1976): 83-90. Reprinted *Poe at Work: Seven
        Textual Studies*. Edited by Benjamin Franklin Fisher
        IV. Baltimore: Poe Society, 1978, pp. 83-90.

        Contends that Poe's successive revisions of "Rue
        Morgue" produced a tale both more grotesque and more
        credible than the original version. He altered the
        description of some clues to further deceive his
        readers.

1476.   Babener, Liahna Klenman. "The Shadow's Shadow: The
        Motif of the Double in Edgar Allan Poe's 'The Pur-
        loined Letter.'" *The Mystery and Detection Annual
        1972* (item 16), pp. 21-32.

        Contends that the strong double pattern in "The
        Purloined Letter" equates the detective and his rival
        morally.

1477.   Bandy, W.T. "Who Was Monsieur Dupin?" *PMLA* 79 (Sep-
        tember 1964): 509-510.

        Argues that Dupin's name was derived from C. Auguste
        Dubouchet and S. Maupin, two of Poe's friends.

1478.   Benton, Richard. "'The Mystery of Marie Roget'--A
        Defense." *Studies in Short Fiction* 6 (Winter 1969):
        144-152.

        Contends that in "Marie Roget," Poe pioneered the
        use of "model building"--the construction of a theo-
        retical model on which an investigation is then based.

Argues that "Marie Roget" is the best of the Dupin stories.

1479. Boll, Ernest. "The Manuscript of 'The Murders in the Rue Morgue' and Poe's Revisions." *Modern Philology* 40 (1943): 302-315.

Emphasizes grammar and punctuation in a close textual analysis of Poe's revisions of "Rue Morgue," but also contends that in changes affecting the formal structure of the story, Poe removes "deceptive guides toward a solution," thus making things fairer for the reader.

1480. Bonaparte, Marie. *The Life and Works of Edgar Allan Poe: A Psycho-Analytic Interpretation.* London: Hogarth Press, 1971. 749pp.

Originally published in 1949, this book contends that the dominant theme of "Rue Morgue" is the archetypal murder of the mother.

1481. Boucher, Anthony. Afterword to *Great American Detective Stories.* Cleveland: World, 1945, pp. 307-308.

Argues that in "Thou Art the Man," Poe deliberately adopts a humorous narrative stance as a way of shocking the reader with his light treatment of the subject of murder.

1482. Buranelli, Vincent. "The Detective Story." *Edgar Allan Poe.* Boston: Twayne, 1977, pp. 81-87.

Poe not only invented a form of literature (the detective story), "he perfected it." Only because Conan Doyle wrote more detective stories than did Poe is Sherlock Holmes more famous than C. Auguste Dupin.

* Cambiaire, Célestin Pierre. "Poe and the Detective Novel in France." *The Influence of Edgar Allan Poe in France* (item 1127), pp. 257-282.

Cites numerous American and French authorities who agree that Poe is the creator of the modern detective story, and points out Poe's influence on Gaboriau, Leroux, and possibly Eugène Sue.

1483. Christopher, Joe R. "Poe and the Detective Story." *Armchair Detective* 2 (October 1968): 49-51. Revised version printed in *The Mystery Writer's Art* (item 54), pp. 19-36.

Contends that Poe not only created the first detective story, but also created sixteen conventions of
the genre, including the eccentric detective, the locked
room mystery, and the unjustly suspected character.

1484.   Davidson, Edward H. *Poe: A Critical Study*. Cambridge,
        Mass.: Belknap Press of Harvard University Press,
        1957, pp. 213-222.

        Maintains that in his mystery stories "Poe's most
        consistent social and moral views" are presented. He
        "was free to construct a totally fictive playground
        of the mind which could still maintain workable like-
        nesses to the world of common affairs."

1485.   Diskin, Patrick. "Poe, Le Fanu and the Sealed Room
        Mystery." *Notes and Queries* 13 (September 1966):
        337-339.

        Details the many similarities between Le Fanu's
        "Passage in the Secret History of an Irish Countess"
        (1838) and Poe's "The Murders in the Rue Morgue" (1841).
        Attributes these similarities to Poe's "unconscious"
        borrowing.

1486.   Engel, Leonard W. "The Use of the Enclosure Device
        in Selected Fiction of Edgar Allan Poe." Ph.D. dis-
        sertation, Fordham University, 1977.

        Contends that in "Rue Morgue" and "Marie Roget" Poe
        uses the device of enclosure "purely and simply as a
        Gothic instrument--to inspire terror."

1487.   Fusco, Richard. "Poe's Revisions of 'The Mystery of
        Marie Roget'--A Hoax?" *Library Chronicle* 41 (1976):
        91-99. Reprinted *Poe at Work: Seven Textual Studies*.
        Edited by Benjamin Franklin Fisher IV. Baltimore:
        Poe Society, 1972, pp. 91-99.

        Contends that Poe's revisions of "Marie Roget" from
        1842 to 1845 indicate a decreasing interest in the
        "bizarre side" of the events surrounding the murder
        of Mary Rogers. Poe's failure to correctly predict
        the solution to the murder caused him to mistrust
        causal conclusions. In "The Purloined Letter," he used
        deduction in solving his crime.

1488.   Gaillard, Dawson F.D. "A Study of Poe's Concern with
        Man's Power of Cognition." Ph.D. dissertation,
        Tulane University, 1970.

Contends that Poe was concerned "with the limitations and the potentialities of man's cognitive powers." His Dupin stories reveal "that man should adapt his method of investigation to the case at hand, rather than adapt the case to the method."

* Grossvogel, David I. *Mystery and Its Fictions* (item 740), pp. 93-107.

Argues that "The Purloined Letter" is an unsatisfactory detective story. The identity of the culprit is given away at the beginning; on the other hand, the contents of the letter are never revealed. Contends that the prime interest in the story is Poe's intentional and unintentional self-revelations.

1489. Hatvary, George Egon. "Horace Binney Wallace: A Study in Self Destruction." *Princeton University Library Chronicle* 25 (1964): 137-149.

Cites Wallace as an important literary influence on Poe. Argues that the "Landor" referred to in "Marie Roget" is Wallace's pseudonym.

1490. Hawkins, John. "Poe's 'The Murders in the Rue Morgue.'" *Explicator* 23 (February 1965): item 49.

Argues that "Rue Morgue" is an account of the superiority of acumen (represented by the game of draughts) over concentration (represented by chess).

1491. Haycraft, Howard. "Father of the Detective Story: Edgar Allan Poe." *Saturday Review* 24 (23 August 1941): 12-15. Revised and reprinted *Murder for Pleasure* (item 36), pp. 1-27.

Contends that Poe was the originator of the detective story and a model for generations of writers. Argues that only the Dupin stories are detective stories. "The Gold Bug" and "Thou Art the Man" contain elements of mystery, but since they withhold essential clues from the reader, they are not, properly speaking, detective stories.

1492. Hipolito, Terrence. "On the Two Poes." *The Mystery and Detection Annual 1972* (item 16), pp. 15-20.

Argues that Poe "places artistic faith in wholly contradictory visions": the ratiocinative and the symbolic.

1493. Hoffman, Daniel. *Poe Poe Poe Poe Poe Poe Poe*. Garden
       City, N.Y.: Doubleday, 1972, pp. 105-125, 132-136.

       Contends that, in the Dupin tales, Poe equates in-
       tellect with strength. Its exercise is moral activity,
       and its action is to disentangle a mystery. The puzzle
       in these stories is not "who is guilty?" It is, rather,
       "how will Dupin infer his guilt?"

1494. Howard, Leon. "Poe's *Eureka*: The Detective Story That
       Failed." *The Mystery and Detection Annual 1972* (item
       16), pp. 1-14.

       Contends that *Eureka* invites comparison with Poe's
       last detective stories.

1495. Hungerford, Edward. "Poe and Phrenology." *American
       Literature* 2 (1930): 209-231.

       Argues that Poe is a believer in phrenology. He uses
       a phrenological term ("ideality") approvingly in describ-
       ing Dupin.

1496. Hurd, C.O. "The Logic of Poe's 'Murders.'" *Harvard
       Monthly* 1 (1885): 7-10.

       Argues that "Rue Morgue" has several logical errors
       in its construction. Poe offers insufficient reasons
       for denying the possibility of a motive for the murders;
       the witnesses should believe that the killer speaks
       their language; and the police should not have suggested
       the suicide.

1497. Keller, Mark. "Dupin in the 'Rue Morgue': Another Form
       of Madness?" *Arizona Quarterly* 33 (1977): 249-255.

       Argues that the character of Dupin evolves from his
       original appearance in "Rue Morgue" through "Marie
       Roget" and "The Purloined Letter." Most of the detec-
       tives's important character traits are delineated in
       "Rue Morgue." In this story, Dupin behaves much more
       eccentrically than he does in the latter two tales; he
       is more of a piece with Poe's other protagonists. His
       abnormal exaggeration of the analytical faculty is a
       form of madness.

1498. Kennedy, J. Gerald. "The Limits of Reason: Poe's Deluded
       Detectives." *American Literature* 47 (May 1975): 184-
       196.

Contends that ratiocination offered Poe a brief "dis-
traction from the recurring nightmare of death and
disintegration" but he finally came to see the detective
story "as a rather superficial and mechanical exercise
in mystification."

1499. Krutch, Joseph Wood. *Edgar Allan Poe: A Study in Genius.*
New York: Russell and Russell, 1965, pp. 106-118.

This study, originally published in 1926, contends
that Dupin bears a number of obvious resemblances to
Poe's other protagonists. Like Roderick Usher, he is
the imaginative projection of Poe's own personality.
Unlike Usher, however, Dupin's mental powers imply no
hint of insanity.

1500. Levine, Stuart. *Edgar Poe: Seer and Craftsman.* Deland,
Fla.: Everett/Edwards, 1972. 282pp.

Argues that Dupin is basically a transcendentalist.
He not only pieces clues together, in doing so "he
creates a beautiful pattern."

1501. "Long Way After Poe." *Nation* 85 (19 September 1907):
251-252.

Maintains that the rules and conventions for writing
detective fiction can be traced back to Poe, who "knew
the art of mystifying without resorting to the conceal-
ment of clues."

1502. Lowndes, Robert A.W. "The Contribution of Edgar Allan
Poe." *The Mystery Writer's Art* (item 54), pp. 1-18.

Notes the first appearance of the ratiocinative
detective in the form of Dupin in "Rue Morgue," and
traces Poe's influence through Conan Doyle and Agatha
Christie. Mystery/detection conventions that Poe
pioneered include: the detective as private citizen;
the detective as eccentric, interested only in unusual
crimes; and the device--perfected by Conan Doyle--of
narrating the story through the perspective of a friend/
foil of the detective.

*   Matthews, Brander. "Poe and the Detective-Story." (item
359).

Credits Poe with originating the detective story. Contrasts the purity of the Dupin tales with the "mystery-
mongering" of Dickens and Balzac. In Poe's stories it

is the process by which the mystery is solved, rather
than the mystery itself, that is the focus of attention.

1503.   Maxwell, D.E.S. *American Fiction: The Intellectual
        Background.* New York: Columbia University Press, 1963,
        pp. 95-96.

        Argues that Poe's detective stories are "for the most
        part ill-presented, wholly artificial puzzles." "Marie
        Roget" is remarkable only for Poe's presentation of
        the nature of the murder.

1504.   Mizuta, Noriko. "Crime and Dream: A Study of Edgar
        Allan Poe." Ph.D. dissertation, Yale University, 1970.

        Contends that Dupin explores the mysteries of the
        external world just as some of Poe's other protagonists
        explore the internal world. Both paths lead "to the
        same autonomous world of symbolic imagination."

1505.   Moore, John Robert. "Poe, Scott, and 'The Murders in
        the Rue Morgue.'" *American Literature* 8 (March 1936):
        52-58.

        Argues that Poe got the idea of using an orangutan in
        "Rue Morgue" from Scott's *Count Robert of Paris.* Thus
        the contention by some critics that Poe's use of this
        exotic animal was indicative of a disordered mind is
        contradicted.

*   Murch, A.E. *The Development of the Detective Novel*
        (item 51), pp. 67-83.

        An extended discussion of the background and character
        of Dupin. Observes that, in addition to his other
        pioneering efforts in the genre, Poe began the develop-
        ment of the detective sequel.

*   Palmer, Jerry. *Thrillers* (item 56), pp. 107-111.

        Analyzes "Thou Art the Man," contending that Poe very
        early hit upon the solution to the problem of reconcil-
        ing character portrayal and criminal motivation. He uses
        irony, creating a distance between the reader and the
        villain.

1506.   Panek, LeRoy. "Play and Games: An Approach to Poe's
        Detective Tales." *Poe Studies* 10 (1977): 39-41.

        Analyzes Dupin in light of Johann Huizinga's defini-
        tions of play, finding many parallels. Dupin is an

amateur; he is completely absorbed in his pursuit, which is undertaken for no material gain and is done solely for pleasure.

1507. Paul, Raymond. *Who Murdered Mary Rogers?* Englewood Cliffs, N.J.: Prentice-Hall, 1971. 271pp.

Sifts through the evidence on the case that inspired "Marie Roget." Contends that Rogers's fiancé, Daniel Payne, was the culprit.

1508. Porges, Irwin. *Edgar Allan Poe.* Philadelphia: Chilton, 1963, pp. 127-131, 142-144.

Contends that, in describing Dupin's methods in "Rue Morgue," Poe was also describing the workings of his own mind. "The detection was Dupin's, but the scientific mind belonged to Edgar."

1509. Quinn, Arthur Hobson. *Edgar Allan Poe: A Critical Biography.* New York: Appleton-Century-Crofts, 1941, pp. 310-312, 355-358.

Argues that Poe did not invent the detective story. His achievement was to create Dupin, a detective who solved crimes by analysis.

1510. Quinn, Patrick F. *The French Face of Edgar Poe.* Carbondale: Southern Illinois University Press, 1957, pp. 223-228.

Compares Poe's detective stories with his tales of psychological terror, contending that Poe identified more strongly with his Roderick Ushers than he did with Dupin.

1511. Ransome, Arthur. *Edgar Allan Poe: A Critical Study.* London: Martin Secker, 1910, pp. 151-167.

Contends that Poe's insatiable curiosity and his brilliant analytical powers led him to write the Dupin stories, which glory in the power of ratiocination. These stories were the valid outlet for the impulse that fueled Poe's obsession with acrostics and cryptography.

1512. Roth, Martin. "The Poet's Purloined Letter." *Mystery and Detection Annual 1973* (item 17), pp. 113-128.

Notes Poe's fascination with cryptography; argues that the cryptographic elements of "The Purloined Letter"

are integral to a proper understanding of the story.
"It is Dupin who dreams the purloined letter into
existence."

*   Sayers, Dorothy L. Introduction to *Great Short Stories
          of Detection, Mystery and Horror* (item 441).

          Contends that five tales by Poe--the Dupin stories,
          plus "The Gold Bug" and "Thou Art the Man"--anticipate
          much of the form and substance of mystery/detection
          fiction, including the figure of the detective, most
          of the basic plot twists, and both the Romantic (sensa-
          tional) and Classic (intellectual) traditions.

1513.   Schwaber, Paul. "On Reading Poe." *Literature and
          Psychology* 21 (1971): 81-99.

          Compares "Rue Morgue" with "The Fall of the House of
          Usher." Both stories accentuate the "tension between
          inductive, logical order and irrationality."

1514.   Sippel, Erich W. "Bolting the Whole Shebang Together:
          Poe's Predicament." *Criticism* 15 (1973): 289-308.

          Argues that Poe's detective stories are based on a
          system of "inexorable causation." Dupin's rationality
          "is the logical outgrowth of order."

1515.   Smith, Allan. "The Psychological Context of Three Tales
          by Poe." *Journal of American Studies* 7 (1973): 285-
          288.

          Contends that Dupin's powers of observation and
          analysis in "Rue Morgue" mirror the principle of associ-
          ation in the philosophies of Locke and Hartley.

1516.   Stone, Edward. *A Certain Morbidness*. Carbondale: Southern
          Illinois University Press, 1969, pp. 140-168.

          Contends that Poe, in his detective stories, "made
          the first measurement and association of ideas in the
          human mind." Dupin's talent is the ability to discover
          links between apparently obscure clues.

*   Symons, Julian. *Mortal Consequences* (item 74), pp. 27-35.

          Contends that Poe's mystery/detection work includes
          "The Gold Bug" and "Thou Art the Man" as well as the
          three seminal Dupin tales. These stories establish many
          of the genre's most important conventions, including

that of the brilliant but eccentric detective and an
admiring but less intelligent narrator.

1517. Symons, Julian. *The Tell-Tale Heart: The Life and Works
of Edgar Allan Poe.* New York: Harper and Row, 1978,
pp. 221-225.

Contends that, while there had been literary detectives before Poe, there had been no detection. Poe
was the first writer to focus on the process of solving
a mystery.

*   Thomson, H. Douglas. "Edgar Allan Poe." *Masters of
Mystery* (item 77), pp. 75-91.

Analyzes in some detail Poe's Dupin stories, singling
out "Marie Roget" as "undoubtedly a masterpiece" of
pure analysis. Calls Dupin the "personification of
analysis."

1518. Wallace, Irving. "The Real Marie Roget." *The Fabulous
Originals: Lives of Extraordinary People Who Inspired
Memorable Characters in Fiction.* New York: Knopf,
1955, pp. 172-215.

An account of Mary Rogers's murder and the writing
and publishing history of "Marie Roget."

1519. Wallace, Robert K. "'The Murders in the Rue Morgue' and
Sonata Allegro Form." *Journal of Aesthetics and Art
Criticism* 35 (1977): 457-463.

Compares the structure of "Rue Morgue" to that of
Beethoven's "Pathétique." Poe negotiated the composi-
tional hazards in his story smoothly, as did Beethoven
in his sonata.

1520. Waller, W.F. ["Rue Morgue."] *Notes and Queries* 5 (12
May 1894): 366.

Argues that a story in *The Annual Register of the
Year 1834* about a theft by a monkey is a possible source
for Poe's "Rue Morgue."

1521. Walsh, John. *Poe the Detective: The Curious Circumstances
Behind the Mystery of Marie Roget.* New Brunswick,
N.J.: Rutgers University Press, 1968. 154pp.

Both a study of the discoverable facts of the murder
upon which Poe's story was based and a study of Poe's

use of the facts he knew (including two revisions of
the work to accommodate new discoveries).

1522. Wimsatt, W.K., Jr. "Mary Rogers, John Anderson, and
       Others." *American Literature* 21 (January 1950): 482-
       484.

       Contends that Mary Rogers died from an abortion.

1523. Wimsatt, W.K., Jr. "Poe and the Mystery of Mary Rogers."
       PMLA 56 (1941): 230-248.

       A close analysis of the murder that inspired "Marie
       Roget." Argues that on the basis of available evidence,
       there is no way of knowing whether Poe's conclusions
       as to the solution of the mystery are correct.

1524. Worthen, Samuel C. "Poe and the Beautiful Cigar Girl."
       American Literature 20 (1948): 305-312.

       Reviews the facts in the death of Mary Rogers. Though
       he cannot positively identify the killer, Worthen con-
       tends that Rogers died during an attempted abortion.
       Poe, relying only on newspaper accounts, lacked the
       facts to solve the mystery.

1525. Worthen, Samuel C. "A Strange Aftermath of 'The Mystery
       of Marie Roget.'" *Proceedings of the New Jersey
       Historical Society* 60 (April 1942): 116-123.

       Reviews the court case resulting from the death of
       Mary Rogers. Argues that Poe failed to come to grips
       with the facts of the case.

POST, MELVILLE DAVISSON (1871-1930). Series character: Uncle
Abner

*   Haycraft, Howard. *Murder for Pleasure* (item 36), pp.
        94-97.

        States that the most serious criticism of Post's
        tales is that many times he fails to make all the evi-
        dence explicit.

1526. Hubin, Allen J. Introduction to *The Complete Uncle
       Abner*, by Melville D. Post. Del Mar, Calif.: Mystery
       Library, 1977, pp. vii-xvi; bibliography, pp. 399-410.

Contends that Uncle Abner "is more distinctly American in acceptance than the hard-boiled story." Annotated bibliography is included.

1527.   Norton, Charles A. *Melville Davisson Post: Man of Many Mysteries*. Bowling Green, Ohio: Bowling Green University Popular Press, 1973. 261pp.

States that Post has been neglected by most critics and recognized by others only for "his superb talents and practical techniques in creating short, entertaining mystery fiction." Norton contends that he should also be recognized for "the profound and prophetic ideas pertaining to legal and social justice" that are in his stories.

1528.   Overton, Grant. "Melville Davisson Post and the Use of Plot." *Bookman* 59 (June 1924): 423–430. Reprinted as "The Art of Melville Davisson Post." *Cargoes for Crusoes* (item 1462), pp. 41–59.

Singles out *The Doomdorf Mystery* as exemplifying Post's artistry: the plot is swiftly-paced; tension is immediately established and is maintained; the prose uses "a somewhat Biblical diction." Observes that "the development of the mystery and its solution side by side" is often considered Post's greatest achievement.

1529.   Williams, Blanche Colton. "Melville Davisson Post." *Our Short Story Writers*. New York: Dodd, Mead, 1922, pp. 293–308.

Contends that Post's most original contribution to the detective short story is his series of stories in which the criminal goes unpunished because of the ability of Post's central character, Randolph Mason, a shrewd, "unscrupulous lawyer."

PRIESTLEY, J.B. (1894-)

*   Shibuk, Charles. "Three British Experiments from the Mainstream" (item 1262).

Contends that Priestley's *Salt Is Leaving* is a "well-written novel with more than its share of wit and charm," but it is marred by a weak and hasty solution.

PROPPER, MILTON (1906-1962)

1530. Nevins, Francis M., Jr. "The World of Milton Propper."
       Armchair Detective 10 (July 1977): 197-203.

       Argues that though Propper's writing contains dull
       narrative and characters who are one-dimensional, his
       work, at its best, has the excitement of the early
       Ellery Queen novels.

QUEEN, ELLERY. Joint pseudonym of Frederic Dannay (1905-   )
and Manfred Bennington Lee (1905-1971). Other joint pseudonym:
Barnaby Ross. Series character also named Ellery Queen

1531. Albany, Francis. "Ellery Queen, le Logicien du Mystère."
       Europe no. 571-572 (November-December 1976): 91-98.

       Observes that the character Ellery Queen is fond of
       cold logic and likes to demonstrate that man's salva-
       tion lies in culture.

1532. Bainbridge, John. "Ellery Queen: Crime Made Him Famous
       and His Authors Rich." *Life* 15 (22 November 1943):
       70-76.

       Argues that Lee and Dannay have achieved continued
       success by "their effective use of an industrial tech-
       nique known as reprocessing, making one murder go a
       long way." Describes the character Ellery Queen as
       falling "somewhere between S.S. Van Dine's Philo Vance
       and a heavily diluted edition of Dashiell Hammett's
       Nick Charles.

1533. Biederstadt, Lynn. "To the Very Last: The Dying
       Message." *Armchair Detective* 12 (Summer 1979): 209-210.

       States that Queen is the master solver of the enig-
       matic message of the dying. Queen has the intellect
       to decipher even the most illogical, misleading final
       communication.

1534. Christopher, Joe R. "The Mystery of Social Reaction:
       Two Novels by Ellery Queen." *Armchair Detective* 6
       (October 1972): 28-32.

       Dannay and Lee wrote two non-Ellery Queen novels,
       The Glass Village and *Cop Out*. Both are novels of social
       comment and both have crimes that are solved.

1535. Douty, Robert W. "Ellery Queen: First Impressions."
      Armchair Detective 12 (Summer 1979): 196.

      Contends that Queen is the antithesis of the hard-
      boiled detective. Queen is "more likable, gentle, a
      suave individual."

1536. Godfrey, Thomas. *"The Lamp of God." Armchair Detective*
      12 (Summer 1979): 212-215.

      States that Queen's *The Lamp of God* is one of his
      best. It skillfully buries its clues, plays fair with
      the intelligence of the reader, and makes effective
      use of atmosphere.

*   Haycraft, Howard. *Murder for Pleasure* (item 36), pp.
      173-177.

      Maintains that Queen's novels are "entirely American
      in their idiom" and a successful blending of Van Dine's
      and Hammett's writing styles.

1537. Nevins, Francis M., Jr. "The Drury Lane Quartet." *The
      Mystery Writer's Art* (item 54), pp. 122-135.

      An analysis of the quartet of novels featuring Drury
      Lane written by Dannay and Lee under the pseudonym of
      Barnaby Ross. Argues that all but the last (*Drury
      Lane's Last Case*) are masterpieces of the Golden Age
      of detective fiction.

1538. Nevins, Francis M., Jr. *Royal Bloodline: Ellery Queen,
      Author and Detective.* Bowling Green, Ohio: Bowling
      Green University Popular Press, 1974. 288pp.

      Contends that the literary career of Ellery Queen
      can be divided into four periods. In the first period
      (1929-1935) he was heavily influenced by S.S. Van Dine.
      In the second period (1936-1939) he was influenced by
      the women's magazines and Hollywood. During the third
      period (1942-1958) he was at the peak of his popularity.
      In 1963 he began a fourth period marked by an "undi-
      mished zest for radical experiment within the strict
      deductive tradition," but his popularity seems to have
      diminished. The major novels of each period are examined
      in detail and a complete checklist of his publications
      is included. A pre-publication excerpt from the book was
      published in *Armchair Detective* 7 (1973): 4-10.

*   Symons, Julian. *Mortal Consequences* (item 74), pp. 121-
         123.

         Points out that the early Queen novels had an in-
         genuity based on the "relentlessly analytical treatment
         of every possible clue and argument."

*   Thomson, H. Douglas. *Masters of Mystery* (item 77), pp.
         269-272.

         States that Queen's *The Mystery of the Roman Hat*
         follows closely the plotting techniques of S.S. Van
         Dine.

RAND, STEVE. See JAY BENNETT

RANDOLPH, GEORGIANA ANN. See CRAIG RICE

RANDOLPH, VANCE (1892-   )

1539.   Clements, William M. "The Red Herring as Folklore."
         Armchair Detective 12 (Summer 1979): 256-259.

         Contends that *The Camp Meeting Murders* (1936) by
         Randolph and Nancy Clemens, a mystery with a Missouri
         Ozarks setting, uses folklore to give one of the con-
         ventions of the mystery--the red herring--a "degree of
         uniqueness."

RAWSON, CLAYTON (1906-1971). Pseudonym: Stuart Towne

1540.   Nevins, Francis M., Jr. "The Diavolo Quartet." *Armchair
         Detective* 3 (July 1970): 243-244.

         Rawson created in a series of novels featuring Don
         Diavolo an unusual atmosphere of "magic, mystery, and
         menace." While the stories are weakened by the hurried
         conception and production, they possess a crude but
         powerful energy that, Nevins contends, makes them ex-
         hilarating.

RAYMOND, RENE BRABAZON. See JAMES HADLEY CHASE

REED, ELIOT. See ERIC AMBLER

REED, ISHMAEL (1938-)

1541.   Carter, Steven R. "Ishmael Reed's Neo-Hoodoo Detection."
        Dimensions of Detective Fiction (item 43), pp. 265-
        274.

        Argues that Reed is one of the leading practitioners
        of experimental mystery fiction (as exemplified by his
        novel *Mumbo Jumbo*), and characterizes this sub-genre as
        combining elements of detective fiction with mainstream
        experimental fiction; examining problems of society
        rather than individuals; "reshaping elements of detec-
        tive fiction to fit a personal vision"; not necessarily
        solving the puzzle or problem posed; and making the
        detective elements play an important part in the work
        as a whole.

REEVE, ARTHUR (1880-1936). Series character: Craig Kennedy

1542.   Cox, J. Randolph. "A Reading of Reeve: Some Thoughts
        on the Creator of Craig Kennedy." *Armchair Detective*
        11 (January 1978): 28-33.

        Argues that Reeve's works are fascinating today "as
        social documents and mirrors of a vanished age" when
        the scientist was a hero. Also lists the books and
        periodical appearances of Reeve.

1543.   Harwood, John. "Arthur B. Reeve and the American
        Sherlock Holmes." *Armchair Detective* 10 (October
        1977): 354-357.

        Contends that the popularity of Reeve's Craig Kennedy
        stories, which emphasized the use of scientific tech-
        niques in crime investigation, influenced the develop-
        ment of modern police procedures.

*   Haycraft, Howard. *Murder for Pleasure* (item 36), pp.
        98-99.

        Maintains that Reeve "had a mobile narrative style
        and a journalistic ability to hold interest and if his
        detection was seldom brilliant, neither was it ever
        wholly bad."

RENDELL, RUTH (1930-)

1544.   Bakerman, Jane S. "Explorations of Love: An Examination
        of Some Novels by Ruth Rendell." *Armchair Detective*
        11 (April 1978): 139-144.

        Identifies three basic kinds of love that are impor-
        tant themes in six Rendell novels: friendship, familial
        love, and sexual love. Concludes that Rendell explores
        these themes skillfully and with "genuine insight."

1545.   Champlin, Charles. "Playing God and Plotting Deaths."
        Los Angeles Times 6 July 1979, part IV, pp. 1, 14.

        In assessing the mystery novels of Ruth Rendell,
        Champlin argues that she is a writer of "uncommon daring,
        grace and firm command of characters, settings and mood,
        who seems increasingly to set herself hard challenges
        for the pleasure of solving them." Also contends that
        Rendell's work is closer to that of Patricia Highsmith
        than to that of Agatha Christie in its psychological
        penetration and sardonic view of human nature.

1546.   Vicarel, Jo Ann Genard. "A Rendell Dozen Plus One."
        Armchair Detective 9 (June 1976): 198-200, 235.

        Provides an annotated checklist of Rendell's novels
        through 1974.

RETCLIFFE, JOHN. Pseudonym of Hermann O.F. Goedsche (1815-1878)

1547.   Plass, Paul. "Concerning *Nena Sahib*." *Armchair Detective*
        6 (May 1973): 157-159.

        Observes that Retcliffe's *Nena Sahib* (1858-1859) con-
        tains an early example of the locked room mystery but
        has little else of interest to students of detective
        fiction. Almost the entire episode is reprinted in the
        article.

RICE, CRAIG. Pseudonym of Georgiana Ann Randolph (1908-1957).
Other pseudonym: Michael Venning

1548.   Dueren, Fred. "John J. Malone (and Cohorts)." *Armchair
        Detective* 8 (November 1974): 44-47.

        States that the Rice books have a large cast of con-
        tinuing characters and analyzes the relationship between

three of Rice's main characters: John Malone, Jake and
Helene Justus.

1549. Jasen, David A. "The Mysterious Craig Rice." *Armchair
       Detective* 5 (October 1971): 25-27, 34.

       Craig Rice wrote two main types of stories: straight-
       forward, fast-paced ones, and introspective, psycholog-
       ical ones. Includes primary bibliography.

RINEHART, MARY ROBERTS (1876-1958)

*   Haycraft, Howard. *Murder for Pleasure* (item 36), pp.
       87-91.

       Contends that Rinehart "represents the quintessence
       of the romantic mood" in the mystery story.

1550. Hoffman, Arnold R. "Social History and the Crime
       Fiction of Mary Roberts Rinehart." *New Dimensions in
       Popular Culture*. Edited by Russel B. Nye. Bowling
       Green, Ohio: Bowling Green University Popular Press,
       1972, pp. 153-171.

       Contends that because of the large number of novels
       she published and their great popularity, Rinehart must
       be considered an important writer of American popular
       literature. This essay views her work both as a "craft
       or art, and as a record of social thought and behavior"
       over a period of approximately fifty years.

1551. Rinehart, Mary Roberts. "Thoughts." *Ladies Home Journal*
       48 (May 1931): 3, 179.

       Rinehart points out that she uses a formula to write
       her mystery stories and states that she believes that
       the biggest weakness of the detective novel has been
       the long anti-climactic explanation at the end.

*   Symons, Julian. *Mortal Consequences* (item 74), pp. 96-
       99.

       States that Rinehart's stories were written to a
       pattern. There was crime, usually murder, and a detec-
       tive, but his activities were less important than those
       of the female character who got innocently involved in
       the crime.

RITCHIE, JACK (1922-   )

1552. Puechner, Ray. "Jack Ritchie: An Interview." *Armchair
        Detective* 6 (October 1972): 12-14.

        Puechner states that Ritchie is perhaps the most an-
        thologized contemporary mystery writer and that his
        stories exhibit a sardonic wit and a "tight, concise
        style." Ritchie describes his "jigsaw" writing method
        as well as discussing his background and the authors he
        admires.

ROBERTS, JAMES HALL. See ROBERT L. DUNCAN

ROBESON, KENNETH. See LESTER DENT and RON GOULART

RODDA, CHARLES. See ERIC AMBLER

ROHMER, SAX. Pseudonym of Arthur Henry Sarsfield Ward (1883-
1959). Series character: Dr. Fu Manchu

1553. Baring-Gould, William S. "'I Shall Live When You are
        Smoke.'" *Armchair Detective* 2 (October 1967): 2-3.

        States that Sax Rohmer's Dr. Fu Manchu was inspired
        by his creator's wanderings through London's Chinatown.

1554. Briney, Robert E. "Sax Rohmer: An Informal Survey."
        The Mystery Writer's Art (item 54), pp. 42-78.

        States that Rohmer's main contribution in his varied
        writing career was the creation of Dr. Fu Manchu. Many
        of Rohmer's books are analyzed in depth.

1555. Frayling, Christopher. "Criminal Tendencies: Sax Rohmer
        and the Devil Doctor." *London Magazine* 13 (June/July
        1973): 65-80.

        Observes that, although Rohmer's books have received
        negative reviews for their literary value, they have
        always been very popular with the general reading public
        which enjoys melodramatic, supernatural plots and
        sinister villains.

*   Prager, Arthur. "The Mark of Kali." *Rascals at Large*
        (item 1315), pp. 45-69.

Points out that the early books of the Fu Manchu series were basically "a string of short stories, loosely connected by some thread of plot, like *The Arabian Nights*." Gives numerous examples to show changes in Fu Manchu's wicked methods.

1556. Rohmer, Sax. "Meet Dr. Fu Manchu." *Meet the Detective* (item 45), pp. 36-41.

States that he was inspired to create the mysterious and remorseless Fu Manchu by his explorations in London's Chinatown section, Limehouse.

* Thomson, H. Douglas. *Masters of Mystery* (item 77), pp. 218-220.

After mentioning the popularity of Orientals in thrillers Thomson proclaims Fu Manchu "the greatest Chinaman of them all" and adds that in the Fu Manchu stories "we at last have an instance of a contest where the villain is more than the equal of the detective."

1557. Van Ash, Cay, and Elizabeth Sax Rohmer. *Master of Villainy: A Biography of Sax Rohmer*. Edited by Robert E. Briney. Bowling Green, Ohio: Bowling Green University Popular Press, 1972. 312pp.

This book began as a collaboration between Sax Rohmer and his wife Elizabeth. After Rohmer's death the manuscript was re-written and completed by Elizabeth and Van Ash, a protege of Rohmer. Later Briney added notes and a bibliography. The book is anecdotal but describes the beginning of Fu Manchu in an article Rohmer wrote on Limehouse, the Chinese section of London. Also maintains that it was "colorful descriptive matter" and "ingenious development of plots" which made Rohmer famous.

* Watson, Colin. "The Orientation of Villainy." *Snobbery with Violence* (item 78), pp. 109-121.

Contends that Sax Rohmer's Fu Manchu novels would not have been best sellers without playing on the latent fear or dislike of Orientals which was common in England at the time.

ROLLINS, KATHLEEN. See BRETT HALLIDAY

ROSS, BARNABY. See ELLERY QUEEN

ROSS, JAMES (1911-   )

1558. Higgins, George V. Afterword to *They Don't Dance Much*,
       by James Ross. Carbondale: Southern Illinois Univer-
       sity Press, 1975, pp. 297-302.

       Ross wrote when the realistic novel was still shackled
       by many constraints and Victorian conventions. Higgins
       contends that "he advanced the craft of fiction as far
       as it could be advanced when he was writing."

RUSSELL, MARTIN (1934-   )

1559. Pettersson, Sven-Ingmar. "Martin Russell: A Profile."
       Armchair Detective 8 (November 1974): 48-49.

       Russell states that he prefers to be called "a delver
       into psychological motivation" rather than a mystery
       writer. He deals with such themes as blackmail and in-
       sanity and also states that he tries to write books
       that are "reasonably well-written ... with a few shocks
       and surprises, reasonably believable characters, and
       not necessarily a happy ending."

ST. JOHN, DAVID. See E. HOWARD HUNT

SAPIR, RICHARD. See WARREN B. MURPHY

SAPPER. See H.C. McNEILE

SAYERS, DOROTHY L. (1893-1957)

1560. Bander, Elaine. "Dorothy L. Sayers and the Apotheosis
       of Detective Fiction." *Armchair Detective* 10 (October
       1977): 362-365.

       Briefly surveys several of Sayers's novels to illus-
       trate her preoccupation with the nature of truth and
       her increasing need to manipulate the detective plot
       to serve the needs of the novel of manners. Contends
       that Sayers ultimately dropped the murder-detection

theme in favor of didacticism in "The Wimsey Papers."

1561. Barzun, Jacques, and Wendell Hertig Taylor. Preface to
       Strong Poison, by Dorothy L. Sayers. New York:
       Garland Publishing, 1976. Also printed in *A Book of
       Prefaces* (item 22), pp. 97-98.

       Argues that this novel is Sayers's preeminent work
       because of its compactness, the inventive way in which
       the murder is committed, and the dramatic mood.

1562. Basney, Lionel. "God and Peter Wimsey." *Christianity
       Today* 17 (14 September 1973): 27-28.

       Though Sayers's detective novels are not explicitly
       religious, Wimsey's personal change from his experiences
       with guilt, innocence, malice, and love "recalls the
       psychological pattern of Christian conversion."

1563. Basney, Lionel. "*The Nine Tailors* and the Complexity
       of Innocence." *As Her Whimsey Took Her* (item 1574),
       pp. 23-35.

       Contends that *The Nine Tailors* is an interesting novel
       as well as mystery story because Sayers successfully
       integrates the detective elements with serious social
       commentary.

1564. Burleson, James B., Jr. "A Study of the Novels of
       Dorothy L. Sayers." Ph.D. dissertation, University
       of Texas, 1965.

       Analyzes each of Sayers's detective novels. Her first
       four established her mastery of plot and style. Her
       two 1930 novels proved her ability to draw character
       and also marked her decision to make her novels "criti-
       cisms of life." In her last detective novels she adds
       a vividly described setting, and the detective element
       is less important than before.

*   Cawelti, John G. "The Art of the Classical Detective
        Story." *Adventure, Mystery, and Romance* (item 150),
        pp. 119-125.

        Argues that Sayers's work is a good example of the
        use of the mystery story formula to present a special
        view of the world. This is particularly evident in
        The Nine Tailors, a classic detective story in which
        characterization, social milieu, and "thematic sig-
        nificance" are "interwoven into the structure of a
        mystery" that embodies Sayers's religious vision.

1565.   Dale, Alzina Stone. *Maker and Craftsman: The Story of*
        Dorothy L. Sayers. Grand Rapids, Mich.: William B.
        Eerdmans, 1978. 158pp.

        In addition to sketching the biography of Sayers,
        Dale details the social background of her life and
        writing and suggests possible models for characters
        in her works.

1566.   Duns, Robert Paul. "'The Laughter of the Universe':
        Dorothy L. Sayers and the Whimsical Vision." *As Her*
        Whimsey Took Her (item 1574), pp. 200-212.

        Contends that in both her detective fiction and her
        religious writing Sayers exhibits "a warm, witty,
        earthy presence."

1567.   Durkin, Mary B. *Dorothy L. Sayers*. Boston: Twayne,
        1980. 204pp.

        In the three chapters devoted to Sayers's detective
        fiction emphasizes "the stylistic techniques" Sayers
        used to elevate the genre "to the literary status of
        the novel of manners," and points out the important
        themes found in all her works--"the integrity of work,
        of the mind, of right relationships with others, one's
        self, and with God."

1568.   Foster, Paul. "Dorothy Sayers." *Writers of To-day*.
        Edited by Denys Val Baker. London: Sidgwick and
        Jackson, 1946, pp. 111-121.

        Argues that Sayers is perhaps the greatest writer
        of detective fiction ever, that both her technique and
        her appreciation of human truths are exceptional. The
        character of Lord Peter Wimsey shows her finest imag-
        inative powers.

1569.   Gilbert, Colleen B. *A Bibliography of the Works of*
        Dorothy L. Sayers. Hamden, Conn.: Archon Books, 1978.
        263pp.

        Primary bibliography. Includes unpublished items in
        manuscript collections open to the public.

1570.   Gilbert, Michael. "Technicalese." *The Mystery Writer's*
        Handbook. Edited by Herbert Brean. New York: Harpers,
        1956, pp. 57-65.

Analyzes Sayers's use of "technicalese" in *Unnatural Death* and *The Nine Tailors*. Includes a substantial excerpt from a letter by Sayers on the latter work. Unfortunately this article is included in only the 1956 edition of *The Mystery Writer's Handbook*.

1571. Green, Martin. "The Detection of a Snob." *Listener* 69 (14 March 1963): 461, 464.

Lord Peter is a fully created character, and one of his chief assets as a detective is his "perfect mastery of English manners." Contends that his popularity with the English is to a large degree due to their fascination with effete upper-class people.

1572. Gregory, E.R. "Wilkie Collins and Dorothy L. Sayers." *As Her Whimsey Took Her* (item 1574), pp. 51-64.

Contends that Sayers's detective fiction shows the great influence of Collins in her plot construction and use of strong women characters. Also the fact that Sayers collected editions of Collins's works as well as books about him attests to his importance to her.

1573. Hamilton, Edith. "Gaudeamus Igitur." *Saturday Review* 13 (22 February 1936): 6.

In this review of *Gaudy Night* Hamilton argues that the "conversational stamina" of women academics of an Oxford College and the cultivated nature of their conversation are the dominant impressions from this skillfully written mystery.

1574. Hannay, Margaret, P., ed. *As Her Whimsey Took Her: Critical Essays on the Work of Dorothy L. Sayers.* Kent, Ohio: Kent State University Press, 1979. 301pp.

A collection of fifteen essays by various authors. Those on Sayers's detective fiction are annotated separately.

1575. Hannay, Margaret P. "Harriet's Influence on the Characterization of Lord Peter Wimsey." *As Her Whimsey Took Her* (item 1574), pp. 36-50.

Contends that Sayers introduced the character Harriet Vane to develop Wimsey's character, to function as an "indirect narrator in love with the hero," and to reveal Wimsey's emotions and personal weaknesses.

1576.   Hannay, Margaret P. Introduction to *As Her Whimsey Took Her* (item 1574), pp. ix-xvi.

Argues that the theme of "work well done" is central to Sayers's work as a novelist, dramatist, translator, and aesthetician.

1577.   Harmon, Robert B., and Margaret A. Burger. *An Annotated Guide to the Works of Dorothy L. Sayers*. New York: Garland Publishing, 1977.

Chiefly a bibliography of works by Sayers but does contain a short section of works about her.

1578.   Harrison, Barbara Grizutti. "Dorothy L. Sayers and the Tidy Art of Detective Fiction." *Ms.* 3 (November 1974): 66-69, 85-89.

Argues that Sayers was a feminist and that both Lord Peter Wimsey and Harriet Vane are feminists.

1579.   Hart, Harold. "Accident, Suicide or Murder? A Question of Stereochemistry." *Journal of Chemical Education* 52 (July 1975): 444.

The chemical information in The Documents in the Case, which Sayers wrote with Robert Eustace, is given in a manner that the layman can understand but that an organic chemist will especially enjoy. Some of the information is now out of date, but it conforms to the ideas of the time. Points out one small error (the color of a sodium flame) but recommends the story for under-graduate organic chemistry students.

*   Haycraft, Howard. *Murder for Pleasure* (item 36), pp. 135-142.

Contends that Sayers made outstanding contributions to detective fiction, but in her commendable attempts at experimentation with the form she often produced novels that are neither good detective fiction nor good mainstream fiction.

1580.   Heilbrun, Carolyn. "Sayers, Lord Peter and God." *American Scholar* 37 (Spring 1968): 324-334. Reprinted *Lord Peter*. Edited by James Sandoe. New York: Avon Books, 1972, pp. 454-469.

Attributes the continuing success of the Wimsey books to superb writing, conversations "in the best tradition of the comedy of manners," sound plots, and intelligent characters.

1581. Hickman, H.P. "From Detective to Theology: The Work of Dorothy Sayers." *Hibbert Journal* 60 (July 1962): 290-296.

Argues that Lord Peter Wimsey, who stands for reason and good sense, finally became inadequate for Sayers, and she turned to theological writing because "the dark tangle of our lives demands a different kind of illumination."

1582. Hitchman, Janet. *Such a Strange Lady: A Biography of Dorothy L. Sayers.* New York: Harper and Row, 1975. 177pp.

In this biography and introduction to Sayers (done without any assistance from Sayers's family or executors) Hitchman points out many connections between Sayers's life and her work.

1583. Hone, Ralph E. *Dorothy L. Sayers: A Literary Biography.* Kent, Ohio: Kent State University Press, 1979. 217pp.

Hone stresses the Christian ethic of Sayers and states that one of the chief virtues of her detective novels is the creation of Lord Peter Wimsey. Also suggests possible connections between passages in the books and the personal life of Sayers.

1584. Leavis, Q.D. "The Case of Miss Dorothy Sayers." *Scrutiny* 6 (December 1937): 334-340. Reprinted *A Selection from Scrutiny.* Edited by F. R. Leavis. Cambridge: Cambridge University Press, 1968, pp. 141-146.

A well-known attack on Sayers which argues against the idea that she is anything more than a "best-seller novelist." States that her fiction is either merely unimpressive detective story writing or "stale, second-hand, hollow," and that she does not deserve her high reputation among educated people.

* Legman, G. *Love and Death.* (item 683), pp. 72-73.

Contends that Sayers is "a bitter feminist, killing off men on paper," and that Wimsey," the most disgusting snob in literature," is the man Harriet Vane "desperately wishes she were."

1585. Myers, Doris T. "Lord Peter Wimsey's Answer to Pilate." *Cimarron Review* 33 (1975): 26-34.

Contends that the plot of each Wimsey story comes from Sayers's central theological convictions: that there is an absolute Truth and that man serves that Truth through what he does.

*   Panek, LeRoy. "Dorothy Sayers." *Watteau's Shepherds* (item 57), pp. 72-110.

Points out how Sayers handles detection in each of the detective novels and how she adapted her technique as she experimented with the detective story form. Observes that in most of her books Sayers introduces the murderer very soon and leaves little doubt of his guilt so that she can show the "causes and effects of evil." Also states that Sayers believed "that the mechanism of murder was a more interesting detective problem than the problem of identity."

*   Peters, Margot, and Agate Nesaule Krouse. "Women and Crime: Sexism in Allingham, Sayers and Christie" (item 536).

The British detective novel is a conservative genre and all three of the women writers treated exhibit conventional sexist attitudes toward women. The "fetish" of Allingham and Sayers, their "hero-worship of the aristocracy," makes them even more conservative. Lord Peter relies on the work of women in his detection, yet gives them none of the credit. Sayers does record the problems but none of the victories of independent women. Harriet Vane is depicted as ultimately inferior and submissive to Lord Peter. Uses examples from several novels.

1586.   Ray, Laura K. "The Mysteries of *Gaudy Night*: Feminism, Faith, and the Depths of Character." *Mystery and Detection Annual 1973* (item 17), pp. 272-285.

Gaudy Night has "the psychological depth of modern serious fiction." It treats the issue of feminism through comments by many characters as well as through the depiction of the Wimsey-Vane relationship as "the union of two discrete and independent individuals in a relationship of tension and support," and it "anticipates the concerns of her later theological writings."

1587.   Reaves, R.B. "Crime and Punishment in the Detective Fiction of Dorothy L. Sayers." *As Her Whimsey Took Her* (item 1574), pp. 1-13.

Argues that Sayers was "concerned that crime and punishment be viewed beyond the narrow scope of simple retributive justice" and cites examples from her novels to illustrate this thesis and Sayers's "artistic accomplishment in integrating these moral concerns" into her work.

1588. Reynolds, Barbara. "The Origins of Lord Peter Wimsey." *Times Literary Supplement* 22 April 1977, p. 492.

With a great many details argues that Lord Peter Wimsey is much like Philip Trent in *Trent's Last Case* (1912) by E.C. Bentley.

* Routley, Erik. *The Puritan Pleasures of the Detective Story* (item 64), pp. 129-145.

Argues that Sayers started a fad for aristocratic detectives with Lord Peter Wimsey and that she excels in the creation of memorable secondary characters and evocative settings. In her best stories the humor, tension, and natural dialog help to prove that style can be achieved without sacrificing the detective element.

1589. Sayers, Dorothy L. "*Gaudy Night.*" *Titles to Fame.* Edited by Denys K. Roberts. London: Thomas Nelson, 1937. Reprinted *Art of the Mystery Story* (item 35), pp. 208-221.

Sayers contends that she tried to write a detective novel that was more a novel of manners than a crossword puzzle and that she got nearer her ideal with each book.

1590. Simonds, Katharine. "Bloodhound into Bridegroom." *Saturday Review* 18 (3 September 1938): 14.

Argues that Sayers has become so obsessed with the character of Peter Wimsey that sentiment is overshadowing the detection in her Wimsey stories and novels.

1591. Soloway, Sara L. "Dorothy Sayers: Novelist." Ph.D. dissertation, University of Kentucky, 1971.

Maintains that the Wimsey novels may be considered as serious literature because they "successfully combine detection with moral and human concerns."

1592. Stock, R.D., and Barbara Stock. "The Agents of Evil and Justice in the Novels of Dorothy L. Sayers." *As Her Whimsey Took Her* (item 1574), pp. 14-22.

Argues that Sayers was a moralist who was interested
in detective fiction as an appropriate means of demonstrating the conflict between good and evil. This conflict can be observed more clearly in her proponents
of good and evil whose characterizations become less
melodramatic as her series of novels progresses.

*   Swinnerton, Frank Arthur. "A Post-War Symptom." *The
        Georgian Literary Scene* (item 1458), pp. 315-323.

Contends that Sayers "writes with distinction" and
"invents with ingenuity," but she is too much the scholar
exercising her scholarship.

*   Symons, Julian. *Mortal Consequences* (item 74), pp. 107-
        110, 128-129.

Although Symons concedes that Sayers's work has merit,
largely because of her incisive mind and wide reading
in mystery literature and her careful craftsmanship,
he argues that she produced long, pretentious, boring
books with stereotyped characters.

1593.   Tillinghast, Richard. "Dorothy L. Sayers: Murder and
        Whimsy." *New Republic* 175 (31 July 1976): 30-31.

Argues that Sayers's novels are a hybrid, "the mystery-
romance." Contends that she is weak on plots but strong
on atmosphere and characterization. Wimsey is "vulnerable
to the point of instability," and his life is not complete until he is accepted by Harriet Vane.

1594.   Tischler, Nancy M. *Dorothy L. Sayers: A Pilgrim Soul.*
        Atlanta, Ga.: John Knox, 1980.

Published too late for annotation. *Publishers Weekly*
states that "the emphasis is on the woman as pilgrim,"
but the detective novels are examined.

*   Watson, Colin. *Snobbery with Violence* (item 78), pp.
        146-148, 153-156, 160-162.

Contends that although Sayers was a snob she was also
an accomplished writer of detective fiction.

SHAFFER, ANTHONY. See PETER ANTONY

SHAFFER, PETER. See PETER ANTONY

SHANNON, DELL. See ELIZABETH LININGTON

SHEPHERD, JOHN. See W.T. BALLARD

SHIEL, M.P. (1865-1947). Sometimes shared a joint pseudonym
with Louis Tracy (1863-1923): Gordon Holmes

1595. MacLaren-Ross, J. "The Strange Realm of M.P. Shiel."
       London Magazine 4 (September 1964): 76-84.

       MacLaren-Ross surveys the works of Shiel, briefly
       analyzing three stories in *Prince Zaleski* that could
       be "roughly classified" as detective. Contends that they
       show some influence of Poe and notes that in two of
       the stories the detective solves the case by pure
       reasoning, without even meeting the participants.

1596. Morse, A. Reynolds. *The Works of M.P. Shiel: A Study
       in Bibliography.* Los Angeles: Fantasy Publishing,
       1948. 163pp.

       In the introduction Morse comments on Shiel's work
       as a whole, but most of the book is a primary bibliog-
       raphy of the various editions of Shiel's novels, and
       his contributions to periodicals and newspapers. There
       is also a short list of secondary sources and a short
       autobiographical note by Shiel.

1597. Moskowitz, Samuel. "The World, the Devil, and M.P.
       Shiel." *Explorers of the Infinite: Shapers of Science
       Fiction.* New York: World, 1963, pp. 142-156.

       Contains a short dismissal of Shiel's detective fic-
       tion as a "pastiche" of Poe and Doyle.

*   Murch, A.E. *The Development of the Detective Novel*
       (item 51), pp. 147-149.

       Contends that Shiel's detective, Prince Zaleski, is
       the "quintessence of the inductive, analytical reason-
       er ... the detective of the intelligensia," and that
       Zaleski's most exotic and striking eccentricities were
       possibly due to Shiel's desire to make his detective as
       different as possible from Conan Doyle's Sherlock Holmes,
       then in his first flush of popularity.

1598. Welby, Thomas Earle. "M.P. Shiel." *Back Numbers.* New
       York: Richard R. Smith, 1930, pp. 98-102.

The chief merits of the tales of Shiel are "the largeness of the central idea and the flaming romanticism of the style." They do not depend on mere ingenuity.

SIMENON, GEORGES (1903-   )

1599.   Austin, Richard. "Simenon's 'Maigret' and Adler." *Adam International Review* no. 340-342 (1970): 45-50.

Contends that Simenon's view of life is much like that of psychologist Alfred Adler. "Man is to [Simenon], as he was to Adler, master of his own fate." Simenon's tragic view of love is, however, quite different from Adler's.

1600.   Becker, Lucille Frackman. *Georges Simenon*. Boston: Twayne, 1977. 171pp.

Argues that Simenon "transformed the rules and techniques of the detective novel and used it ... to express the most important themes of the twentieth century: guilt and innocence, alienation and solitude." Using frequent quotations, also analyzes such themes as "the clan," the "identity of opposites," and "salvation through paternity."

1601.   Bishop, John Peale. "Georges Simenon." *New Republic* 104 (10 March 1941): 345-346. Reprinted *Collected Essays of John Peale Bishop*. Edited by Edmund Wilson. New York: Scribners, 1948, pp. 359-362.

Contends that Simenon is a serious writer, "serious in a way that Conan Doyle could never have dreamed of being." Simenon's detective fiction is one with real, convincing, credible characters, but he carefully observes the conventions of the genre.

1602.   Bode, Elroy. "The World on Its Own Terms: A Brief for Steinbeck, Miller, and Simenon." *Southwest Review* 53 (Autumn 1968): 406-416.

Argues that "reality" is the key word to explain the art of Simenon. Praises his style and creation of atmosphere.

1603.   Boileau, Pierre. "Quelque Chose de Change dans le Roman Policier." *Simenon* (item 1630), pp. 190-192.

Argues that Simenon goes beyond the traditional detective story plot of a crime, an investigation, and a solution. Through the eyes of Maigret, his protagonist, Simenon sees these characters in all their humanity.

1604. Brophy, Brigid. "Jules et Georges." *New Statesman* 67 (10 April 1964): 566-568. Reprinted as "Simenon." *Don't Never Forget: Collected Views and Reviews.* New York: Holt, Rinehart and Winston, 1967, pp. 145-149.

Argues that *The Train* is a literary masterpiece in which Simenon uses his favorite method of exact, particular descriptions of people and settings together with one of his favorite themes (personal moral failure contrasted with national moral collapse) to evoke the fall of France in 1940.

*   Cawelti, John. G. "The Art of the Classical Detective Story." *Adventure, Mystery, and Romance* (item 150), pp. 125-131.

Argues that in Simenon's Maigret novels detection is grounded in the complexities of human behavior, thus bringing "the various interests of the classical formula into a highly effective unity."

1605. Cobb, Richard. "Maigret's Paris." *Listener* 82 (25 September 1969): 403-405.

"Simenon's endless attraction is his sensitive rendering of atmosphere, his feeling for locality, the acuity of his social observation."

1606. Collins, Carvel. "The Art of Fiction IX: Georges Simenon." *Paris Review* no. 9 (1955): 71-90. Reprinted as "Georges Simenon." *Writers at Work: The Paris Review Interviews.* Edited by Malcolm Cowley. New York: Viking Press, 1958, pp. 143-160.

In this interview, which is often referred to in Simenon criticism, Simenon describes his method of writing and states that his novels are about characters pushed to their limit and that two of his primary themes are communication and escape. He says that his detective novels bear the same relationship to his other novels that a sketch bears to a painting.

1607. Courtine, R.J. "Simenon ou l'Appetit de Maigret." *Simenon* (item 1630), pp. 204-219.

Argues that Simenon is, among other things, a true gastronome, and that the many culinary traditions of

France are represented in his work. Many important conversations in his novels take place around the dinner
table.

1608. Debray-Ritzen, Pierre. "Mon Maître Simenon." *Simenon*
       (item 1630), pp. 59-68.

       Argues that though Simenon's characters may often be
       pathological cases, they are presented as human beings,
       not as psychological subjects. In Simenon, there is
       harmony between the visceral brain ("cerveau ancien")
       and the human brain ("cerveau nouveau").

1609. Deniker, Professor. "Georges Simenon, Clinician de l'Ame."
       Simenon (item 1630), pp. 69-70.

       Argues that Simenon unveils the psychic evolution
       of his characters through the course of his work. These
       characters are often enigmatic, and Simenon withholds
       the full truth about them until his denouement.

1610. Dubois, Jacques. "Simenon et la Déviance." *Littérature*
       (University of Paris) 1 (1971): 62-72.

       States that individuals who deviate from the norm of
       their groups are important in Simenon. Examines six
       novels.

1611. Dubourg, Maurice. "Géographie de Simenon." *Simenon* (item
       1630), pp. 139-156.

       In an analysis of the geographical settings of
       Simenon's works (both French and exotic locales), argues
       that Simenon's own very extensive experience as a trav-
       eller is reflected in the authenticity of these back-
       drops.

1612. Dubourg, Maurice. "Maigret & Co.: The Detectives of
       the Simenon Agency." [Translated by Francis M. Nevins,
       Jr., from the essay published in the December 1969
       Mystère-Magazine.] *Armchair Detective* 4 (January 1971):
       79-86.

       Dubourg traces the development of the character of
       Maigret through several books Simenon wrote before the
       Maigret series.

1613. Duperray, Jean. "Au Nom du Père." *Simenon* (item 1630),
       pp. 99-129.

In an analysis of familial relationships in Simenon, argues that individual members of the family often live in solitude. There is little love or communication between them.

* Eames, Hugh. "Jules Maigret—Georges Simenon." *Sleuths, Inc.* (item 30), pp. 48-97.

Contends that "among problem solvers in criminal fiction, Jules Maigret seems the most original" and most enlightened, partly because of his ability "to identify himself, sympathetically and intuitively, with the victim."

1614. Eisinger, Erica M. "Maigret and Women: La Maman and La Putain." *Journal of Popular Culture* 12 (Summer 1978): pp. 52-60.

The French detective novel is by, for, and about men, with women relegated to minor roles. Simenon is "the champion of men," and in his work women represent either the mother or the whore.

1615. Fallois, Bernard de. *Simenon*. Paris: Gallimard, 1961. 305pp.

Reportedly this book is regarded by Simenon as the best study of his work.

1616. Frank, Nino. "Hypothese à Propos de Maigret." *Simenon* (item 1630), pp. 193-196.

Argues that Maigret is, in reality, Simenon, who uses his protagonist to examine genuine, sympathetic human beings.

1617. Freustie, Jean. "Une Petite Tente au Milieu du Jardin." *Simenon* (item 1630), pp. 52-58.

Argues that solitude is the dominant theme of both *La Prison* and *Il y a Encore des Noisetiers*. The destiny of the major character in each novel (Alain Poitaud and François Perret-Latour) is fulfilled.

1618. Galligan, Edward L. "Simenon's Mosaic of Small Novels." *South Atlantic Quarterly* 66 (1967): 534-543.

States that the Maigret stories reveal the basic qualities of the mind of Simenon. Nearly all are "fables demonstrating the ways of the creative, or intuitive intelligence" and are not "mere mystery stories." The effort to understand is crucial to these works.

1619.   "The Geography of Simenon." *Times Literary Supplement*
        12 December 1968, pp. 1397-1399.

        Simenon's chief virtue is his "sensitive rendering of
        atmosphere." His plots are, however, weak.

1620.   Grella, George. "Simenon and Maigret." *Adam International
        Review* no. 328-330 (1969): 54-61.

        Argues that the detective Maigret represents the
        creative artist. He "must get inside the skins of other
        human beings" to solve crimes just as a writer must do
        to create fiction.

1621.   Grunwald, Henry Anatole. "World's Most Prolific Novelist."
        Life 45 (3 November 1958): 95+.

        The message of virtually all his stories is that
        escape is not possible. Points out that "corpulent and
        middle-aged" Maigret is "all wrong for a fictional
        detective." Much biographical material.

1622.   Harris, Lis. "Maigret le Flâneur." *New Yorker* 55 (2
        April 1979): 122-124.

        The setting and atmosphere of a Simenon story are so
        attractively described that they are nearly characters
        in their own right. Also, Simenon's world is neatly
        divided into decent people and bad ones.

1623.   Henry, Gilles. *Commissaire Maigret, Qui Êtes-vous?* Paris:
        Plon, 1977. 284pp.

        Not available for annotation but listed in the *Arm-
        chair Detective* bibliography for 1977.

1624.   Highsmith, Patricia. "Review." *New York Times Book Review*
        16 March 1969, pp. 5, 50.

        In this review of *Simenon in Court* (item 1642) High-
        smith points out that Simenon takes the individual out
        of society, which is the reason his novels "do not and
        will not date."

1625.   Jacobs, Jay. "Simenon's Mosaic." *Reporter* 32 (14 January
        1965): 38-40.

        Simenon is "essentially a fine novelist." His early
        working schedule gave him a rapid pace and clean style.
        Disdains the "bizarre twist" and operates by understand-
        ing how an ordinary human might be driven into committing
        a crime.

1626. Juin, Hubert. "Un Roman Ininterrompu." *Simenon* (item 1630), pp. 77-88.

Argues that Simenon's work is a single, uninterrupted novel. His characters, particularly Maigret, go through "solitude, the burden of living, and dispossession of self," but through it all, they have a capacity to survive.

1627. Kanters, Robert. "Sur la Vieillesse et sur la Mort." *Simenon* (item 1630), pp. 71-76.

Argues that Simenon's depiction of old age is an important element in his work.

1628. Koskimies, Rafael. "Novelists' Thoughts About Their Art." *Neuphilologische Mitteilungen* 57 (1956): 148-159.

Simenon states in *Les Memoires de Maigret* that "only by selecting, arranging, and simplifying can reality be made 'believable' and 'real.'"

1629. Lacassin, Francis. "Simenon et la Fuge Initiatique." *Simenon* (item 1630), pp. 158-183.

Argues that the fugue is an important metaphor in much of Simenon's work. Analyzes several novels which are composed of a prelude (usually consisting of some sort of humiliation suffered by a major character); an escape, which is a transition stage; and the return of the character, more self-assured, to his original world.

1630. Lacassin, Francis, and Gilbert Sigaux, eds. *Simenon*. Paris: Plon, 1973. 481pp.

A collection (in French) of essays on Simenon's work, texts by Simenon, portions of correspondence between Simenon and André Gide, and a bibliography. The critical essays are annotated separately.

* Lambert, Gavin. "Night Vision: Georges Simenon." *The Dangerous Edge* (item 42), pp. 171-209.

Argues that his mother's dread of poverty and his own ambivalence about middle-class values influenced Simenon's mystery writings, which are designed to show people pushed to their limit. Simenon's strong point is sustained concentration on a single character.

1631. Lewis, C. Day. "In Praise of Simenon." *Listener* 79 (8
       February 1968): 177.

       Describes Simenon's working method and states that
       "the stories are as streamlined as the process which
       makes them."

1632. Mambrino, Jean. "Le Mot du Coffre." *Simenon* (item 1630),
       pp. 23-51.

       Argues that Simenon's novels, taken as a whole, con-
       stitute the true Simenon Novel. Analyzes several re-
       curring images: rain and fog, the sea, sunlight, church
       bells ringing on Sunday, and human hands in water.

1633. Mauriac, Claude. "Georges Simenon et le Secret des
       Hommes." *Preuves* no. 67 (1956): 79-85. Reprinted as
       "Georges Simenon." *La Littérature Contemporaine.*
       Paris: Albin Michel, 1958, pp. 135-151. Translated
       as *New Literature.* New York: George Braziller, 1959,
       pp. 133-150.

       Contends that the themes of guilt and alienation are
       found in all Simenon's work. Also gives examples of
       sensuousness connected with anxiety.

1634. Messac, Ralph. "Georges Simenon: Romancier-Nez." *Simenon*
       (item 1630), pp. 130-138.

       Argues that olfactory imagery is an important element
       in Simenon's work. Analyzes odors relating to cooking,
       the sick and the dying, and sex and humanity.

1635. Mortimer, John. "The Great Detective." *Spectator* 2 April
       1965, p. 443.

       Contends that Maigret is an "archetypal middle-class
       deity" and is a bit too dispassionate.

1636. Narcejac, Thomas. *The Art of Simenon.* London: Routledge
       and Kegan Paul, 1952. 178pp. [First published in French
       as *Le Cas Simenon.*]

       Argues that Simenon's huge volume of work is "a per-
       fectly co-ordinated whole" and that his detective stories
       differ from the norm in that they emphasize character
       over plot. Narcejac emphasizes such concerns of Simenon
       as sympathy and conquest of oneself.

1637. Narcejac, Thomas. "Le Point Omega." *Simenon* (item 1630),
       pp. 18-22.

Argues that Simenon is more a painter than a writer
and contends that all of his important characters
eventually ask the existential question "Who am I?"

1638.   Nicolson, Harold. "Marginal Comment." *Spectator* 23
        March 1951, p. 380. Reprinted as "Simenon and Maigret."
        Spectator Harvest. Selected by the Editors of *Spectator*.
        London: Hamish Hamilton, 1952, pp. 56-59.

        Contends that Simenon is "frequently impossible" but
        never improbable and that the character of Maigret is
        "so vivid and convincing" that other fictional detectives
        seem to be "mere puppets."

1639.   "Novels by the Hundred." *Time* 66 (15 August 1955): 76.

        In the context of a review of *Destinations* (two novels
        in one volume) discusses Simenon's stature as a mystery
        writer (his fans think of him as a real novelist with
        a special outlook on life) and his working methods,
        which are swift and simple. Simenon does not believe
        that fast writing is necessarily bad writing. Simenon
        lives and writes according to the maxim: "Live joyously
        and be very careful not to take yourselves too seriously."

1640.   Oberbeck, S.K. "Simenon Maker." *Newsweek* 75 (27 April
        1970): 102-103.

        Simenon has written 408 novels and has both popular
        and critical success. His chief character, Inspector
        Maigret, is "the minimal hero." The novels are contem-
        plative and eschew flamboyance and sensation.

1641.   Parinaud, André. *Connaissance de Georges Simenon*. Paris:
        Presses de la Cité, 1957. 416pp.

        Relates Simenon's life to his writing and maintains
        that much of his power as a novelist comes from his
        style, his ability to create an atmosphere with his plots,
        the psychological depth of his characters, and his
        penetrating philosophy.

*   Parsons, Luke. "Simenon and Chandler" (item 691).

        Because of their "serious purpose and ... relation-
        ship to life" the detective stories of Simenon and
        Chandler are literature.

1642.   Raymond, John. *Simenon in Court*. New York: Harcourt,
        Brace and World, 1969. 178pp.

Contends that Simenon is "one of the most poetic of living novelists" and in his best works "the most significant and least difficult writer of our time." Includes a short biographical section and analyses of several of the novels. Contends that generalizations about Simenon are difficult and states many of the "contradictions and paradoxes" of his work.

1643. Richter, Anne. *Georges Simenon et l'Homme Désintégré.* Brussels: La Renaissance du Livre, 1964. 113pp.

Studies the "disintegration" of modern man in the novels of Simenon.

1644. Ritzen, Quentin [pseudonym]. *Simenon: Avocat des Hommes.* Paris: Le Livre Contemporain, 1961.

Argues that an important theme in the work of Simenon is the consequence of uncovering truth. Also contends that Simenon is a spokesman for the ordinary person.

1645. Rolo, Charles J. "Simenon and Spillane." *New World Writings: First Mentor Selection.* New York: New American Library, 1952, pp. 234-245. Reprinted *Mass Culture: The Popular Arts in America.* Edited by Bernard Rosenberg and David Manning White. Glencoe, Ill.: Free Press, 1957, pp. 165-175.

Argues that Simenon's Maigret, whose goal is *understanding* the criminal, reflects the psychoanalytic outlook of the modern age.

1646. Schraiber, Eleonora. "Georges Simenon et la Littérature Russe." *Simenon* (item 1630), pp. 184-189.

Tracing the influence of Chekov and Dostoevsky in Simenon's work, argues that many of his novels are sociopsychological, reflecting Simenon's view of man as a struggling being who refuses to give up the struggle. Though for Simenon "to be a man is a difficult task," his viewpoint remains basically optimistic.

1647. Sigaux, Gilbert. "Lire Simenon." *Simenon* (item 1630), pp. 13-17.

Argues that Simenon's work is a galaxy of portraits which constitute a picture of man. His purpose is not to ask who is the murderer; rather, Simenon asks where is man going and what is the meaning of his adventure?

1648. Steinhoff, William R. "Georges Simenon: The Most Popular Novelist in the World." *Michigan Quarterly Review* 2 (25 April 1963): 85-89.

Argues that Simenon's chief accomplishment is the creation of a protagonist of a detective story who is ordinary and modern rather than an old-fashioned hero. Maigret is appealing to readers because he is "extraordinarily human."

1649. Stéphane, Roger. *Le Dossier Simenon*. Paris: Robert Laffont, 1961. 142pp.

Not available for annotation but recommended by some critics.

1650. Sullerot, Evelyne. "Les Hommes, les Hommes." *Simenon* (item 1630), pp. 89-98.

In an analysis of the themes of sexuality and virility in Simenon's work, argues that while his characters may confront their concept of virility, true manhood need not inevitably be demonstrated through the sexual act, as evidenced by his depiction of Maigret.

1651. Symons, Julian. "Compulsion." *New York Review of Books* 25 (12 October 1978): 34-37.

"Simenon is not in the ordinary sense of the words a detective story writer at all." He lacks interest in the apparatus of clues and deduction; Maigret "has no method but operates by instinct." Symons regards the Maigret tales as second class compared to the rest of Simenon's work, though he contends that Maigret himself is the most fully realized character in all of Simenon's work.

*   Symons, Julian. "Simenon and Maigret." *Mortal Consequences* (item 74), pp. 145-150.

Argues that Simenon's preeminence in detective fiction is due largely to his creation of Maigret and other memorable characters as well as the ambience of the novels.

1652. Thoorens, Léon. *Qui Êtes-Vous Georges Simenon?* Limbourg, France: Gerard, 1959. 159pp.

Observes the importance of rebellion and flight in the work of Simenon.

1653.   Vandromme, Pol. *Georges Simenon*. Brussels: P. de Méyère,
        1962. 80pp.

        This short study concentrates on the "heroes" in
        Simenon's work and their conflict with the world in which
        they find themselves.

1654.   Whiteley, J. Stuart. "Simenon: The Shadow and the Self.
        An Interview with Georges Simenon." *Mystery and
        Detection Annual 1973* (item 17), pp. 221-236.

        This is a report of a television interview of Simenon
        by two British medical experts. At the end Whiteley, a
        psychiatrist, notes that the interview became a psychi-
        atric session concerned chiefly with Simenon's vacilla-
        tion between freedom and restraint. Whiteley ascribes
        the Maigret books to the restrained part of Simenon's
        psyche.

1655.   Wolf, Jürgen. "Technik der Schilderung und des Romanauf-
        baus bei Georges Simenon." *Die Neueren Sprachen* no. 11
        (November 1969): 548-551.

        Argues that Simenon is different from practitioners
        of the *nouveau roman*. Though his stories are centered
        in the plot, he is also concerned with characterization
        and with the attempts of his detective to put himself
        in the criminal's position.

1656.   Young, Trudee. *Georges Simenon: A Checklist of His
        "Maigret" and Other Mystery Novels and Short Stories
        in French and English Translations*. Metuchen, N.J.:
        Scarecrow Press, 1977. 153pp.

        A primary bibliography of the books Simenon published
        under his own name.

SIMPSON, HELEN (1897-1940)

1657.   Sayers, Dorothy L. "Helen Simpson." *Fortnightly* 149
        (January 1941): 54-59.

        Chiefly concerned with Simpson's personality but does
        state that her fiction was usually stimulated by histori-
        cal or personal fact, a characteristic which sometimes
        gave it an air of remoteness.

SIMS, GEORGE. See PAUL CAIN

SJÖWALL, MAJ. See PER WAHLÖÖ

SMITH, ERNEST BRAMAH. See ERNEST BRAMAH

SNOW, C(HARLES) P(ERCY) (1905-1980)

1658. Barzun, Jacques, and Wendell Hertig Taylor. Preface to
       Death Under Sail, by Charles Percy Snow. New York:
       Garland Publishing, 1976. Also printed in *A Book of
       Prefaces* (item 22), pp. 99-100.

       Contends that one of the chief interests of the novel
       is the way Snow skillfully constructs the plot and
       manipulates "material and psychological clues."

1659. Cooper, William. *C.P. Snow*. London: Longman Group, 1971.
       39pp.

       Argues that *Death Under Sail* is a "remarkable beginning"
       for Snow's career and that it is different from most
       other detective stories in that "the plot grows out of
       the characters rather than the characters out of the
       plot."

1660. Greacen, Robert. *The World of C.P. Snow*. London: Scorpion
       Press, 1962, pp. 20-21.

       States that *Death Under Sail* is an ordinary detective
       novel but says that it shows high spirits. Also quotes
       William Cooper's comment on characterization (item 1659).

1661. Mayne, Richard. "The Club Armchair." *Encounter* 21
       (November 1963): 76-82.

       In a general discussion of Snow's fiction Mayne notes
       that the world of "powerful, well-thought-of, rather
       stately" men of Snow's non-detective novels is like
       that of pre-war detective stories. Points out that Snow's
       first published novel, *Death Under Sail*, is a detective
       story, and that it shares many characteristics with
       Snow's later works.

1662. Rabinovitz, Rubin. "C.P. Snow as Novelist." *The Reaction
       Against Experiment in the English Novel, 1950-1960*.
       New York: Columbia University Press, 1967, pp. 196-211.

       Treats *Death Under Sail* primarily as a foreshadowing
       of themes and stylistic devices, especially suspense,
       Snow was later to use in his non-mystery novels.

*   Shibuk, Charles. "Three British Experiments from the
       Mainstream" (item 1262).

       Contends that *Death Under Sail* is a formal detective
       story with excellent writing, plotting, and character-
       ization.

1663. Shusterman, David. *C.P. Snow.* Boston: Twayne, 1975,
       pp. 41-45.

       Quotes Cooper's comment on characterization (item
       1659) and argues that the novel has a number of touches
       which are typical of Snow's later (non-detective) works.

1664. Snow, C.P. "Author's Note." *Death Under Sail.* London:
       Heinemann, 1959, pp. vii-viii.

       In his preface to this slightly revised version of
       his 1932 detective novel, Snow calls the book "a
       stylized, artificial detective story very much in the
       manner of the day." It was fun to write, he notes, but
       he decided to devote his time to "proper" novels. He
       believes the detective story could be more like a
       realistic novel.

1665. Thale, Jerome. *C.P. Snow.* New York: Scribners, 1965,
       pp. 8-9.

       States that *Death Under Sail* "was not an especially
       promising beginning" of Snow's career as a novelist
       but is a good example of the highly stylized detective
       story of its time (1932). States that it has few charac-
       teristics of Snow's later (non-detective) novels.

SOUTAR, ANDREW (1879-1941)

1666. Soutar, Andrew. "Meet Phineas Spinnet." *Meet the Detective*
      (item 45), pp. 106-115.

      Admits his close identification with Spinnet, whom he
      says created himself and is not a composite of different
      people, a "method," Soutar contends, that is a dangerous
      one for an author to adopt.

SPAIN, JOHN. See CLEVE F. ADAMS

SPILLANE, MICKEY (1918-   ). Series character: Mike Hammer

1667.   Banks, R. Jeff. "Spillane and the Critics." *Armchair Detective* 12 (Fall 1979): 300-307.

Contends that most critics limit their attention to Spillane's first seven books and only one of his detective heroes. Banks singles out as a chief example John Cawelti (item 1670) and attempts to refute his contentions about Spillane's violence and the motivations of his detective, Mike Hammer.

1668.   Banks, R. Jeff. "Spillane's Anti-Establishmentarian Heroes." *Dimensions of Detective Fiction* (item 43), pp. 124-139.

Argues that Spillane's heroes' distrust of the Establishment is shown by the conflict between the willingness of his heroes to circumvent the "good policeman," destroy the "bad policeman," and to save the country in spite of officials or agencies that are not acting in the national interests.

1669.   Barson, Michael. "Just a Writer Working for a Buck." *Armchair Detective* 12 (Fall 1979): 293-299.

Contends that Spillane's work has been unduly neglected and derided by the critics and that more than any other mystery writer, Spillane has shown the dark side of the American character and experience. An interview with Spillane is appended.

1670.   Cawelti, John G. "The Spillane Phenomenon." *University of Chicago Magazine* 61 (March/April 1969). Reprinted *Journal of Popular Culture* 3 (Summer 1969): 9-22. Revised version published as part of "Hammett, Chandler, and Spillane." *Adventure, Mystery, and Romance* (item 150), pp. 183-196.

Argues that it is not so much the emphasis on sex and violence which makes Spillane so popular but rather it is his near evangelical denunciations of corruption and immorality and the extra-legal punishment of evildoers. States that the books are "atrocious" by literary and artistic standards.

1671.   Cowley, Malcolm. "Sex Murder Incorporated." *New Republic* 126 (11 February 1952): 17-18.

Cowley states that the popularity of Spillane's "so-
called detective stories," the ingredients of which are
sex, sadism, and some masochism, frightens him: "I am
not used to having Jack the Ripper presented as a model
for emulation." States that Spillane's style is "a mixture of Raymond Chandler and the hard-boiled comic
books" and that his stories and violent criminals are
"part of the same moral configuration."

1672.   "Dames and Death." *Harpers* 204 (May 1952): 99-101.

Argues that in Spillane's books "the element of sex
is secondary and is fulfilled only through violence,
no other way."

1673.   Fetterley, Judith. "Beauty as the Beast: Fantasy and
        Fear in *I, the Jury.*" *Journal of Popular Culture* 8
        (Spring 1975): pp. 775-782.

Argues that underlying the novel is the belief that
femininity is "simply a performance that women put on
in order to pursue goals of their own which are distinctly
threatening to men." Thus Charlotte Manning can be
both the "ultimate sex object" and the "ultimate killer."

1674.   Johnston, R.W. "Death's Fair-Haired Boy." *Life* 32
        (23 June 1952): 79+.

In a long article mainly devoted to Spillane's
personal life and the immense popularity of his books,
Johnston suggests that Spillane's fantasy world of sex
and violence is appealing to many people in the post-
war world who are "baffled by problems that seem too
big to solve." Johnston also states that Spillane has
neither style nor taste.

1675.   La Farge, Christopher. "Mickey Spillane and His Bloody
        Hammer." *Saturday Review* 37 (6 November 1954): 11-12,
        54-59. Reprinted *Mass Culture: The Popular Arts in
        America*. Edited by Bernard Rosenberg and David
        Manning White. Glencoe, Ill.: Free Press, 1957, pp.
        176-185.

Argues that the theme of Spillane's novels--a man
should try to cure whatever seems wrong by whatever
means he chooses--is the logical conclusion of McCarthy-
ism. The writing is "grotesque" and "the worst sort of
lurid." La Farge concludes by asking, "What has come to
our country that it can support and applaud these
attitudes?"

*   Palmer, Jerry. "The Hero: Alone, Sexy, Competitive."
         Thrillers (item 56), pp. 24-39.

         Argues that Spillane and Fleming "seem to exhaust the
         possibilities of sex in the thriller" by insisting on
         the isolation of the hero whose relationship with women
         to whom he is drawn must be competitive "in the sense
         that the hero has to prove that he is *above* what they
         can offer: the erotic love that characterizes normal
         adult relationships."

*   Rolo, Charles J. "Simenon and Spillane" (item 1645).

         Argues that Spillane's Mike Hammer appeals to people
         who feel frustrated because an individual is helpless
         against such great evils as communism and organized
         crime.

*   Ruehlmann, William. *Saint with a Gun* (item 65), pp.
         90-99.

         Contends that Spillane's detective, Mike Hammer, acts
         from private motivations and that he embodies the
         "middle-class man's suspicion of government and faith
         in the will of 'the people.'" Hammer's adventures satisfy
         the public's desire for vengeance.

1676.   "The Thriller Writer Mickey Spillane Appears with His
         Wife on the 'Parkinson' Show." *Listener* 89 (12 April
         1973): 481-483.

         In a short interview Spillane says that he writes only
         for money, that his early work as a crime reporter gave
         him material for his books, that women are all sex ob-
         jects to him, and that sex and violence in his books
         are like exclamation points.

1677.   Weibel, Kay. "Mickey Spillane as Fifties Phenomenon."
         Dimensions of Detective Fiction (item 43), pp. 114-
         123.

         Argues that Spillane in his novels reflected the
         cultural attitudes of the 1950s in his portrayal of
         woman as both mother and sex object.

1678.   Wylie, Philip. "The Crime of Mickey Spillane." *Good
         Housekeeping* 140 (February 1955): 54-55, 207-209.

         Wylie cannot understand why millions are reading these
         terribly written books about "brutality, bestiality,
         and dirty sex," in which pain is glorified as a means

of revenge. In each book are "a dozen or so chillingly antisocial speeches," and the culprit is punished, not by the law, but by Hammer, who makes himself sole judge of right and wrong. Wylie also objects to the insulting implication that bestiality is attractive to women and concludes that "the crime of Mickey Spillane ... is that he stands *in contempt of humanity.*"

STARK, RICHARD. See DONALD E. WESTLAKE

STEIN, AARON MARC. See GEORGE BAGBY

STEVENSON, ROBERT LOUIS (1850-1894)

1679.   Borowitz, Albert. *Innocence and Arsenic: Studies in Crime and Literature.* New York: Harper and Row, 1977, pp. 26-32.

Argues that the split personality of Stevenson's Dr. Jekyll was based in part on William "Deacon" Brodie, an 18th-century resident of Edinburgh. Brodie was a respected carpenter by day and a thief by night.

1680.   Buitenhuis, Elspeth MacGregor. "Fractions of a Man: Doubles in Victorian Fiction." Ph.D. dissertation, McGill University, 1970.

Argues that the popularity of the theme of the split personality exemplifies the schizophrenia of the Victorian age. Analyzes Dr. Jekyll and Mr. Hyde as a prime example of this genre.

1681.   Butts, Dennis. *R.L. Stevenson.* New York: Walck, 1966. 72pp.

Argues that although *Treasure Island* is first and foremost a historical romance, it "does say something about the condition of man's nature."

1682.   Chesterton, G.K. *Robert Louis Stevenson.* London: Hodder and Stoughton, 1927. 259pp.

Defends Stevenson against the critics of the day, arguing that his work is well written and profoundly moral. His defect as a writer "was that he simplified so much that he lost some of the complexity of real life."

1683.   Daiches, David. *Robert Louis Stevenson*. Norfolk, Conn.:
        New Directions, 1947. 196pp.

        Arguing that Stevenson's writings are worth serious
        examination, Daiches contends that Stevenson's mystery
        stories combine his love of adventure with his sense
        of character and atmosphere. Major commentary on *Treasure
        Island*, *The Wrecker*, and *Kidnapped* is included.

1684.   Egan, Joseph J. "Artistic Design and the Ambivalence
        of Reality: Craft and Idea in the Fiction of Robert
        Louis Stevenson." Ph.D. dissertation, University of
        Notre Dame, 1965.

        Analyzes *Treasure Island*, "The Body Snatcher," "Mark-
        heim," and *Dr. Jekyll and Mr. Hyde*, arguing that Steven-
        son depicts his characters as having contradictory emo-
        tions "in order to emphasize the ambiguous nature of
        good and evil in human life."

1685.   Egan, Joseph J. "Grave Sites and Moral Death: A Reexamina-
        tion of Stevenson's 'The Body Snatcher.'" *English
        Literature in Transition (1880-1920)* 13 (1970): 9-15.

        Argues that "The Body Snatcher" has been unjustly
        criticized for its use of the supernatural for shock
        effect. The story "concerns itself with the mythic pre-
        sentation of man's moral-psychological predicament."

1686.   Egan, Joseph J. "'Markheim': A Drama of Moral Psychology."
        Nineteenth-Century Fiction 20 (1966): 377-384.

        Argues that Stevenson intended to write more than a
        mere short story. "Markheim" is a "moral fable in the
        form of an exploration of his main character's mind."

1687.   Egan, Joseph J. "The Relationship of Theme and Art in
        The Strange Case of Dr. Jekyll and Mr. Hyde." *English
        Literature in Transition (1880-1920)* 9 (1966): 28-32.

        Denies that Jekyll and Hyde are total opposites. Dr.
        Jekyll himself is both good and evil. This theme is re-
        inforced by Stevenson's imagery, particularly those
        symbols involving houses.

1688.   Eigner, Edwin M. "The Double in the Fiction of R.L.
        Stevenson." Ph.D. dissertation, State University of
        Iowa, 1963.

        Analyzes *Treasure Island*, *Dr. Jekyll and Mr. Hyde*,
        and *The Wrecker*, relating Stevenson's fiction to the

19th-century literary tradition of the doppelgänger.
Argues that Stevenson uses this device to show the in-
compatibility between conscientiousness and action.

1689. Eigner, Edwin M. *Robert Louis Stevenson and the Romantic
       Tradition.* Princeton, N.J.: Princeton University Press,
       1966. 258pp.

       Comments on *Kidnapped,* "Markheim," and *The Wrecker,*
       with an extended analysis of *Dr. Jekyll and Mr. Hyde.*
       Argues that Stevenson's fiction is in the tradition of
       the 19th-century prose romance.

1690. Girling, H.K. "The Strange Case of Dr. James and Mr.
       Stevenson." *Wascana Review* 3 (1968): 65-76.

       Argues that the moral allegory of duality in *Dr. Jekyll
       and Mr. Hyde* can be applied to "the duality of alterna-
       tive purposes--call them realistic and romantic--open
       to novelists." Seen in this light, Henry James, the
       realist, is Dr. Jekyll; Stevenson, the romantic, is Mr.
       Hyde.

1691. Gossman, Ann. "On the Knocking at the Gate in 'Markheim.'"
       Nineteenth-Century Fiction 17 (1963): 73-76.

       Contends that Stevenson was influenced by *Macbeth* and
       by DeQuincey's critical comments on the play. Argues
       that Stevenson uses the knocking at the door in the
       same way that Shakespeare used the knocking at the gate
       in *Macbeth*--he is telling the story from the point of
       view of the murderer, not the victim.

1692. McKenzie, Mary. "Experiments in Romance: Theory and
       Practice in the Fiction of Robert Louis Stevenson."
       Ph.D. dissertation, University of Toronto, 1974.

       Explores Stevenson's own literary theory, arguing that
       Treasure Island and *Dr. Jekyll and Mr. Hyde,* among other
       works, exemplify Stevenson's dictums about adhering to
       the truth while obeying "the ideal laws of the day-
       dream!" The result is romance, a genre at which Steven-
       son excelled.

1693. Miyoshi, Masao. "Dr. Jekyll and the Emergence of Mr.
       Hyde." *College English* 27 (1966): 470-474, 479-480.

       Argues that *Dr. Jekyll and Mr. Hyde* is worthy of close
       scrutiny. Notes the Hyde-like characteristics implicit
       in Dr. Jekyll's personality.

*   Murch, A.E. *The Development of the Detective Novel*
      (item 51), pp. 142-145.

      Contends that, although *The Wrecker* contains elements
      of the detective story, it is properly considered a tale
      of adventure. *The Wrong Box* is a parody of French detec-
      tive fiction.

1694. Saposnik, Irving S. "The Anatomy of *Dr. Jekyll and Mr.
      Hyde*." *Studies in English Literature, 1500-1900* 11
      (1970): 715-731.

      Argues that critical analysis of *Dr. Jekyll and Mr.
      Hyde* has been simplistic; that the story is not merely
      a "myth of good-evil antithesis," but rather "an imagina-
      tive exploration of social and moral dualism." The
      central issue in the story is the necessity for moral
      flexibility in a society that dictates moral rigidity.

1695. Saposnik, Irving S. "Aspects of Evil in the Works of
      Robert Louis Stevenson." Ph.D. dissertation, Univer-
      sity of California, Berkeley, 1965.

      Emphasizes the Calvinist Christian basis of Stevenson's
      major works, including *Dr. Jekyll and Mr. Hyde*, *Treasure
      Island*, *Kidnapped*, and "Markheim." Argues that the
      various aspects of "moral cowardice" in Stevenson's
      characters stem from Stevenson's belief in man's inherent
      evil.

1696. Saposnik, Irving S. *Robert Louis Stevenson*. New York:
      Twayne, 1974. 164pp.

      Surveys Stevenson's literary career, with commentary
      on all of his mystery fiction. *Dr. Jekyll and Mr. Hyde*
      is an apt metaphor for the "inescapable sense of division"
      that haunted Victorian man.

1697. Saposnik, Irving S. "Stevenson's 'Markheim': A Fictional
      'Christmas Sermon.'" *Nineteenth-Century Fiction* 21
      (1966): 277-282.

      Argues that the religious elements in "Markheim" are
      fictionalized versions of the ideas found in Stevenson's
      essay "A Christmas Sermon," which urges that the Christ-
      mas season be a time of self-examination. Markheim
      refuses to engage in this sort of self-examination and
      commits murder on Christmas Day.

1698.   Stern, G.B. *Robert Louis Stevenson*. London: Longmans,
        1952. 52pp.

        In this general survey of Stevenson's career the longest
        explications are given to *Treasure Island* and *Dr. Jekyll
        and Mr. Hyde*.

1699.   Swinnerton, Frank. *R.L. Stevenson: A Critical Study*.
        New York: George H. Doran, 1923. 195pp.

        Argues that Stevenson's writing evolved from romance
        to realism. His later work is superior to his early
        adventure stories.

1700.   Wallace, Irving. "The Real Dr. Jekyll and Mr. Hyde."
        *The Fabulous Originals: Lives of Extraordinary People
        Who Inspired Memorable Characters in Fiction*. New York:
        Knopf, 1955, pp. 126-171.

        Notes the fact that William "Deacon" Brodie, an 18th-
        century Scot, was the inspiration for Stevenson's story.
        Provides a detailed history of Brodie's activities and
        an account of the composition of Stevenson's story.

1701.   Watson, Harold F. *Coasts of Treasure Island: A Study of
        the Backgrounds and Sources for Robert Louis Stevenson's
        Romance of the Sea*. San Antonio, Tex.: Naylor, 1969.
        231pp.

        Studies the 19th-century nautical novel, citing
        Treasure Island as "an example," and in some sense "the
        culmination" of the genre.

STEWART, J.I.M. See MICHAEL INNES

STOCKTON, FRANK R. (1834-1902)

1702.   Bowen, Edwin W. "F.R. Stockton." *Sewanee Review* 11
        (October 1903): 474-478.

        Argues that Stockton is one of the most brilliant of
        American authors. States that his stories for adults are
        weak in plot and characterization but have many strengths:
        wit, dry humor, wholesome moral tone, and simple style.
        Observes that "The Lady or the Tiger?" is Stockton's
        best known short story but argues that "Rudder Grange"
        is possibly his best longer short story because of its
        simplicity and style.

1703. "Francis Richard Stockton." *Harpers Weekly* 46 (3 May 1902): 555.

Contends that Stockton was not a stylist but that his writing had a unique quality that is partly attributable to his ironic sense of humor.

1704. Griffin, Martin I., Jr. *Frank R. Stockton: A Critical Biography*. Philadelphia: University of Pennsylvania Press, 1939, pp. 64-70.

Argues that the epilogue of "The Lady or the Tiger?" raises it above the level of a trick to an "exposition of human strength and human frailty."

1705. Howells, William Dean. "Stockton and His Work." *Book Buyer* 20 (February 1900): 19-21.

Contends that Stockton writes amusing stories about wild capers performed with sobriety and that "his personality delights when other things somewhat fail."

1706. Mabie, Hamilton W. "Frank R. Stockton." *Book Buyer* 24 (June 1902): 355-357.

Reports that James Russell Lowell contends that Stockton's humor relies on the contrast between the extraordinary event and his modest style that gives it a "fresh, captivating quality."

1707. "A Stockton Memorial Sketch." *Bookman* 17 (July 1903): 448, 450.

States that Stockton's practical and inventive mind would probably have invented machines had it not invented plots.

1708. Werner, William L. "The Escapes of Frank Stockton." *Essays in Honor of A. Howry Espenshade*. New York: Thomas Nelson, 1937, pp. 21-45.

Contends that Stockton escaped from the poverty and restrictions of childhood into a fantasy-land which he created in his writing. Later, after the success of "The Lady or the Tiger?" made him financially independent, he escaped from writing by traveling and living in "fanciful houses."

STOUT, REX (1886-1975). Series characters: Nero Wolfe and
Archie Goodwin

1709. Baring-Gould, William S. *Nero Wolfe of West Thirty-Fifth
       Street: The Life and Times of America's Largest Private
       Detective*. New York: Viking Press, 1969. 203pp.

       Not an examination of the writing of Rex Stout but a
       "biography" of the character Nero Wolfe, written as if
       he were a real person.

1710. Barzun, Jacques, and Wendell Hertig Taylor. Preface to
       Too Many Cooks, by Rex Stout. New York: Garland Pub-
       lishing, 1976. Also printed in *A Book of Prefaces*
       (item 22), pp. 101-102.

       Contends that Stout's creation of Nero Wolfe and
       Archie Goodwin is a "classic partnership" that ranks
       with the Holmes-Watson association.

1711. Corbet, James J., and J. Susan Milton. "Who Killed the
       Cook?" *Mathematics Teacher* 71 (April 1978): 263-266.

       Uses mathematical probability theory to support the
       deduction of Nero Wolfe in *Too Many Cooks*. Done as an
       exercise to interest students in the concepts of prob-
       ability.

1712. Gerhardt, Mia I. "'Homicide West': Some Observations on
       the Nero Wolfe Stories of Rex Stout." *English Studies*
       49 (1968): 107-127.

       The device of having all the Nero Wolfe stories told
       in the first person by the character Archie Goodwin
       makes the books more lively and more convincing than
       would a third-person narrative. Like most detectives
       Wolfe is skeptical about the society in which he lives,
       but he is in many ways an old-fashioned romantic hero.

1713. Jaffe, Arnold. "Murder with Dignity." *New Republic* 177
       (30 July 1977): 41-43.

       Argues that Nero Wolfe embodies "social and philosoph-
       ical relativism."

1714. Johnston, Alva. "Alias Nero Wolfe." *New Yorker* 25 (16
       July 1949): 26-28, 33-38; 25 (23 July 1949): 30-34,
       39-43.

       In this long biographical profile of Rex Stout, John-
       ston makes a few observations on Stout's detective
       novels. He contends that the specialty of Nero Wolfe
       is detecting fallacies and that Stout uses his wide
       knowledge and experience without encumbering his stories

with "miscellaneous erudition." Stout, he states, is
like Wolfe in one respect--both are good debaters.

1715. Knight, Arden. "An Appreciation of Archie Goodwin."
       Armchair Detective 12 (Fall 1979): 328-329.

       Contends that Stout's creation of Archie Goodwin as
       Nero Wolfe's assistant is important because Goodwin's
       character "provides the underlying thread that not only
       is the basis for various subplots but also acts as the
       showpiece for Stout's own personal style and wit."

1716. Lochte, Richard S., II. "Who's Afraid of Nero Wolfe?"
       Armchair Detective 3 (July 1970): 211-214.

       A wide-ranging interview done in 1967 in which Stout
       gives his opinion of mysteries, Edmund Wilson's critic-
       ism of the genre, and the differences between British
       and American mystery writers.

1717. McAleer, John. Introduction to *Justice Ends at Home and
       Other Stories*, by Rex Stout. New York: Viking Press,
       1977, pp. ix-xxviii.

       Contends that one of Stout's favorite themes is the
       conflict between mind and heart and points out his
       commitment to an equitable, well-ordered society.

1718. McAleer, John. *Rex Stout: A Biography*. Boston: Little,
       Brown, 1977. 621pp.

       Argues that Stout's beginning as a writer in a wide
       range of genres laid the groundwork for his detective
       stories. Also contends that Stout's novels attack social
       evils while they entertain and suggests that Nero Wolfe
       and Archie Goodwin are two sides of Stout's personality.
       Also contends that the Nero Wolfe novels combine the
       best elements of the hard-boiled and classical detective
       stories.

*   Rauber, D.F. "Sherlock Holmes and Nero Wolfe: The Role
       of the 'Great Detective' in Intellectual History"
       (item 1013).

       Just as Sherlock Holmes reflects the assumptions of
       classical physics, Nero Wolfe reflects the changes in
       that science produced by the emergence of sub-atomic
       phenomena. The difference is chiefly that Wolfe does not
       use straight, clear logic based on physical objects as
       does Holmes.

*   Ruehlmann, William. *Saint with a Gun* (item 65), pp. 43-
       48.

       States that Stout's detective, Nero Wolfe, fits into
       neither the "aesthetic," nor the "working" categories
       of private detectives. Points out Wolfe's similarities
       to Sherlock Holmes's older brother, Mycroft: corpulence,
       lack of energy, and superior powers of observation and
       deduction.

STRATEMEYER, EDWARD L. See CAROLYN KEENE

STREET, CECIL JOHN CHARLES. See MILES BURTON

STRIBLING, T.S. (1881-1965)

1719. McSherry, Frank D., Jr. "Rare Vintages from the Tropics:
       T.S. Stribling's *Clues of the Carribees*." *Armchair
       Detective* 6 (May 1973): 172-178.

       Contends that Stribling's book has never achieved
       the popularity that it deserves because, although it
       uses many conventions of the detective story genre, it
       is really "mainstream fiction using the form and struc-
       ture of the detective story."

STUBBS, JEAN (1926-   )

1720. Forrest, Alan. "Mistress of Period Crime." *Books and
       Bookmen* 18 (April 1973): 39.

       Stubbs writes period mysteries and has created an
       1890s sleuth called Linnott, based on a real Victorian
       policeman, whom she later discovered was also used as
       a model by Wilkie Collins and Charles Dickens. She says
       that a theme of all her books is that people "share
       their lives without really knowing each other."

SUE, EUGENE (1804-1857)

1721. Brooks, Peter. "A Man Named Sue." *New York Times Book
       Review* 83 (30 July 1978): 3, 26-27.

       States that Sue began his novel *The Mysteries of
       Paris* (which was published serially in 1842 and 1843)

using the Paris underworld chiefly for its strange and
mysterious atmosphere, but as he learned more about
the underworld, he became concerned about the effects
of urbanization, industrialization, and capitalism on
society.

* Murch, A. E. *The Development of the Detective Novel*
(item 51), pp. 59-62.

Contends that although *Les Mystères de Paris* (1842-
1843) is not a detective novel, Sue "had some influence
on later detective fiction, especially in France," and
on M.P. Shiel, whose protagonist in his novel *Prince
Zaleski* (1895) seems to owe much to Sue's fictional
hero, Prince Rodolphe.

* Palmer, Jerry. "The Literary Origins of the Thriller."
Thrillers (item 56), pp. 118-122.

Maintains that Sue's hero, Rodolphe, in *Les Mystères
de Paris*, is an avenger who "clearly anticipates the
thriller hero."

SYMONS, JULIAN (1912-)

1722. Carter, Steven R. "Julian Symons and Civilization's
Discontents." *Armchair Detective* 12 (Winter 1979):
57-62.

Contends that Symons's chief contribution to the crime
novel is "that he has proven how flexible a vehicle it
is for presenting a personal vision of the stresses of
modern western civilization." Carter analyzes a number
of Symons's works to support this thesis.

1723. Lauterbach, Edward S. "Wise Detective Stories." *Armchair
Detective* 5 (April 1972): 146-147.

States that Julian Symons's *Bland Beginning* is based
on the real life case of Thomas J. Wise, who forged
rare books.

1724. Symons, Julian. "Progress of a Crime Writer." *The Mystery
and Detection Annual 1973* (item 17), pp. 238-243.

Symons recalls his early fondness for detective stories
and points out that what he has consciously tried to
do in most of his mystery novels "is to use an act of
violence to point up my feelings about the pressures of
urban living." Concludes that a novel built around a

crime may be just as memorable and meaningful as another kind of novel.

TAYLOR, H. BALDWIN. See HILLARY WAUGH

TAYLOR, PHOEBE ATWOOD (1909-1976). Pseudonym: Alice Tilton

1725.   Dueren, Fred. "Asey Mayo: 'The Hayseed Sherlock.'" *Armchair Detective* 10 (January 1977): 21-24, 83.

Traces the changes in Taylor's detective, Asey Mayo, from 1931 to 1951, contending that his "greatest change is from simplicity to a sophistication concealed by simplicity," and that he is more active in the later novels. Cites numerous examples from the novels to support his contention.

TEMPLE, PAUL. See FRANCIS DURBRIDGE

TEY, JOSEPHINE. Pseudonym of Elizabeth MacKintosh (1896-1952) Other pseudonym: Gordon Daviot

1726.   Aird, Catherine. "Josephine Tey." *Armchair Detective* 2 (April 1969): 156-157.

Argues that Tey's range and versatility is truly outstanding considering her restricted background.

1727.   Davis, Dorothy Salisbury. "On Josephine Tey." *New Republic* 131 (20 September 1954): 17-18.

Compares Tey's work to that of Dashiell Hammett and argues that Tey took detective fiction back to the "vicar's garden." States that Tey's work is distinguished by her ability to evoke character, atmosphere, and manners through people's conversation. People in Tey's novels speak naturally and speak well. Concludes that there is "practically no stratum of English society with which she was not conversant" and briefly reviews *Three by Tey* (which contains the novels *The Franchise Affair, Miss Pym Disposes,* and *Brat Farrar*).

1728.   "The Last of Tey." *Newsweek* 42 (7 September 1953): 89.

An obituary containing a biographical sketch. Briefly discusses her work, emphasizing the ingeniously constructed plot of *The Man in the Queue*, her first detective novel. Concludes that Tey seems to have had a "balanced view of the world, unlike many mystery story writers, but her curious elliptical style is sometimes irritating."

1729. Roy, Sandra. *Josephine Tey*. Boston: Twayne, 1980. 199pp.

Devotes a full chapter to each of Tey's mystery novels and points out that Tey's work reflects the traditional approach to the detective story as well as the later hard-boiled style. States that Tey stresses style and characterization over plotting and excels in dialog and symbolism.

1730. Sandoe, James. Introduction to *Three by Tey*, by Josephine Tey. New York: Macmillan, 1955, pp. v-x.

Maintains that "Tey was not an innovator" but that in her eight mystery novels she succeeded in compellingly evoking character.

1731. Smith, Myrna J. "Controversy: Re: Richard III." *Armchair Detective* 11 (July 1978): 237.

This is Smith's point-by-point response to Guy M. Townsend's rebuttal (item 1733) of Smith's reply (item 1732) to Townsend's original article (item 1734) on *The Daughter of Time*.

1732. Smith, Myrna J. "Controversy: Townsend, Tey, and Richard III." *Armchair Detective* 10 (October 1977): 317-319.

Argues against Guy M. Townsend's article on *The Daughter of Time* (item 1734) by disputing a large number of Townsend's individual points, such as the reliance on a report by William Wright and George Northcroft that human bones discovered in 1674 were those of the princes.

1733. Townsend, Guy M. "Controversy." *Armchair Detective* 11 (April 1978): 130-131.

A point-by-point rebuttal of Myrna J. Smith's reply (item 1732) to Townsend's article on Tey and Richard III (item 1734).

1734. Townsend, Guy M. "Richard III and Josephine Tey: Partners in Crime." *Armchair Detective* 10 (July 1977): 211-224.

Argues that *The Daughter of Time* is "neither a good
detective story nor an accurate portrayal of the historical episode which it purports to illuminate," the murder
of the princes in the tower. Extensively documented.

THAYER, LEE (1874-1973)

1735.   Breen, Jon L. "On Lee Thayer." *Armchair Detective* 5
        (April 1972): 148-150.

        Though Thayer's novels follow the conventions of the
        classic detective story, her "writings are really like
        no one else's," particularly in their denouements. In-
        cludes checklist.

1736.   Nevins, Francis M., Jr. "Death Inside the Cow: A Few
        Notes on the Novels of Lee Thayer." *Armchair Detective*
        5 (April 1972): 151, 155.

        Contends that Thayer's novels are written for refined
        elderly rich ladies and are extremely slow paced with
        poor plotting, characterization, and dialog.

THAYER, TIFFANY (1902-1959)

1737.   Stone, Edward. "Whodunit? *Moby Dick!*" *Journal of Popular
        Culture* 8 (Fall 1974): 280-285.

        Describes Thayer's *Thirteen Men* as a sensational and
        sleazy murder mystery. Also claims that a tirade against
        Moby Dick by the murderer in the book inspired many
        readers (including Stone himself) to read Melville's
        book.

TILTON, ALICE. See PHOEBE ATWOOD TAYLOR

TINKER, BEAMISH. See F. TENNYSON JESSE

TORRIE, MALCOLM. See GLADYS MITCHELL

TOWNE, STUART. See CLAYTON RAWSON

TRACY, LOUIS. See M.P. SHIEL

TRAIN, ARTHUR (1875-1945)

1738.   "Vale." *Saturday Review* 29 (5 January 1946): 16.
This obituary states that Train's work is as memorable as that of more pretentious writers and that his writings "rose to genius" in the creation of characters. Also observes that whatever he wrote about he knew his subject well and that he exhibited typical American idealism.

1739.   Van Gelder, Robert. "Interview with Mr. Arthur Train." *Writers and Writing*. New York: Scribners, 1946, pp. 169-172.
In an interview in which he describes his working methods, Train states that he uses a formula similar to a three-act play: (1) statement of the problem, (2) apparent impossibility of justice triumphing over legal technicalities, and (3) triumph of justice.

TREVOR, ELLESTON. See ADAM HALL

TREVOR, GLEN. See JAMES HILTON

TWAIN, MARK. Pseudonym of Samuel Langhorne Clemens (1835-1910)

1740.   Baetzhold, Howard G. *Mark Twain and John Bull: The British Connection*. Bloomington: Indiana University Press, 1970, pp. 298-304.
Traces the influence of Conan Doyle and the Sherlock Holmes stories on Twain's career, citing parallels between *A Study in Scarlet* and Twain's burlesque, "A Double-Barrelled Detective Story." Argues that Twain's story was too farcical to be an entirely effective satire.

1741.   Baetzhold, Howard G. "Of Detectives and Their Derring-Do: The Genesis of Mark Twain's 'The Stolen White Elephant.'" *Studies in American Humor* 2 (1976): 183-195.
Notes Twain's love-hate relationship with detective fiction, and contends that Twain was prompted to write

"The Stolen White Elephant" to burlesque the sensational
newspaper accounts of a grave robbing incident in New
York in 1878. Indicates parallels between the press
coverage and Twain's narrative.

1742.   Baldanza, Frank. *Mark Twain: An Introduction and Inter-
        pretation*. New York: Barnes and Noble, 1961, pp. 94-
        99, 121-123.

        In an analysis of *Pudd'nhead Wilson* and *Tom Sawyer,
        Detective*, notes Twain's fascination with the ratiocina-
        tive detective story, and argues that Twain, in *Pudd'n-
        head Wilson*, was the first to make fictional use of
        fingerprint evidence.

1743.   Banks, R. Jeff. "Mark Twain: Detective Story Writer."
        Armchair Detective 7 (May 1974): 176-177.

        Analyzes *A Double-Barrelled Detective Story*, "The
        Stolen White Elephant," and *Simon Wheeler, Detective*,
        contending that the sardonic humor in each is intended
        to show the vindictiveness of mankind.

1744.   Bay, J. Christian. *"Tom Sawyer, Detective*: The Origin
        of the Plot." *Essays Offered to Herbert Putnam by His
        Colleagues and Friends on His Thirtieth Anniversary
        as Librarian of Congress, 5 April 1929*. Edited by
        William Warner Bishop and Andrew Keogh. New Haven,
        Conn.: Yale University Press, 1929, pp. 80-88.

        Contends that Twain based his novel on Steen Steensen
        Blicher's *The Minister of Vejlby*, a Danish account of a
        17th-century crime.

1745.   Briden, Earl F. "Idiots First, Then Juries: Legal Meta-
        phors in Mark Twain's *Pudd'nhead Wilson*." *Texas Studies
        in Literature and Language* 20 (1978): 169-180.

        Argues that Twain's use of metaphors rooted in the
        legal processes reinforces one of *Pudd'nhead Wilson*'s
        fundamental themes--"that personal identity is all but
        a fiction," and that the judgment of others is often
        the prime determinant of this identity.

1746.   Cooper, Lane. "Mark Twain's Lilacs and Laburnums."
        Modern Language Notes 47 (February 1932): 85-88.

        Argues that a passage at the beginning of Chapter 4
        of "A Double-Barrelled Detective Story" parodies *The
        Seamy Side*, by Walter Besant and James Rice.

1747. Davis, Chester L. "'Simon Wheeler, Detective' Published."
      Twainian 23 (March–April 1964): 1–3.

      Traces the history of Twain's manuscript. Argues from
      clues in the text that the novel is set in Florida,
      Missouri.

1748. French, Warren. "*Simon Wheeler, Detective*." *American
      Notes and Queries* 3 (September 1964): 14–15.

      Argues that *Simon Wheeler, Detective* is very poor
      Mark Twain and did not warrant reprinting. Scholars
      would have been better served by a facsimile reprint.

1749. Kraus, W. Keith. "Mark Twain's 'A Double-Barrelled
      Detective Story': A Source for the Solitary Oesophagus."
      Mark Twain Journal 16 (Summer 1972): 10–12.

      Notes similarities between a passage in Twain's story
      and Conan Doyle's *A Study in Scarlet*, which Twain paro-
      dies. The reference to a "solitary oesophagus" seems to
      be based on Doyle's mention of a "solitary traveller."

1750. La Cour, Tage. "The Scandinavian Crime-Detective Story."
      American Book Collector 9 (May 1959): 22–23.

      Notes the similarities between *Tom Sawyer, Detective*
      and *The Vicar of Vejlby*, by Steen Steenson Blicher; also
      records a denial by Twain's secretary that Twain had
      ever read the earlier Danish work.

1751. McKeithan, Daniel Morley. *Court Trials in Mark Twain
      and Other Essays*. The Hague: Martinus Nijhoff, 1958,
      pp. 26–40, 91–103.

      In chapters on the trials in *Pudd'nhead Wilson* and
      Tom Sawyer, Detective, contends that, although Twain
      knew a good deal about trial procedure, he was not
      aiming for literal realism in these scenes, but rather
      for "presenting his characters vividly and dramatically."

1752. Olds, Nathaniel S. "A Mark Twain Retort." *Saturday
      Review* 7 (7 May 1932): 722.

      Recapitulates an earlier exchange between Twain and
      Olds, who, in reviewing "A Double-Barrelled Detective
      Story," had suggested that the incident in which a
      pregnant woman was tied to a post and attacked by dogs
      was implausible. Twain responded with a letter explaining
      that the account was based on a real event.

1753.   "The Origin of *Pudd'nhead Wilson*." *Literary Digest* 45
        (26 October 1912): 740-741.

        Contends that a palmist named Cheiro interested Twain
        in handprints, a theme which Twain incorporated into
        Pudd'nhead Wilson.

1754.   Orth, Michael. "*Pudd'nhead Wilson* Reconsidered; or, The
        Octaroon in the Villa Viviani." *Mark Twain Journal* 14
        (Summer 1969): 11-15.

        Argues that much of the detection (including the use
        of the science of fingerprinting) in *Pudd'nhead Wilson*
        was anticipated by Mayne Reid's *The Quadroon* (1856) and
        Dion Boucicault's *Octaroon* (1859).

1755.   Pettit, Arthur G. *Mark Twain and the South*. Lexington:
        University Press of Kentucky, 1974. 224pp.

        In an analysis of race relations in Twain's work,
        argues that the character of Toby in *Simon Wheeler,
        Detective* is "a stereotyped darky," and a complete
        failure. The mulattoes in *Pudd'nhead Wilson*, however,
        while not perfectly drawn, do represent an honest effort
        by Twain to come to grips with his attitudes on the
        race question.

*   Ritunnano, Jeanne. "Mark Twain vs. Arthur Conan Doyle
        on Detective Fiction" (item 1015).

        Points out that Mark Twain's "A Double-Barrelled
        Detective Story" is a pardoy of Conan Doyle's Sherlock
        Holmes story *A Study in Scarlet*. Bases her conclusion
        on a comparison of the two plots and maintains that the
        Conan Doyle story "depicts man as a free agent who acts
        with noble and unselfish motives" and that "man's
        intellect is a valuable tool in overcoming difficulties."
        Twain's parody, however, demonstrates that man is mean,
        selfish, vindictive, and not a free agent.

1756.   Rogers, Franklin R. Introduction to *Simon Wheeler,
        Detective*, by Mark Twain. New York: New York Public
        Library, 1963, pp. xi-xxxviii.

        Argues that Twain's delight in *Simon Wheeler, Detective*
        "derived not from an artist's satisfaction with his work
        but from a satirist's gleeful previsions of his target's
        discomfiture." Identifies the targets as Allan Pinker-
        ton's detective stories and the Bedford Brothers, Canadian
        publishers who had pirated Twain's work.

1757. Rowlette, Robert. *Mark Twain's Pudd'nhead Wilson: The
       Development and Design*. Bowling Green, Ohio: Bowling
       Green University Popular Press, 1971, pp. 38-61.

       In a chapter on "Mark Twain and the Detective," argues
       that, although Twain burlesqued Conan Doyle mercilessly,
       he was indebted to Doyle and used Sherlock Holmes's
       ratiocinative methods, especially in *Pudd'nhead Wilson*
       and *Tom Sawyer, Detective*, in which "he employs the
       mode of detection to reveal truths of broad social
       import."

1758. Smith, Henry Nash. *Mark Twain: The Development of a
       Writer*. Cambridge, Mass.: Belknap Press of Harvard
       University, 1962. 212pp.

       Argues that Twain identifies with his detective figures,
       who approach life calmly and intellectually, thus dis-
       tancing themselves and their author from the wretched
       human race.

1759. Stone, Albert E., Jr. *The Innocent Eye: Childhood in
       Mark Twain's Imagination*. New Haven, Conn.: Yale
       University Press, 1961, pp. 188-195.

       Argues that *Tom Sawyer, Detective*, and, to a lesser
       extent, *Pudd'nhead Wilson*, were written to cash in on
       the Conan Doyle-inspired vogue for detective fiction.
       Tom Sawyer, Detective is Twain's worst short story, but
       in *Pudd'nhead Wilson* Twain was able to use the detective
       genre to exploit his penchant for switched identities
       and to thereby illustrate the evils of slavery.

1760. Wigger, Anne P. "The Source of the Fingerprint Material
       in Mark Twain's *Pudd'nhead Wilson and Those Extra-
       ordinary Twins*." *American Literature* 28 (January
       1957): 517-520.

       Argues that Twain's source was Sir Francis Galton's
       Finger Prints.

UPFIELD, ARTHUR W. (1888-1964). Series character: Napoleon
  Bonaparte

1761. Barzun, Jacques, and Wendell Hertig Taylor. Preface to
       The Bone is Pointed, by Arthur Upfield. New York:
       Garland Publishing, 1976. Also printed in *A Book of
       Prefaces* (item 22), pp. 103-104.

Observes that in this novel the episode of the bewitching of Upfield's half-aboriginal detective, Napoleon Bonaparte, "is perhaps the most memorable part of a complex narrative full of strong contrasts."

1762.   Cawelti, John G. "Murder in the Outback: Arthur W. Upfield." *New Republic* 177 (30 July 1977): 39-41.

Contends that Upfield, when writing at his best, could create a psychological mystery blending the aboriginal culture and the "extraordinary social and geological landscape of the Australian outback."

1763.   Donaldson, Betty. "Arthur William Upfield: September 1, 1888-February 13, 1964." *Armchair Detective* 8 (November 1974): 1-11.

Observes that Upfield used many incidents in his novels which happened to him while working and traveling in Australia in his youth. Also maintains that his female characters never seem quite real, but that his male characters are always totally believable. An annotated checklist of Upfield's novels is included.

1764.   Fox, Estelle. "Arthur William Upfield, 1888-1964." *Armchair Detective* 3 (January 1970): 89-91.

States that Upfield, an Englishman, learned about the customs and language of the aborigine and then used this knowledge in his novels featuring his half-caste detective, Napoleon Bonaparte. A checklist of Upfield's novels is included.

1765.   Hawke, Jessica. *Follow My Dust: A Biography of Arthur Upfield*. London: Heinemann, 1957.

Although this biography devotes little attention to Upfield's writing, it provides a background for understanding his detective stories because he used so many incidents from his own life in them.

1766.   Sarjeant, William Anthony. "The Great Australian Detective." *Armchair Detective* 12 (Spring 1979): 99-105.

Contends that Upfield's outstanding achievement in his creation of his half-aborigine detective, Napoleon Bonaparte, is that he makes us see his detective as a part of the Australian landscape. Cites biographical details from the novels in order to create a composite picture of the detective.

VAN DeWETERING, JANWILLEM (1931-)

1767.   White, Jean M. "Murder by Zen." *New Republic* 179 (22
        July 1978): 34-35.

        Observes that Van DeWetering's detective stories are
        Zen mysteries using the police procedural device and
        are dominated by "mood, character, and atmosphere."

VAN DINE, S.S. Pseudonym of Willard Huntington Wright (1888-
1939). Series character: Philo Vance

1768.   Bartlett, Randolph. "Man of Promise." *Saturday Review*
        13 (2 November 1935): 10.

        Since *The Greene Murder Case* the quality of Van Dine's
        detective novels has deteriorated "until now all there
        is to the novels is the formula."

1769.   Beaman, Bruce R. "S.S. Van Dine: A Biographical Sketch."
        Armchair Detective 8 (February 1975): 133-135.

        Argues that Philo Vance is modeled on Wright's own
        character. Includes checklist of Wright's work under
        his own name and as Van Dine.

1770.   Braithwaite, William Stanley. "S.S. Van Dine--Willard
        Huntington Wright." *Philo Vance Murder Cases*. New
        York: Scribners, 1936, pp. 29-45.

        Braithwaite gives the critical and aesthetic background
        of Wright and draws parallels between Wright and Philo
        Vance, especially in their "rare personal charm" and
        knowledge of art.

1771.   Hammett, Dashiell. "Benson Murder Case." *Saturday Review*
        3 (15 January 1927): 510. Reprinted *The Art of the
        Mystery Story* (item 35), pp. 382-385.

        Contends, in this review, that Philo Vance "manages
        always, and usually ridiculously, to be wrong," and
        that rudimentary police routine would have solved the
        case promptly.

*   Haycraft, Howard. *Murder for Pleasure* (item 36), pp.
        163-168.

        Argues that the literacy with which Van Dine's mystery
        novels were written and their careful attention to
        verisimilitude were largely responsible for their enor-

mous popularity. Later, these same qualities made the
novels date badly and lose their popularity.

1772.   Lachtman, Howard. "Willard Wright's Philo Vance: A Dandy
        in Acid." *Los Angeles Times Book Review* 3 June 1979,
        pp. 3, 25.

        Argues that Wright created a classic detective in
        Philo Vance, gave mystery fiction the literary stature
        it had lacked since Poe, "reconciled murder and good
        manners for the masses," and laid the groundwork for
        the development of a "truly American style of mystery
        writing."

1773.   Lowndes, Robert A.W. "Dear Me, Mr. Van Dine." *Armchair
        Detective* 7 (1973): 30-31.

        Lowndes tries to put the Philo Vance novels of S.S.
        Van Dine into a "coherent chronological order" and find
        consistency in the dating of the cases but discovers
        instead many inconsistencies.

1774.   Maurice, Arthur Bartlett. "The History of Their Books:
        VI. S.S. Van Dine." *Bookman* 64 (June 1929): 414-416.

        Willard Huntington Wright was an editor of several
        magazines and author of nine books on various cultural
        subjects when he suffered a nervous breakdown. After-
        wards he was not allowed to read anything for two years.
        When he was finally permitted to read only detective
        stories, he studied the genre exhaustively and began to
        write detective stories himself when he was well enough.
        Maurice suggests that this intellectual approach to the
        detective story has influenced Wright's books.

1775.   Rosenblatt, Roger. "The Back of the Book: S.S. Van Dine."
        New Republic 173 (26 July 1975): 32-34.

        The most interesting thing about Philo Vance was that
        he had money. Rosenblatt contends that the mind of Vance
        is more intuitive than strictly logical and that he is
        impossible to like. Van Dine "was not creating fiction,
        but a kind of riddle."

*   Ruehlmann, William. *Saint with a Gun* (item 65), pp. 37-
        43.

        Argues that Van Dine's detective, Philo Vance, resembles
        Doyle's Sherlock Holmes in physical appearance, cold-
        bloodedness, erudition, and in having his adventures
        told by a biographer and companion.

1776. Seldes, Gilbert. "Van Dine and His Public." *New Republic*
       59 (19 June 1929): 125-126.

       Argues that Van Dine's stories are far more interest-
       ing than his detective and that their strength is the
       emphasis on deduction. Contends that Van Dine shows a
       contempt for the public in his excessive pedantry.

*   Symons, Julian. *Mortal Consequences* (item 74), pp. 110-
       113.

       Contends that Van Dine's detective, Philo Vance, is
       similar to Dorothy Sayers's snobbish detective, Lord
       Peter Wimsey, but is a more fully realized character
       with real erudition.

*   Thomson, H. Douglas. "The American Detective Story."
       Masters of Mystery (item 77), pp. 262-269.

       Cites examples from Wright's novels to illustrate his
       aesthetic-psychological method and basic plot structure.

1777. Tuska, Jon. "The Philo Vance Murder Case." *Views and
       Reviews* 1 (Winter 1970): 54-62; 1 (Spring 1970): 38-
       46; 2 (Summer 1970): 45-54. Reprinted *Philo Vance:
       The Life and Times of S.S. Van Dine*. Edited by Jon
       Tuska. Bowling Greeen, Ohio: Bowling Green University
       Popular Press, 1971, pp. 5-34.

       Argues that Van Dine reached an apex with *The Bishop
       Murder Case*, after which his writing finally degenerated
       into self-parody.

1778. Wright, Willard Huntington [under the pseudonym S.S.
       Van Dine]. "I Used to be a Highbrow but Look at Me
       Now." *American Magazine* 106 (September 1928): 14+.
       Essentially the same article reprinted as Introduction
       to *Philo Vance Murder Cases*. New York: Scribners, 1936,
       pp. 1-28, 74-81. Part reprinted as "Twenty Rules for
       Writing Detective Stories." *The Art of the Mystery
       Story* (item 35), pp. 189-193.

       Wright's own account of his nervous breakdown and
       subsequent change from a poor highbrow to a wealthy
       detective story writer. Includes his twenty rules for
       the "intellectual game" of the detective story, such as
       determining the culprit by logical deductions and having
       no love interest.

VAN GULIK, ROBERT (1910-1967)

1779.   Atchity, Kenneth John. "Robert Van Gulik." *The Mystery
         and Detection Annual 1972* (item 16), pp. 237-245.

         The stories of Van Gulik feature the Chinese magistrate
         Judge Dee, an historical figure, and have plots which
         are to some degree based on real cases. Atchity evalu-
         ates Van Gulik as "an amateur author who will be remem-
         bered more for his several literary strengths than for
         a successful artistic integration of content and tech-
         nique," and singles out *The Haunted Monastery* (1963),
         Necklace and Calabash (1967), and *Poets and Murder* (1968)
         as his most successful novels.

1780.   Lach, Donald F. Introduction to *The Chinese Bell Murders*,
         The Chinese Lake Murders, *The Chinese Maze Murders*,
         The Chinese Nail Murders, and *The Chinese Gold Murders*.
         All published by the University of Chicago Press in
         1977.

         This introduction, which was printed in each of the
         above volumes, states that Van Gulik's novels are not
         strictly accurate, but that they present Imperial China
         as a vivid, living culture. Van Gulik used an historical
         character, Judge Dee, as his central figure, and used
         plots and information from the whole range of Chinese
         literature to embellish his novels.

VENNING, MICHAEL. See CRAIG RICE

VIDAL, GORE. See EDGAR BOX

VULLIAMY, C.E. (1886-)

1781.   Shibuk Charles. "Notes on C.E. Vulliamy." *Armchair
         Detective* 3 (April 1970): 161; 5 (April 1972): 145.

         Vulliamy is a relatively unknown mystery writer whose
         wit, sense of the absurd, and pessimistic view of man-
         kind make him a skillful and entertaining writer. Three
         of his novels are briefly discussed.

WADE, HENRY. Pseudonym of Henry Lancelot Aubrey-Fletcher (1887-
         1969)

1782.   Barzun, Jacques, and Wendell Hertig Taylor. Preface to

The *Dying Alderman*, by Henry Wade. New York: Garland
Publishing, 1976. Also printed in *A Book of Prefaces*
(item 22), pp. 105-106.

Contends that although Wade wrote in the classical
English detective fiction genre, this novel demonstrates
that he "belongs neither to the genteel tradition nor
to the glorification of the Establishment" and shows
his virtuosity in inventing plots.

1783.   Shibuk, Charles. "Henry Wade." *Armchair Detective* 1
        (July 1968): 111-115; 2 (October 1968): 45. Revised
        and reprinted *The Mystery Writer's Art* (item 54), pp.
        88-97.

States that Wade was an advocate of the classical detective novel but also wrote some stories partly or
wholly from the criminal's viewpoint. He has done more
to "explicate the psychology and mores" of the English
than any other writer in the genre. The bulk of the
article is a list of Wade's books with comments on each.

WADE, ROBERT. See WADE MILLER

WAHLÖÖ, PER (1926-1975). Wrote all his detective novels with
Maj Sjöwall (1935-   )

1784.   Duffy, Martha. "Martin Beck Passes." *Time* 106 (11 August
        1975): 58-E3 [*sic*].

Article, written one month after Wahlöö's death, is
an overview of the Martin Beck novels. Contends that
this series of thrillers (written by Wahlöö and his
wife Maj Sjöwall) is unusual in that it has a number of
interesting recurring characters. Argues that a critique
of Sweden's welfare state is an important part of the
books, and that the series becomes "increasingly radical,"
with the victims in the later novels as villainous as
their killers.

1785.   Occhiogrosso, Frank. "The Police in Society: The Novels
        of Maj Sjöwall and Per Wahlöö." *Armchair Detective* 12
        (Spring 1979): 174-177.

Argues that the ten Sjöwall/Wahlöö novels "contain
an evolving vision of society" in which the attitude
toward police becomes ambivalent.

*   Palmer, Jerry. "After the Thriller." *Thrillers* (item
        56), pp. 218-220.

        Classifying Sjöwall and Wahlöö's *The Abominable Man*
        as an anti-thriller, the author goes on to define this
        sub-genre as one in which the conspiracy entirely dom-
        inates--"competitive individualism has been eliminated,
        and the individual is reduced to solitary inadequacy
        or to a bureaucratic function."

*   White, Jean M. "Wahlöö/Sjöwall and James McClure: Murder
        and Politics" (item 1382).

        Wahlöö and his wife Maj Sjöwall decided to examine
        Swedish society by writing a series of crime novels.
        Argues that Beck does get somewhat tiresome in his con-
        tinual attacks on the Swedish Establishment, but finds
        that a crime novel can be "far more incisive and telling"
        than a "serious" work.

WALKER, HARRY. See HILLARY WAUGH

WALLACE, EDGAR (1875-1932)

1786.   Chesterton, G.K. "On Detective Story Writers." *Come to
        Think of It*. New York: Dodd, Mead, 1931, pp. 33-38.

        Points out that Wallace's work is entertaining, but
        it generally should be classified as adventure fiction
        rather than detective fiction.

1787.   Hogan, John A. "An Exhumation of *The Tomb of Ts'in*."
        Armchair Detective 6 (May 1973): 167-171.

        States that in *The Tomb of Ts'in* (1916) Wallace used
        materials from his own novel *The Island of Galloping
        Gold* (1916), itself an unacknowledged version of his
        Captain Tatham of Tatham Island (1909). Speculates that
        Wallace did this in order to get *The Tomb of Ts'in* pub-
        lished more quickly.

1788.   Morland, Nigel. "The Edgar Wallace I Knew." *Armchair
        Detective* 1 (April 1968): 68-71.

        Contends that the secret of Wallace's successful
        writing was his absorption in his work and his lack of
        pretension about his novels as art.

*   Thomson, H. Douglas. "The Thriller: The Wallace Collec-
      tion." *Masters of Mystery* (item 77), pp. 222-229.

      States that Wallace's work has a variety of theme and
      style. Argues that his strengths are straightforward
      narrative, exciting atmosphere, inimitable and humorous
      characters, intimate knowledge of police methods, and a
      familiarity with criminal slang. His weaknesses are too
      many improbabilities, sensationalism, imperfect grammar,
      and the over-use of the not likely person device.

*   Watson, Colin. "King Edgar, and How He Got His Crown."
      Snobbery with Violence (item 78), pp. 73-84.

      Contends that the very qualities in Wallace's writing
      that offended critics made him popular with the public:
      his refusal to write explicitly about sex or anything
      offensive or upsetting, his stereotyped characters that
      offered an escape from reality, and his ridiculous plots
      that led to a happy ending.

WARD, ARTHUR HENRY SARSFIELD. See SAX ROHMER

WAUGH, HILLARY (1920-   ). Pseudonyms: H. Baldwin Taylor, Harry
   Walker

1789. Waugh, Hillary. "Fred Fellows." *The Great Detectives*
       (item 60), pp. 99-108.

       Fellows was carefully created to fill the role of de-
       tective in the small town police procedurals which the
       author likes to write. He must solve many crimes over a
       period of years without using up his resources or wear-
       ing out his welcome with the reader.

WEBSTER, HENRY KITCHELL (1875-1932)

1790. Barzun, Jacques, and Wendell Hertig Taylor. Preface to
       Who Is the Next?, by Henry Kitchell Webster. New York:
       Garland Publishing, 1976. Also printed in *A Book of
       Prefaces* (item 22), pp. 107-108.

       Argues that this novel is made pleasurable by Webster's
       deft narration, skillful handling of family relation-
       ships, and a successful flouting of one of the genre's
       conventions--the introduction of romance into the mystery
       story.

1791.   Taylor, Wendell Hertig. "Henry Kitchell Webster: The
        Emergence of an American Mystery-Writer." *Armchair
        Detective* 5 (July 1972): 199-201.

        Argues that the fact that women dominated mystery
        writing in America between 1918 and 1930 delayed Web-
        ster's entry into the field. Includes brief summaries
        of his mystery novels.

WELLS, CAROLYN (1870-1942). Pseudonym: Rowland Wright

1792.   Breen, Jon L. "On Carolyn Wells." *Armchair Detective* 3
        (October 1969): 77-79.

        States that Wells is now nearly forgotten. Her stories
        are highly conventional but she was "an honest and sin-
        cere practitioner with an obvious and infectious enthu-
        siasm" for the detective story form. Includes primary
        bibliography.

WEST, JOHN B.

1793.   Turner, Darwin T. "The Rocky Steele Novels of John B.
        West." *Armchair Detective* 6 (August 1973): 226-231.
        Reprinted *Dimensions of Detective Fiction* (item 43),
        pp. 140-148.

        West, a black writer, published six novels between
        1959 and 1961 that featured Rocky Steele, a white de-
        tective modeled on Mickey Spillane's Mike Hammer because
        at that time black detective heroes and black culture
        had not become popular.

WESTLAKE, DONALD E. (1933-   ). Pseudonyms: Tucker Coe, Timothy
    J. Culver, Richard Stark

1794.   Bakerman, Jane S. "Patterns of Guilt and Isolation in
        Five Novels by 'Tucker Coe.'" *Armchair Detective* 12
        (Spring 1979): 118-121.

        Argues that Westlake's novels written under the pseudo-
        nym Tucker Coe are more serious than his other works
        and that they center on the theme of "coming to terms
        with isolation and guilt."

1795.   Nevins, Francis M., Jr. "Walls of Guilt: Donald E.
        Westlake as Tucker Coe." *Armchair Detective* 7 (May
        1974): 163-164.

Contends that the mystery novels Westlake wrote under
his pseudonym of Tucker Coe (featuring Mitchell Tobin,
an ex-cop turned detective) are among the best mystery
novels of the 1960s.

* Palmer, Jerry. "After the Thriller." *Thrillers* (item
56), pp. 212-215.

Contends that Donald Westlake's novels written under
the pseudonym of Richard Stark are "enforcer stories,"
which some critics believe constitute a distinct genre
from thrillers. "Enforcer stories" are characterized
by the legal isolation of the enforcer, who operates
entirely outside the law because it gives him emotional
or financial satisfaction to do so.

1796. Serebnick, Judith. "New Creative Writers." *Library
Journal* 85 (1 June 1960): 2205.

Quotes Westlake as saying the basis of *The Mercenaries*
is the idea that a crime syndicate is a *business*.

WHEATLEY, DENNIS (1897-1977). Collaborated with J.G. Links on
four Crimefiles

1797. Gadney, Reg. "The Murder Dossiers of Dennis Wheatley and
J.G. Links." *London Magazine* 8 (March 1969): 41-51.

An account of four murder stories by Wheatley and
Links which were published in the 1930s in the form of
dossiers that included such clues as a photo of the
victim, a bit of bloodstained curtain, photostats of
telegrams and reports. The solution to each case was
sealed, and the reader was to solve the case himself
before breaking the seal.

1798. "New Thrill for Armchair Detectives: With a Crimefile
of Clues, the Fan Works Out Own Solution." *Literary
Digest* 122 (3 October 1936): 25.

Describes the Crimefile called *File on Bolitho Blanc*
(see item 1797) and states that it is no better than the
usual detective story except for its unusual presentation.

WHITE, T.H. (1906-1964)

1799. Crane, John K. *T.H. White.* New York: Twayne, 1974, pp.
31-42.

Devotes some attention to White's two detective novels, *Dead Mr. Nixon* and *Darkness at Pemberley*. The former was written in collaboration with R. McNair Scott and Crane contends that it is a cleverly conceived English version of a 1930s American gangster movie but is "not particularly good from a literary standpoint." *Darkness at Pemberley*, Crane argues, seems to address some serious issues and themes, but they are obscured by an excess of contrivance.

WIBBERLEY, LEONARD PATRICK O'CONNOR. See LEONARD HOLTON

WILKINSON, ELLEN C. (1891-1947)

1800. Barzun, Jacques, and Wendell Hertig Taylor. Preface to *The Division Bell Mystery*, by Ellen Wilkinson. New York: Garland Publishing, 1976. Also printed in *A Book of Prefaces* (item 22), pp. 109-110.

Points out that Wilkinson skillfully uses "the alternate separation and convergence" of two strands of action—one inside the House of Commons and one outside—to add to the suspense and plausibility of her story.

WILLIAMS, JOHN B. (1827-1879)

1801. Bleiler, E.F. "John B. Williams, M.D., Forgotten Writer of Detective Stories." *Armchair Detective* 10 (October 1977): 353.

Argues that Williams seems to have been the first American "to write a collection of stories based on the exploits of a professional detective"—*Leaves from the Note-book of a New York Detective* (1864-1865).

WILSON, ROBERT McNAIR. See ANTHONY WYNNE

WINTERTON, PAUL. See ANDREW GARVE

WITTING, CLIFFORD (1907-)

1802. Barzun, Jacques, and Wendell Hertig Taylor. Preface to *Measure for Murder*, by Clifford Witting. New York:

Garland Publishing, 1976. Also printed in *A Book of
Prefaces* (item 22), pp. 111-112.

Argues that the success of Witting's book is largely
due to his use of a two-part division of the book. The
first half is "a diary kept by one of the principal
characters" and the second half is the verbatim testimony of the various characters introduced in the first
half.

WOOLRICH, CORNELL (1903-1968). Pseudonyms: George Hopley,
William Irish

1803.   Nevins, Francis M., Jr. "Cornell Woolrich." *Armchair
        Detective* 2 (October 1968): 25-28; 2 (January 1969):
        99-102; 2 (April 1969): 180-182.

        Surveys Woolrich's work, citing examples from various
        of his mysteries to prove his thesis that Woolrich is
        one of America's greatest mystery writers. Argues that
        in his major works Woolrich "reverses the convention
        of the suspense story, ending not with the dissolution
        of terror but with the revelation that nothing but
        terror exists." He also evokes love with equal intensity.
        Concludes that Woolrich's best work is artistically
        equal to that of Poe. Includes a primary bibliography
        of Woolrich's writings.

1804.   Nevins, Francis M., Jr. "Cornell Woolrich: The Years
        Before Suspense." *Armchair Detective* 12 (Spring 1979):
        106-110.

        Surveys Woolrich's early writing and finds many of
        the themes and characteristics of his later suspense
        works such as descriptions of movie palaces, maternal
        motifs, and love leading to horror.

1805.   Nevins, Francis M., Jr. Introduction to *Nightwebs*, by
        Cornell Woolrich. New York: Harper and Row, 1971, pp.
        ix-xxxiv.

        Argues that Woolrich is one of the genre's greatest
        masters of suspense and sees even his apparent weak-
        nesses—careless plotting and "feverish emotionalism"—
        as contributing to the intensity of his work. His abil-
        ity to portray fear, desperation, and police brutality
        is matched by his ability to evoke love's destruction
        and perversities.

WRIGHT, ROWLAND. See CAROLYN WELLS

WRIGHT, WILLARD HUNTINGTON. See S.S. VAN DINE

WYLIE, PHILIP (1902-1971)

1806.   Keefer, Truman Frederick. *Philip Wylie.* Boston: Twayne,
        1977. 168pp.

        Argues that *The Smiling Corpse* is both "a lively and
        ingenious murder mystery" and a satire on the mystery
        genre. *The Spy Who Spoke Porpoise*, Keefer says, is "the
        work of a professional at the height of his powers." It
        combines entertainment and Wylie's vision of life. Its
        high quality Keefer attributes partly to the fact that
        Wylie was not trying to write an "important" novel.

1807.   Lauterbach, Edward S. "Invisible Man, U.S.A.: Some Pulp
        Prototypes." *Armchair Detective* 3 (July 1970): 241-
        242.

        Contends that Wylie's *The Murderer Invisible* has many
        elements of the pulp thriller, "super villains, super
        heroes, and super laboratories" and that it set a
        pattern for the pulps themselves.

WYNNE, ANTHONY. Pseudonym of Robert McNair Wilson (1882-   )

1808.   Wynne, Anthony. "Meet Dr. Eustace Hailey." *Meet the
        Detective* (item 45), pp. 139-147.

        States that the philosophy of crime embodied by Hailey
        can be summed up in the following comment: "The really
        interesting crimes ... are those committed by people
        who, in ordinary circumstances," would never commit a
        crime.

YATES, DORNFORD. Pseudonym of Cecil William Mercer (1885-1960)

*   Usborne, Richard. "Dornford Yates." *Clubland Heroes*
        (item 629), pp. 58-79.

        Argues that Yates's fictional character, Jonah Mansel,
        is a "true clubland hero" and "a mania man" compared
        to Chandos, another series character, who is more roman-
        tic though not as sophisticated a hero as Mansel. Con-

cludes that Mansel is "perhaps the bossiest hero of
thriller fiction since Sherlock Holmes."

YORK, JEREMY. See JOHN CREASEY

ZANGWILL, ISRAEL (1864-1926)

1809. Adams, Elsie B. *Israel Zangwill*. New York: Twayne, 1971.
       177pp.

       Devotes only two paragraphs to Zangwill's detective
       story, *The Big Bow Mystery*, stating that "a series of
       ironies makes the story a better-than-average example
       of its genre."

1810. "Short Stories." *Athenaeum* no. 3935 (28 March 1903):
       400.

       Contends that Zangwill's *The Big Bow Mystery* seems to
       be a detective story written by a clever young person
       who does not especially like the form. The resulting
       book is neither good nor satirical but merely badly told.

Index of Critics